GROWING UP WITH THE GAULEITER

GROWING UP WITH THE GAULEITER

My childhood before, during and after
the Second World War

RICHARD LORD

Matador
9 Priory Business Park,
Wistow Road, Kibworth Beauchamp,
Leicestershire. LE8 0RX
Tel: 0116 279 2299
Email: books@troubador.co.uk
Web: www.troubador.co.uk/matador
Twitter: @matadorbooks

ISBN 978 1788036 719

British Library Cataloguing in Publication Data.
A catalogue record for this book is available from the British Library.

Printed and bound in the UK by TJ International, Padstow, Cornwall
Typeset in 11pt Aldine401 BT by Troubador Publishing Ltd, Leicester, UK

Matador is an imprint of Troubador Publishing Ltd

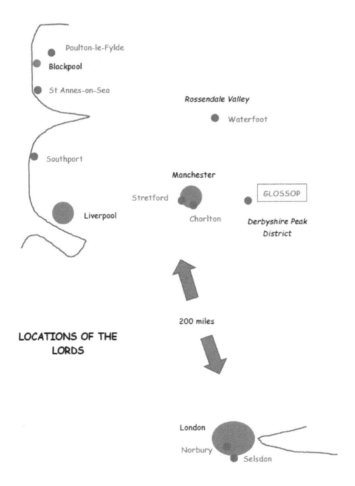

Poulton-le-Fylde

Blackpool

St Annes-on-Sea

Rossendale Valley

Waterfoot

Southport

Manchester

Stretford   GLOSSOP

Chorlton

Liverpool   Derbyshire Peak
                 District

200 miles

**LOCATIONS OF THE
LORDS**

London

Norbury

Selsdon

CONTENTS

A FOREWORD FROM THE GAULEITER'S GRANDDAUGHTER

'*Growing up with the Gauleiter*' is an autobiographical account by my late father, Richard Antony Lord of his childhood in Manchester and Glossop. Central to the narrative is Richard's relationship with his father Cecil Lord – a powerful and at times overbearing figure within both his family and the wider community of Glossop, where the family lived during the 1930s, 40s and 50s.

The story took 30 years to complete. Being at once a social commentary on the institution of the grammar school, an historical account of northern England in the mid twentieth century and a personal memoir of life with an extraordinary character, it is difficult to classify and not easy to market. When Richard had completed a draft he was happy to put before the public he found it difficult to attract the interest of publishers and literary agents, due to the book's diverse nature. Eventually he decided upon self-publication and was about to finalise the contract with Matador, when he became ill. Richard died in February 2016 and it falls to me, the 'Gauleiter's Granddaughter', to explain the 'circumstances of production' (a phrase Richard liked to borrow from Marxist historians when discussing anything from a book or film to a painting or country house).

When Cecil Lord died in 1980, Richard was principal of Skelmersdale College in West Lancashire and was coming to the end of his 30 year career in the state education sector. In that career he taught in the RAF, comprehensive and grammar schools, higher education and further education institutes. He would then embark on what he said was his best teaching, working as a tutor for the Open University in the 1980s and 1990s.

Richard believed that learning was an essential human need – as satisfying as food and sex when teaching was done well, but he thought it was often done badly in English schools (an analogy with school dinners and sex education here would probably be going too far, so I won't continue with the metaphor). Ignoring his warnings, I followed him into the profession and am now a deputy headteacher, so we continued our discussions on what good learning is during the following decades.

On his early retirement in 1985, Richard found he had time to reflect on the lives of his parents and in doing so began exploring the extensive diaries his father had kept during his tenure as Headmaster of Glossop Grammar School. The early drafts of the book were a treatise on the institution of the grammar school (and all that Richard thought had been wrong with it). In writing about his own experiences, however, he began to see a good deal that was right in the way he was taught. At the time, my university choices were being impeded by poor A level grades (something which confounded my father, until I confessed on a visit to Chatsworth House that despite studying British History in the seventeenth century we hadn't finished the syllabus and got to the Glorious Revolution). This may have confirmed for him that the comprehensive system he had been so positive about during the 1960s and 1970s had failed, at least in one case. He gave up on Marxism around the same time, following a visit to the Democratic Republic of Germany.

So the tone of the book changed from anti – to pro-grammar school, a traditional syllabus and what was affectionately termed the 'mallet process' by Cecil Lord's deputy, Sammy Holt (or rote learning, recently given a renaissance by Mr Gove). What I find interesting about this account is not that the grammar schools had better teachers or methods (you will meet some fairly terrible characters in the book), but that teachers who have a love of their subject and who are able to foster understanding through dialogue are the most successful. Richard himself was a great teacher. He listened as a much as he spoke. Wow!

But 'Growing up with the Gauleiter' is more than just a book about teaching. It is ultimately an affectionate account of a relationship with someone who was clearly quite a difficult man. Cecil Lord could quote eloquently the words of Cranmer's prayer book in the morning assembly and give a blustering tirade against 'bloody parsons' at teatime. He could rage tyrannically against the 'thankless child' in the evening only to wake the next morning and acquiesce to all the unreasonable demands of his adolescent son.

The relationship between father and son was at times dysfunctional, but it was also loving, strong and in our modern age of introspection, tremendously interesting. Richard came to believe Cecil existed in two forms: 'Gauleiter' and 'Holiday Dad'. Gauleiter was a man of his times. He had served in World War I and like some veterans on both sides of that conflict he felt there was unfinished business. His railing against 'Prussian Militarism' made the nickname seem very amusing. His first nickname amongst the Glossop pupils had been Joe (Stalin), but once operation Barbarossa turned the Soviets into the good guys and British people came to understand the internal organisation of the Nazi party, the Gauleiter cap seemed to fit. What we must remember is that at the time there was limited knowledge of the atrocities committed by both the Nazi and Soviet regimes and certainly the teenagers of Glossop would have been unaware of the concentration camps. But Cecil did run the school as a quasi-dictatorship and photographs show he was short of stature and sported a very fetching moustache...

Holiday Dad was a devoted parent and altogether more engaging character. He doesn't make many appearances in the book, but can be found tramping with Richard around Mossy Lea or showing off his motor car in (1930s posh) Southport or (1930s smart) South London. His biggest soliloquy is when he tells Richard about his heroic adventures advancing from Misery to Pissy (near Amiens) and showing Ludendorff the door. I don't think Cecil realised how much his Great War stories impressed and influenced Richard. When he left his campaign medals to my cousin Oliver, Richard was hurt, but by that stage Cecil and Richard hadn't spoken much for decades, so perhaps he shouldn't have been too surprised?

Growing up with the Gauleiter ends with a letter written by Richard to his father in 1991, 11 years after Cecil's death. Richard never redrafted this. It is not about teaching or life in a northern town, but it tells of a son's love for his father, which was not fully expressed during the latter's life time. I challenge you to read it without a tear. Cecil Lord was a distant character in my childhood, but through this book I have got to know my grandfather in his flaws and in his triumphs. I also hear the voice of the father I love, who was honest, enquiring and funny. I hope you enjoy meeting them both too.

Susannah Lord-Cloke, June 2016

Prologue

HOW THE BOOK CAME TO BE WRITTEN

My father was not really a Nazi party boss. Instead between 1937 and 1960 he was the headmaster of a nice little grammar school at Glossop, a mill town in the Derbyshire hills, fourteen miles from Manchester. 'Gauleiter' was his nickname. Towards the end of the war, as the Allied armies invaded Germany, the word was often on the lips of BBC newsreaders and it got attached to Dad. Which was not altogether fair because he was not a brute and indeed had more in common with Captain Mainwaring than the Führer. He was a charismatic classroom teacher seeking to spread 'sweetness and light' – a lot of Shakespeare with a dash of science – among the boys and girls he served, some of whom came from quite poor homes. He could however be fierce, was riddled with prejudice and was capable of tyranny and that must be why the name stuck. It replaced 'Joe', meaning Stalin, so the kids had a point, and it was not just that Dad and both the dictators concerned had moustaches. His totalitarian tendency was picked up by colleagues as well as pupils, as you can see from *Plate 1* which shows a cartoon, drawn to amuse the staff-room in a school he once taught at.

Dad was a grammarian. His life [1898-1980] coincided with the heyday of the grammar school – say from 1902, when the species was initiated by a Conservative government, until 1965 when Labour announced its demise – during which time every town harboured an elite academy, nurturing those identified as the brightest of its sons and daughters. Maybe the system offended against modern views of equality but it did a lot for social mobility and it was too hastily abandoned. Dad thought it an affliction to be working class but that, in suitable cases, the condition could be cured. That, at least in part, was what his school was for. He had been a beneficiary himself. As a boy he had attended three different grammar schools and at the last of them he met my mother. Then, after an interlude in the Great War trenches and some student years, he taught at two more such schools before getting his headship at Glossop. When he retired the comprehensive hurricane was still only a distant cloud on the social weather map.

I did not mean to tell Dad's story. I began writing in order to find out what it was that had caused me to run away from my own career in education. I had been principal of a further education college when, at the age of only fifty two, I asked for early retirement and, with disconcerting alacrity, my request was granted. I was bothered about learning. I mean the unencumbered satisfaction of curiosity with a view to getting to the heart of something that matters to the learner. I thought that sort of open enquiry not only useful but also just about the greatest pleasure life offers and I had become disillusioned that not much of it seemed to happen in schools and colleges dedicated instead to certification. Passing exams was OK in its way but it was a lesser reward than feeling the earth move. Depression on that score was not the only thing prompting my bid for freedom but I think it was the chief one. Having escaped, I looked around for something to do and predictably resolved to write a book. I would describe my own early experience of learning, both the instruction I received in classrooms, including those at Glossop Grammar School, and what I picked up off my own bat outside school. I had little doubt that the latter would turn out to have been more productive than the former.

It did not turn out quite like that. First, it emerged that I acquired a lot of factual knowledge at school and also some good habits, often by methods that, in my days as an educational progressive I derided as 'rote learning'. Second, the book lost its pedagogic focus and with it, fortunately, its polemical character. Instead of a sermon it became an open-ended enquiry into how things used to be when I was young, in my family and in the wider world, as well as at school. Much of my childhood was spent during the war, a phenomenon that came to dominate the memories I conjured. It was not that I was in any kind of danger or suffered significant hardship. Glossop was never bombed and I was over-fed by an indulgent mother who had a way with shopkeepers. The war however, as viewed from the stands, proved a sporting event infinitely more riveting than the

World Cup and the Olympics combined. I could not get enough of it and the outbreak of peace in 1945 left me bereft. The third unexpected turn taken by the emerging book was that my father came to occupy centre stage. He had died a few years before I began to write and in his dotage we had recovered something of the companionship we had known long ago as together we listened to news bulletins and pored over war maps. Later our relationship turned sour and degenerated into our own thirty years war. I was sad about that and was looking to discover what had gone wrong. There was unfinished business.

Thus a sermon became an autobiography. It gushed out in rapid spurts over several years until other preoccupations nudged it into touch. In retirement I began to teach again, first as an Open University tutor and then as a National Trust room guide, in conditions much more conducive to real learning than I ever encountered in schools or colleges. That experience proved so absorbing and rewarding that the book got confined to a metaphorical drawer, in which it lay untouched for a couple of decades. Last year I took it out again thinking to offer it for publication but found that, being insufferably long-winded, it would not do as it stood. So I have rewritten it. Much of the original text has been incorporated however and the episodes related are mostly the ones I recalled twenty five years ago when my memory was more reliable than it is now. For this is not an oldie's rambling essay in nostalgia. Rather I offer memories unearthed in middle age as a primary source for how it was when I was young. I am aware for example that what I remember about the war differs markedly from how wartime life is often represented. I had it cushy. I never slept in an air raid shelter, was never evacuated, never went hungry and enjoyed myself between 1939 and 1945 more than I ever did before or afterwards. The book is also a serious contribution to current social debate. About grammar schools, for example. Should they be brought back?

Richard Lord, September 2015

Chapter 1

ORIGINS

On 2 September 1898, at Omdurman in the Sudan, the concentrated rifle volleys of Kitchener's army, sent to avenge the martyred General Gordon, annihilated a horde of 'dancing Dervishes'. According to Wikipedia, ten thousand were killed at a cost to the British of 47 dead. Lieutenant Churchill was present and so was Major Haig. The latter does not seem to have registered the extreme vulnerability of infantry advancing across open ground in the face of modern fire power and hence the sacrifice of twice the total of slaughtered Dervishes on Day One of his Somme offensive in 1916. They included five hundred 'Pals' from Accrington, a tram ride from where my parents then lived.

My father, aka 'the Gauleiter', was born near Bolton two days after Omdurman and, in that high noon of empire, and despite the socialism professed by his father, they called him 'Cecil' after Cecil Rhodes, prophet of imperialism and one of the instigators of the Boer War, which broke out while Dad was learning to walk. It seems then that his cradle was rocked to the brave music of distant drums and that fits what he grew up to be quite well. What his parents were doing in Bolton I do not know for they came from the Rossendale Valley, some twenty miles away. Richard William Lord, usually Dick, who was twenty eight when his third child and second son was born, was however a restless young man who, as we shall see, was prepared to travel to better himself. According to his daughter Marion, in some jottings recorded in 1957, he had started work at the age of twelve when he was apprenticed to his father, a warper in a cotton mill. Dick's grandfather, Samuel Lord [b1806] seems to have

1

owned his own mill. It may, of course, have been a small concern, the distinction between 'workshop' and 'factory' being flexible, but he must at least have been his own boss. Later the Lords lost their independence and began to work for other people. This seems to have happened in the 1860s so maybe they were victims of the 'Cotton Famine' attendant upon the American Civil War. Warping however was a skilled occupation that conferred status a cut above what most cotton operatives enjoyed. That anyway is an impression I formed in 1948 when I was in the sixth form of Glossop Grammar School ['Virtus, Veritas, Libertas' Headmaster: C Lord BA] and as an end of term treat we were given a tour of Sumner's Mill, a vast slab of regularly fenestrated granite that dominated the lower reaches of our town. It was hard times grim. The overwhelming din, dust and heat were scarcely tolerable to a fastidious visitor and the dates displayed on the machines suggested not much had changed at Sumner's since about 1880. However the warpers seemed comparatively privileged. There were only a few of them and, although their workplace was smelly, they had plenty of space and it was mercifully quiet. Their task was to stiffen yarn for weaving by chemical treatment. It seemed to require knowledge and judgement and they carried themselves with the confidence of skilled artisans, members of the 'labour aristocracy'.

That I guess was no comfort to Dick who took a dim view of the industrial scene and had conceived a plan to turn his back on capitalism. He would opt instead, like William Morris, for a rural, pre-industrial idyll. Morris in 1896 had published *News from Nowhere*, a sort of *Country Life* edition of Marx's *Das Kapital*, depicting a utopia in which money had withered away, along with human greed, and the comrades freely supplied each other's needs through the exchange of craft skills and artistic talents. Ironically Dick's Morrisite revolt against the industrial revolution was made possible by industrial progress which, by the 1890s, had delivered the three essential ingredients in his escape plan – photography, the bicycle and the seaside holiday. He put it together like this. More and more people were going to Blackpool. When people are on holiday they like to tell their friends they wish they were there and the picture postcard was a perfect medium for such felicitations. In the Fylde, the countryside around Blackpool, unlike in most parts of the country where agricultural depression was deeply established, farming still flourished – Blackpool boarding houses and mill town chippies relied on spuds from the Fylde

– so there a certain rural felicity survived. The district also lay within pedalling distance of the Golden Mile so Dick, setting up as a high street photographer, could cultivate the postcard trade while also obliging his neighbours with parlour portraits. For a bicycle is an adaptable vehicle. With the aid of straps and carriers, baskets and panniers, capes and clips it will serve as a mobile studio, delivery van and company car. That clinched it. So in 1900 Dick, his wife Ada, five year old Leslie, three year old Elsie and Cecil the toddler voted with their feet against industrial society and settled amid green fields at Poulton-le-Fylde

...small market town, and par. With ry sta ... near river Wye ...915 ac .. pop 2223; P.O., T.O. Market day Monday ...

according to J G Bartholomew [ed] *The Survey Gazetteer of the British Isles* [1904]. Rustic Poulton then is where my father grew up. So his early memories carried a pastoral tinge imparted by fields, woods, riverbanks and the big skies of the flat Fylde. Thus he responded readily to pastoral elements in English literature, the discipline that came to mould his sentiments. The founding idyll however proved relatively brief. When he was fourteen, in rather unhappy circumstances that will keep till later, he was yanked back to Rawtenstall amid the Rossendale smoke.

Thus it happened that in 1913 Cecil became part of the first intake of pupils to the brand new Bacup and Rawtenstall Secondary School, a state grammar school set up, like a thousand others, under the terms of the 1902 Education Act which inaugurated that remarkable species. It also happened that another pupil called Lord joined the pioneer cohort. Nellie and Cecil Lord were not related. It is just that Lord, a fairly unusual surname in the country as a whole, is locally common in east Lancashire. In due course – it took nearly twenty years – they became my parents but, although they took their time about procreation, I think they must have become a couple quite soon after they first met *[Plate 2 middle left]*.

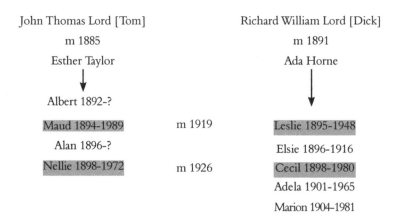

Lord and Lord
A simplified family tree

John Thomas Lord [Tom]		Richard William Lord [Dick]
m 1885		m 1891
Esther Taylor		Ada Horne
↓		
Albert 1892-?		↓
Maud 1894-1989	m 1919	Leslie 1895-1948
Alan 1896-?		Elsie 1896-1916
Nellie 1898-1972	m 1926	Cecil 1898-1980
		Adela 1901-1965
		Marion 1904-1981

Nellie's older sister Maud and Cecil's older brother Leslie were more precipitate. They married immediately after the Great War in 1919 [*Plate 2 bottom right and Plate 3 top*] and had a baby the following year. I need to fill you in on all that because otherwise you will find the genealogical situation baffling. In brief, two brothers called Lord married two sisters, also called Lord, as the table above shows.

By the time Nellie was born, also in 1898, John Thomas Lord, her father and my grandfather, was in his late thirties and had become a substantial businessman. His success was due to his boot straps, not to a silver spoon, for he and his wife Esther had both been child workers in cotton mills. She used to tell me she started when she was seven, which would have been in 1869, although for a while she spent part of the working day in school, a privilege that cost her parents twopence a week. The local mechanics institute had been a staging post in Tom's rise but it was his membership of a chapel congregation that proved truly instrumental. At the Bethel Baptists in Waterfoot, one of the Rossendale townships and the location of the new grammar school just mentioned, he fell in with the chapel's chief patron, an inventor and entrepreneur called Henry Trickett. Trickett is credited with devising the carpet slipper, inspired, so it is said, by the practice of mule spinners, who rather than walk always barefooted behind machines that had to be trundled forever backwards and forwards during their operation, wrapped their feet in pieces of felt. He adapted Gaghills Mill, a former cotton factory, for the manufacture of footwear, made globe-trotting sales trips and became known, across the British Empire, so it is also said, as the 'Slipper King'. In 1910, for services to the Liberal Party, he acquired a further title, becoming Sir H W Trickett Bart *[Plate 2 top right]*. My grandfather travelled deftly in the Trickett slipstream, rising from the shop floor – he did time as secretary to the slipper-workers union – to a place on the board. Soon after Nellie was born, at Gaghills Terrace, above the mill, Tom moved his family to a four square residence, complete with servants' quarters and a shrubbery, called Warthe House. It calls to mind Stone Lodge, the home of Dickens's Mr Gradgrind. It stood discreetly back from the road but remained handy for the mill, the Liberal Club and of course the chapel. The doings, sacred and secular, of Bethel Baptists dominated my mother's early life and it is an immersion to which we shall pay homage in a later chapter. For the moment let us say she acquired an ethic that was Protestant but not austere. She had no doubts about what was right and wrong but did not feel she was her brother's keeper. Which was just as well for Albert [b 1892] and Alan [b 1896] were chalk and cheese. Albert stuck to the slipper maker's last, becoming in time a caricature tycoon. When he visited us in Glossop, after the Second World War, he arrived in a chauffeur driven Daimler and a ten gallon hat, accompanied by Major, his large furry dog, Ivy, his large furry fancy woman and her lean 'companion' in blue gabardine. He once boasted of receiving 't' biggest bloody gas bill i' Morecambe'. Alan however achieved gentility. As a doctor on a cruise liner he met the daughter of a baronet and went off to live in a manor house in Wales. I do not know where my mother received her early schooling for it was not a matter she deemed interesting. She never much rated book learning. However in 1911 they sent her to Ackworth, the Quaker school in Yorkshire where Alan was already a pupil. She only stayed two years. She was quite glad to have had a brief experience of boarding school but her recollections were not ecstatic. I guess home-sickness – even chapel sickness – dogged her. So the new grammar school, erected just behind Ross Mount, the even more des res Tom and Esther had now moved up to, probably brought Nellie blessed relief. They let her come home and go there instead of packing her box again for another sad sojourn on the wrong side of the Pennines.

Thus my parents found each other but, as I say, they took their time about moving their relationship on. Things got in the way. First there was Dad's involvement in the war *[Plate 2 bottom left]* and then his university years. By then their families had migrated from Rossendale. Remarkably Dick, about the end of the war, at the age of around fifty, managed another dramatic career change, landing a job as a photographer with Sport and General, a Fleet Street agency *[Plate 10]*. The achievement seems remarkable but how he pulled it off I do not know. Thus he, Ada and their two younger daughters [Elsie had died] went off down south and I came to know them as 'Granny and Grandpa London'. *Plate 4 top* shows them lined up on Clapham Common with the boys there as well.

I knew my other grandparents also by a geographical label, that of 'Southport', the then superior resort on the Lancashire coast to which they retired in 1919. Actually Tom's retirement proved premature when his savings evaporated in a post war slump. That was the story anyway but I guess he also missed his job. Anyway he went back to work and soon became Chairman of Sir H W Trickett Ltd, an office he still held on his death in 1943. But they stayed in Southport and he commuted by train. This suited Cecil as well as Nell for he was a frequent visitor at their comfortable villa. They used to speak nostalgically of picnics on the beach, tennis in the parks and a quasi-Parisian round of cafés, cinemas and thés dansants along Lord Street, the tree-lined avenue that, far from aping the French capital, claimed plausibly to be the model for its boulevards. Although they delayed their marriage, they 'anticipated' it – according to Maud's later-life partner who, for good reason, disliked Cecil and enjoyed reporting his embarrassing boasts. So presumably their rather surprising un-chaperoned holidays in Switzerland, which began as early as 1920, were everything their mothers must have feared.

At last in 1926, by which time my father had become a schoolmaster, they got married *[Plate 3 bottom]* but that did not signal the start of 'a family'. Clearly their approach to contraception was as modern as their attitude to pre-marital sex. My father kept a book by Marie Stopes in his bedroom drawer, together with a German revolver, about which more in a later chapter. I used to read it surreptitiously but it was maddeningly imprecise. The author confessed to being defeated by 'feelings too intimate to describe' and the illustrations revealed nothing more than the exterior of an outlet for surgical goods somewhere in Soho. But whatever Nellie and Cecil did or did not do it worked and my birth was long delayed, thus permitting further Alpine excursions and the acquisition of a 'Baby Austin' *[Plate 4 middle]*. Not that I should complain. More hasty parents could have landed me with an uncomfortably direct role in the Second World War. However, after a final visit to Switzerland and notwithstanding a major political crisis to do with Labour and the gold standard, I was duly conceived at the start of the new school year in 1931. It is a season when teachers commonly resolve to make changes to their lives.

Just before their marriage my father had been appointed Senior English Master at Stretford Grammar School, another of the new breed of academies. It was tastefully housed in neo Georgian brick, amid playing fields, opposite Old Trafford Cricket Ground, three miles from the centre of Manchester. They set up house, within cycling distance of his place of work, at Chorlton-cum-Hardy, a good class suburb the features of which reinforced the illusion of rusticity conjured by its name. So it had [and has] a village green with a lych gate and a pub that looks old and the street names – Rye Bank Road, Great Stone Road, Barlow Moor Road – perpetuate the truly rural myth. They lived at 11 Polruan Road, on a newly built estate of little bow-fronted semis that after the Great War had billowed out beyond the Victorian 'village' centre. Polruan is a fishing harbour in Cornwall, so you see what I mean. I was born in a nursing home in Edge Lane, Chorlton on 16 June 1932. It was hot they said and haymaking was going on beneath the windows in 'the meadows', a swathe of watery cow pasture flanking the River Mersey. The lanes between the meadows are now closed to traffic, the area having been designated the 'Mersey Valley Country Park', a somewhat grubby pedestrian paradise, but in the flaming June of 1932 my parents were able to drive their open-topped Austin furiously up and down those byways in an effort to coax me from a womb I had occupied too long. I showed an early preference for repose against activity.

When I first set out to recover the incidents of early life, memory seemed to serve me well and out came the coherent, though not necessarily reliable, account of what happened to me between the ages of two and four that occupies much of this chapter. For times before that only hearsay and pictorial evidence is available. I was however a much photographed infant, as you can see from the evidence of *Plates 5, 6 and 7*. Uncle Leslie as well as Grandpa London being professionals and ever ready with their lenses, tripods, flash bulbs and black hoods. For, a few years before I was born, Leslie, toiling hitherto to build up a motor cycle business in Rossendale, repeated the dazzling Fleet Street coup achieved by his father a decade earlier. He somehow got a job on *Reynolds News*, a Victorian Sunday scandal sheet which was transformed into a respectable left wing weekly rant, when it was acquired by the Co-operative Wholesale Society. It brought him, Maud and Barbara the nice house in the Surrey woods at Selsdon which will figure later in this chapter. Leslie delighted *Reynolds* readers with photographic strip cartoons and sometimes, as flaxen haired toddler or mousy three year old, I starred in them. Little man soaps face and tries out Daddy's razor [*Plate 6 top right*]. Naughty boy smashes Cinderella's palace built by Mummy with toy bricks. Well, it paid the mortgage while they waited for the Revolution.

The fallout from all that posing and snapping was a bulging box of family photographs which, through perpetual perusal, stamped in an abiding sense of family solidarity. This is who we are. This is where we come from. This is what we do. But is the evidence of the photographs reliable? In a major respect it is certainly at variance with what I remember. A constant feature of these images of sun-kissed childhood – played out on lawns and beaches, in woods and parks, while building sandcastles and snowmen, with balls and quoits, rubber fish and a real dog, toy trains and pretend ice-cream carts – is mostly missing from my actual memories. It is my father. In the pictures he is always there – a laid back, ever smiling, open-necked, unfailingly affectionate playmate. But I cannot believe the photographic evidence revealed on *Plate 5 bottom* and *Plate 6 top*.

Was Dad ever laid back? Did he really smile a lot? It is not how I remember him. In fact, despite surprisingly good recall of my infancy, I have only fleeting recollections of him until a crisis exploded when I was three and a half. Instead the centre of my being was someone who figures less frequently in the photographs. I grew up with my mother. Which may not come as a sensational revelation. Have I not heard the earth is round and what goes up can be expected to come down? Well, yes but I fear it took me a long time to realise that how you get on with your mum when you are young makes a difference to how you turn out. I arrived at that peak in Darien by a coldly academic process when, in my mid-thirties, I was called upon to give lectures to trainee teachers on 'The Sociology of the Family'. It was a subject I knew nothing at all about but, since nothing concentrates the mind like a topic you have to teach next week, I learned fast and, as a spin off, began for the first time to look at my own origins with an attempt at detachment. By the canons of 1960s sociology the scene I contemplated was depressing. For my first three and a half years I was an only child in a classic nuclear family, separated by geography from daily contact with relatives and not much in touch, so far as I can remember, with the local community, if any such existed on the raw estate we were encamped upon. So there we were, my mother and me, in solitary confinement in a claustrophobic semi, the tedium of our dull lives relieved only by visitations from a largely absentee breadwinner. According to the books my mother was a captive wife with minimal opportunities for personal growth and my environment was so un-stimulating that I was threatened with mental retardation. But it was not like that. You can't always trust what you read in books. Indeed the sociology version is even less convincing than the photographs. So let us dig deeper and try to find the mother I remember.

Although she habitually bustled, Mum was not a slave to perpetual chores. The house in Polruan Road was compact and 'modern' and therefore 'labour saving'. We had up to date domestic equipment. We not only had a mincing machine but also a sort of hand pump that manufactured the synthetic cream without which a jelly was naked. And we had a kitchen cabinet with flour dispenser and a permanent shopping list you marked up by swivelling red arrows. We had an electric fire with imitation coals to supplement the open hearth and an electric iron, which Mum plugged into the light socket and wielded with verve across a purpose built ironing board. Granny Southport on the other hand heated a set of smoothing irons to scorching point on the hob of her cast iron range before snatching them away with a piece of scorched flannel to make a rapid transit of clothes spread out on a blanket on the living room table. Poor Granny was not modern. And her with her lumbago too. She even persisted with a Ewbank whereas we, of course, had a tubular vacuum cleaner with attachments. We also had a gas cooker and a gas clothes boiler with a built-in mangle that took the sting out of washing day, which was Monday of course. It had neat rubber rollers, unlike those of Granny's mangle which were gargantuan, wooden and all but immovable. The most important labour saving device was called Kathleen. She came from Ireland and smelled nice and used to take me for walks. I liked her. She came every day and Mum said she was a good worker. But she had to go. One weekend when we were at Southport there was a message from Mr Young next door and we went home early. I noticed beer bottles in the front room but it was evidence in the bedroom that grabbed my parents. A flushed but defiant Kathleen left in a hurry and I was sad.

So although my mother turned her day into a breathless round, it was not a cycle of unremitting toil. The chores were alleviated, giving her scope to develop the finer points of 'household management'. She had an updated version of Mrs Beeton's classic, with photographs instead of the mouth-watering colour plates that decorated Granny's Victorian edition. It was an opportunity she took up with zest. I am sure she did not hanker for the world of paid employment. If she thought about that at all she would have been profoundly thankful that, at no stage in her life, had there been the remotest possibility that she might herself have to follow her mother into the mill. To my mother's generation of northern women, acutely aware of a century old tradition of working mums in textile factories, to be a full time housewife was a token, not of deprivation, but of liberation. She used her freedom fully. Cooking was her first love. Over the years, cowed by health warnings, I have tried to wean myself from her cuisine. She was heavily into cream and pastry and doing things with very hot fat. But I like the way she did it. What she communicated in the kitchen was creative fulfilment. She was not just making a fruit cake for tea, she was doing something that lit up her whole person and made her, for the moment, beautiful. Her élan was the more exciting for being unconscious. To watch her beat a batter, peel a potato or judge the temperature of the chip fat just so – well usually, she twice set the house on fire – was to sit with an artist at work. Not that she was universally accomplished. In some fields her skills approached what she could do in the kitchen. She had green fingers and loved gardens and because shopping goes with cooking, and because, before there were supermarkets, you had to socialise with shopkeepers, she excelled along the high street. But in other fields she was no great shakes. She could wield a frying pan more deftly than a needle. But that did not put her off. She did not restrict herself to hemming and darning but engaged in a permanent festival of knitting, dressmaking, embroidery and the production of shawls, blankets and cushion covers, made of crocheted 'medallions' sewn together. Furthermore, in all that, she was in charge. Nobody challenged her sovereignty. The home was hers to dispose of as she saw fit. She arranged things to suit herself. She did as she pleased. I call that good work.

The contrast with how we live now does not need spelling out. Perhaps my mother and I, in a Manchester suburb in the 1930s, were very lucky.

We exploited a window of bourgeois bliss that began to unravel when war came, was briefly knitted together again afterwards in the 1950s, but then plunged into oblivion. Had my mother been born a generation later she would have been lucky to escape university and an exhausting tussle between career and family. Had she been born three generations later then I would probably have been consigned to a nursery and given a collective upbringing. I admit that does not seem to have done my granddaughter irreparable harm but I am glad it did not happen to me. Instead I was for several years the focus of my mother's love and chief beneficiary of her creative housewifery. She was my only friend. Until I started school I had no regular contact with other children. But the friendship – perhaps more a love affair – was so warm and so stimulating that I craved no other company. Maybe I lacked opportunities to acquire social skills but my mother gave me something I rate higher than affability. It is self-esteem. Despite abundant knocks and repeated failure I have always maintained a superlatively high opinion of myself. I know deep down that, whatever happens, I am all right really. I got that confidence from my mother when I was very young. Thanks Mum.

Bliss was not of course unalloyed. I have bad memories as well as good ones. I cannot remember my own toilet training but, judging from the horrors that attended efforts to tame my sister into premature continence, I guess it was rough. Perhaps that was why bed-wetting plagued my childhood. They thought I could help it but I knew I could not. Also I had problems with food. It seems I was subjected to the regime of Dr Truby King, guru and martinet, and in obedience to his prescriptions they used to leave me to yell between scheduled feeding times for King forbade comforting as well as out of hours snacks. Once apparently I cried continuously for 24 hours and in panic they called the doctor. Was it was OK to pick me up? He diagnosed hunger, prescribed an immediate feed and the cure was instant. That must have been my uptight, interfering fusspot of a father, turning the nursery into a schoolroom. It was he who told the tale and did so without shame or irony. Left to herself Mum would never have been so daft. The agony in the cot is of course beyond recall but I do remember a painful scene a year or two later. It was dinner time – that is 12-30 midday, when we had our main meal and Dad came home to devour it. I piped up with a suggestion. Let's skip the main course and go straight to the Queen of Puddings. It was my favourite and I knew it was to follow, having licked out the dish. Fletcher

Christian could not have defied Captain Bligh with greater presumption. It was mutiny. Thus I was force fed a churned up mixture of spiky potato and grisly mince. I yelled but neither fads nor tantrums would be tolerated. That was heavy handed Dad again. My mother was more crafty. She had this theory that rice pudding is 'just like ice cream'. I knew she was wrong and tried to argue the case but she remained incorrigible. Porridge was another problem. She laced it with syrup but still it would not go down. Then she showed me the caber tosser on the Scots Oats packet but I lacked any ambition to be big and strong and wield a telegraph pole. I still retch at the mere sight of the stuff. And I find the smell of oranges distressing. That stems from memories of Mum, spreading thighs mottled by a roaring fire, half a fruit held by suction to her voracious lips, showering juice around her person like a marathon runner taking a sponge. I am a lifelong chaotic eater. My appetite rages independently of the biological need to restore consumed energy. I assume it has to do with long gone porridge and the oranges of yesteryear.

Those were the bad bits but it is memories of good times alone with my mother that mostly stick. We played together a lot. I remember bricks with mother. They were shiny and came in assorted colours and included architectural pieces, like classical columns and curved lintels. We did jigsaws and played cards. Or looked at cards anyway – Happy Families and also Lexicon, so I must have known about letters early on despite anxieties to come when I was slow to read. We had picture books and I learned verses. There were nursery rhymes but I preferred A A Milne. Soon I knew by heart a lot of the poems in *When We Were Very Young*. They often seemed to be about royals and their retinues so they must have been anathema to my socialist relatives. There was the one about the king, by no means 'a fussy man', who fancied 'a little bit of butter for his bread' and then there was Alice who was 'marrying one of the guards' knowing that 'a soldier's life is terrible hard'. Indeed the very earliest thing I can properly remember is standing on a stool, reciting to Mrs Clark, Kathleen's predecessor:

I often wish I were a King/And then I could do anything

Distrust of democracy being endemic, I went on wishing it for many years until experience showed the wish to be an illusion. The second line does not infallibly follow from the first.

Drama was on the syllabus as well as poetry and politics. We acted out situations with my ice cream cart, a replica of one of Walls' 'Stop me and buy one' trolleys, ubiquitous on the streets of pre-war Britain, usually in the form of a tricycle pedalled by a man in blue and white stripes with uniform cap – a Pied Piper, more glamorous than the butcher's boy and less sinister than the rag and bone man. Mine was only a hand cart but it was otherwise authentic. Under a tight fitting 'ice box' lid I had a store of wooden pieces representing choc-ices, strawberry and vanilla briquettes, and the paper wrapped triangular water ices that foreshadowed the post war ice lolly. I liked the rituals of retailing and wanted to be a shopkeeper. I also had a toy rake and a toy roller but that did not make me want to be a gardener. I had a tricycle too, with white tyres and a bell and, as I recall with alarm, when Mum heard the 'twelve o'clock hooter', announcing dinner time at Metrovics engineering plant in Trafford Park, two miles away, she sometimes let me go off on my own, traffic and paedophiles notwithstanding, along Polruan Road to the lamppost at the corner of the street, to wait for Dad as, on his grown up bike, he pedalled down Great Stone Road towards his dinner [*Plate 6 middle left* – note that the bell is not working]. I suppose it freed her to dish up in peace.

Indoors there was a choice of equipment for situation drama. I had a clockwork train set with trees, tunnel, a signal box and a station [*Plate 6 middle right*]. Although made in Liverpool, it was clearly a rural branch line and the lead passengers I stood on the platform were commuters with furled umbrellas and shopping ladies going up to town. Also I had both a farmyard and a zoo, each with appropriate fencing. Thus I learned to classify. Like was corralled with like – lions on the left, lambs on the right. At that very moment they were doing the same thing in Dachau – red triangles for communists and purple for homosexuals. I had bath toys and take to bed toys. The rubber fish you have seen and I also had boats for bath time. But, despite the hegemony of Pooh in my mental life, I had no teddy. I think Dad censored it but I do not know why. I did have a gollywog though, which in the minds of correct thinking readers will confirm the worst impressions already formed. He was called Sambo and he came to a sad end, being burnt before my very eyes on Granny Southport's living room fire. He was infectious because I had whooping cough. It was Whitsun 1935 and the King was having his Jubilee and it was on the wireless. What a crazy thing to do to a child. Dad again? Probably, but Mum was there as well and she did not stop him. Their reverence for medicine, his anyway, was quasi-religious. I am sure they did not mean to hurt. They did though.

But back to the good times. Sometimes we played away, visiting the wider world beyond Number 11. Beyond the streets with the whimsical names was Longford Park and on fine afternoons I often went there with mother. It was no mere municipal plantation but the grounds of real country house adapted by the municipality. So it had a grand leafy avenue and acres of spreading grassland shaded by spreading trees. Municipal adaptations must have been going on in the 1930s for I remember a new café in the rose garden and they were draining the lake. At least I assume that is what happened because there is no lake there now, only a depression in the grass. But I know there was one once because a horror snapshot lives on in my head. One afternoon my mother and I stood behind the railings on Edge Lane and stared appalled at an island, where scurrying rats swarmed in the sunshine. Like she said, it was 'alive with them'. The sight thrilled me but I was not really afraid because I was safe with my mother and there was an expanse of water between us and them. I think that viewpoint became habitual. The world was full both of fascination and danger but if I stayed close to mother I could have the former without the latter. I became a voyeur savouring sundry holocausts, always safely insulated from the action. I soon found a better insulating medium even than water. It was print. The pages of books, magazines and newspapers, adult ones as well as children's, became a favourite focus. I mean pictures not words. Scrutinising them became a passion. It reached its peak during the war, a paradise for a young voyeur but I was hooked before that. I remember, for example, the animal book I had at Christmas 1935. On the cover there was a big brown bear and the image was so powerful it entered my dreams as well as my waking life. We shall meet him again.

I think I learned to think by looking. Take my next encounter with rats. It came after the period of this chapter but it nicely illustrates the process. These other rats came with *Picture Post* the news magazine launched in 1938. I was 'reading' one of the early numbers with my father. That is I was closely examining the pictures and Dad was telling me about them. We were looking at a slum courtyard in Glasgow. Dad said the reporter had seen 18 rats [or was it 23?] in broad daylight on that very spot. The light must have been too dim for the camera, because you could not discern any wild life even if you peered and peered at the grainy page. But I could 'see' the rats nevertheless. The image came out of a store inside my head. Rats from Longford Park were transferred to Glasgow slum yard that needed to be populated with them. My mind then retained the resulting photo-montage as well as the original images and I could retrieve that too whenever I felt like calling it up. Thus my brain was both a camera and a photograph album. Mixing the images it contained to create ever more complex mental constructions was profoundly satisfying. I was learning how to think. And all without words, please note. Looking and thinking worked so well I felt no need of the printed word. Why read if you can get so much from pictures? Later perhaps I deliberately chose not to read lest it diminish the pleasure of looking and thinking. If so, I was storing up trouble with Dad and other teachers, whose minds seemed differently wired.

But back to Chorlton when I was three. My mother and I went to the 'village' as well as the park. Did I walk? I think I remember a push chair. I certainly remember knocking over a big swinging mirror in a dress shop. I was making it swing faster, then suddenly it shattered and there was broken glass everywhere. I was shocked. Mum was cross. The shop lady was not amused. There are impressions of other shops too – icing on cakes, bananas on hooks and cash tubes that whizzed overhead. I liked the smell of the fishmongers and of Dr Philbin's surgery. Once at the doctor's they gave me the actual glass phial that had contained the needle with which I had been immunised against diphtheria. Can that really have happened? I did not get smallpox jabs because my parents, participating in a current medical debate – they would wouldn't they? – considered the risks of vaccination greater than the chance of infection. And I was immunised against whooping cough, as we have seen, by whooping and coughing, thus sealing Sambo's fate. Later I had mumps and measles and chickenpox, though not all at once. But, unlike quite a lot of school friends, I never had to go into hospital. It is now quite rare for children to have children's diseases but before the war we all grew up assuming that life would from time to time be interrupted through the not always unpleasant process of illness? Sometimes though illness led to death, even in young people. I saw Muriel Young, the teenager who lived next door, carried out on a stretcher. A little later my mother, unusually quiet and urging stillness also on me, drew the front curtains and peeped out from behind them, as neighbours were doing up and down the street, at something very solemn going on outside. It seemed to involve a lot of men and cars.

We used to go to 'town' as well as the village. That meant taking a tram and I liked those friendly jumbos. They had stalks on top that sparkled like fireworks. They were in the charge of manly men in long dark overcoats with peaked caps, metal badges and leather straps. The conductor had a long pole he used to turn the stalk round at the terminus. Then he ran upstairs and reversed all the seat backs so that passengers would go into town facing the right way. The driver meanwhile stayed calm at his post, presiding over his shiny brass controls. The inside had a special feel, secure and serene. Womb like? The dim light was soothing. It came through windows decorated at the top with panes of red and purple, pierced by cut glass stars, and from flickering bulbs in what I would come to know as art nouveau holders. Pasted on the partition behind the driver's compartment, there was a small oval picture of the Manchester Ship Canal. I loved that mysterious name. A tram ride was ideal for looking and thinking. Like watching the rats, it combined a good view with security and detachment. So, safe with mother, nose glued to the window, I sailed to town through Hulme, where the slums were. What did I see? I saw a lot of traffic including great horse-drawn drays. There were pubs with fancy glass, churches with elegant spires and brightly lit shops. Before Christmas Allenscots in Stretford Road was hung with poultry and game, spotlighted among the holly. To left and right of the main road, if you looked sharp you could pick up dim narrow streets with the front doors close together – presumably the slums. But I suspect my recollections have been invaded by Friedrich Engels' famous description of an earlier Manchester, as laid out by cunning capitalists. He said the plan – broad highways, flanked by a cosmetic display of well-lit shops, radiating from the commercial centre to respectable suburbs – had been deliberately devised to shield the eyes of commuters from the proletarian squalor behind the facades. Well ... perhaps there is something in it.

Once in town we went to the big shops. Lewis's was the prime target but there was also Affleck and Browns and Pauldens and posh Kendal Milnes. Lewis's was best. It was Aladdin's cave set in an opera house. You stood in the middle of the ground floor, beside the kiosk of the 'Ask Me' girl, and looked up at the tiered sales areas above. You could go up in big lifts with clanging grilles and uniformed drivers who obliged with commentary on the diverse attractions of the passing levels. Behind the grilles the lift shafts, furnished with gliding cables and big flat counterweights, were open to my fascinated inspection. But I much preferred the moving staircase. Riding the escalator was as good as going on the tram. It had the same solid slatted floor. It gave the same even transit. It too offered a time out of life, dedicated to standing and staring, with the added dimensions of movement and ascension. The whole world was laid out before you but you were safe from its perils and excused its obligations. Until you reached the top, that is, when you had to negotiate the tricky bit, where the staircase disappeared underground and you had to jump off and make your legs work by your own efforts. Thus began a lifetime attachment to shopping. How I envy modern three year olds whose induction into that delight takes place in megastores, malls and out of town centres of a scale, magnificence and technical sophistication that far exceeds the steam age marvels of Lewis's in my day. I never even got a ride in a supermarket trolley.

Sometimes when we went to town Dad came too but it was not the same. Probably to free Mum for a bit of shopping on her own, he took me off to inspect the city beyond the shops. In itself a good plan surely. One day we went to the new Central Reference Library just opened by the very king who was having his jubilee the day Sambo was burnt. You had to go in through a revolving doorway which meant I had to let go his hand and for a horrifying moment was trapped in solitary but mobile confinement. Trauma is too weak a word to describe my terror. Once inside we were assailed in a big space by an echoing alternation of light and shade as we climbed a rubber staircase watched by a sad lady in marble with her clothes all dishevelled. I was getting to tell old buildings from modern ones but here you didn't know where you were. The rubber was reassuringly modern but the sculpted figures had hauled themselves from some time long, long ago. Finally we reached a vast and awesome temple whose great dome shed a pervading green light, on all sides round. I was pole-axed and yelled. So I was hustled back down the bouncy steps and thrust again through the mincing machine into the light of common day. Dad was furious. My behaviour was wilful. His embarrassment was acute. I was a wicked boy and did not deserve treats. I was only three but was no stranger to righteous indignation. It was like the forced feeding. He

17

was totally unreasonable, incapable of understanding. He just did not get it. He should have remembered what Canterbury Cathedral had done to me last summer. The terror that place induced was just like what had beset me at this alarming library. I had yelled then as well and been frog marched out of evensong. I did not of course know it was Canterbury or a cathedral but I knew terror when it grabbed me. Yet architecture was to become a grown-up passion despite this unfortunate induction so maybe I should be grateful to Dad after all. However I still get bad dreams in which I am humiliated by manly men in circumstances of architectural grandeur.

To be fair, in the trips he planned, Dad sometimes got it right. Other cathedral-like edifices in Manchester indeed were enchanting, not frightening. I mean the railway stations – wonderlands of sounds, sights and smells under soaring roofs. Victoria was to be experienced at three different levels. There was a tiled cavern running under the very tracks where you could feel in your temples the pounding weight of the passing trains. And above ground level the scene took off into theatrical fantasy. A uniformed young man piloted a wickerwork parcels trolley that fluttered like a bird beneath the high roof. There must have been tracks but, shrouded in all the smoke and steam, the daring young man appeared to be flying, like the fairies in *Peter Pan* at the Opera House. At London Road – renamed 'Piccadilly' in a post war jeu d'esprit – the engines made even more impact than the architecture. They were huge and painted red. There was a walkway above the buffers from which you could look them in the face, which was scary because they were capable of roaring back in a great steamy ejaculation that engulfed us onlookers. But I knew these monsters were friendly. Once the engine driver talked to us and I was lifted onto the footplate. It was very hot.

But it is time to go home to Polruan Road, to tea as the lamps are lit, to sardines on buttered toast and cherry cake or one of those squashy confections, with a crust of marbled greeny-blue icing over a deep well of cream, that came from Lowes, on the station approach, the best cake shop in Chorlton. The drawn curtains shut out the perils and dangers of the night yet a sense of harm lurking beyond them never quite went away. For in the black night beyond the curtains lay the dark and sinister gable ends of larger houses in Grange Road. They scowled across an overgrown back passage into the neat garden where Mum hung the washing while I played with my ice cream cart. Later I would identify Grange Road as Victorian. The rear quarters of the houses there – they were of the design called 'tunnel backs' – projected towards us like gun barrels. Although built of brick, they were smoke-dimmed and their black slate roofs glistening in the drizzle. They scared me. Grange Road must harbour wretched folk living, not the brave modern lives we enjoyed, but a blighted, nasty-minded and old fashioned existence. For I grew up convinced that somehow, not long before I was born, there had been a seismic cultural shift. The world had suddenly become a cleaner and better lit place. An enlightened era had arrived and the fog that had enveloped earlier and less fortunate generations had been blown away. In time I came to think of the divide as 'Modern' [good] and 'Victorian' [bad]. In due course, because I liked my old fashioned Southport grandparents, I developed a sneaky regard for some things Victorian but I never doubted that modern was best. So Victorian Grange Road was sinister and I had no sympathy for the troglodytes who squatted there.

Grange Road was often in my sights because we lived mostly in the dining room at the back of the house. There was also a 'front room' – not a 'lounge', my parents were not vulgar. That apartment harboured a cut moquette suite, some misty mountain water-colours and a folding mahogany three tier cake stand without which no home was complete. But, like the 'parlour' respectable Victorians kept spotless but unsullied by daily intercourse, we hardly ever used it and that showed how precarious modernity was. Grange Road attitudes had not been wholly eradicated even from our bravely modern lives. The unused front room, along with a kitchen of such ludicrously inadequate dimensions that it bore the shameful name 'scullery' and the absence of central heating, combined to compress our waking activities almost entirely into the cramped 'dining room'. Thus our classic semi was in practice as overcrowded as the classic slum. If 11 Polruan Road was 'a machine for living in', it was a defective one. Still, while there were only three of us and Dad was out most of the time and we spent the weekends in a big house at Southport, the heavily used dining room was cosy and fire-lit rosy. The furniture was 'Jacobethan'. There was a leafed table, with grooves that collected crumbs and matching chairs with high backs and saggy leather seats. Dad's chair had baronial arms but Mum and I sat in lesser state. There was a veneered sideboard in the Old English style, on which the radio stood and a drop leaf bureau, whose polished surface I once deeply scratched, maliciously, they said. In a fireside alcove there were Dad's books in an oak-looking case. Although there were two lamps, one floor standing with a frilly shade and the other a table model with a barley sugar shaft and a shade of scorched parchment, Dad preferred the centre light. Since it was hidden behind marbled glass of formidable opacity he had to keep bumping up the wattage to floodlight the *Manchester Guardian*. A cased clock ticked on the mantle-piece, and the tiled hearth, as well as assorted irons, sported a gypsy tripod coal scuttle in imitation copper. On each side of the fire was an easy chair in leather with brass studs, while a matching settee confronted the glowing coals. That suite too was Jacobethan as was my little wicker-seated stool with barley sugar legs that completed the ensemble.

I suppose we might blame William Morris. Our furniture was debased Arts and Crafts. Indeed the suburban semi itself is linearly descended from the Kentish 'Red House' at which Morris took a sabbatical from the industrial revolution. When the 'vernacular' furniture he crafted became fashionable, capitalism got its own back by mass producing derivatives and hence the tat that cluttered our dining room. Not that my parents were aware of any of that. They were not arty or crafty. They just bought an affordable property and filled it in accordance with the prevailing fashion, which just happened to be a debased Arts and Crafts. For me though our furniture was evidence of modernity. You would not find the like of it in Grange Road and it contrasted with the big fancy pieces Granny and Grandpa Southport lived among. I took much pride in the modernity all around me. I rejoiced that I lived among cars and cameras, vacuum cleaners and wireless sets. We ate tinned fruit and bottled sauce. We had rubber hot water bottles and I slept on a rubber sheet. My father had a typewriter and so did Uncle Leslie. I took electricity for granted and knew it came from Barton power station which we passed on the way to Southport, just before the swing bridge, where the Ship Canal cut masterfully through the scrubby countryside. Soon after that we joined the 'New Road', wider even than the canal and just as straight, with leaping bridges, broad carriageways, cycle tracks and roundabouts. It was truly modern. Great lorries hurtled imperiously down this East Lancs Road with the same indifference to the surrounding fields as the big ships sailing on the alley alley oh. So I knew, by that remarkable osmosis by which children discover a cultural identity, that I lived in a modern world, that modernity was underpinned by technology and that technology went with industry and industry went with towns and cities.

I was equally aware however that the urban and industrial scene was not always modern. There was the dark shadow of Grange Road, where benighted Victorian ways lingered like a fog that would not lift. The fingers of that pollution spread wide. They encompassed the slums of Hulme. They tangled even with the brave new drive to Southport, their grip being evident in the clapped out collieries and brooding mills you saw from the East Lancs Road. And the 'Little Canal' – it was actually the very one with which an 18th century Duke of Bridgewater had inaugurated the industrial revolution – whose banks the Austin navigated immediately after the swing bridge, was totally in their possession. Here rotting hulks protruded from dark brown scummy water, awash with sundry detritus, into which, on summer Sundays, pale proletarians could be seen projecting themselves from diving boards improvised from step ladders. Just how I was aware at the age of three of the affront to modernity represented those plucky slum dwellers, and by the attendant ruins of Victorian industry, I do not understand. But I am sure I picked up some such message. I grew up to the clash of cultures.

Not that worrying about the precarious character of modernity seriously got me down. Nor to be fair did the occasional episode of force feeding or a couple or frog marches out of awesome edifices. I was actually a pretty contented three year old. In particular I relished the love nest I shared with my mother, my best and only friend. That bliss was surely ours forever. Unfortunately I was wrong. It went in a flash and all too soon. It is clear in retrospect that the dismantling of my bliss began when they moved me into the box room, the diminutive chamber above the front door, common to the semi as a genre. Until then I had slept safely in a cot which I think of as standing near the bow window in my parents' sunny front bedroom. But perhaps I have got that wrong for it seems against common sense to let a growing child stay in your bedroom when two other rooms are available. So perhaps I only went into my parents' room as a visitor and my cot was really in the back bedroom and that room was equipped as a nursery. If so I now had to vacate it in deference to a sinister project of which I was wholly unaware. They needed the cot as well as the back bedroom so I had to exchange it for a proper bed without protective sides. I would surely fall out. Monsters would get me.

I was scared. And I was scared of being scared because they said I was a big boy now and that was why all these changes were needed. The box room was even provided with a chest of drawers called a 'tallboy', in celebration, I assumed, of relentless maturity. It followed that I was not to cry anymore because big boys don't. But I needed to cry because the box room plan was truly upsetting. Anyway I couldn't help crying any more than I could help wetting the bed. They couldn't stop me. When I began to ponder my predicament, fear and sadness turned to anger. Being told I must not cry was unreasonable. Protest beckoned. I would scream and yell.

The first determined demo was provoked by a trip to the pictures. One evening, soon after I was banished to the bed without arms in the shadow of the tallboy, my parents planned a visit to one of Chorlton's three cinemas. Charlie Chaplin perhaps or maybe the ominous *Things to Come*? A baby sitter had been engaged and that was surely a first. But I rumbled the plan and trumped it. From the fastness of the box room I held the household hostage. I cried. I screamed. I threw myself about in histrionic raptures. My wrong footed parents dithered fatally between guilt and anger. In the end he stomped off to the Picturedrome on his own, leaving her to follow, if and when the tyrant of the box room could be pacified. I do not remember what happened in the end. Perhaps I fell into the sleep of the just, knowing I had made my point. Then perhaps Mum bustled along Oswald Road to catch what was left of the big picture. Not that she deserved even that. How *could* she? Going out with him instead of watching over my slumbers? How fickle. How could I trust her again? Particularly after that lie about rice pudding and ice cream. My victory then was hard won. It came with recognition that I was not the only apple of my mother's eye. I had a rival.

About this time I had a recurring dream. I called it 'bears climbing over' and sometimes used to 'order' it – saying its name while banging my head into the pillow before going to sleep. For, although it was scary, it was fascinating. It projected an image of the exterior of 11 Polruan Road clear in all its familiar outline. But over the roof, coming from the darkness of Grange Road, a huge bear-like creature towered like King Kong. His – I knew the bear was male – neck was extended, nose sniffing the night air, as he gripped the sides of the house between great paws, strong enough to crush its fragile walls. Even the bear was familiar. He came off the cover of the animal book mentioned above. I had unwrapped it, sitting rapturously in my mother's arms in their bed, on the first Christmas Day I can remember, which was 1935. The dream experience was realistic and yet unreal. Indeed it was 'surreal'. In my dream painting I had fallen in with contemporary cultural fashion. Think, for example, of Magritte's vision of a real train steaming into a sitting room through a carefully delineated fireplace. Everything is realistic except the situation.

I suppose the train's penetration of the fireplace is sexual and so probably was my bear's possession of our house. He embodied aggressive masculinity and the frail but protective house was feminine and maternal. Were the bear's intentions destructive or creative? Was he engaged in crushing the house or making love to her? Or both? No wonder I repeatedly called up this dream. For the first time, but unfortunately not the last, I was trying to make sense of sex, to explain things I was aware of in myself or might even have glimpsed from my cot. Whose side was I on? Although, on the whole I identified with the female house and feared the male bear, his masculinity was not entirely unsympathetic. It betokened an alternative way of life, active rather than contemplative, that maybe I would have to adopt now I had been declared a big boy. There was plenty there to think about so no wonder I often banged my head on the pillow and asked for 'Bears climbing over'. Often I was rewarded – or was it punished?

Then in January 1936, only a fortnight after the happy Christmas just recalled, my life was changed utterly. On a night of gales and tumbling chimney pots my mother's heartless infidelity, evident already since the night of the Picturedrome fiasco, was massively confirmed. For suddenly, quite out of the blue, taking me completely by surprise, there she was, grinning toothily in her dressing gown, clutching to her bosom this, wriggling, wrinkly, whining, red thing she introduced as my sister. I should have known something bad was happening for this strange woman had taken up residence and there had been lights on at all hours. That the cause was the birth of a baby was beyond my understanding. I think I knew babies sometimes happened but had been led to understand that they invariably arrived, as I had done, at a remote location called a nursing home. For the phenomenon to occur in our house, in the very bedroom from which I had been expelled was deeply disconcerting. Yet, once again, as in the affair of the box room, I was expected to rejoice. I most decidedly would not and could not. The whole business was not only exceedingly

23

distasteful in itself but, as became painfully apparent over the next few days, this new red thing got all the doting attention Mum had previously kept for me. Well, I was not going to put up with it. Had I not already discovered, à propos the trip to the pictures, that intolerable situations need not be tolerated? So forget looking and thinking, the time had come for action. Thus one afternoon, as I clearly remember, I entered my mother's bedroom with a weapon in my hand. It was a piece of track from my Hornby train set – two strips of aluminium held together by tinplate 'sleepers'. There the thing was, in *my* cot, in *my* place by the window. From just inside the door I took deliberate aim and flung the projectile at the baby. I do not know whether it hit the target. Probably not. But the intent was murderous.

This is not the first time I have written about the culminating event of my infancy. In 1945 as I was approaching my thirteenth birthday, a decade after the trauma, I confided in Miss Hughes our English teacher. Most weeks in term time she had us do a 'composition', a piece of free writing, and doing such an essay had become part of my normal Sunday routine. This week the title was 'A Journey' and I had chosen to describe the enforced trip to London, to stay awhile with my aunt, that was the consequence of my alarming behaviour. Before recounting the journey itself I provide an introduction – 'very interesting and well expressed but rather too long', in Miss Hughes's judgement, and 'do try to be tidy' – in which I recalled my feelings about the arrival of the new baby. It seems worth quoting in full because, out of the mouth of a child speaking much closer in time to the event, it provides confirmation of the old man's recollections just offered. Note that the essay only came to light *after* the above account of my sister's birth was put together. At the time of writing I did not know I had already visited those events long before.

On a dark and stormy night, in January 1936, my sister was born. It was, I believe, one of the worst storms experienced in Manchester for some years and the Lord Mayor had advised people not to go outside that night, unless strictly necessary, as there was a danger of chimney tops being blown off and falling in the roads. I have often thought since that it was an ideal time for my sister to be born as the character of the night has been firmly installed in my sister's character.

About half an hour after she had been born I was allowed to look at my new sister. When I first saw her I was amazed to think that everyone was admiring a thing that I thought was ugly, slimy, flat-nosed and devoid of hair, and I immediately formed a temporary but nevertheless strong prejudice against my sister. I was also indignant to think that the spotlight of affection and interest that had, up to now, focused entirely on myself had been switched over to this new creature that had thrust itself into my life. I therefore resolved to make things as difficult as I could for everyone in the house but especially the new baby and the nurse, whom I detested because she treated me as a baby and I thought myself very much beyond such treatment. So to show my annoyance I brought snowballs into the house to throw at the nurse or put on the fire, locked myself in the bathroom and screamed, threw parts of my Hornby railway at my sister, tried to knock her cot over and so many other similar things that it was decided, much to my delight, to send me to my auntie's house in London for a few weeks.

The situation it seems was worse than I remember. The assault with the toy railway track was only one incident among many, the nurse as well as the baby being subjected to sustained abuse. Furthermore, according to the schoolboy historian of the insurrection in Polruan Road, the aggressive episodes were not spontaneous outbursts but the systematic execution of planned subversion. Anyway the effect was devastating. Enough was enough and the boy would have to go. So on a winter afternoon my father and I set off for the tram stop opposite Chorlton Baths at the start of an epic journey. We went on one of those big trains from London Road station and then on the Underground and then on a bus and then another tram. I remember being icy cold somewhere he said was Brixton. It was long past bedtime and we were sheltering in a doorway opposite a big building with a clock tower. Not that I minded. It was hugely exciting and furthermore I was getting special treatment again, albeit from the wrong parent. When Dad asked the conductor if the tram went to the 'Swan and Sugar Loaf' I knew for sure we were bound for fairyland. Actually we fetched up at Auntie Maud's in Selsdon. The wireless was on and they were saying the King was dead. He had a habit of turning up at critical points in my life, for it was the same chap who had opened the Central Library and whose jubilee had attended the burning of Sambo. Next day there was more snow. It carpeted the terraces of the garden and garlanded the woods beyond. Wearing wellingtons and a beret I went out into the white wonderland with a girl called Margaret who must have been my first playmate. They made us a snowman [*Plate 6 bottom*] but note the fallibility of memory – in the photograph I am wearing a beret but not Wellingtons. Then back indoors, where they had a piano with a long stool topped in red velvet, and my big cousin Barbara read me Pooh stories I had not heard before, because they had *Winnie the Pooh* whereas we only had *The House at Pooh Corner*. Paradise regained. It was so good I do not remember my father leaving.

It seems I was away three weeks. Although I have no recollection of the process I suppose I then came to accept the accomplished fact of Helen's arrival. So the temporary exile to fairyland had worked. The hurt however was never entirely assuaged. My sister and I never became close and Mum became a useful adjunct to my life rather than its very centre. I had reduced expectations of her. She had let me down once too often, and this time cruelly. Inevitably I turned to Dad and in so doing passively consented to being a boy. He had after all taken me on that amazing long distance trek through the winter night – a great adventure, the trip of a lifetime. So for the first time I willingly accepted his company. In return he accorded me the front seat in the car – yes, at the age of four and without seat belts and I did sometimes bang my head on the windscreen – while my Mum and Helen, mere females, lounged in the back. Dad was much more talkative than Mum and a lot of what he said was undoubtedly riveting. He was keen enough to answer questions but told me things anyway even if I had not asked. I was perhaps aware that learning had taken on a new form, different from looking and thinking. Instead of puzzling things out for myself, seemingly at random while Mum sat benevolently by, he directed my curiosity. I was no longer following my nose but was being led by it. I suppose you might call it growing up. 'Shades of the prison-house' were closing in. Thus Wordsworth.

As a coda to this account of how I exchanged infancy for childhood I offer some analysis. The Freudian overtones of the above narrative were not pre-planned. It was only *after* writing that I recognised them myself and looked for confirmation in what Freud wrote. The work consulted was *Introductory Lectures on Psychoanalysis* [1917]. This is what is to be found there. We start with the theory of infant sexuality. Very young children enjoy a 'copious sexual life'. Since such an assertion shocked respectable Vienna, Freud felt obliged to describe what infants get up to as 'perverse'.

It was the task of 'education' to put them straight. In particular young children are quite without inhibition about incest. Thus a boy routinely becomes passionately fond of his mother. He may exhibit towards her 'undisguised sexual curiosity' and 'even make actual attempts at seducing her'. That is usually a bad move. The lad will suffer, not only his mother's rejection but also agonies of jealous anger towards his father and rival suitor. In an age when classical knowledge was widespread Freud dubbed that network of inflamed family feelings the 'Oedipus complex', after the Greek hero who 'unknowingly' in adult life realised his infant desires – he killed his father and slept with his mother. All that causes a lot of bother to kids aged between two and five but it is subsequently 'repressed'. 'The sense of guilt by which neurotics are so often tormented' stems from the Oedipus complex but in adult life we don't know that – unless analysis unlocks it. Events, as is their wont, are apt to make matters even worse. Thus a new baby 'usually meets with a very unfriendly reception' from a child displaced from his mother's undivided attention. '*Even murderous assaults are not unknown*' [my italics]. Apart from attempts at homicide, what can the poor boy do about it? He can for a while escape by standing apart from his mother and identifying with his father. This usually works during the 'latency period', that time of diminished sexuality that normally arrives about the age of five. But you do not permanently escape. At puberty the urgent imperative of the engorged libido requires that again you confront the Oedipus complex.

But I guess we can leave all that for later. Let us stick for now with 1936, with me pushing four, a new king on the throne and Herr Hitler about to send his troops into the demilitarised Rhineland. But before I spare you further potted psychology here are a few further insights from the 'degenerate' psychologist soon to be forced by Hitler into exile. They concern dreams, the interpretation of which was his forte. Let us try Freud on my dream about the bear, the elements of which offer some persuasive explanations. A wild animal represents someone in 'an excited sensual state' while a house is a representation of the human figure. If it has smooth walls it is male, but projections render it female. Freud, who knew not the English inter-war semi, suggested balconies as female characteristics but bow windows are even more voluptuous. Climbing implies sexual intercourse. Thus my bear, excitedly pursuing his passion, was from the rear, from the smooth walls of the male houses in dark Grange Road –

remember they extended towards us with phallic potency – embracing the pair of semis with the bosomy bows. His twitching nostrils are not sniffing the night air but savouring orgasm. The house is my mother. The bear is me. I became the bear I first met in my mother's bed, on the cover of my book the Christmas just before my sister was born. So let's face it. When I was very young I fell in love with my mother. I wanted to possess her exclusively and physically. But she rejected me in favour of my brutal father. Then, without warning, she produced my sister and the hurt became intolerable. So I wished my new rival dead and took practical steps towards that end. They failed and, in the aftermath, my mother's rejection became final. She let my father carry me off to a never-never land. That turned out to be a surprisingly pleasant experience, in the course of which I licked my wounds, distanced myself from my mother and became reconciled with my father. He began to teach me to be a man and that was quite interesting. His instruction may have included advice about incest and murder. They are best avoided. Something a boy should know.

It all fits? Well ... maybe some of it seems to. Maybe also they had bred a spoiled brat who led them a merry dance.

Chapter 2

EXILE

Thus my engagement with Oedipus was adjourned and the rest of 1936 passed quietly enough, giving the new bond with my father time to develop. In the spring we moved house to Stretford, a couple of miles away [*Plate 7 top*]. Perhaps the move was prompted by Helen's birth. Perhaps it betokened a good salary, for despite the Slump those with a safe job in the 1930s had it pretty good. Perhaps it was compensation for the headship that eluded Dad. He regularly got short-listed but then failed to convince panels he had what it took. That hurts, so maybe a nicer house and a new car were consolation. So the squat second hand Austin Ten, bought in 1934, was replaced by a brand new streamlined 1937 version [sunroof, walnut effect facia, green leather seats]. It easily did sixty on the East Lancs Road – at our considerable peril on that single carriageway with a central, lethal 'overtaking' lane [*Plate 7 bottom*]. A load of new gear came with the new house. There was a blue tubular steel electric fire with a reflecting arc of brilliant silver. Instead of imitation coals the undisguised element flashed you a beam of warmth and light. I loved it. I knew it was truly modern long before I had heard of its cradle, the Bauhaus. We got a new Hoover too. It had a headlamp for penetrating the undersides of sideboards and settees. It even had a baby called a 'Dustette', just the job for stairs and chairs. And we got our first long-handled tin opener and a fiendish little wire device for slicing hard boiled eggs – Mum's salads came undressed but were naked without an egg. Modernity extended to ornament as well as utility, although my parents were not actually modern enough to abolish the distinction. Hence two startling objets d'art – a girl trundling a green hoop, dressed only in green paint, and a table lamp with a big milky globe instead of a shade that came on at a touch on a button. Wow! It was difficult to decide what the lamp was made of. It was not exactly wood but not exactly metal either. Perhaps it was 'Bakelite', like my beaker and the wireless set. The modernity of plastics was mind-exploding.

134 Urmston Lane, Stretford was certainly a better address than 11 Polruan Road, Chorlton and it came with a separate brick garage and also an immersion heater. Not with a thermostat however, as we discovered coming back from Southport one Sunday afternoon straight into a Turkish bath with scorched and blistered paintwork. The neighbours also were a step up. Albert Dakin himself [MA Cantab], Dad's boss, lived nearby in Gladstonian austerity behind a shrubbery. Another colleague, a polymath called Len Whittaker [Senior Master, Senior Maths and senior enough music-wise to get gigs with the Halle], lived more affably, all Mansion polish and coffee cake, diagonally opposite us, next door to somebody important at the University. There was visiting and bridge was played because we had also acquired a folding card table with brown baize. But what pleased Dad best about our new situation was the family next door. The occupants of the corresponding semi were a doctor, his wife and their baby daughter. Not only a doctor but Scottish too, although unfortunately from Glasgow not Edinburgh. I think Dad fancied the doctor's bonny wee wife but she was of course reassuringly unavailable. Nevertheless his enthusiasm for her Scotch pancakes seemed to irritate Mum. And Stretford in itself, or at least the Urmston end of it, was posher than Chorlton. Not that today you would think so, for sometime in the later twentieth century the town centre got swallowed up into a big shed called the Arndale Centre. But in the 30s it was a bustling borough separate from Manchester. The town hall, next door to Dad's school, was a smooth Scandinavian version of Manchester's craggy equivalent, then universally reviled by persons of taste as a 'Victorian monstrosity'. In modernity however it was eclipsed by the promised art deco extravagance of the Longford Cinema, nearing completion in 1936. Of course at the time I did not know it was art anything but I knew it stood for the future and wasn't I lucky to live nearby?

Dad told me Old Trafford cricket ground, also next door to where he worked, was famous but I don't think he ever mentioned Manchester

United. I did however know about Hamilton Academicals, Cowdenbeath and Airdrieonians because I liked their names when they were read out on the wireless on Saturdays by a man with a melodiously modulated voice. Listening to the football results was part of identifying with Dad, of tuning into the male world of public events – of the news. There was plenty of news about in 1936 and it was mostly it was to do with kings, of whom there also seemed to be a surfeit that year. They came and went more rapidly than Dad's cars. I was sorry to see King Edward go. I liked his fresh young face on the new stamps and his multi-sided three-penny bit was achingly modern. How I liked modern things. The new coins and the clean stamps were, I knew, of a piece with our new gadgetry, the Longford Cinema and the white chocolate you could buy at that shop on the station approach. The new man on the throne seemed pretty wet though. I was not enchanted either with the little princesses, being at that time disenchanted with girls generally and indeed with the whole female sex. Mum and Dad mocked George VI. They had both grown up among speeches, sermons, recitations and elocutions in Edwardian chapels, so you can imagine their contempt for a king with a stammer. Something in the ether at our house, perhaps also connected with chapels, told me that disability was culpable.

What else came out of the wireless along with sport and the royals? Science did. I remember an autumn evening, just before poor Edward abdicated, when the voice in the Bakelite said there was going to be an interesting astronomical event, a conjunction of the moon with a single bright star. Dad said I could stay up till seven to watch it. He did have moments of inspired spontaneity. We went out into the darkness and there it was, just as predicted, a very bright moon and a single piercing star, alone in the cold, still sky. It was moving. What about world events? They must have been reported on the wireless but for me they got lost behind the kings and the weekly incantation concerning London Welsh, West Bromwich Albion, Glasgow High School FP and Forfar Athletic. However I knew there was trouble in Abyssinia and also in Spain, to which destination Dad said Mr Madison should take himself off. I agreed. I was once taken to play with young Peter Madison and it was once too often. He was bossy and smug and had a better train set than me. It seems Madison senior had already dodged the Great War on the grounds that he was too young. Youth, like disability, was culpable. He was a maths teacher and Dad's chief opponent in staff room political debate. Being both a socialist and a pacifist put him in a spot over the Spanish Civil War, a spot Dad mercilessly exploited. Dad was not a pacifist. He had been at Passchendaele and despised 'conchies'. In Dad's demonology they were worse than 'pansies' and 'bloody parsons'. He really did talk like that. Let us have another look at the cartoon in the Prologue above which shows him holding forth from a soap box. It is the work of the art master who, like the rest of the common room, was apparently riveted by the verbal fisticuffs exchanged between storm-trooping Dad and Comrade Madison. My father's physical resemblance to another veteran of the Ypres Salient is perfectly captured and the all-black garb implies affinity with Sir Oswald Moseley. Note however that the caption dates the cartoon to 1935, when leaning to the right did not incur automatic eviction from the human race.

Despite Dad's alleged sympathies, I carry no memories of Hitler's triumphs in 1936. I do not remember the reoccupation of the Rhineland intruding on our preparations for the move to Stretford, nor do I recall the BBC's coverage of the Berlin Olympics. It was not until 1938, and Mr Chamberlain's mission to Munich, that for me the Führer hit the headlines. Instead the wireless was full of a forthcoming attraction called the Coronation. The good news was that, despite the Abdication and the new king's stammer, it had not been cancelled. Before King George's big day however I was scheduled to make my own entry into public life and that appointment with destiny overshadowed even the forthcoming attractions in Westminster Abby. My debut came one dread morning in the spring of 1937 when I was four and three quarters. At an ungodly hour I was dragged from the breakfast table, dragooned unto my overcoat and marched along Manor Road and round the corner to Moss Park School. It induced raptures in Mum and Dad. It was new and very up to date and had dinky little lavatories tailored to infant bottoms. I like the building I see today. It is prettily set in a leafy little park. It has warm red bricks and big sash windows with rounded tops. I remember colonnaded courtyards and a pond with goldfish. There may even have been a fountain. But locked in anguish the charm of the architecture passed me by. Instead it triggered regression and I did a box room. I yelled and screamed and rampaged around the tasteful cloisters before seeking sanctuary in the girls' toilets. I remember a tweedy lady, from beyond the door of cubicle, urging reason, like a nice guy cop sweet-talking a gunman. In the end I came quietly. But not happily. I had been taken prisoner.

Then, mercifully I got mumps and for a week or two I was safe. I sat up happily in bed, amid pillows, hot water bottles and an upturned tea tray, assembling my Frog aeroplane and doing my Coronation cut-out. Heavily leaded windows kept the naughty world at bay. My room was a refuge also from the unwholesome mother and baby chaos of the rest of the house. Not that I was isolated because as soon as he got in Dad used to rush upstairs to bring me a news update, help with the cut-out or read to me, something nowadays Mum seemed never to have time for. I was well shut of her. But after a few days of bliss they began to hassle me. There was officious attention to temperatures and pulse rates. I was prodded and interrogated. In the end I was formally charged with wilful constipation. It was a grave offence, the failing being seen as moral, not physical – as wilful not involuntary. Like disability and undue youth it was deeply culpable. Dad himself was much into prunes and All Bran and, with a regularity exceeding clockwork, every day – rain or shine, workday or holiday, war or peace – he purposefully mounted the stairs immediately after breakfast, with his pipe and the *Manchester Guardian*. Restoring mobility in his son was a sacred duty.

Mum too was battling with intransigent intestines – not mine but my little sister's. How her world had contracted. She, my erstwhile companion on those mind blowing adventures down the tram tracks, now gave her all to the taming of a baby's gut. A year old and still in nappies! A disgrace! So everywhere there were potties and at fixed times there were 'holdings over' at the kitchen sink. When not pilloried to a pot my sister was incarcerated in a cage called a 'playpen'. But the kid had guts. She fought back. Sometimes she turned the pen into a pot, which certainly got them jumping. Even more impressive was her capacity to wrench the pen from its fastenings. The battle of the hinges ever escalated. My parents having exhausted Woolworths' range, from dainty brass fittings to heavy steel clamps, resorted to specialist ironmongers. Again and again, they screwed, she wrenched, she won. Perhaps it was after losing their struggle against Helen that their alimentary offensive was turned against me. In my case they turned to Boots not Woolworths. All that famous pharmacy could supply was deployed. Ex-Lax ['just like chocolate'] was superseded by California Syrup of Figs [fancy label], which in turn yielded place to Liquid Paraffin [plain and unadorned – irresistible force needed no advertisement]. My pneumatic hot water bottle was usurped by a cold ceramic conch called a 'bed pan'. There was no response. It was mutiny. Only the ultimate weapon was left. Suddenly a strange woman in white invaded my bedroom trundling a collection of glass bottles and rubber tubes and box-room time was here again. Like Napoleon's guard I came on in the same old way. But like Wellington's Buffs they stood steady. I was locked down and an enema was forcibly administered. Then they all slunk away, smitten I hoped with guilt, leaving me alone again. My understandable riposte was self-harm. I attacked myself with scissors. Perhaps I had castration in mind but in the event only a large section of front hair suffered amputation. Was I, like Oedipus, aiming at the eyes? Then I contemplated the green satin counterpane stretched over a well-filled eiderdown. Aroused again, my scissors lost control. I cut and slashed and slashed again. A snowstorm of feathers enveloped a rough cut mess of jagged green strips.

It is remarkable how calm and storm, construction and destruction, war and peace, life and death can coexist. Despite all that drama there was still time during my eventful progress through the mumps for some learning in repose. And it happened even through the medium of the demonic scissors. I had them with me in bed for the entirely respectable purpose of doing a cut-out of the Coronation procession. In Woolworths at the time you could get cut-outs of many things. It might be a Spanish galleon or the battleship *Nelson* or a zoo or a pantomime or a figure on which a change of clothes – dresses perhaps or uniforms – could be hung. But the principle was always the same. Flat sheets of card had components printed on them in colour. You cut out the components, taking care not to snip off the tabs by which you glued them into shape at the end to form 3D objects that might be arranged, as on a theatre set, against a background that came with the outfit. I loved them. The focus of the Coronation cut-out was the golden coach in which the King would ride with its bedecked horses and outriders. It was accompanied by cohorts of uniformed men, mounted as well as on foot, wearing turbans as well as helmets, the armed forces of the Empire, in step behind their King-Emperor. It was destined for the window ledge of the front room which, being bowed, had space for a suitably extended parade. Thus the spirit of Empire possessed me. In time I was to rebel against it, but not yet. We ruled the world and wasn't the world lucky? Although, as I worked on my cut-out, the fall of Singapore was only five years in the future, and in another five its Indian jewel would be plucked from the imperial crown, in infancy clairvoyance was not granted me. The Coronation taught me the British mission to civilise the world. As both Hitler and Churchill insisted – the 'thousand year Reich' and the 'Empire and Commonwealth' that might 'last a thousand years' – the lifespan of empires was to be counted in millennia.

Then suddenly Dad got lucky. One morning just before the Coronation, and just after we got the Bauhaus fire, I woke up to a buzz of excitement. Last night, after I had gone to bed, Dad had come home in triumph, as headmaster designate of the grammar school at Glossop, a town fourteen miles away, and it seemed we were to move house again. His euphoria had been marred by a 'blatantly deliberate' scratch on the boot of shiny new 60 mph DND 838 received while it was parked outside the Municipal Buildings, where the interviews had been held. Was it some anonymous lout or was it Mr Casey, the chemistry master, who had thought himself in line for the job? It did not too much dampen Dad's spirits but, as I took in the implications of this unexpected happening, mine gradually began to dip again. I could do without further change.

The rest of the summer was an anti-climax. Coronation Day was wet. In the afternoon we squelched around a muddy field down a snicket opposite our house where a glum funfair was inconveniently encamped. I had candyfloss which stuck to my hair, or what was left of it after the DIY barbering. Next day we drove to London, in convoy with the doctor next door, who, being Scottish, could not be expected to know the way. A Union Jack fluttered at the end of the bonnet. I guess it celebrated Dad's promotion as much as the Empire's joy. 'Pag pying', my precocious sister, whose guttural effusions were teetering on the brink of verbalisation, reiterated in a remorseless determination to communicate. She was rewarded by indulgent chuckles from her complacent parents. New car, new job, new prodigy. It made me sick. The journey made my sister sick as well. With stupefying frequency her conversational gambits were cut short by urgent pumpings, releasing the acrid scent of vomit. Indeed for years our car journeys were thus punctuated, so the back seat was permanently littered with flannels and crumpled paper bags and a smell lingered in which unpleasantness was mixed with exhaust fumes. Even today the expression 'family car' disgusts me.

It used to take all day in the car to get from Manchester to Selsdon, the journey culminating in an exciting passage into central London along the Edgware Road to Marble Arch. This time we got stuck in a traffic jam in Hyde Park and that thrilled me because we were following the actual route of the Coronation procession my cut-out had represented. I could stare from the stationary car straight into the very scaffolding that had carried yesterday's crowds. Amazing – the news made flesh. I still had to imagine the crowds and the marching soldiers, but conjuring a vision in my head to impose on what my eyes could see somehow made the scene more rather than less vivid. Then on to family gatherings. Grandpa London had brought home full plate glossy photographs from Northcliffe Newspapers where he now worked. They published the *Daily Mail* but I think he was on the tabloid *Daily Sketch*. There was a bird's eye view of the action on the Abbey floor, taken from high up amid the vaulting. It was so sharp you could make out all the details of the trains of the King and Queen. I stared and stared and took it home and stared again and again and something Gothic entered my soul. Photographs of the family were also duly taken with shiny DND 838 as a centre-piece to most of them *[Plate 7 bottom]*. Dad wore his new holiday casuals – blue suit and silk tie. He had arrived.

I do not remember anything about school after the Coronation, in honour of which all the kids in Stretford were given a pewter mug inscribed 'Albert Smith Mayor'. It also carried a medallion depicting the King and Queen. I got one too so I must have put in some sort of appearance after mumps. Perhaps in view of the intending move, and since I was not yet quite five, some of my sentence at Moss Park was commuted. Or perhaps I just got used to it. We kept going over to Glossop to look at tumbled down stone mansions with mouldy conservatories, in one of which we disturbed an owl with an enormous wing-span and that was scary. It seems these mill-owners' palaces were going for a song, hard times having hit the cotton trade. Mum and Dad seemed to like them but to me they were jumbo versions of the eerie houses in old fashioned Grange Road that had given me bad dreams when we lived in Chorlton. For a modern boy from the suburbs this small town dereliction was upsetting. I took against Glossop and did not want to go. I cheered up later when we went on holiday to Cleveleys, near Blackpool, close to Poulton and Dad's boyhood haunts. We had been there before and it was good because there was an amusement park beside our boarding house and the trams had their very own tracks like proper trains – truly modern. We saw the Isle of Man steamer arrive at Fleetwood and observed the operations of the Knott End ferry. I think actually the holiday came after the tumult of the house move. Which would make sense, wouldn't it? Get it over with and then relax.

Glossop is only fourteen miles from Manchester but to me in 1937 it might have been two hundred. Indeed if we had moved two hundred miles from south Manchester to a south London full of relatives, trams and semis, I should have felt on more familiar ground. And if the move had taken place today it would not have been traumatic at all, for Glossop has adapted smoothly to the way we live now. After a wartime revival the cotton industry slipped into terminal decline and now few traces of it remain. Marks and Spencers have colonised the last vestiges of Woods' Mill and Tescos have settled amid the ruins of Sumner's. The once ubiquitous chapels scarcely survive except as flats and houses. Although chippies are still frying, Asian restaurants have given a different flavour to the High Street and have penetrated the pubs. The Globe has even gone vegan. Opportunities to eat out or take away are now so extensive that little cooking must occur in artisans' dwellings which, like their equivalents on Coronation Street, have become bijou residences. Modern Glossop is so full of southern comfort that northern grit is confined to nostalgia, as in the photographic display that amuses commuters at the spruce station as they await rapid transit to Manchester. It is all far removed from the slump-stunned, northern mill town that became my place of exile in 1937.

What exactly hit me that was so different? Let's start with the weather. We left the plain and went to live in the hills, at the foot of the Snake Pass, a dramatic turnpike cut in the early nineteenth century to speed mail coaches across the bleak Pennines dividing Manchester from Sheffield. So the climate was different. Manchester, despite its reputation, is not all that wet, its annual rainfall being less than that of Bristol. But Glossop is. You hardly ever see snow in Manchester but Glossop gets cut off. I got to like the rain and snow but I really missed the urban gloom I had grown up with. Manchester then was still coal-burning so fog was never far away.

The subsequent abatement of the smoke, although no doubt good for life expectancy, has killed the beauty of wet pavements under lamplight diffused by murk. It survives in the fogscapes of Adolphe Valette in the city's art gallery but you can no longer, with blinking eyes and a catch in the throat, know it for real. In Glossop the gloom was never there, even before war and welfare worked a social revolution. The well-washed moorland air was too clean so the light never reached the critical level of greyness. Pollution never had a chance.

But although I missed the Manchester murk, the visual splendour of my new home town began to make its mark. Its setting was spectacular. I registered that cardinal fact soon after our arrival when Dad, who needed to get his bearings, started taking me on extended walks. Thus we discovered Mossy Lea [Plate 8 middle]. The soft, pastoral appellation disguises a genuine engagement with mountain scenery. The walk began with a sharp ascent past Shire Hill Quarry, where miniature railway trucks, full of broken stone, lurched down a steep incline under their own power, seemingly by magic. Then, as Sheffield Road became the Snake Pass, we turned off onto a rough track, from the top of which a spread of moor and sky, all grey and brown and green and purple, suddenly filled the full wide field of our vision. Usually there was rain in the air and if a wind was up as well the sense of being taken out of yourself and caught up in elemental forces was overwhelming. It is what Romantic poets called 'sublime'. Dad would have known all about that but I don't suppose even he thought the notion could be communicated to a five year old. He didn't need to. I could feel it in my face and legs and lungs. I had to admit I liked it. I went on liking it ever afterwards. The way home lay along a wild valley until we crossed the rocky brook by a single plank without a handrail – wow! – scaled a steep hillside beside a long black stone wall to the edge of an oak wood, and made our way back to civilisation at the curiously named Pyegrove, near our house. Thus I found consolation in the stones of Glossop. They are of 'millstone grit', a type of granite, which welds the buildings to the moors the stones have come from. Although brick and concrete have made inroads Glossop still bristles with the stuff. When the houses stop, dry stone walls go onwards and upwards, networking the moors – for a purpose that is not immediately apparent – until they merge imperceptibly with dark cliffs, hanging boulders and the rocky beds of rushing brooks. Even on the peaty tops you still find stone put to human use as sheep pens or shooting butts and as a neat stretch of road once supposed to be Roman.

The shock of my translation was social as well as physical. We moved from affluence into poverty. Not of course in the micro-economic climate of the Lord family. The rent of the draughty stone lodge my parents chose for us was only £28 a year, which made scarcely a dent in Dad's salary of £600. So we were more than comfortably off. The poor however were always with us and around us and we caught up with the Slump. Glossop was not working. Unemployment defined the place. Dad said half the workforce was jobless and a recent check on the statistics shows that he was right. Some of the mills were empty and so were quite a lot of shops. Since the welfare system was leaky as well as abbreviated want and squalor were unconcealed. You really did see bare-footed kids in the streets, even in winter, and some of the classmates I sat among wore disintegrating boots or eroded clogs and had gaping holes in their patched and filthy jerseys. They had bad teeth, grubby cotton wool blocked their ears, and they gave off a strong smell. Teachers distributed second hand clothing and each day a man came from 'the Clinic' with free sandwiches for targeted clients. Free school meals did not exist because neither did school meals. It was not only personal poverty my antennae picked up. The whole town was in economic retreat and emitted an air of dereliction. Even the mills still in reduced use seemed to be chugging along without much confidence that the corner would be turned. At the end of *Sing As We Go*, Gracie Fields had let out a joyful shout – 'Coom on lads and lassies, t'factory's oppen' – but audiences at the Empire cinema knew she was whistling in the dark. It was not just the mills that looked sad. So did the chapels and Sunday schools which seemed to shun the unemployed. Theirs was a work ethic, not an out of work one. So too it seems was the ethic of the clubs – political, working men's, and 'friendly' [the Oddfellows and the Foresters] – whose imposing premises exuded an air of melancholy that also hung around half derelict insurance offices, unfrequented herbalists, under-patronised pie shops and a host of establishments that were too seldom frying tonight. It was pervasive. The market was run down. The theatre was derelict. A few huddled spectators at the football ground perched dangerously on rotting timbers and upturned dustbins. And yet, at half cock, the show *did* go on. Surely in the end something would turn up. The station lion said it all *[Plate 8 bottom]*. Grass grew tall in the sidings beneath him but his tail was out-stretched. Maybe the angle implied diminished virility, but he was not finished yet. He was right. Something *did* turn up. It was the Second World War. It put the bounce back into Glossop, as we shall see.

Glossop had not always been the way it was now. As I explored the alien environment I had been catapulted into by a random twist in my father's career, I soon came to realise that before the dire straits there had been a golden age. I read it in the stones fifty years before I learnt about it from books. As a semi-literate schoolboy I learned to read buildings more fluently than I could decipher words. It was the mills that got me started. Five of those stately dreadnoughts lay at anchor in a line along an east-west axis through the town. Compact Hurst's Mill, up Sheffield Road, was followed along High Street East by a cluster of doughty installations known collectively as 'Woods'. The eminence of Shepley's Mill rose above you as you walked down High Street West, and then, when the shops ended, you suddenly beheld Wren Nest. Some wren! Some nest! Here was Sumner's Mill, an immense, multi-storey slab of looming granite, punctuated by great windows that made it, like famous Hardwick Hall, more glass than wall. Then, moving on, before you reached the sprawling Print Works you were stunned by Dinting Arches, a railway viaduct that miraculously vaulted the valley. Those structures amazed me. That I was contemplating products of human genius wrought in heroic times now gone away, I did not doubt. Everybody else did though. I don't remember being told the mills were 'satanic' but that was the general feeling. They were ugly and dirty and horrible and their presence was a cross we had to bear. But I did not let what people said shake my conviction that glory in ancient time had shone around Wren Nest. What people say, as I eventually discovered, is usually rubbish.

It was not just the mighty mills that thrilled me. There was another sort of architecture to be savoured as well. Quite a lot of buildings announced themselves as important from the way they were put together. I knew these edifices were old but perhaps not quite as old as they had been made to appear. They had been given a hoary look deliberately so we would respect what went on in them. So catching a train under the eyes of the station lion was a ritual, not just an everyday occasion. Around Norfolk Square a whole assembly of dignified premises were gathered. There was the Town Hall of course, and the Market behind it and the nearby Post Office, together with the Norfolk Arms, the District Bank, the Liberal Club and the big Co-op with its various departments. There were venerable piles in other parts of Glossop as well. They abounded in cobbled Talbot Street where the Victoria Hall stood beside two pointy churches and Dad's Grammar School, which had a special quiet dignity you could not ignore and which made you behave yourself, even without anybody telling you to. Up in Howard Park there was Woods' Baths along with Woods' Hospital and the Partington Maternity Home. I was not sure what maternity was but you could tell it mattered just by looking at the place. In the same way you knew education was important because the schools all over Glossop had a venerable look. When Mum and Dad said they were a disgrace and old fashioned, unlike up to the minute Moss Park, I disagreed. I liked going to school in a fancy old building. Dad warned me off the churches too. He didn't agree with what went on inside them, but they looked interesting to me. Some were fairy tale fancy with stained glass, while others were plain, but sort of Greek, with columns and pediments. At the age of eight I went through a Greek phase. I am saying I found real and ever increasing pleasure in architecture. But again it was a private passion. My parents and everybody else seemed to spurn the feast in the streets. They were indifferent to the stones of Glossop or disparaged them as a blight on the town, not a cause for pride and joy. It turned out they were 'Victorian' and thus incorrigibly inconvenient as well as ugly and when better times came along – a millennium eventually known as 'after the war' – they would be pulled down and good riddance. Fortunately, with the sad exception of the mills themselves, that prophecy was not fulfilled. Most of the fine structures I secretly loved as a child are still there and now they are suitably celebrated. Glossop today flaunts its Victorian 'heritage'. It has generated a shelf-full of books that prove I got it right as a child when I sensed a golden age. The urge to tell you about it cannot be resisted but I will try to be brief.

Although we did not know it, wild Mossy Lea, that Dad and I discovered, was important in the history of the town. For it was thereabouts, towards the end of the 1700s, that the machine spinning of cotton yarn first shook up a remote little settlement now known as 'Old Glossop'. Likely lads had sussed out that bobs aplenty were to be made by harnessing fast flowing water to drive spinning 'frames' and, as Dad and I had noticed, there was a lot of rapid water swirling around up Mossy Lea. At which point you may sigh, expecting another gritty northern saga of rags to riches – but you would be wrong. For the Glossop phenomenon – involving a twentyfold explosion of population in only fifty years – was a product, not of brash capitalism, but of good old fashioned benevolent feudalism. It was inaugurated, not by acquisitive go-getters pulling on their bootstraps, while damming streams and rigging sluices, but by the largesse of a great aristocratic family, the head of which had long been styled the 'highest peer in the land'. The man who made golden Glossop possible, who first conjured there mighty mills and noble architecture, was none other than Bernard Edward Fitzalan Howard, 12th Duke of Norfolk, whose principal seat was Arundel Castle, two hundred miles away in lush Sussex. The enterprise was continued with no slackening of the pace by his son, the 13th Duke, who got *his* younger son to forsake the soft south and actually come and live in rugged Glossop, the better to guide its burgeoning fortunes. For his pluck the boy was in 1869 rewarded with a peerage in his own right, as Lord Howard of Glossop.

It had all come about because, sometime way back, the manor of Glossop, a substantial but agriculturally inferior acreage, had become part of the voluminous Howard estates and had been placed in the care of agents, whose job was to maximise the rent yield. That must have been a challenge but about 1820 Matthew Ellison, the incumbent agent, rose to it magnificently. Having noted the success of the likely lads up Mossy Lea, he decided to supplement his salary by opening a cotton mill of his own, not among the lads in the hills, but on broader, flatter land further down the valley – at a spot called Wren Nest. At that time of course what we call the industrial revolution was steaming ahead, literally so since steam power was fast replacing water. With an engine you could operate many more machines in the same mill, provided there was space enough for the necessary installations, which might include an expanse of single storey weaving sheds as well as tall spinning blocks. Wren Nest had the necessary elbow room and so did a string of other possible factory sites, all owned by the Duke, spread out along the Glossop valley. All had abundant water supplies – still needed even for a steam-driven mill – as well as space for development. All that was lacking, from the point of view of an entrepreneur looking to set up and make a fortune, was 'hands' to mind the machines. For at that time practically nobody lived in arctic Glossop Dale. Hence Ellison's proposition. Let His Grace build a new town to accommodate the many thousand hands that would be needed to make Ellison's project happen. Then capitalists would clamour for leases and the elevated rents they willingly shelled out would swell the ducal treasury, eclipsing the modest returns he got from farm land up and down the country.

The canny Duke said yes and the miracle unfurled. From the 1820s onwards, four generations of Howards, assisted by two generations of Ellisons, established a new Glossop and gave it an infrastructure. They tried to call it 'Howardtown' but the fancy moniker did not catch on. They did not expand the original village but built a mile away around a strategic cross roads, where two turnpikes intersected. There a younger Ellison laid out Norfolk Square and built the town hall. Around it a network of streets was constructed, its nomenclature doing homage to family genealogy and thus to English history – Norfolk, Howard, Fitzalan, Surrey, Talbot and Shrewsbury – and immortalising the Christian names of the current Howard brood – Edward, Bernard, Henry, Thomas and Charles. There was also an Ellison Street. The new streets were watered and drained by the ducal waterworks and illuminated through the agency of the ducal gasworks, which in my time still perfumed a thoroughfare we mispronounced as Ar*u*ndel, instead of *A*rundel. The greatest benefaction however was the branch line, brought to Glossop Central in 1847 at the personal expense of the 13th Duke, when the Manchester, Sheffield and Lincolnshire Company had the temerity to by-pass the new town. In 1852 the arrival of that Duke's younger son, as a hands-on squire, who rebuilt the modest manor house as a stately chateau, made Glossop truly the Howards' town, in spirit if not in name.

In 1866 Glossop ceased to be a manorial fief and, with the Duke's blessing, matured into a self-governing borough. Henceforth the entrepreneurs whom the Howards had attracted, and who had duly filled the interstices of the street plan with mills and workers' cottages, became the dominant force in local life. The two biggest mill-owners were the Wood Brothers of Howardtown Mills and Francis Sumner of Wren Nest, each of whom employed some two thousand workers and disposed of looms and spindles in a mass that is statistically mind numbing. The Woods were local people who had come in from the cold up Mossy Lea but Francis Sumner was an incomer from Coventry who bought Wren Nest from Matthew Ellison. In the 1870s another foreigner hit the town running and brought diversity to the local economy. Edward Partington, an inventor as well as a capitalist, adapted Turn Lea Mill to manufacture paper from wood pulp. It was the way Partington's raw material got carted from the station yard to Turn Lea that for me, at the age of five, first brought the industrial revolution snarling into fiery life. Trailers piled-high with stripped logs were hauled through the town by a fleet of steam traction engines, each carrying the name 'Tiger' on a brass plate attached to the boiler. With spinning fly-wheels, belching sparks and Guinness-hued smoke from tall chimneys they rattled across the station cobbles, shuddered down Norfolk Street and then charged up Victoria Street with momentum enough to scale the Nab, the mini-mountain that presides over Glossop. It was magnificent but not of our time. Why ever did they not use motor lorries? I am glad they didn't though.

The mill-owners, along with the Howards, governed Glossop as well as enriched it. They did so under rival political banners. The Howards and Sumner were Whigs while the Woods were Tories. The arrival of Partington gave new life to the local Liberal Party and for a while Partingtons and Woods alternated as MPs for the High Peak, a constituency that awkwardly married gritty Glossop to balmy Buxton. Mock wars of religion were also fought. The Howards were famously Catholic and so was Sumner, but the Woods were Anglicans while Partington was a Unitarian. The harvest of that diversity was a burst of ecclesiastical architecture ranging from Neo-classical All Saints, to French Gothic St Mary's, to an elegant essay in Early English placed by Captain Partington – he commanded the local Volunteers – in Fitzalan Street, opposite the Victoria Hall, the public library he donated. The 'Vic' came into existence during a lavish bout of competitive philanthropy conducted by the rival benefactors during and after 1887, the year of the Queen's Jubilee. Among the lawns, grottoes and cascades of Howard Park, newly gifted by his lordship, the bountiful Mrs Anne Kershaw Wood, grandest of grandes dames, established not only an elaborate monument to her own family but also the resplendent Woods' Baths, its boiler smoke vented from a soaring campanile. At which Captain Partington, declaring that healthy bodies should support healthy minds, planned the library aforementioned. Mrs Wood's riposte was Woods' Hospital set above the Baths. Partington trumped that with a convalescent home, a cricket pavilion and a rugby club. Touché – or so he must have thought. The Woods however slashed back. They bought

Glossop North End and squeezed it briefly into the First Division of the Football League, entertaining the likes of Manchester United.

I find that an inspiring tale. It celebrates a group of powerful men *and women* acting *co-operatively* to do themselves a lot of good and serve their people in the process. It undermines the dispiriting assumption of class struggle that hung over the history I was taught at university and subsequently imbibed in half a century of historical reading. According to Marxist theory an emergent bourgeoisie should have been in revolutionary confrontation with a declining landed aristocracy. But it was not like that in Victorian Glossop. The Howards and the entrepreneurs were in cahoots not conflict. Even while doing time in the history gulag I sensed that an alternative scenario might be asserted. My scepticism stemmed, not from books, but from vivid memories of Glossop's mighty mills and fine architecture. They surely betokened peace not war – the legacy of a vanished golden age. I was never told about that happy time. Local history had no place at either St Luke's or the Grammar School and, although his predecessor as headmaster had been a pioneer local historian, my complacent father showed no curiosity about Glossop in the dark ages before his own accession. I only began to discover the facts in the 1980s when I started to examine my origins. By then, as I say, Glossop had discovered it had a heritage and more and more of it was being put in the public domain by diligent investigators. I gratefully lapped up their products. Thanks.

But what about the workers? Did Marx at least have a point? If the Duke and the mill-owners had a ball was it not at the expense of an exploited proletariat? Sure, the 'hands' got a health service of sorts and a swimming bath, a public library, a football team and a grammar school, plus of course the opium of religion in fifty seven varieties. But at the end of the day they had to go back to ... well, slums. Or so I came to suppose. I know that by the age of seven I had discovered social class. For at that age – it was the first Christmas of the war – I fell foul of my hitherto bossy but indulgent Aunt Marion, my grandfather's daughter and his political disciple. She turned very nasty indeed when I said I was glad I was not working class because I would not like to live in a slum. I thought it was unfair for her to get cross because she lived in London so knew nothing about slums. I did though and not only from looking at *Picture Post* with Dad. For unlike my prickly, cocky aunt I visited one quite often. The slum in question was just next door to the Commercial, the pub down the road from our house, and it was occupied by Olive and her family and I knew they were working class because my parents said so. Olive was the young girl who every weekday from nine until six, for a few shillings a week and some left overs, helped my mother. Sometimes that assistance extended to taking me, and presumably Helen too, back to their house for a few hours, letting Mum go off to the golf club or, in a child-free environment, entertain ladies who played bridge. Although the Battersbys treated me kindly I hated going there for an overpowering reason. It was the smell. An unequivocally nauseating stench pervaded their cottage. And it was not peculiar to Olive's place. I often picked up corresponding whiffs of proletarian lifestyle as I passed the doorways of other artisans' dwellings, innumerable terraces of which snaked all over Glossop. Furthermore it assaulted my nostrils from the persons of kids I had to sit next to in class at St Luke's. Eureka! I had sniffed out an incontrovertible truth which, concurrently and unbeknown to me, had been pronounced also by George Orwell. In 1936, somewhere along the road to Wigan pier, he observed that 'the working classes smell' and in four words said more about the class struggle than four million of Marxist-Leninist rhetoric. Fragrant people and the smelly ones cannot happily coexist. Simple. But get rid of the smell and class will wither away. I think, sometime after the war, that actually happened.

Let me try to analyse the smell, as I first knew it at Olive's and then confidently projected it so that, in my mind, it festered also behind the comely granite facades of all the cottage homes of Glossop. Where did it come from? Perhaps it started with the outside privies. They were almost universal. They lay along windy paths or across gritty backyards, amid dustbins and coal places, where repellent wildlife was said to lurk. Not all were flushed by water. Horse drawn tumbrels loaded with night soil dallied in the streets beyond daybreak. Since, particularly after dark, there was a disincentive to use outdoor facilities that were inaccessible as well as noisome, they were generously supplemented indoors by chamber pots and slop pails, emptied as and when. Thus a lingering miasma of stale excrement gave the slum stink its foundation. Bathrooms were known to cottagers only as futuristic and erotic visions sometimes glimpsed at the Empire, the local cinema, so a big galvanised iron tub hung outside many back doors. However the use of this device, traditionally in the glow of the kitchen range, was also subject to disincentive. Filling it – with much humping of heavy pans between cold tap, hob and bathtub – was laborious and so too was emptying it of dirty water. It was too demanding a ritual, following a hard day's work, to be undertaken more than ... well, probably not the once a week cherished in nostalgia. In the meantime a good all-over wash at the kitchen sink, that is in the middle of a densely populated living room, was not easy to arrange. The consequence was a profound accumulation of stale body odour, circulating constantly in a confined space. It was probably scarcely perceptible to the hardened nostrils of residents, but it was overwhelming to a well-scrubbed and fastidious visitor like little me. The cold water tap in the kitchen constituted the only indoor plumbing. It surmounted, not a sink, but a slop-stone, an eroded shallow masonry tray with a plug-hole that more readily accommodated big pans, kettles, buckets – and no doubt chamber pots. As well as for personal hygiene, food preparation and the brewing of tea, the cold tap served also for doing the laundry, another activity too burdensome to be promiscuously engaged in. Hence an endemic disinclination to change even under garments which, when they did go to the wash often got little more than a quick rinse in a bowl of not very soapy water. The detergent revolution was a post war phenomenon. Domestic electricity was something else for New Jerusalem. It too was known to pre-war slum dwellers only on the silver screen. Nevertheless most kitchens were lit by gas. The mantles however often leaked, thus adding an inorganic ingredient to the bio-fug. In those circumstances family life revolved around the cast iron, coal-fired kitchen range. It was the sole source of hot water. It was the means of baking puddings and pies, simmering peas and lentils, frying bacon and eggs and stewing a hot pot. It offered a light to smokers and lit the candles and oil lamps that occasionally illuminated darker regions beyond the gas-lit kitchen-living room. It was an efficient waste disposal unit. And it was crucial to any serious laundering that was attempted, acting first as a boiler, then wafting warm air to the clothes maiden and the ceiling rack, and finally heating the flat irons. Also of course it maintained the living room in the state of torrid humidity to which cotton operatives were accustomed at work.

Thus the ingredients of the stench begin to identify themselves. Body smells were laced with the tang of soot and with the rancid smell of hot fat repeatedly re-used. That mix was enriched by whiffs of gas, tobacco smoke and wet washing. To make matters worse, the foetid soup was trapped and perpetually recycled by a battery of insulating devices deployed against the hurricane of draughts generated by the roaring fire of the range. Hence a battle royal against demon draughts, held to be bringers not only of lumbago but also of galloping consumption and death-dealing fevers, as well as chill discomfort. Thus an urge to block every orifice. Since opening a window would break its seal ventilation was taboo. Doors as well as windows were heavily curtained. The internal one at the foot of the stairs was specially fortified. As well as a thick curtain and a 'sausage' at its base, it was insulated with rubber tubing tacked inside the door frame. Even the damp rising through the cracks between the kitchen flags was defied by a profusion of rag rugs supplemented by last week's *Glossop Chronicle and Advertiser*. Unfortunately for me, immured to abundant fresh air by my genteel upbringing, the draught defences were all too effective. They trapped the stink that suffocated me.

A conviction that the insupportable pong stemmed, not from insufficient connection to the public utilities and particularly to the electricity grid, but from the very fabric of the 'slums', was confirmed when Mum, responding to the war effort, began hawking a collecting tin on behalf of the Red Cross Penny a Week Fund and often recruited me as her reluctant lieutenant. Our beat covered High Street East and its tributaries. It included a dank terrace below water level at Corn Mill Bridge that I knew to be the lair of the dreaded, red-headed Dawson boys, and the eponymous Milltown, a maze of little streets clustered under Woods' tall chimneys. Sure enough many doors that opened to us released a blast of sick-making pungency. Sometimes to my horror we were invited in. Please don't let them offer us a brew! However prissy little stuck-up snob that I was, I was a thoughtful stuck-up little snob. The habit of looking and thinking had not gone away. The niggling voice of truth could not be indefinitely ignored. The thing was I could not honestly suppress the knowledge that not every two-up, two-down stone cottage in Glossop qualified as a slum. For some of them did not smell. Some of the nice people who opened their doors to Mum did not in the process release choking clouds of nastiness. Sometimes also I went to Mrs Brown's cottage in Thomas Street and I couldn't, cross my heart, say that it really had a smell either, well not more than just a little perhaps and that mostly of 'Gloss-up' polish, the local speciality. Mrs Brown had replaced

Olive who had, I guess, like a million British women, escaped from the ill-paid drudgery of domestic service into the well-heeled Elysium of war work. Mrs Brown, a policeman's widow living on her own, proudly kept her dwelling spick and span. Circumstances, I began to realise, alter cases and theory sometimes falls foul of facts. Also I was sometimes invited to classmates' birthday parties and some of them lived in apparent slums. But the stone cottage Fred Clough lived in, near Hadfield station, did not smell at all. Neither did Geoffrey Sims's cottage opposite our school in Talbot Street. Nor did Maureen Garlick's next door.

It was when I got to know Douglas Swallow that my theory about cottages and slums finally collapsed. Doug and I did not really like each other and our 'friendship' owed more to our fathers' sponsorship than to actual affinity. But the acquaintance taught me a lot because it gave me frequent access to a quite different 'slum' from the one inhabited by Olive and her family. At least slum is what their cottage at Gamesley ought to have been. It was part of a terrace, it was two-up, two-down, it was built of stone and it had an outside privy. Yet it was charming. Not only was there a total absence of unpleasant odour but it was neater, tidier, better scrubbed and more brightly polished than our house was, even with the help of Olive and Mrs Brown. The Swallow cottage made the house of Lords seem shabby. Furthermore a bathroom had been carved out of the back bedroom. Although that meant Doug's quarters were reduced in area to something like my old box room at Chorlton, his dad was an accomplished handyman, so the resulting pad felt like a cabin on a ship. It was compact and convenient, with ingeniously contrived stowage for all Doug's belongings, including a mushrooming collection of butterflies and moths, all filed away in glass-topped display drawers in a cabinet devised by the talented Mr Swallow. The cottage had been cleverly expanded. A loft conversion provided a spacious playroom and the living room had gained in space, without losing in cosiness, when the range was removed and cooking, washing up and laundry operations were transferred to a glass-roofed extension built behind the original back door. Electricity had of course been installed and the effect of that was revolutionary. A Hoover banished dust and dirt, supplementary heaters reduced the need for stifling insulation, and everything was bathed in even light. Although the loo was indeed outdoors it was a pleasure to walk past the rain-water butt and through a flower garden to an installation that was immaculate and of course water-driven. Beyond was a vegetable plot with associated greenhouse and tool shed. Not a slum but a gem.

By this time, during 1943 and 1944, the end of the war was focusing minds. It was to be followed by 'New Jerusalem' a planned paradise, all fair shares and free false teeth, a cardinal feature of which was to be 'slum clearance'. They would have to go, all the little stone houses of Glossop – and of everywhere else as well – because they were insanitary and unfair to the workers who had won the war. I had seen the shape of things to come in glossy manifestos I devoured at bedtime, instead of Biggles or the *Hotspur*, because I was still not a fluent reader and the post war planning books were mostly pictures. It seemed the slums were bad not only because they were smelly but because they were horizontal when the future was vertical. So dwellers in terraced cottages were going to be re-housed in tower blocks, raised on stilts so that the ever spreading Eden in which post war workers would perpetually sunbathe need not be interrupted by streets. Well, I supposed the planners must know best, working as they did at drawing boards under those angle-poise lamps that were so breathtakingly modern. But as an habitué of the Swallow cottage I had my doubts right from the start. I knew there was no need for rebuilding. All that was wanted to turn a slum into a bijou residence was electricity, better plumbing, a conservatory and a loft conversion. Perhaps it was also necessary for the occupiers to be the owners as I think the Swallows must have been. He was something at one of the mills and seemed to be more a manager than a foreman. Also they were Particular Baptists and that would have been helpful too. Their tight little ship, with a place for everything and everything in its place, was a product of the Protestant ethic. And of family planning, for Doug was an only child. In a two-up, two-down, two or three may be company but five or six would be a crowd. But with those reservations I was an early sceptic about slum clearance. Improvement instead of demolition would be more popular as well as cheaper. It would preserve communities and bring down the speed of change from a mad rush to a comfortable jog. But the planners won over the politicians and much vandalism ensued. The customers however were not won over and hence a great irony. In 1960, while the bulldozers were doing their worst, 'Coronation Street' was born in celebration of the life-style the planners had condemned. Note that the soap has outlasted the tower blocks.

Miraculously however the stone cottages of Glossop survived post war planning. When, after a long absence, I briefly returned in 1975, I found them still there. The bulldozers had spared the town. A hundred handsome terraces smiled at me in the summer sun and there was not a slum in sight – or smell. The stonework had been cleaned. The roofs had been fixed and fitted with Velux windows. New paint glistened in rainbow colours on a parade of front doors. The electrical revolution had long since worked its magic. Beneath Habitat blinds you could glimpse open staircases, fitted kitchens and decks of hi-fi. Clematis and honeysuckle bloomed in backyards cleared of privies and converted into patios. Then, on dozens of 'For Sale' boards, I read a familiar name. Fred Clough, whose birthday party in a fragrant cottage I had once attended, had become a house agent. Obviously he too valued properties like the one he had grown up in. You could tell that from the astronomical prices posted in his high street window.

But back to how Glossop was when I first knew it. Interspersed among the little houses were shops and pubs and chapels. There were shops everywhere, not just along the main High Street West. It seemed that every third door was open to trade and that families must keep the wolf at bay by the equivalent of taking in each other's washing. Consider the immediate retail opportunities available to the Battersbys, Olive's family. They had the Commercial next door, with an alternative source of a pint at the nearby Rose Green Working Men's Club. All the meat and groceries they could afford were to be had at the Stores [the Co-op] opposite. The Stores adjoined the chip shop, beyond which was Bennets the newsagents, where sweets were sold out of jars, Woodbines came in packets of five, and you could buy the local rag and the *News of the World*. A bit below Bennets was Mr Goodwin's pie shop and, just up Sheffield Road Mrs Hampson baked bread and cakes. All within a radius of a hundred yards, just like in Coronation Street. A farmer with a horse drawn float delivered milk straight from churn to jug while the rag and bone man supplied donkey stone, for the front steps, in exchange for old iron or disintegrating cast-offs. Nostalgia rules OK? No, not at all. As a modern boy from the city I despised all that primitive trading and bartering. Where I came from you shopped in the 'village' not in somebody's front room round the corner. High Street West was more like it. Here a touch of class could be found with Edwin Bailey, the draper, or Finlay McKinley, who traded by appointment to Lord Howard, whose arms were emblazoned above the big flasks of coloured liquid in the windows of his chemist's shop. And Vernon Lord's Café was almost Viennese, what with his elaborate confectionary and his kudos as a chess master. He used to play the combined talents of the grammar school simultaneously and win. The talent did not include me. To start with, before I could read what it said on the painted boards that relieved their plain facades, I found chapels and pubs hard to distinguish, although it was clear that Dad was better disposed towards the latter than the former. There were plenty of each sort embedded among the cottage terraces. Eventually I twigged that Chesters, Boddingtons, Robinsons and Bents brewed beer while Wesleyans, Baptists and Independents saved souls. I also discovered that not only were some Baptists Particular, like the Swallows, but some Methodists were Primitive. Beyond that I gave up on both those forbidding sets of premises dedicated to mysterious grown up rites. What went on there was not my business.

Beyond the cottage terraces, which were clustered in a broad band around the town centre, lay the houses of the better off. On Glossop's far perimeter were some palaces erected in the golden age for the ruling millocracy. The grandest of these was Moorfields where the bountiful Mrs Wood had kept house for her husband Samuel and his bachelor brother Daniel. The house was well named, for its grounds had been extracted by a tour de force from the wild moors of the Kinder Scout massif, the highest part of the Peak. The Sumner and Partington palaces stood apart from the habitations of their people less insistently and Lord Howard himself was content with Glossop Hall, only half a mile from the station. Between the terraces and the palaces were the houses of the bourgeoisie. Many of them lay beyond the railway line in the north west quarter of the town, much of which had been developed in the twentieth century. Here brick had challenged the supremacy of millstone grit and semis and bungalows had blossomed. They delighted me. In North Road, Park Crescent or Spire Hollin I could imagine being back in Chorlton or Stretford. So why oh why did my parents reject suburban charm and settle instead for a bleak stone lodge in Sheffield Road, at the eastern end of the town? Not that Sheffield Road – not anyway as far up it as our house – was part of the slums and there were some interludes of brick to relieve the succession of hard cold frontages. But it *was* austere, especially in winter when blizzards blew in down the Snake. Eventually, as we have seen, I got to like it but it was a shock to start with. And 'Holly Wood', our house, itself presented a complete contrast to the semi-detached cosiness in which I had been bred and in which Mum and Dad had thus far spent their married life. So why did they choose Victorian grandeur? Perhaps because the more convenient semis and bungalows were popular with Dad's colleagues, including Mr Casey, and he cherished what he called the 'differential'. Or did Mum remember her childhood in the best houses in Waterfoot?

Holly Wood – the name perhaps described the expanse of sometimes prickly foliage that shielded us from vulgar gaze – was erected in 1852 and its unadorned facade was determinedly four square [Plate 8 top]. It was stone built and slate roofed and the regularity of its windows and chimneys, and the gravel path leading up to its door, made it look like a child's drawing of a house. The parsonage at Haworth is a close lookalike. It stood in perhaps an acre of ground, its outbuildings comprising a carriage house/garage, a washhouse, a greenhouse and buildings equipped for the shelter of hens and goats. The latter were not, in our time devoted to animal husbandry although wild creatures too often suffered in a once elegant summer house in which I set up a mini-zoo but neglected its inmates [two rabbits plus an occasional hedgehog, with tadpoles and sticklebacks confined to jam jars]. Beyond the walled garden was a wilderness my father called the 'Paddock'. In response to the 'Dig for Victory' campaign he made commendable progress in taming its weedy fecundity, until defeated by a pugnacious rivulet determined to escape the prison of its leaky culvert. The interior accommodation – four beds, two rec, kit and bath – was more than enough for two adults and two children. Its cubic capacity was impressive. Not only were the rooms large but they were tall as well and an astonishing amount of floor area was given over to circulation [of draughts as well as people] – porch, hall, majestic staircase and a landing that, in its dimensions, resembled the long gallery of a Tudor manor house. There was also an interesting attic and a vast semi-basement larder fitted with broad stone slabs, butcher's hooks, wall cupboards and a defunct Victorian ice box. 'Victorian ice box' would aptly describe the ensemble for, apart from a defective gas fire in the dining room and the itinerant Bauhaus heater, now called upon for heroic service, our only defences against hypothermia were an open hearth in the 'study' [sitting room] and another, its back boiler generating a fitful flow of tepid water, in the kitchen. It would not have been enough at the best of times which, by conventional criteria, these were not, for our sojourn at Holly Wood coincided not only with war and austerity but with at least two notoriously severe winters [1940 and 1947]. Thus the draughts were icy, the rising damp approached the ceilings, the pipes froze and the windows, in their rotten frames, were awash with condensation when they did not bloom into gardens of frost flowers. Yet after the initial shock I quickly adapted. Twelve years in the sub-arctic mini-climate of that Bronte-esque habitation gave me a tolerance of – even a preference for – a dank and chilly domestic environment that has ever afterwards rendered living with me a perilous undertaking.

Why did I like it? Well, in a glum sort of way it was handsome. It had an architectural quality I responded to that sprang from its granite solidity and its noble proportions. Its weathered and weather-beaten fabric was satisfying to touch, prod and smell. Its fixtures and fittings, many of them old and some of them ruinous, fed a growing curiosity about the past. I was an historian by the time I was seven. The garden and Paddock teemed with animal and vegetable life, bidden and unbidden, that also aroused curiosity and prompted observation. The unpredictable behaviour of the errant stream was a constant source of fascination. But mostly what I liked about Holly Wood was that it afforded me so many opportunities to be alone with my thoughts. I had an abundance of hideaways. There was the summer house, the washhouse, and the dusty, dung-encrusted chicken-wire entanglements of a never-never land up the henhouse ladder. I could withdraw into the rhododendron thicket, to the banks of the stream or into the branches of a favourite tree in the Paddock. From the fastness of my back bedroom, already well insulated from the rest of the house, I could retreat further up the attic stairs or hide under them. Compared with many schoolmates, who could find solitude only in the outside loo, I enjoyed privacy on a princely scale. It seemed I needed solitude at least as much as company and at Holly Wood my craving was generously satisfied.

Why did I need to be alone? Partly because of the contemplative persona, addicted to standing apart rather than joining in, that already characterised me. But it was also because our family life was so abrasive. Perhaps the pursuit of happiness is not the prime purpose of a family, so why should I expect ours to have delivered it? It didn't though. Although basic parental duties were not neglected and we enjoyed occasional relaxed moments together, it would be stretching the remembered facts too far to describe as happy the web of relationship that held us together. The prevailing atmosphere at Holly Wood was one of storm or gathering storm. At our house if trouble was not brewing it was probably happening. Physical violence was infrequent, and I am grateful for that, but rows and ranting were endemic and verbal abuse exploded in many forms. Barrages of defamation, denunciation and condemnation regularly echoed through the voluminous spaces of the house. Confrontation was a preferred form of communication and, although the mood was sometimes lightened by humour, gentleness was rare and expressions of affection unusual. In response I developed the habit of flight. I learned to weather whatever storm was raging by retreating from it, taking advantage of the boltholes just indicated, where usually I was left unmolested, Dad being too busy to give chase and Mum being inclined to let sleeping dogs lie. But always running away was not good for me. It did little to develop my social skills or capacity to work with other people. And it was lonely. It was not, as we shall see, that I entirely lacked companions and I did forge one close friendship that remarkably has survived through eight decades and may it flourish a few years longer. But I never fitted into the crowd and never felt comfortable in the rough and tumble of a group with a common outlook. I always felt different. In particular I sensed I never properly belonged to Glossop. Sure, I came to like the climate, glory in the scenery, commune with the stones and admire the architecture. But unlike most folk around me I was keenly aware of life beyond Dinting Arches, in the general direction of Manchester and even London. In my mind I remained in exile.

So I failed in my youth to appreciate a feature that in retrospect seems precious. Glossop when I lived there was a city state. It was self-governing. It revelled in a quasi-Athenian autonomy. It is true that we arrived after the golden age and after the benevolent despots had gone away. For when the Second Lord Howard died in 1927 his heir sold the Hall. Edward Partington had died two years earlier and the Woods, recognising that cotton had no future but that banking did, flitted to London, diverting their patronage from Glossop North End to the Arsenal. Yet despite the additional body-blow of the Slump the local ship of state stayed afloat. Notables of lower rank but not necessary of lesser capability – like Alderman Doyle, socialist, journalist and manager of the Co-op shoe shop – took over from the departed captains and most public services continued to be generated locally. Many of them were carried out by the Corporation, a body of solid citizens installed in the handsome Municipal Buildings, abutting the Town Hall, where the Mayor had a parlour and aldermen and councillors sat in dignity in their chamber. They employed a solid corps of professionals, some with exotic titles, like Town Clerk, Borough Surveyor or Sanitary Inspector. Those public servants included the Chief Constable of the borough's independent police force and the Chief of its own Fire Brigade. They included Dr Milligan, the Medical Officer of Health, who defended us all from infection, infestation and unfitness. 'Marcus Milligan's got the flu/Mind he doesn't give it you', kids used to sing in playgrounds. They included the manager of the borough waterworks and the superintendent of the borough's market. They also included my Dad who, at least in theory, was at least nominally responsible to the Borough Education Committee, which ran a dozen or so other establishments as well as the Grammar School. The borough's own magistrates held petty sessions at the Town Hall. The Glossop Gas Company served only Glossop. Although electricity was imported, the consortium that supplied it – the grandly named 'Stalybridge, Hyde, Mossley and Dukinfield Transport and Electricity Joint Board', which also operated bus services – had its headquarters only a few miles away. The hospitals were locally owned and managed and so was the institution that until recently had been the workhouse. Public baths, public parks and public libraries functioned munificently in the care of the borough which of course lit its own streets, collected its own refuse and buried its own dead. In my day we Glossopians benefitted from firm but well intentioned government exercised on the spot by local people. We enjoyed a measure of genuine autonomy.

After the war autonomy withered away. Successive 'reforms' took services out of local hands into those of faceless ones in other places. The NHS absorbed the medical services. The County Council took the schools away and later pinched the libraries as well. The supply of gas and electricity, following nationalisation, came to be administered from far away. One by one the old titles were dropped. The Chief Constable disappeared and so did the Medical Officer of Health. Presumably their duties were somewhere still performed but nobody much in Glossop knew by whom or in what manner. Eventually even the Mayor and the Town Clerk had to recycle their robes and clear their desks. For the

Borough of Glossop itself ceased to exist, absorbed into something hybrid and over-extended with a logo instead of a motto. The modern Borough of the High Peak must be difficult for Glossopians to identify with because it extracts its predatory taxes from a base in alien Buxton, a spa town bristling with conference hotels and opera houses, separated from Glossop by history and culture as well as by fifteen miles of mountain roads. It all seems a great pity.

Chapter 3

SCHOOLING

In September 1937 I entered Miss Merry's reception class at St Luke's Church of England Elementary School. This time there was no trauma. I just went and got on with it. I was not even put off by the Grange Road grimness of the building, so unlike the pert modernity of Moss Park. It seems Glossop's Victorian ambience, much vaunted in the last chapter, must already have entered my soul and even moderated my erstwhile addiction to what was up to date. I do however remember some reservations about the rusty, dusty tin cans I found sitting on our desktops that first morning. Long ago they must have held baked beans or tomato soup. I thought they were for drinking milk out of but then Miss Merry distributed slates and put chalks in the cans. So that was alright.

Although Mum seemed indifferent to the issues involved – as I say, she never rated book learning so what did it matter which school I went to? – Dad agonised about St Luke's all through our first weeks in Glossop, even though, simultaneously and anxiously, he was preparing his debut as 'headmasterglossopgrammarschool'. He habitually mouthed it staccato as though it might get away if he didn't keep a grip on it. There was the building to start with. No Victorian ambience had entered *his* soul. Like all enlightened members of his generation he believed something nasty and lingering had infected architecture round about the 1840s, just as the Irish potato crop, with dire consequences, was also struck by blight. So to him St Luke's, like the Town Hall and Sumner's Mill, was a monstrosity. It was insanitary too. It was no place for his first-born. But what could he do? *All* the elementary schools in Glossop were Victorian monstrosities.

Worse still they were all in thrall to 'bloody parsons', a breed condemned in Dad's 'Inferno' – along with Germans, 'conshies', opticians, 'nancyboys' and sundry other untouchables – to the lowest cycles of the damned. The parsons prevailed because the Howards and the mill-owners, in their competitive philanthropy, had endowed so many of the local churches with day-schools that there was no need in Glossop for 'board schools', the secular alternative ushered in by the famous 1870 Education Act. It is true that all the local schools were 'aided', that is they received state funding, channelled through the Borough Education Committee, and were subject to the scrutiny of His Majesty's Inspectors. However the churches retained substantial control and, under the supervision of their clergy, saw it as their duty to induct pupils into whatever sacred truth, with attendant liturgy, was embraced by each particular denomination. Which did not suit Dad at all. He had undergone a counter-conversion from the Methodism in which he was bred and now knew for sure that all religious faith was superstitious, if not actually occult. Thus he was determined to protect his children from the tocsins dispensed by 'bloody parsons'. He also fretted about his image. If he sent his lad to a denominational school would that not compromise the rational ethic, standing aloof from religious claptrap, that he intended to maintain at the Grammar School? But there was no alternative. So after a quick sniff at the Duke of Norfolk's School in Old Glossop, cowering in the obnoxious shadow of the parish church but a bit nearer our house, he opted for St Luke's. It was next door to the Grammar School so the boy could walk in with his Dad who might, during those daily marches, provide decontamination from the poisonous discourse of parsons. Also J W S Fielding, Head of St Luke's, must be a sound chap because he had lost a leg in the war.

Technically there was another option. He might access the private sector. He could certainly afford it but at five I was still too young to be sent away to boarding school, although that alarming prospect did subsequently from time to time disturb the passage of my childhood. Believe it or not, Kingswood, the Methodist public school near Bath, was at one time under consideration and that project surely undermines any notion of Dad's religious position as the product of cool and rational humanist conviction. It seems more likely he was just plain mixed up and was actually haunted by the 'bloody parsons' he affected to despise. Which is scarcely surprising since the circumstances in which he lost his faith might be considered post traumatic. For in 1918, as we shall discover, he had at great peril taken part in the final defeat of the German army on the Western Front and it was in the aftermath of that heady triumph that he liberated himself from 'bloody parsons'. They had somehow been in league with 'Prussian militarists' and yellow 'conshies'. Poor Dad! Was he perhaps permanently shell-shocked and is that a clue to his personality? Anyway in 1937 he might have sent me, not to Kingswood, but to Kingsmoor. It was a private school, advertising itself on a big board at the top of Norfolk Street as 'Preparatory to University Entrance', and its owners had taken possession of Glossop Hall when the Howards sold up in the 1920s. For a day or two that August Kingsmoor must have been a live possibility and I have an impression that Mum rather favoured it. She probably thought it catered for a better class of parents and she was probably right. So one rainy afternoon I was taken to peep at the premises through a locked gate. I saw a big garden with a fountain and beyond it a grand house with a little church tacked on the end of it [the former private chapel]. I was mildly apprehensive but nothing followed the recce. I suppose snooty Kingsmoor would be even worse for Dad's image than denominational St Luke's, for it had a secondary department as well as a prep school and thus operated in direct competition with the Grammar School. Sending me there would have been like running a restaurant and going out for lunch. Thus the associates of Kingsmoor soon joined Dad's menagerie of bêtes noires, along with the parsons and Prussians. The shoddy upstart establishment lacked academic credibility yet it seduced the golf club set from its duty to support the local grammar school by sending its progeny there. Actually the golf club set seemed to prefer the PPS [Private Preparatory School] that Mrs Thomas conducted in an upper room of the exclusive Glossop Social Club, which displayed its well-polished brass plate on a door in Ellison Street, near the Fire Station. It was a providential location in view of the barred window of the schoolroom and the single flight of steep stairs that was its only means of access. Eventually my sister went there with no perceptible damage to her body, mind or psyche. Which suggests Dad's doubts about St Luke's had not been resolved. Yet that school served me well.

The building Dad despised had been erected by the High Church, High Tory Wood family to celebrate Queen Victoria's Diamond Jubilee in 1897 *[Plate 9]*. Its foundation stone was laid just before that of the technical school which soon began to rise up next door, further along Talbot Street. The latter was the latest benefaction of Liberal, Catholic Lord Howard and soon it transmuted into the Grammar School over which Dad now presided. The original St Luke's building lasted until the 1980s, when a boring new structure with better plumbing replaced it, but the fabric survives, albeit at the unpredictable mercy of the local authority, which has adapted it for some bureaucratic purpose. With a touch of flattery what we see might be called 'Arts and Crafts'. Well, the roofs are high and the windows are big, so airy and light was probably the progressive intention. The plan was a 'T' made up of two long rectangular spaces, the cross piece being the Junior School while the upright housed the Infants. Apart from cloakrooms and the Head's room, the arrangement was open plan, the teaching areas being divided only by folding timber and glass partitions, suspended from ceiling tracks and bolted to the floor. In the Infants Miss Wild's older class and Miss Merry's younger ones were separated by such a contraption, with mutual access through a sort of wicket gate that was not easy to open. In the Juniors Miss Lee's Standard I and Miss Little's Standard II were partitioned off at the two ends, while the space in the centre was shared by Standards III and IV. By the time I got as far as that Mrs Newton presided over Standard III. Since there was a war on she was allowed to be married yet carry on teaching and that fact, together with her habit of enforcing numeracy through the not quite playful application of a flexible ruler to the learner's outstretched palm, gave her an aura that was distinctly erotic. Her fleshpot was separated from the territory of Miss Max's Standard IV only by a line of plywood screens, perhaps five feet high. Thus in the higher standards you always knew what was happening in the other place. You were aware also of the comings and goings of Mr Fielding, the Head, who as well as having a private office, kept a large solid desk in front of the cast-iron fireplace, under a big map of the British Empire, with our possessions splashed in bright red across a world otherwise represented in dull buff. Mr Fielding's use of this station was ceremonial rather than administrative. It was here that he received VIPs. The Mayor of Glossop himself once honoured us in his civic regalia. It was from this podium too that Mr Fielding addressed general assemblies of the whole school on Friday mornings and also on solemn occasions such as Armistice Day in November, Empire Day in May and the outbreak of renewed hostilities in September 1939. It served also as a scaffold when he judged an offence so heinous that only the ultimate penalty would do. The resulting ceremony seemed the more awesome because Captain Fielding's wooden leg drummed rhythmically on the bare boards of the schoolroom as he ushered the miscreant to his fate. A profound hush would descend to be broken at length by the repeated swish of a long yellow cane, meticulously green corded at the handle, like a golf club. When I was eight I was fairly appalled. Now I am eighty I still am. 'The stick' overshadowed life at St Luke's. Although they wielded it less formally and more tentatively, it was seen as an essential classroom resource by the assistant teachers as well. They would have said, truthfully enough, that it was not employed promiscuously but the fact that it was there at all was not just alarming it was emotionally disturbing. It didn't seem right.

J W S Fielding, the tall moustachioed war hero with that purposeful gait, looked very like General De Gaulle and the wooden leg was only one of his trappings of authority. Others derived from his tenure of the office of Chief Air Raid Warden. This merited an official plaque on his front gate and he often appeared at school wearing a white helmet with a superior 'Services' respirator, in a designer canvas container, slung by a wide webbing belt across his broad shoulder. How different from us. Our bog standard gas masks came in cardboard boxes with rough string that cut into your neck. His presence indeed was godlike. I knew about gods for this was my Greek phase, when the inhabitants of Olympus felt like next door neighbours. Stanley Fielding was surely Zeus, ruling a court of female deities including kinky Mrs Newton as Aphrodite and wise, if ratty, Miss Little as Pallas Athene. But was he a greater god than my Dad? That question perturbed me. It was true my father was head of a secondary school whereas St Luke's was only elementary but Mr Fielding had three Christian names while Dad had only just the one. And although our house was big there were slums nearby, like the one Olive lived in, whereas the Fielding villa was in Fauvel Road – the émigré Père Fauvel had been given refuge by the Howards during the Napoleonic Wars – in the heart of a residential district that was undoubtedly exclusive. Moreover Mr Fielding's house was modern. It had gables, a glazed porch and was pebble-dashed and built of brick. Its truly suburban character agonisingly recalled Manchester. Nor did Dad stand up well on a physical comparison. Although he too had a moustache, he was not tall and, despite having been in the war, both his legs were made of ordinary flesh, as I knew because I often saw him with his trousers off, a situation in which I had never beheld Mr Fielding. I used to imagine it though. Where exactly did the flesh stop and the wood start and how exactly was the latter attached to the former? And Dad, although briefly serving as Billeting Officer, distributing smelly evacuees among Glossop's reluctant householders, was not in the ARP [Air Raid Precautions], defending Glossop against the worst the Luftwaffe might hurl at us. As the war went on however Dad gained in belligerent credibility. The Luftwaffe snubbed Glossop – we were favoured by not a single little incendiary throughout the whole war – and that dimmed the lustre of the Chief Warden. Then Dad set up the ATC [Air Training Corps] which made him a Flight Lieutenant. That not only gave him a helmet and a Services' respirator but a whole smart uniform as well. But it was a pity he was only a Flight Lieutenant because that meant that, at town parades, he had to salute Major Lancely, boss of the Turn Lea paper works, who as well as deploying the Tiger tractors, was CO of the Glossop Home Guard.

Above Mr Fielding's big desk and the map of the Empire, and along most of the back wall of the Juniors, stretched the Honours Board. Thereon in neat black script were inscribed for posterity the names of all those St Luke's pupils who, year by wonderful year, since before the Great War, had brought glory to us all and benefit to themselves by passing 'the Scholarship'. That appealing name was later usurped by the expression 'Eleven Plus' which, was more or less the same thing. On the wooden panels, the names of an elite few were starred as having distinguished themselves from the ruck of 'Free Place' holders by winning a 'County Minor Scholarship'. Getting one of those was seriously big. It was a bit like having a VC, or at least a DFC. It brought instant celebrity and I began to fancy I would rather like some of that for myself. There was however a snag that I could not honestly discount. To get a County Minor you had to be able to read, and right up to the time when, at the age of nine, I got into Miss Max's Scholarship Class, the crème de la crème of Standard IV, I had to admit I was no great shakes in that department. It bothered me less than it did Dad and my teachers but I knew that socks would have to be pulled up and maybe it was longing for a star on the Honours Board that brought me at last to achievement of a halting literacy. Achievement was the thing. It mattered a lot at St Luke's and motivation to accomplish it was paramount in the 'hidden curriculum', the set of desired cultural norms indicated by the way the school operated. Do well in class and you got praise plus sometimes a coveted stamp to stick into your exercise book. Those tokens depicted scenes of pastoral felicity – thatched cottages and horses ploughing – together with the legends 'Excellent', 'Very Good' or at least 'Well Tried'. Do badly however and you got the rough end of Miss Little's tongue or the correctional sting of Mrs Newton's ruler. Miss Little even made Standard II sit every week in order of merit as determined by the marks we accumulated. One Friday I came second, so next week I shared the top table with a tall girl recently arrived from a distant Camelot the name of which impressed our teachers. It was 'Coventry'. The willowy but bossy girl was called Marcia Field and when she grew up she was made Lady Falkender for services to Harold Wilson.

Achievement motivation then was central to a hidden curriculum which also taught me about sex. That is, I discovered that society is segregated by gender as well as by merit. So there was a separate girls' playground that, even though it had to be shared with the 'mixed infants', was smaller than the boys'. What happened there had a distinctive feminine character, involving skipping, dancing and the playing of soulful, singing games like 'Sally lies a-weeping'. Although I could do without skipping and dancing, as a mixed infant I liked the tranquillity of the girls' yard where I was left alone to get on with the solitary looking and thinking to which I was accustomed. But when, aged six and three quarters, I became a junior, I was plunged into the furore of the more extensive asphalt jungle allocated to the boys and dominated by gangs that imported rituals to the playground from their bases in nearby mean streets. There rougher, conflict oriented play was de rigeur. I was OK about 'Cops and Robbers' and actually liked 'Tiggy off the Ground'. But I dreaded 'Ghost Train'. You lined up one behind the other, holding the coat-tail of the boy in front, while our leader made for the bottom of the yard where, beside a basic urinal, wholesomely exposed to the elements, there stood a dark, stinking, half derelict shed with two entrances, among the festooned cobwebs of which toilet cubicles could be dimly discerned. Here the 'ghosts' lurked and fell upon the 'train' as it attempted a fumbling progress between the two doors. The outcome was a brawling, bruising mêlée confined within the insanitary space. It was not nice. I learned something else about sex as well. Men are in charge. The only two adult males on the premises, the Caretaker and the Head, were accorded an automatic deference by mere adult females, even by feisty Miss Little and sultry Mrs Newton. Mr Fielding's position was indeed privileged. He only occasionally did any teaching himself and, despite the absence of a general staff room, had a private office. Furthermore his whims were law to his simpering harem. Thus, despite its popularity, unless our master was known to be off the premises, we missed out 'Ho Ro my Nut Brown Maiden' when we came to it in the song-book. 'Mr Fielding doesn't like it'. Just that. I wonder what he had against it? Was he perhaps a pioneer anti-racist? It is an interesting thought that only now, after three quarters of a century, occurs to me.

Class, as well as gender and merit, was on the hidden curriculum. It separated me from my schoolmates. For although I felt no particular animus against them – they were alright in their way – I knew they were not like me. After a day at school, conforming, willingly enough and up to a point, to expected behaviours, I went home to something quite different – a better off, more comfortable, cleaner, more spacious, better equipped, more cultivated, middle class world, to which my peers did not belong. Following a stint of sums and scripture, effort stamps and marks out of ten, public executions and the Ghost Train, it was relaxing to seek out one of the hiding places at Holly Wood and ponder it all in blessed solitude. During my brief interlude during the 1960s as a pretend sociology lecturer I came across an expression that nicely encapsulated my role at St Luke's. It was 'participant observation' and it was what American anthropologists did in the south Pacific, camping among Samoans or Trobriand Islanders and affecting to join in, before slipping discreetly back to the straw huts where they kept their notebooks. That was me at St Luke's. I observed and participated but it was not my proper scene. I felt fundamentally different even from boys like Geoffrey Sims, Tommy Waghorn or Charles Yolland who were neatly turned out, did not smell and came from respectable homes. As for the great unwashed ... well, their plight was a sight to be observed. That high profile poverty was on display at St Luke's has already been noted. I have said that many children wore tattered clothes, stank of stale sweat and excrement, had green teeth, snotty nostrils and suppurating ears, and were disfigured by sores and rashes. Also the 'Olive' smell lingered despite the caretaker's generosity with Jeyes Fluid, and although teachers fervently promoted the virtues of cleanliness. We were regularly inspected for head lice and once I was found to be infested. At least my shocked mother thought so and hence a brutal assault on hair and scalp, a prolonged course of fine combings over white paper spread on the kitchen table, and the application to my cropped head of something purple and shameful. We have seen also how, by order of the Medical Officer of Health, the officially undernourished were called out each morning to the front of the class, there to consume, on the spot, before our very eyes, a penitential 'Swedish Sandwich', constructed from extra-thick brown bread with a pay-load of hard-boiled egg and salad, dispensed at arm's length by a studious looking young man from 'the Clinic'. All that I observed, noted and pondered. It was certainly interesting. But did I care? Was compassion part of my response? Not much I think. Poverty was mildly distasteful but it was not really my business. Schools were not welfare agencies, I thought. Not of course that I would have put it like that. Their function was to promote learning not to relieve poverty and being poor or even smelly did not stop you thinking. Such attitudes, if they are rightly recalled, came surely from the hidden curriculum, not of the school, but of my own family. The Lords believed in self-help. When my grandparents were babies, Samuel Smiles' book of that name had stood beside the bible on millions of cottage mantelpieces. Whether or not they actually read Smiles, my grandparents, by their actions, proved the efficacy of his thesis. They rose by their own efforts from rags to riches and knowledge of that achievement somehow informed my childhood judgement. Thus I knew poverty was, with effort, reversible. That truth applied even to a boy called Stanley who came from Edward Street, Glossop's most notorious slum, and gave off a pungent stink. Our teachers must have thought so too for with therapeutic purpose his grubby palms were forever tickled by the corrective cane. I *think* I grasped something of all that when I was about seven, the instruction of Granny Southport being a major factor in my enlightenment. More later.

So much for hidden curricula, institutional and domestic. What about the open variety? Did they actually teach me anything at St Luke's? They certainly tried. Our teachers worked hard. They were organised and systematic. We trusted them. They inspired confidence in what they told us to do. I do not doubt they believed in their mission and found satisfaction in its pursuit. I remember them as enthusiastic, usually cheerful and normally kindly. They were indeed dedicated professionals.

The school day moved forward in almost exactly the same sequence whatever day of the week it was and whether we were infants or juniors and that was a comfort. Always the morning was for real work – the three Rs – while more trivial pursuits might enliven the afternoons. But, exactly as Dad had feared, before the three Rs, came religious instruction. What we got was the genuine Anglican article, containing nothing fudged and nondenominational, and certainly nothing comparative, suggesting that heretics like Methodists or Catholics, heathens like Jews or Mohamedans, or naked savages like Red Indians or Zulus, were to be embraced as our brothers and sisters in faith. St Luke's stood in an uncompromising historical tradition that dated back to the 'National Society' founded in 1817 'for the Education of the Poor in the Principles of the Established Church throughout England and Wales'. Sure National schools taught the three Rs as well, but as an aid to salvation, not as an end in themselves. So every day at St Luke's began with Prayers. Eyes shut, hands together. On Mondays, Wednesdays and Thursdays we prayed with our own teachers in our own classrooms but on Fridays we gathered at the feet of Mr Fielding – or at his solitary foot perhaps – who on those occasions turned his scaffold into a pulpit. On most Tuesdays mornings however something special occurred. Then the whole school went in a crocodile of pairs, like the animals approaching the ark, down the lane past the Grammar School huts, over Fauvel Road and up the path into St Luke's Church. It is a late Gothic structure dating from about 1905 but to me it felt profoundly old, in a nice way, not a scary one like the houses in Grange Road of yore. Ever since 1937 when I first passed its portals that edifice has served me as a stereotype for 'church', the film set on which I place any appropriate scene I read about or hear described. There was a high roof and a prominent chancel arch with a text inscribed upon it, although my reading was never good enough to make any sense of it. And there was an organ that I think somebody played to accompany our hymns, and a pulpit the Rev Mr Chivers stood in, immaculate in white robes, with a sort of black scarf and a collar the wrong way round. He looked good up there so you could believe what he was saying was OK even though he must be one of those 'bloody parsons' Dad disapproved of. We sat in front of him in nice little boxes that held perhaps ten of us at a pinch. There was a strip of red carpet to make sitting on the wooden bench a bit more comfortable and some of those well stuffed cushion things for kneeling on. At the entrance to each of these 'pews' the owner's name, on a visiting card, was slotted into a little metal frame. One of them read 'Mr and Mrs J W S Fielding' so it seemed that on Sundays every local family had a little home from home at church and I liked that. Indeed I liked the whole scene more than I admitted to Dad. By the font there was even a 'Children's Corner' with books and activity materials. When we left, Mr Chivers said an individual goodbye to each one of us while his snow-white vestments billowed in the wind.

After Prayers came Scripture. The name was appropriate. Our religious studies were not only exclusively Christian but rooted in Christian texts. We were told a lot of bible stories. As well as the Christmas and Easter narratives and sundry parables – 'an earthly story with a heavenly meaning' we were told, though we were not told what that meant – I came to know the tales of Moses in the bulrushes, Samson bringing the house down and David felling Goliath, at least as well as I knew Jack and the Beanstalk or the Labours of Hercules. Also we learnt basic texts by heart and then chanted them in unison while Miss scanned our lips for hesitation. There was the Lord's Prayer of course and the Ten Commandments and some psalms and the Creed, all naturally in the Authorised or 1662 versions, and I got to know some hymns. I remember noticing that many such passages found a welcome in my head even though I had only a hazy idea what they meant. The words sounded good and were exciting to say and I had a sense that gradually, in time they would make more sense, and indeed they sometimes did. Thus incomprehension did not invalidate learning. Perhaps our teachers shared that conviction because they did not hasten to enlighten us about the meaning of what we parroted. However I think I can remember Miss Wild exploring temptation.

What I picked up then was an incomplete body of Christian knowledge that I never subsequently filled out through church-going. It was better however than the none at all children often get today, in schools that are sometimes aggressively secular or obsessively multi-cultural. How can you make sense of a western civilisation that is fundamentally Christian without that sort of knowledge? How otherwise can you do history? – that is get inside the heads of people, a hundred generations of them, who quite unlike most of us, struggled with the prospect of an after-life and were thus governed by a need to find favour with God. For example, Henry VIII apparently dominates modern classrooms but what kids get is the sexy bit of the story extracted from its boring religious context. Which is a wicked distortion. Sure, Henry fancied Anne but that fateful warming of the loins occurred in a stormy religious climate so that private passion became the catalyst for public cataclysm and that is the point of teaching the topic. Without knowledge of the debate about Protestantism the story of the Reformation, arguably the key event in English history, is hopelessly trivialised. And how can you understand western literature, music or art without a knowledge of Christian mythology? At least, when I did Eng Lit for Higher School Cert, and had to confront Milton's urge to 'justify the ways of God to man' I could call to mind the bible stories Miss Little taught us, and the passages from the Book of Common Prayer she made us memorise. And when at university I discovered art history and, in tackling Renaissance painting, beheld a sequence of annunciations, adorations, ascensions and assumptions, I had further cause to thank my teachers at St Luke's. Modern students however, insulated from Christianity by their schooling, must find utterly baffling much of the subject matter of western art.

Engagement with one particular Christian text brought taught me a lesson that was not intended. It encouraged me in scepticism. We were studying the Catechism and of course learning it by heart. 'What is thy name?' was the first of a whole battery of questions with only one correct answer that made up the Catechism. I was supposed to recite that my name had been given me by my godfather and my godmother at my baptism. But I could not truthfully do that because I knew I had not been baptised and lacked godparents. Dad was insistent on the point and Mum said she had got to be fourteen before the minister at Bethel plunged her fully clothed, more or less, into a mini-pool somewhere behind the organ. So in my case the Prayer Book must surely be wrong. I put the dilemma to the class. Encouraged by mischievous Miss Little they insisted Dad was teasing me and Mum was a story-teller. Everybody got christened only you could not remember it happening because you were only a baby at the time. I would not be shaken. I had not been baptised and did not have godparents yet I knew I had a name. So there. It was a confusing but useful experience that served to show that public opinion, even when backed by the authority of a teacher, could be wrong. It did not do to swallow whole everything 'they' came out with. A blessed occasion.

At 9-30 Sums followed Scripture. Not just Sums but 'Mental', which

I dreaded more than anything in the school day apart from Ghost Train. 'Richard Lord, what are nine eights?' If I could take my time I could work it out and if she had asked me eight eights, '64' would have come out pat. But that was the point of Mental Arithmetic, you were not allowed time to think. Everything had to be done instantly, by reflex. Even the 'problems' we were set in Mental had to be done at the double. For it was not just times tables that were flung at us. They were at least memorable, though not as easily as psalms. But we also had to do lightning calculations about the price of apples or the speed of trains. As with the Catechism there was only one correct answer and woe betide you if you did not spit it out. Just do it!

If six pounds of apples cost a shilling, what do two pounds cost? – *Four pence.*

Fair enough. That was easy. But try this one.

If one train leaves Manchester for London at ten o'clock, travelling at an average speed of 50 mph and another leaves London at the same time for Manchester, travelling at exactly the same speed, and the distance between the two cities is 180 miles, how far will the northbound train have travelled when it meets the southbound express? – *90 miles.*

Sure, the penny drops if you have time, but time you were not given. Quick, quick! No holding back! Get on with it! It was the same, ten years, later doing square-bashing during National Service at RAF Henlow.

Squadron Leader and ranks above approaching your post, to the front salute.

No messing, no thinking – just jump to it and present arms a bit smartish. One ...left, right ... two ... left, right ... three. Our instructor made the pedagogic principle very clear.

But Corporal, I thought ...

Think! You 'orrible little man!! You're not 'ere to fucking well think!!!

It worked too. After a while I got quite good at saluting squadron leaders and enjoyed being good at it. I even got ninety per cent in a drill test. But the satisfaction was scarcely intellectual. Rather than stimulating the mind drill anaesthetises it and by the time I was eighteen maybe I had got to like being sometimes zonked out. But to a dreamy eight year old, accustomed to free range looking and thinking with oodles of time to spare, it was all very upsetting. My brain seemed to seize up and my tongue stuttered uncontrollably. Even if I managed to understand the sum with that particle of my mind that escaped general cerebral paralysis, I could not get the answer out. Yet the confusion it wrought in me does not necessarily invalidate Mental. Yes, it was unadulterated drill but useful skills – like saluting squadron leaders – can be efficiently acquired that way. Also, at the time concerned, long before the age of the pocket calculator, let alone the computer, the ability to do complex calculations instantly in your head much improved your job prospects and was indeed a practical necessity in many of the ordinary tasks of life.

Sums proper followed Mental at the prime time of ten o'clock. I think we mastered the basics of adding up and taking away before we left the infants, leaving multiplication and division for Standards I and II, when presumably our brains would have developed sufficiently to cope with those more demanding operations. What it mostly boiled down to was breaking down a number into its constituent hundreds, tens and units. Get hold of that and even long division need not defeat you. Getting a sum to work out was actually rewarding in itself so moments of joy as well as gasps of anguish punctuated many mornings. 'HTU' having been mastered it was on to higher things. I got on well with fractions but found decimals more difficult, which they should not have been if I had properly got the point of HTU. However you could imagine a bar of chocolate being divided into halves and quarters, which is what Mum did all the time, but 0.25 of a Dairy Milk was harder to imagine. Then there was LCM. It seemed clear enough when Mrs Newton explained it but what it is and why it matters have since eluded me. Not so the 'Rule of Three' or 'if', 'then' and 'and' – *if* a dozen eggs cost sixpence, *then* one egg costs a halfpenny *and* seven eggs must cost seven halfpennies, i.e. three pence halfpenny – still seems an elegant way of thinking and useful to have at one's disposal. The whole gamut of imperial measures, including perches and pecks, chains and furlongs, acres and square feet, gills and quarts slipped down easily enough. Having memorised tables of measures we used them to calculate the likes of areas and volumes. Again I enjoyed the poetry of the words. And a certain factual fall-out was stored away for use along life's journey. When for a while I followed the horses it was handy to know a furlong is longer than a short head and if you took a girlfriend to the Royal Oak you needed to appreciate that her femininity demanded a gill, not a pint. However that is about all I can remember about sums and it does not seem all that much, considering that we devoted more than an hour a day over a period of five years to this king of the three Rs. I was left with a lingering sense of innumeracy. I wonder why. Perhaps it was because we were too much drilled in procedures without having underlying principles explained. My daughter, who teaches maths to juniors, says they do better today and I hope she is right. Or perhaps the sense of inadequacy lay somewhere else, inside me beyond the reach of teachers. For I am not really innumerate. I prefer statistics to rhetoric.

About eleven, after milk and play, it was reading and writing. Or rather it was writing for I do not remember being taught to read. If that happened it did not work, not at least for a long time and perhaps I have suppressed knowledge of a painful struggle. It is true that by the time I left St Luke's when I was ten, I had acquired a limited literacy but I still read slowly and sotto voce pronounced all the words. It had been touch and go and Dad had suffered. Eventually, as will be related, I took pity on him and taught myself to read, independently of any schemes my teachers may have attempted to expose me to. Paradoxically illiteracy did not impede my progress in writing. I remember moving smoothly from chalk to pencil and on to pen and ink with little trauma and considerable satisfaction. Except that they said I was untidy. They were still saying it long after I started at the Grammar School. 'If you had a coat of arms,' said Mr Casey, who kept a jaundiced eye on the son of the usurper who had done him out of his headship, 'it would be a blot rampant on a field of ink'. This witticism much amused him – excessively so, I thought. At the time I couldn't see that it mattered much but perhaps I was wrong. Sometimes writing meant doing a 'composition', although only as a reward after a decent spell of punctuating or distinguishing adjectives and adverbs. You felt Miss thought composition an inferior activity and maybe she would not bother with it if it were not something that had to be done in the Scholarship. A composition was something you made up freely, like a story or an account of an episode in your life. I liked it, except that they knocked marks off for untidiness and bad grammar. I lost out on the former of course but not the latter. For my grammar was already perfect. I just wrote the way we spoke at home. I knew exactly how to talk correctly because I had picked up that skill at my mother's knee without even knowing it was difficult. So unlike nearly all the other children in the class, I had no need to learn school-talk, a foreign tongue to be used in class and particularly when doing writing. It was one of the ways I knew I was different from them, perhaps the most important one. Not that the knowledge made me complacent because in the playground the tables were turned. There the local patois defeated me and they thought my accent lah-di-dah so I was often left on my own – not maliciously, I think, but simply because the linguistic barrier was too high to be jumped over in the middle of a game of Cowboys and Indians. My own addiction to solitude of course intensified my isolation. The trouble was I preferred being on my own and did not particularly like Cowboys and Indians. Anyway I thought there was something to be said for the Indian point of view. But there I go again, 'fucking well thinking'. It is no way to make friends. Being habitually grammatical was a problem in class as well as during play. My fluency in standard English made writing lessons boring. All that banging on about apostrophes and inverted commas and ID checks on parts of speech. Sure, I didn't know what a verb was until Miss Little told me but I never made up a sentence without one – as will be apparent if you will re-read the last one I gave you. Then there were all those bits of writing we had to comprehend. My problem there was guessing what the words were. If she would read it aloud instead of making us read it for ourselves making sense would present few problems. I am saying grammatical instruction seemed gratuitous to an eight year old already fluent in the King's English – more fluent actually than the poor stammering monarch himself.

At twelve o'clock we all went home for dinner, school meals not being available until about half way through the war. Even then they were, as far as I could see and smell, nauseatingly unappetising and I was relieved that my parents made no effort to wean me from Mum's chip-pan. Going home and back was a round trip of two miles so some of the excessive calories got burnt off. Sometimes I walked home with Dad but increasingly, for the first part of the journey, my companion was Chris Gillings who lived next door to his granddad's billiard hall, half way along High Street East. Was Chris's house a slum? The problem perplexed me. It was bigger than most cottages and it did have a bathroom but, even though his dad was a French polisher, it retained vestigial odours. Perhaps that was because Gillings Senior at the commencement of hostilities gave up polishing and became a policeman before, later, joining the navy. PC Gillings was firm but fair. He used a razor strop to instil into his son the elements of right-thinking decency and to the same end regaled him with cautionary tales about judicial floggings administered at the police station on the orders of the magistrates. But when pushy Chris, claiming first sight, took sole possession of a half crown he and I had simultaneously spotted in a gutter while homeward bound from St Luke's, Mr Gillings came hot-foot to our house bearing my legitimate prize money of one and three-pence. Sharing, even Stevens, was one of the elements of decency and finders must have been keepers in the book of the Glossop Constabulary. Assurance sat comfortably on Chris's stocky shoulders. He knew what was what and where it was at and was seemingly learned about things that by rights belonged exclusively to the world of grown-ups. So I found him a useful if not always reliable work of reference and deferred to him as my guide to the culture of the streets and back-yards. That way I fell into the way of doing his bidding. So sometimes after school, in the gathering dusk, I turned my cap round like him, made clicking sounds as though urging my steed, and trotted off behind him towards Manor Park, the dread haunt, he assured me, of ferocious Catholic gangs, like the one led by the Dawson boys. Fortunately we never found any lurking heretics before black-out time came along and we could each go home for tea. Actually Chris was a bully. Once for insubordination he twisted my arm and made me write out twenty lines and in our wash-house too, where he was my guest. He was clever though. He could devour the *Hotspur* comic whole, in great silent gulps, while I stumbled over the balloons emitted from the mouth of Korky the Cat, on the front page of the *Dandy*. He was ambitious too and in the wide blue yonder duly fetched up as an HMI, a schools inspector. Although I expect his judgements would have been fair enough I bet he enjoyed telling head teachers their schools required improvement. We shall join Chris again soon.

Fortified by something and chips, at half past one it was back to school for the afternoon session and the bits of the curriculum that did not matter much, not anyway by comparison with the three Rs of the morning. Perhaps it is because of that covert inferior billing that only a random collection of arbitrarily remembered data seems to survive from what we did in afternoon lessons labelled 'Nature', 'Poetry', 'Geography', 'History' or 'Music'. We recited verses and sang songs. We went up the airy mountain and down the rushy glen. We sailed a quinquerime of Ninevah and on mad March days butted up the Channel. We asked after grey-coated John Peel, asserted Bobby Shafto's honourable intentions but, in obeisance to Mr Fielding, forbore to patronise a certain nut-brown maiden. By way of geography we scanned the world, or rather the British Empire, which was more or less the same thing. We learnt about sheep farming in Australia and logging in Canada and also established the location of the principal British coalfields. We made posters for Spitfire Week and mastered production skills connected with the manufacture of paper chains. So much for art and craft. All I can remember about history is the names of Robin Hood's band. Can that really be true? Perhaps I have dim recollections also of Queen Boadicea with whom, I guess, Miss Little felt an affinity. Nature Study has left more traces. In September we did spiders and learned to distinguish them from the insect kingdom. In February it was pussy willow and we noted also the distinguishing features of certain birds of winter passage. In April we collected frog spawn and during the subsequent bluebell season, when jam-jars chock-full of the droopy things littered our classroom, the principal parts of a flower were demonstrated. Most days towards four o'clock tensions relaxed. Sometimes she read to us, though apart from a weekly contribution to the *Children's Newspaper* by a hitherto unknown author called Enid Blyton, I can remember none of the works narrated. Sometimes also at this witching hour we had silent reading. Chris anyway was silent – totally absorbed as he scanned page after rapid page of an apparently exciting story but me, I just tried to stop Miss noticing that under my breath I sounded all the pitifully few words I got through. Sometimes I let my finger run along the line as well. Friday afternoon however was different. Then, lest you fell into holiday mood in the firm's time, you felt the lash of 'Penmanship'. She wrote something in rhythmic, loopy copperplate on the blackboard and we had to reproduce it in our books with corresponding cursive competence. Chris seemed to manage that as well but, as you can imagine, my notorious untidiness let me down.

In September 1941 Chris and I moved up from Miss Newton's Standard III into Miss Max's Standard IV. By then the war was offering such intoxicating draughts of living history that it is not surprising the deeds of Robin Hood and Boadicea seemed small beer. Not only had the *Bismarck* been recently sunk but Hitler, to Dad's astonishment as well as Comrade Stalin's, had invaded Russia and that September his panzers were shown in the *Manchester Guardian* war maps executing the most dramatic pincer movements right across the limitless steppes of the

Ukraine. Wow! It was beautiful. Going into Standard IV however was not itself devoid of drama for it was now that we were formally subjected to a great selection. Selection was the flavour of the time, particularly behind the eastern front where Jews had to be separated from Slavs and, on the ramp at Auschwitz, prisoners fit for work had to be sorted from those finger-jerked direct to eternity. For while Chris and I were in Standard IV, although we knew it not, western civilization reached its nadir. The British wartime state did not carry the logic of selection as far as mass murder but it systematically selected and rejected its conscripted citizens, both male and female, and directed them to suitable roles in the war effort and it seemed axiomatic that schoolchildren should be similarly mobilised. What that meant for Miss Max's class was that her elite sheep, bound for the Grammar School, must be separated from rubbish goats due to languish at West End Central School. Why it was called that mystified me for it was situated at least half a mile from Norfolk Square. Entry to the Grammar School was a glittering prize since getting in led on to a career instead of just a job. Of that there was no doubt. So aspiring parents vehemently urged their children onwards and upwards. Like Mrs Gillings, for example – she wore the trousers now Chris's dad was away in the navy – who on the kitchen table kept a pile of careers manuals obtained by mail order. They told you what you had to do to get on in a whole range of callings, ranging from cliché bull's eyes, like doctor or lawyer, to more exotic avocations like sanitary inspector, commercial artist or quantity surveyor. She and the whole Gillings extended family – they occupied adjoining houses as well as the upper reaches of the billiard hall – perused them constantly. The 'Go' position for all the careers on that tantalising board was the Grammar School. Get in and the world was your oyster. But even before reaching 'Go' there was a pre-selection to be accomplished. You needed to get into the 'Scholarship Class' the safe fold in which abided Miss Max's sheep. Joining it was the first step on a long road.

Actually doing 'the Scholarship', the portmanteau name for a whole sequence of selections, was more like being subjected to an industrial process than just travelling along a road. In retrospect, a few years later, it reminded me of an illustration in one of the Puffin Picture Books that beguiled me at bedtime. Even at twelve my situation literacy-wise remained embarrassing and I still preferred pictures to words. The much thumbed slim volume in question was called *The Magic of Coal*. It celebrated the contribution of our plucky miners to final victory and as a reward promised them pithead baths after the war. By a lucky fluke I have the book still so here is the cut-away drawing concerned and it is reproduced as *[Plate 9 bottom left]*. It shows how coal is mechanically sorted by size at the pithead. A brief text explains how …

> … *the coal is jiggled along shaking plates which are pierced with holes. The biggest holes are in the top plate so all but the biggest pieces fall through to the next floor. Pieces too big to fall through pass right out of the building and down a chute.*

How ingenious. Wow! The process however seemed familiar. It struck me that the screening of coal was very like the screening of children that had been carried out when I was with Miss Max in Standard IV. The less valuable bigger lumps that were discarded early were obviously the kids who failed the Scholarship, or never even took it. However the dinky 'nutty cobs', like me and Chris Gillings, sitting pretty in a railway truck bound for the Grammar School, were the bright ones who had survived successive jigglings and shakings.

As just indicated the first and most crucial, of those convulsions took place right at the start of Standard IV when the Scholarship Class itself was constituted. For although no doubt all the children at St Luke's were legally entitled to have a go for the Grammar School, the only ones who actually did were those admitted to that elite group. It was the infallible judgement of our teachers, unaided by formal testing and without consultation with parents, that determined who was chosen and sometimes no doubt the criteria they applied, consciously or not, were social rather than academic. Bright boys and nice girls in, the rest nowhere. Henceforth we favoured ones sat snugly and smugly at the front of the class where Miss Max provided a rigorous teaching programme that diverged sharply from the less demanding routines by which she pacified the rejected remnant of the class, now inescapably destined for off-beat, off centre West End. There they would mark time until, at fourteen, they left school to take up their allotted places in the mills. In what remained of their time at St Luke's they 'sat at the back and did basketwork'. It is the poignant phrase of the late Thora Hird. Meanwhile the Scholarship Class prepared to face selection. The great sorting out would take the form of a two stage external examination, Part One being scheduled for February, with Part Two to follow in March. In order to sit Part Two you had to pass Part One, so there was a mini-selection within the selection. The Scholarship was not for those of a nervous disposition and there turned out to be some such amongst us. The moral fibre even of cocky Chris Gillings began to fray as the February reckoning approached. Not that our situation bothered me one jot. I never had any doubt that I was bound for the Grammar School. Despite being untidy and not quite literate I was an obvious sheep. Boys from nice homes invariably got in and anyway, as we shall see, if anything by some improbable mischance went wrong, then Dad would bail me out. However I was not immune to schadenfreude and rather relished the squirming of Chris under the pressure of family expectations. Serves him right. The bossy know-all had bullied me so let him suffer for a change.

Members of the Scholarship Class contemplated no fewer than six different chutes down which, at the end of their ordeal, they might be dispatched into the rest of their lives. First but not very likely, the Scholarship examination might identify you as a super brain-box. In that case, amid hurrahs, you would be awarded a 'County Minor Scholarship,' the source of the selection's endearing appellation. Only eight of these were available among all the schools of Glossop so that golden chute saw little traffic. Many more, perhaps two thirds of each intake, arrived at the Grammar School via the second 'Free Place' chute. Getting a Free Place lacked the kudos of winning a County Minor but it got you in nevertheless. It meant you had passed the Scholarship but had not won one. But what if you failed? If you were young enough, not yet eleven, it was not too bad. You could have another go. You might choose the third chute, labelled 'Re-Sit', which would tumble you into next year's Scholarship Class and another trip along the jiggling plates. Until the 1944 Education Act introduced fair play – thus intensifying the misery of rejection – there was however an alternative path for those found wanting. Smart parents whose offspring had let them down by failing the Scholarship might, when the immediate high tide of shame receded, take a sniff at a fourth chute that carried the intriguing label 'Entrance Exam'. Remarkably it cut out the whole Scholarship razzmatazz and led straight to the back door of the Grammar School. The snag was you had to pay to get in when you got there. However the annual fee was only £10. That sum of course was worth a lot more in those days, but now the war had brought back full employment, it was well within the budgets of all but the most feckless families. And in Dad's opinion – and he was the referee – there was no point in letting the progeny of the feckless get past the stately gates of his school. Yes, its mission was indeed, in suitable cases, to rescue working class children from the affliction of their inferior social condition, but the operative word was 'suitable' and those with 'poor home backgrounds' just were not suitable. They would lower the tone for the rest and then probably commit the unforgivable offence of 'early leaving'. So, although potential fee-payers took a written Entrance Exam, much depended upon an accompanying interview, conducted by Dad himself. His antennae naturally were well tuned to the subtleties that signalled 'good home background', so time and again, regardless of the inky confusion of their efforts on paper, he cleverly identified a sheep-like character in some of the alleged goats paraded before him. I am saying, until the Eleven Plus came along and spoiled things, if you failed the Scholarship but came from a good home, you would probably pass the entrance test for fee-payers. Perhaps a quarter of each annual intake came down that soft chute. It was one of the ways the old system was more merciful than what replaced it. And it delivered some excellent material. Among the fee payers of my time was my all-time best mate Jas Holt, of whom much more anon. I have never encountered his intellectual superior yet he not only failed the Scholarship but for several decades afterwards managed consistently to conceal his genius from officialdom.

If you failed the Entrance Exam however, and were already eleven, or if your parents would not or could not avail themselves of its mercy, it was curtains. You went down the fifth chute, labelled 'Reject', to await dispatch to West End along with the basket-working mass of big lumps never admitted to the Scholarship Class in the first place. There was one more chute, the sixth, and it involved a particularly cruel selection. That penitential passage was labelled 'Girls Only' and was reserved for able females, well qualified for Free Places, but deemed to belong not quite in the top drawer. The problem was that girls were rumoured to 'mature' more quickly than boys so they consistently did better than boys in the Scholarship exam. Which, to the powers in being, was a patently unacceptable situation that demanded rapid correction. For it stood to reason that the education of boys was more important than that of girls.

Future breadwinners should not be denied a superior education in favour of mere future housewives. Not to worry. The backroom boys knew a trick or two. So round at the education offices every year they fixed things. The raw order of merit was adjusted so that the same number of each sex was admitted to the Grammar School, even though some of the boys deemed to have 'passed' had actually performed less well than some of the girls who had 'failed'. Which is presumably why some obvious sheep, like Sylvia Hancock and Maureen Garlick, found themselves pitched mercilessly onto the West End transports. Taking the Scholarship could be agonising.

We took Part One just as Singapore fell in the middle of February 1942. For the fiendish Japanese had joined the war and stabbed us in the back. Which was a good thing really because it brought the Yanks in, but not for our boys at Singapore, among whom was Mr Bell, the art master at the Grammar School. Still, life had to go on and the Scholarship was the Scholarship. And Chris was still nervous. Which is probably why, the afternoon before Part One, as we were going home down Ellison Street, past the Elim Tabernacle, he blurted out a word I had never heard before. 'Fuck', he said. I admitted I did not know what it meant and I was not sure he did either. I was getting wise to Chris's bombast. It was clear however that this expression was in a different league from 'bloody' or even 'bloody hell'. Dad often said 'bloody,' even in front of Mum, though not in the presence of either of the grannies. But the aura with which Chris vested the new word separated it firmly from family usage and the world of childhood. I felt I had crossed a threshold not unconnected with the following day's reckoning. Next morning we of the Scholarship Class got red carpet treatment. The teachers were specially gentle, all rattiness suspended, and Mr Fielding himself acted as invigilator. Instead of our usual pitch on the concourse shared by Standards III and IV, we took over the Standard I classroom behind the yellow partition. It was warm and quiet and the desks were thinned out and separated so we each had a private space. We had new blotting paper too. We were special. Soon I began to enjoy myself. The sums were very easy and the only word I did not know was 'lathe'. Mr Fielding afterwards explained what it meant, so that was two new words in two days. Mr Fielding today was rather free with explanations and did not invariably wait until afterwards. As he walked up and down he looked over shoulders. Sometimes a clue was murmured or a finger pointed. H'm! As I say, you could only take Part Two if you passed Part One so several weeks of anxious waiting now ensued, during which the Japanese conquered the Dutch East Indies and invaded Burma and still there was no news about Mr Bell.

Both Chris and I duly passed Part One and thus contemplated the more demanding part of the selection process. There would be 'Problems' as well as ordinary sums and you had to write a Composition. Still there was the accompanying Intelligence Test to look forward to. We often did practice IQ papers and they turned out to be fun as well as easy-peasy. In any case it was not the actual papers that worried me about Part Two but the location of the exam. You had to sit it, not in the familiar comfort of St Luke's, but at West End itself, along with all the Part One survivors from all over the borough. Was that meant as a spur? Look around you, kids, because this is where you will fetch up if you don't shape. The facts seemed indisputable. West End was where failures went. Since only poor children failed and the poor were often dirty, the place must be a slum. Who knew what you might pick up there? It was like going downstairs at the pictures. However I braced myself, like Churchill said we all should. There was a war on and pluck was called for. So all nonchalance, on the Friday night before Part Two, which happened on a Saturday morning, I strode out as usual, through the blackout, with Mum, Dad and Helen, to the Empire cinema. It was Walt Disney's *Three Caballeros*, which mixed real characters with cartoon figures. It was OK but not such a big deal. Why bother, we thought. Then in the morning, fortified with a chocolate bar, no less – because of the U-boats they were getting to be quite rare – I braved the darkness of West End. Anti-climax ensued. It was actually a good deal cleaner than St Luke's and smelt of disinfectant rather than bodies. And they had indoor lavs! Not even the Grammar School thus cosseted its pupils, not the boys anyway. We took the exam in the Hall, a large space filled with the cream of all the Glossop schools. If I had engaged in numerical reasoning, not only in the IQ test, but also to measure the extent of the competition, I might have given myself a few qualms. But the papers, if more taxing than those in Part One, gave me no real trouble so my confidence was not dented. There was something funny about the Composition paper though. By a remarkable co-incidence the essay titles were exactly the same as Miss Max had given us for homework, only last week. Funny, that. However I duly polished some remembered sentences and presented them cheerfully to the examiner. Mine was not to reason why.

It turned out someone had indeed blundered. This year's titles had been accidentally published as part of the report on last year's exam. Maybe Miss Max or Mr Fielding had been smart enough to spot the mistake and turn their inside knowledge to our advantage. But to no avail. A new Composition paper was ordered, to be taken just before the Easter holidays, just as the gas chambers at Auschwitz-Birkenau became operational. By then I had chicken-pox and was happily at home in quarantine, so Miss Lee, who lived nearby and every day came home at dinner time, was released early from her morning lessons and stopped off at our house, where she sat with me, by the landing window, while I wrote my composition on an upturned tea tray. This time it was me who acted smart. One of the titles invited candidates to tell the story of a great invention that had benefitted mankind. Wow! You won't believe this but, a year or so earlier, while teaching myself to read, I had painstakingly learnt by heart the first chapter of my aeroplane book. Lightning struck. That chapter matched the title exactly. So out it all tumbled. 'For a thousand years,' I breathlessly scribbled,

... man has pondered the mystery of flight, but it was only on 17 December 1903, at Kitty Hawk, North Carolina, that a heavier than air machine first left the ground under its own power. Wilbur and Orville Wright ...

or some such polysyllabic confection of hard fact and resonant platitude, reminiscent of the voice on Gaumont British News. An impressively extended script emerged. I ruled off, read it through as directed and, after correcting the odd error, handed it to Miss Lee, who popped it in her shopping basket and went off up Sheffield Road to her lunch, congratulating herself perhaps on a welcome variation in her daily routine. And that was that. The Scholarship was over. The screening process had been completed and all we had to do now was wait for the results. They would come out, round about Whit, in the middle of the summer term. I will tell you how I got on in a later chapter.

I fear I have not been quite fair to St Luke's. Too much of what you have just read stems from the habit of disparagement that with me became a default position during the 1950s when I grew up to be an 'angry young man'. Rightly or wrongly we angries perceived an over-mighty establishment and set about its demolition, using satire like a JCB. In that climate the urge to mock detracted too often from fair play, an establishment value that came in for more than its fair share of ridicule. Thus any school was a potential source of merriment as a gathering of pompous gits peddling trash. St Luke's was categorically not that and being there did me a power of good. For five years I fitted, up to a point, into an ordered community that was doing its best to endow all its often disadvantaged clients with marketable skills, while at the same time much improving the prospects of its more promising alumni by helping them through the mill of the Scholarship. I learned more there, I guess, than has been suggested above. I became a more efficient calculator than I realised at the time and learned well how to give formal expression to the correct English I brought with me from home. If it is true they never managed to teach me to read, that was surely a quirk stemming from my own psyche rather than from any deficiencies in Miss Little's pedagogic toolbox. But the chief benefits I took with me from St Luke's were social rather than academic. I rubbed along with kids whose backgrounds were mostly very different from mine, in a spirit that contained more in the way of mutual respect than of class antagonism. Chris Gillings inducted me into the culture of aspiration as well as into the ways of the backyards and I am grateful for that.

Then there was that aspect of St Luke's that had caused Dad to hesitate about sending me there. It was an Anglican community. In a spirit that was charitable, in the best Christian sense of the word, it promoted the Ten Commandments. We not only learned to recite them but the culture of the school conformed to them. Thus lying and stealing were truly bad – indeed up there in the frame along with murder – and needed to be punished. Today, having survived into a world in which calculated, self-serving dishonesty has become a moral imperative, I couldn't agree more. As for sexual irregularity, well ... I had not really come across it when I was eight but now I am eighty I can see there is a case to be made out against it and certainly it has caused me bother personally. Likewise not getting on with your parents, a major theme of this memoir. Then there is believing in God. At St Luke's I think they all did and that made a crucial difference. I am glad I went there.

Chapter 4

LEARNING

Thus my five years with Mr Fielding and his ladies did me much good but it emerges that what I picked up at St Luke's had more to do with social training than with mental progress. I learnt that society is a complex and interesting phenomenon and that it is necessary to fit in, up to a point, with the community you find yourself part of. I learnt, most valuably, that lines can and should be drawn between right and wrong and that widely agreed rules governing morality cannot be lightly transgressed or ignored. I learned particularly that honesty is the best policy, in thought as well as in behaviour. It is interesting that I associate moral education with school rather than home. They knew what was what at St Luke's but Mum and Dad seemed less sure of themselves. I also learned some useful academic skills like counting, writing and punctuating but not how to read. And I picked up a smattering of general knowledge though, except in the field of biblical studies, where my debt to St Luke's is substantial, its sum was unimpressive considering the number of classroom hours devoted to its acquisition. The last is the point of departure for this chapter. It is difficult to remember much from the body of factual information they put before me at St Luke's. Not a lot seems to have stuck. That is not surprising you might think. It was a very long time ago and old men forget. But if so why is it I struggle to remember what I was taught in school but I recall vividly what I learnt when I was *not* in school? In the latter case, instead of struggling to remember, the problem is what to leave out. Between the ages of five and ten the data base I carry in my head was hugely expanded, but very little of it was sourced at school. Another feature of that massive extra-curricular accumulation is worth noting. Gathering it in seems to have been more to do with finding out than with being told. It was me that did it, not them. I am going to call it 'learning' as opposed to 'schooling' and in this chapter will toy with the idea that good thinking stems from the former and may actually be impeded by the latter. Here then is a selection of amazing things that grabbed me *during* the St Luke's years but not *at* St Luke's. There will be more of the same in the next chapter which concerns itself with an extra special learning opportunity that, because of the date of my birth, I was lucky enough to enjoy. I mean the Second World War.

Let's take nature study first. Glossop, as we have seen, brimmed over with nature. I tangled daily with elemental substances – water and stone, wood and turf, smoke and fire. I smelt them, felt them, scrutinised them and frequently subjected them to chemical change by burning them, boiling them or melting them. Weather too was happening all the time, quite often in extreme forms. And the light was stunning. As we have seen, continuing regrets for Manchester murk did not dull an ever-sharpening appreciation of Pennine clarity. The pedestrian character of my comings and goings enhanced that exposure to natural forces. In 1941 a dwindling petrol ration finally gave out and DND 838 was laid up for the duration. For four years it stood dustily in the garage with vital bits removed so it would be useless to any German parachutists who happened to drop in. Meanwhile it offered an additional Holly Wood hideaway. Mostly we had always walked anyway, the car being principally for trips to visit grandparents at the seaside. You see a lot more on foot and everywhere I walked – provided I walked alone, as even as a seven year old I mostly did, traffic in wartime being sparse and the theory of ubiquitous paedophilia not yet floated – I did a lot of looking and thinking. I tramped a good mile to and from school twice a day [home for dinner], wet or shine, frost or snow. I preferred snow to sun and wet days to dry ones. After Corn Mill Bridge there was a choice of routes. Instead of following High Street East, past the mill chimneys and Chris's granddad's billiard hall, you could nip up a steep path by some allotments onto the Royle, a heath divided by a cinder track between hen runs and pigeon lofts affording a panoramic prospect of hills and sky. Wow! Walking was not the only blessing I received at the hands of war. Another was the blackout. Not only did it enhance the charm of indoors, giving extra warmth to a fire and extra magic to lamplight, but it gave the outside night back to nature. Stars and the moon came into their own when shops were unlit, street lamps were extinguished and only the occasional vehicle groped past with dimmed lights. Waters on a starry night were beautiful and fair. Wordsworth said that. He too grew up among northern hills and rills not negated by neon and noticed is effects long before I did. The only rival to God's candles was the pocket torch and what cameos it captured in its beam – crystalline gravel, glistening flagstones, rainwater swirling in gutters, the details of a doorway. Sometimes on a cold night I would cup the torch to my eye and savour the incandescence of the element itself. Thus I learnt about the properties of matter.

I learnt a lot more about them when we played out. 'We' usually meant Jeffrey and Alan Holt, the twin sons of S E Holt MA, Second Master at the Grammar School and Dad's best friend, his only friend actually, in Glossop anyway. I always think of Jeff by his later nickname of 'Jas', short for 'Jasper', which I shall henceforth use, albeit anachronistically. It suggests the raffish villainy of a predatory squire dangerous to village maidens. Although unfair, his intentions being almost invariably innocent, the nickname suited him, for something about him communicated indifference to authority. Even before he opened his mouth those in charge felt affronted. So it is not surprising he upset Dad. Indeed my father could not abide Jas. Constantly he disparaged 'the Holt boys', a collective noun that resonated with moral reservation. And the inclusion of gentle, biddable Alan in the supposed conspiracy was entirely unjust. I had been introduced to the twins in August 1937, only a few days after we moved into our new house, and since we were almost next door neighbours – they lived at Moorlands, a big stone semi further up Sheffield Road from Holly Wood – soon became frequent playmates. Despite Dad's best efforts to nip it in the bud, a rapport soon emerged between Jas and me that remarkably has endured through three quarters of a century. Dad's animosity towards my friend became apparent after only a few weeks, in circumstances that nicely illustrate Jas's vulnerability to the charge of dumb insolence. We were up in our attic, one of the hideaways I had already established. While looking and thinking in that stimulating environment, littered with junk left there by the previous householder, I had discovered the solitary pleasure of repeatedly ramming the cylindrical metal tip of a rod, some component of an abandoned Venetian blind, into the yielding plaster of the walls. While Jas, in his already scholarly way, was quietly exploring some old papers in a far corner of the attic, I introduced Alan to the battering ram game. Mayhem followed. We yelled ecstatically as time and again our rods penetrated the wall, leaving it pitted all over, as though smitten with a pox. Jas, absorbed in archival research, totally ignored the mindless, orgiastic vandalism perpetrated by his companions. Dad however did not. Attracted by sounds of revelry he rushed upstairs and leapt nimbly to the wrong conclusion. You could pick out the ringleader for sure just by the surly look on his arrogant face. Assuming Jas's guilt he condemned him instantly, not only for an act of criminal damage but for corrupting his brother and me as well. Thus the delinquent Holt boys were barred from Holly Wood and no doubt their father too had grounds to quake. He had bred an unsuitable son. Don't let it happen again. Meanwhile I got off quite lightly. But I was to beware getting into bad company.

The ban of course did not last long, although Dad's animosity did. Soon Jas and Alan were back at Holly Wood and stayed for the duration. We made dens in the rhododendrons and in springtime 'swaled' [set fire to] the dry grass of the Paddock. In that enclosure also Jas encouraged the unruly stream in its deviant course, an unwise intervention because Dad nurtured his own plans for the taming of that pelting rivulet. We explored the properties of matter also in the outbuildings. We set up a museum in the summer house and turned the washhouse, which had gas as well as water, into a research establishment. There we investigated poisonous substances and probed rotting flesh. That is, we melted lead toys and old pipes and decapitated dead birds and small mammals so that their flayed heads might be soaked in peroxide to provide skull specimens. There was fun to be had in the garage as well, where laid up DNB 838 might serve as the getaway vehicle for an imaginary car chase or the bonnet might be lifted for Jas to explore the intricacies of the internal combustion engine. Perhaps after all you could see where Dad was coming from. Anyway he usually hovered not far away and his stifling vigilance, coupled to his obvious disapproval of my guests, determined that, more often, we played at Moorlands instead of Holly Wood.

Although Mrs Holt was not to be trifled with, Sammy was a much more easy going parent than Dad and he seemed to have no particular animus against his sons' friend. So at Moorlands I felt at home. Our room to manoeuvre there was almost unlimited for we enjoyed playing rights, not only within the half-wild Holt garden but also across an extended neighbouring complex of lawns, terraces and tennis courts, furnished with pavilions, arbours and a swimming pool. These pleasure grounds belonged to a clutch of local notables. J W Darlington Esq [solicitor], Mrs Lee [town clerk's widow and mother of Miss Lee of Standard I], Mr and Mrs Townsend [Glossop Gas Company], Mr and Mrs Oliver ['Plumbers, Boiler Makers and Sanitary Engineers'] and Miss Leech [independent means] seem to have thrown down their boundary fences and formed a horticultural collective. With admirable grace they tolerated our unruly intrusions with only an occasional complaint. We mostly congregated on the banks of the Cowbrook over which there was a footbridge leading to the fields of Bennets' Farm, where also we were allowed to wander freely. In the brook, under Jas's direction, we built dams, constructed stepping stones and bombarded objects and/or each other, but often we just gazed at the river, in pleasure mixed with awe. The steep-sided Cowbrook had plunged down the valley from the Broombank Reservoir – deep dark water, surrounded by high heathery moors – above the golf course, a mile or so upstream. In its time it had driven the wheels of cotton mills and I guess the big waterfall, the potency of which enthralled us, had been a weir serving the now disappeared Cowbrook Mill. Talented Mr Townsend had adapted the mill-race to create a water garden of smooth-sliding canals, gurgling sluices, tinkling cascades and chic little bridges. Here we held regattas, giving fanciful names to roughly shaped pieces of firewood and here also we launched a Woolworths' version of the battleship *Nelson*. When all that tired the farm was at our disposal. I do not remember us ever being challenged as we made lairs in hedgerows, charged down grassy banks releasing model gliders, or engaged in environmentally disreputable activities like birds' nesting or harvesting wild flowers. We had access even to the slurry-washed farmyard. It was picturesque but, remembering the state of the milking shed, I am glad my mother opted for pasteurised, in bottles from the Co-op, in preference to the deliveries, direct from churn to outstretched jug, offered by the Bennets from their horse-drawn float. I am not claiming my childhood was a rural idyll. It was not these romps along the Cowbrook that principally made me during the Glossop years but they got me frequently into the open air and, as a loner without inclination to join street gangs and banned from them anyway by parental vigilance, they let me sample the joy of 'playing out' with other children. Jas, Alan and I constantly explored an extended natural habitat that we were left to investigate and manipulate without supervision. In those activities, without being consciously scientific, we were often systematic. Playing out was good for our minds as well as our bodies. So we observed, collected, hypothesised, experimented and recorded. We displayed specimens in jam jars and shoeboxes and kept notebooks. Sometimes too we argued learnedly about our findings. Thus I guess I learnt as much science along the Cowbrook as I did in the Chemistry lab. Not that the two were mutually exclusive. The brook complemented the laboratory.

I think there are two reasons why Jas and I have always got on and the more I ponder them the bigger the bearing they seem to have on the pursuit of happiness, on what makes for a good and useful life. First, I share his inexhaustible curiosity, his ever robust and constantly regenerated appetite for knowledge. We shared that intellectual hunger in 1937 and do so still. Secondly, I admire his attitude to the system, to the way public life is at any one time conducted, and sometimes, but not always, I wish I shared that too. In brief he is indifferent to the system but it bugs me. More shortly, but let us first celebrate curiosity. Knowledge-wise young Jas just followed his nose, as I did mine. It is what I have called 'looking and thinking'. You observe, you accumulate, you speculate. You do not ask whether what turns you on is important or trendy, and thus to be cultivated, or unworthy or unfashionable, and thus to be eschewed. You just go for it regardless. I have watched Jas go single-mindedly for many things in our time. Hydrodynamics is one – manipulating the Cowbrook or the stream in Dad's Paddock. In retirement that youthful obsession resurfaced and his water feature turned gardeners green all over Clacton-on-Sea. Train spotting and football were more conventional boyhood preoccupations. Jas, whose mind is infinitely open, has no prima facie objection to what is conventional. Football meant the fortunes of Blackpool FC, a team well worth supporting in wartime because Stanley Matthews wore the No 7 shirt. Later it was girls that got him jumping and simultaneously tennis, in both of which fields he leapt from rabbit to tiger in what seemed like a fortnight. Then it was geology and then meteorology, followed by mini-cars. The science of not spending money has brought him life-long satisfaction although domestic economy cohabits with unbounded generosity and a fierce compulsion to buy the first round. But during the time I am recalling – say 1942 give or take a couple of years – it was the 'Aircraft of the Fighting Powers' that made Jas tick. That was the title of the plane spotters' bible and, although it was a big and glossy book and not cheap, his dad had bought him his own copy and it was ever open on their kitchen table – like the 'how to get on in life insurance' manuals they took with their tea, chez Gillings. The way Jas went about plane spotting, how one thing led to another like it does in a good learning experience, is instructive, so let us make it a case study.

During the war aircraft recognition was a necessary military accomplishment. Before shooting down an apparent Junkers 88 it was important to make sure it was not one of ours, say a Mosquito. But the cult spread far beyond the circles immediately affected – like fighter pilots, aka ack gunners or Observer Corps personnel – and took hold of the general public as well. It had all the appeal of bird watching plus the sense that in pursuing a hobby you were somehow helping the war effort. So a mushroom crop of black aircraft silhouettes invaded the newspapers and decorated the walls of public buildings, like libraries, post offices and British Restaurants [subsidised off-the-ration nosh]. Enthusiasts could indulge their addiction also through specialist magazines, which suggests the government, which tightly controlled the supply of newsprint, must have decided to indulge the patriotic craze. I myself bought the *Aeroplane Spotter* every week at Coggins on High Street East. To Jas however the *Spotter* was just for starters. He relished rather the red meat of *Flight* and *The Aeroplane*, high tech journals that only advanced students could make sense of. In mastering the literature of the discipline, Jas by the age of thirteen had even graduated from *Aircraft of the Fighting Powers* to *Jane's All the World's Aircraft*, in which experts spoke only to experts. The fat volume was packed with plans, stuffed with statistics and spilled over with specifications. He gobbled the lot. A myriad well sorted facts found lodgement in his bursting brain. You could not fault him. I could tell a Spitfire from a Hurricane and a Lancaster from a Halifax but that was about it. Jas however would, at the drop of a hat, explain exhaustively from memory the exact modifications that distinguished a Spitfire Mark IV from a Spitfire Mark V. And he could supply comparable data for the Fockewolf 190, the Flying Fortress, the Zero, the Storch, the Catalina, the Beaufighter or successive generations of the Messerschmitt 110. It came as no surprise when later, as an ATC cadet, he won a national aircraft recognition contest.

What do you do with a load of knowledge? If you do not apply it to some purpose it is apt to go stale. Jas did not let that happen. His grasp of the aircraft of the fighting powers made him an artist. If he reads this he will indignantly deny it. He doesn't do art. Modern art is rubbish, he says – isn't it? Well, maybe some of it is, but a lot of it isn't, at least I don't think so, and some of it I like a lot, or quite a lot, I think. 'Bullshit!' he replies. Anyway, as well as recognising planes he began to model them. Nobody told him how to do it but it was a skill he wanted so he got it and quickly too. He began with kits but as the war went on kits became rare on Woolworths' shelves and anyway, in Jas's expert judgement, kits left a lot to be desired in accuracy. So he began to work direct from the precise plans printed in Jane's and in *Aircraft of the Fighting Powers* and the resulting replicas looked especially good because they exuded authenticity. Then the supply of balsa wood stopped. They said it came from Japan. So he turned to junk and firewood. He would examine a bundle of kindling or size up bits of a broken chair to find pieces suitable for a fuselage, a wing or a tail plane. It was like watching Michelangelo rummaging in the marble quarries at Carrara. Then it was back to the kitchen/studio to begin work. First he would strip away with a penknife, then do fine cutting with a razor blade and, having checked the piece against the plan, apply sandpaper with the satisfaction of a job well done. Then came gluing and painting and mounting, all of which similarly bristled with nice problems generating satisfying solutions. Matt black in an abstract metaphor or realistic camouflage with markings and roundels? Suspended from a ceiling or a table model on a stand? All the while, in the manner of an old master, inducting apprentices into the craft, he would offer a commentary and even let Alan or me perform a few minor tasks ourselves.

I have expanded upon my friend's love affair with aeroplanes because it rams home a vital point. Children don't have to go to school in order to learn. Surely we all know that because we have all been children and must have memories of how it was when we were about ten and soaked up knowledge, like Jas did, wholly without adult supervision. It may be that this 'free' learning is, for many or even most of us, more effective than formal education. I am sure that has been my experience, as will be further demonstrated later in this chapter. Yet the provision of schooling, the education system, commands so much respect and attention and consumes so much of our national treasure. Is it worth it? Might there be better ways of equipping kids for life? I do not of course propose to engage with that preposterous question. The system is there. It is bigger than us and we cannot just turn our backs on it. As I acknowledged when, at St Luke's, I surrendered meekly to the schooling I had so furiously resisted at Moss Park. Which brings us back to Jas and his adventures with the system. It treated him abominably. I have never met his mental superior or anyone of greater intellectual honesty. Yet he failed the Scholarship. Not that it mattered very much, since the Grammar School was scarcely going to spurn the fees proffered by its Deputy Head on behalf of both his sons. Then Dad judged his performance in the Grammar School first year to be so far below standard that he was kept down and made to do the year all over again. It might seem he was still paying for that damage to our attic walls of which he was wrongly convicted. Even if you don't mean it, or can't help it, dumb insolence gets you into lasting trouble. Jas survived eight years under the Gauleiter, but always in 'B' forms of whose inmates not much was to be expected. He even went on to take a good degree but that did not redeem him in Dad's eyes because it was at Hull which, Dad insisted, was not a proper university. Then, being due for national service, he offered his continuing familiarity with the aircraft of the fighting powers to the RAF, which rewarded him by slinging him off the officers' training course. After that he became a teacher but quickly offended another 'gauleiter' who, maddened by the arrogant young pup's insufferable dumb insolence, refused to sign him off from probation. Honest, guv, he never, meant no harm! Predictably, in the end he proved a tutor of exceptional talent, channelling a flood of students to Oxford and Cambridge from a small Yorkshire grammar school in 'Summer Wine' country. One year he bagged five places, one more than Glossop managed throughout the 1940s. In his spare time he did research in meteorology but his supervisors repeatedly rejected his thesis. Then he took refuge in teacher training and inevitably upset sundry deans and principals. However during the turmoil in higher education that accompanied university expansion he contrived to snatch early retirement. At forty seven! The system owed him that.

I too have suffered at the hands of the system, although it took me five years longer than Jas to wrest from it the palm of early retirement.

That however was fair enough because I consistently provoked the system. I thought it flawed. I thought it suppressed learning. I thought the intellectual awakening Jas and I experienced through our own unaided efforts on the banks of the Cowbrook surpassed any enlightenment that came our way in classrooms and I wanted others to know the same felicity. I wanted to promote learning even during the process of schooling, to liberate schools so that children might learn the way we had done. So I set about conquering the system in order to obtain the power to change it. I failed. I got some way up the greasy pole but that did not in itself deliver the clout I needed. The system was too strong. You cannot decree cultural change. Mostly they didn't know what I meant and anyway they wouldn't be buggered about. I should have known that. Jas did even in the early days, which is why he suffered the system's slings and arrows with remarkable patience. They did not exactly bounce off him but he did not care all that much either. He just did his own thing sustained by that delight in learning for its own sake he had discovered as a boy as he made a model Lancaster or plotted to dam the Cowbrook. The joy of learning is supreme. Once you discover it, it changes your life. There is not much that beats it. It certainly beats climbing greasy poles. At least so it seems to me, although many I know would deny it. Like Chris Gillings for example, whose attitude to the system was totally different. Whereas Jas shrugged off the system and I tried to change it, Chris just *worked* it. He got to the top and we did not. Do we care? I am not sure.

That's enough philosophy for now. Let's get back to my own DIY learning spurt between the ages of five and ten. I made a lot of progress just lying in bed, a location in which I was very active throughout my childhood. I had the smallest and cosiest of the four bedrooms at Holly Wood. They were all of generous proportions but the floor area of my room was reduced to make way for the attic stairs. Perhaps I chose the room because it gave access to that favourite hideaway and offered another, as a bonus, in the boxed-in space under the stairs which had its own door. Its main attraction however was the remarkable view, which new every morning, enthralled me as I drew back the curtains and returned to my pillows, the better to contemplate it. The early morning works for me. When the body is in repose but the mind is alert thoughts come dripping fast. The backdrop to the scene was a moorland plateau that began towards the top of the window on the right hand side, inclined gently towards an eminence called Peak Naze [1250 feet] and then made a majestic downward sweep to the left hand border of the window. At least that is how it looked when I first knew it but it was remodelled before our very eyes on 29 May 1944, the day of the Great Glossop Flood, an event that for locals rather eclipsed D Day, which followed a week later. Below the mountain lay undulating ground on which were laid out fields, buildings, shacks, tracks and streets among which a regular pattern of human activity could be daily observed. As I rubbed my eyes lights went on in a predictable sequence, signalling the start of the working day. It began for different families at different times but the folk who lived in the stone cottage next door to the chapel in Manor Park Road always lit their lamps first, ahead of the tardier inhabitants of the neighbouring modern houses of red brick and pebbledash, the assertively suburban character of which sometimes induced tears of nostalgia. By seven o'clock there was frenetic activity around the asbestos-clad garage of the North Western Road Car Company, at the end of York Street, as red and cream buses prepared to carry workers to their workplaces. Despite its name they would not, I knew, take passengers to the big stone building in the middle distance. Its huge bow window, projecting from the facade like an Edwardian bosom, was ablaze with light in the early morning. It was a warming sight, except that I picked up sinister vibes from Olive and also from Chris Gillings, that panjandrum learned in all things disreputable, disturbing and off-beat. It seems it was called the 'workhouse' but the people who lived there did not actually work. That was puzzling. Was it perhaps Mickleover, where Chris said I would fetch up if I did not mend my ways? They would come for me, he said, in a yellow van and carry me off there. Decades later I discovered that Mickleover is a village near Derby where the County Lunatic Asylum once stood. So my uncomfortable association of the brightly lit workhouse with sinister oppression was well enough conceived. Among many things I owe to Chris is knowledge of a pervasive fear, then rampant among ordinary families, of what 'they' – the agents of the state – might do to them were they to be afflicted by poverty, sickness or mental confusion. Such dread haunted the workers' terraces. I suppose the arrival of the welfare state, during and after the war, dispelled it. Then, subjects were transformed into consumers and a liberating, yet increasingly aggressive, sense of entitlement took the place of impotent dread. For better or worse it really was a social revolution.

Beyond the bus garage and beside the modern houses lay the ground of the Old Glossop Cricket Club. It had well-manicured grass, framed by white-washed walls, a pavilion striped like a blazer, and an assortment of interesting equipment, like nets, a scoreboard and a big iron roller. I already knew I was no good at games [how?] so I looked wistfully upon that classic scene. I sensed gatherings of gentle and gentlemanly men engaged in orderly contest demanding mental agility as well as physical prowess. Could I ever find a place on some such hallowed strip of turf? Probably not, I thought, and that prediction proved dead right. However I had no wish to join in the rowdy antics that polluted a neighbouring field where rough men of the Vol Crepe Football Club pigged it in a plain, unpainted shed instead of an elegant pavilion. The company manufactured synthetics in a mill building let go by the Woods, so they were diversifying the local economy. They must have had modern views also on workers' welfare and hence the works' football club. I knew football scores came only in single figures and thus did not tax the supposedly simple wits of the players so a scoreboard was not needed. Where did that piece of snobbery stem from? Dad, I suppose. The Little Hill rose behind the Vol Crepe field. It was diminutive by contrast with Peak Naze but it suited the Observer Corps, which as war approached, dug in there behind sandbags. We went to their open day and I envied them their cosy den, furnished with easy chairs, a primus stove and copies of *Picture Post*. Their job was to spot approaching Stukas and then set the siren off to warn Glossopians they were about to be dive-bombed. I bet I knew as much about aircraft recognition as they did, although not as much as Jas of course, so I could have given them a hand. On the other side of the Vol Crepe field, bordering our Paddock, was a long field too big for the modest company of hens kept there by Mrs Bennet and her sister. Those ladies turned up daily at seven carrying buckets of feed and so layered in winter they looked like mobile snowmen. They lit lamps inside the chicken coops, which was nice, and held long conversations with the birds. The pep talks did not do much good though because the disloyal hens often strayed and laid their eggs on our side of the fence. Not that we were complaining. The excessive free ranging permitted to the pampered Bennet hens contrasted with the regimented living conditions of the birds kept by Walter Hurst, Glossop's principal man of feathers, whose veritable poultry farm also lay next door to our Paddock. In those precise pens Black Leghorns were strictly segregated from Rhode Island Reds.

It was not just the view I pondered in bed. In that productive station I also consumed books. For a long time that meant a lot of looking at pictures and not much in the way of reading words. Images were so engrossing I had little incentive to tackle text and it was without the benefit of literacy that I made a great intellectual leap. In my room with a view, when I was seven, just after the war began, I began to think chronologically. It was magic. Arrange things you know about in the order in which they happened and suddenly they make sense in a big way. It was such a rewarding discovery that I submitted instantly and eagerly to a discipline that was to mould my thought processes ever afterwards. Before I could read I found history. I used to suppose my precocity unique but I have recently read an account of a similar early awakening so my arrogance is clearly misplaced. In her memoir *My History*, Antonia Fraser, who is my exact contemporary, reports a remarkably similar experience. It was not her schooling that made her an historian but an Edwardian children's book and, despite learning to read years ahead of me, it was the *illustrations* in that work that first sounded the history trumpet for her. Her herald was Henrietta Elizabeth Marshall author of *Our Island Story*. In my childhood I never came across that famous chronicle but I became the proud possessor of a similar work, of a similar vintage, which had a similar life-changing impact. It was called *The Young Briton's History Reader*. Who the author was, I cannot say, the title being unknown to Google and the book itself being long gone. Its blotchy red cover was coming loose even when I first got it. It was Dad who gave it me. He had won it as a prize at Sheaf Street School, Poulton-le-Fylde when he too was about seven and there was a splendid label inside the cover proclaiming that achievement. He passed it on because he had noticed what I enjoyed when we went to the pictures, which we often did. *Owd Bob* was OK – a canine weepy made long before Lassie came home – and *Snow White*, although a bit soppy, was watchable but the movies that really had me goggle-eyed and jumping out of my seat were tales of empire like *The Drum*, *Gunga Din* and particularly *The Four Feathers*. So he thought I would like *The Young Briton's History Reader* and he couldn't have been more right. The last two pictures in the book even showed the 'Death of Gordon' and the 'Battle of Omdurman', scenes straight out of *The Four Feathers*. It was like going to the pictures without getting out of bed. I was amazed, gob-smacked even. Giving me *The Young Briton's History Reader* was maybe the best thing Dad ever did for my education.

For years I pored over the coloured plates in the riveting *Reader*. They penetrated my brain and will never leave it while I keep my wits. First came the centurion, leaping down from Caesar's galley to defy the painted Britons, thus shaming his craven legionaries. Here was noble Caractacus led fettered through the streets of Rome. Pope Gregory found Anglian angels in the slave market. The sandals of St Columba crunched the pebbles of Iona. Alfred sat trance-like by the oven door. The Conqueror, crowned at Westminster, looked strangely disgruntled despite having done so well. Richard the Lionheart charmed Saladin but his shifty brother John was forced to grant Magna Carta. The barons had trouble making it stick though until Simon de Montfort invented parliament. The Black Prince won his spurs. The peasants revolted. Drake played bowls while Raleigh flashed his cloak and sundry Tudor and Stuart ladies extended swan like necks over big, black blocks. Wolfe and Nelson in well-cut uniforms dealt death to frantic Frenchmen but Captain Cook was done down by swirling south sea savages. Something bad happened at Cawnpore. At last Kitchener avenged Gordon at Omdurman and history gave way to modern times. You could tell that because Kitchener's cavalry wore khaki, just like Dad had done in the Great War. Sure, there is a lot missed out in that quick trot through our island story, but when you are only seven there is plenty of time to fill in the gaps. I have been doing it ever since.

Those inexpungable images not only told me what had happened in history but, equally important, also carried useful hints about how history is best done. The first was that history is fun so lie back and enjoy it. What could be nicer than lounging comfortably in bed while alternately speculating about the nature and purpose of the workhouse and scrutinising yet again the scene of poor Gordon's martyrdom? As he stood defiant at the top of that staircase, did his rapier skewer down the throat of the Dervish on the left before the spear of the Dervish on the right pierced him through the heart? You could never quite tell. You never knew for sure. An alternative version of what had happened always seemed admissible and that turned out to be the way history always was. It was perpetually subject to revision. I did not of course put it like that when I was seven but I think I got the rough idea. History was a story with alternative endings. That the past was indeed a story, a very long one that started way back and went on and on until it reached modern times, was another fundamental discovery. There was another thing too. As the narrative unfolded, you could see that although it consisted of one thing after another, nevertheless often one thing *led* to another. There was cause and effect and scope to exercise judgement. Sometimes a particular explanation carried all but absolute conviction – until new evidence cropped up and you were back to square one, which was a nice place to be because it meant you did not know where you might fetch up next. There was no final answer but revision was perpetual. That was a basic charm of history.

The most important discovery of all was the value of a framework. Although I kept finding out more and more about what had happened in history – as I examined other sources of information as well as the *Young Briton's History Reader*, and even, as literacy dawned, I began to get the drift of the text as well as the pictures – the original chronological framework I got from the sequence of pictures joining Julius Caesar to General Kitchener, proved indispensable. That organising framework was like something fashioned from the bits of a Meccano set. Meccano – you made things by bolting together perforated metal strips – was to my generation what Lego, and then Minecraft, was to be for those that came after. The structure I put together from the pictures in the *Reader* became a framework on which I could hang all the new things I learned. The original simple framework could be infinitely extended and adapted to take in what had happened before or after the time-span of the *Reader* and to accommodate things not included in its story but which turned out to be happening also at the various times explored in the book. Playing with my history Meccano was infinitely satisfying. The more complicated it got the more fascinating it became for, with a familiar framework to hang on to, history need never overwhelm you. Whatever new things you found out could be bolted in somewhere in the structure. *Just so long as you always checked the dates.* History did not work without dates. Without them it was Meccano without the nuts and bolts. The structure would always fall apart. But, so long as chronological order was strictly observed, with my history Meccano new knowledge did not get lost but instead served as the starting point for new journeys which in turn would require further adjustments to the ever adaptable framework. The Meccano metaphor seems to capture nicely the way I learnt how to store and retrieve data. Which is surprising because, although they bought me a Meccano set, I was not enchanted by it the way some of my contemporaries were. I was not nimble with a screwdriver. But in exploring the past – and the present – I know I consciously organised what I learnt into complex but adaptable structures. Thus the toy I neglected turned out a good buy.

The first modifications to my history Meccano came when Dad gave me another book. It was not as enticing as the *Reader* because the pictures were not in colour and, apart from a solitary photograph of bi-planes flying over the pyramids, they were not realistic. Instead of offering the drama of an artist's impression they were faithful representations of museum artefacts. Furthermore, except for a Greek galley as depicted on a vase, they were mostly objects of everyday use – like a boring Roman comb and a fiendishly uncomfortable Egyptian headrest – as dug up by meticulous archaeologists. I was not much into everyday life. There was a war on and I found it more exciting than peace. Also the title of the book was mysterious. It was *From Ur to Rome*. Whatever did that mean? I had heard of Rome. It was where big, fat Mussolini came from – 'Mussolini he's a silly ass/Like old Goering he's filled up with gas', George Formby used to sing. But 'Ur' … well err … I never fathomed what it meant. But I persevered with the unexciting pictures and was rewarded. For the new book permitted a backwards extension to my history Meccano. The *Reader* started with Julius Caesar but *Ur etc*, having surveyed the Babylonians, Egyptians and Greeks, stopped with that top Roman. All that new knowledge had to be bolted into the ever-accommodating Meccano. It nicely obliged. Thus history came to have a prequel called 'Ancient Times' and soon I was to discover it had a sequel as well – indeed two sequels actually. More in a moment. Another good thing about *Ur etc* was that it had maps as well as pictures and with me and maps it was love at first sight. They were now bursting out all over Dad's newspaper as well and suddenly, before I could read, I began to devour the *Manchester Guardian*, which went in for maps as eagerly as *Ur etc*. Thus I found the Germans and Russians carving up Poland and grasped, from maps of the Baltic, that the predatory Russians were bent on doing likewise to Finland. From *Ur etc* I discovered another land-locked sea called the Mediterranean, just in time for a new shift in the war which soon had us and the Greeks taking on Hitler, Mussolini and a shifty lot called the Vichy French, all around its shores. That littoral was convoluted but, having plotted the shape of the Roman Empire, it was already installed in my history Meccano so I had no trouble following the conflict in the Mediterranean theatre.

I liked the laid back Greeks much better than the stiff Egyptians and actually better than the pompous Romans. I found out more about my favourite Greeks about the time of my eighth birthday, which coincided with the Germans marching into Paris. It was then that 'volumes' entered my life as well as books. My main present was the self-important *Children's Encyclopaedia* which came in a Bakelite case and in ten volumes bound, in my case, in red 'Rexine' which was posher than cloth but not as expensive as 'half calf'. Well, there *was* a war on. For me the *Children's Encyclopaedia* did not actually work the wonders Dad said it would. Its format was confusing and its pictures were titchy and fuzzy and drowned in blue and green tints. Those about the Greeks were all vases [again!] and statues of limbless ladies. The Holts however had *Pictorial Knowledge*, an alternative set of volumes that I much preferred. Pictorially was how I liked to get my knowledge but I did not tell Dad he had backed the wrong horse, knowing he would rubbish *Pictorial Knowledge* on account of its provenance. Anyway it had an excellent section on the Greeks, illustrated in full colour, and had crystal clear maps as well. I even managed to decipher some of the text the text and worked out the inspiring story of Phidippides. He ran twenty six miles from Marathon to Athens to tell the citizens they had won the war against the Persians, and then gamely jogged on through the olive groves to Sparta to deliver the same glad tidings. Wow! It killed him but what a way to go, cheers resounding in his failing ears! There was something about the loneliness of the long distance runner that specially appealed to me. Being alone was best. One of my Christmas presents that year – they came along with the Manchester blitz – further filled out the Greek section of my Meccano, for it was all about the Greek gods who lived on Mount Olympus and quarrelled with each other a bit like kids in a playground and seemed to be much driven by less comprehensible but intriguing passions as well. Whatever was Zeus up to with Europa and why did I find the picture of sleeping Psyche so compelling? Since during the Battle of Britain, the previous summer, I had achieved a halting literacy, I got the hang of most of these tales without much help and very useful those efforts proved. They gave me a basic acquaintance with classical mythology to set beside the bible stories I learned at St Luke's. Thus I discovered what, at the Grammar School, they were to tell us were the two tributaries, Hellenic and Hebraic, that flowed together to make western civilisation. It is an interesting idea that seems to have lost currency.

Thus my Meccano was becoming more and more complex. It comprised 'History', as related in *The Young Briton's History Reader*, and also 'Ancient Times' as delineated in *Ur etc* and also in *Pictorial Knowledge* and the book of myths. Soon it acquired another section called 'Modern Times' that began where History stopped, that is at Omdurman on 2 September 1898. We have seen that this, the first big event in Modern Times, happened two days before my father's birth. Thus it was above all to Dad that I turned for the story of modernity. He had been around all the time it was happening so he must know about it. In particular he had been in the 'Great War' which was the main event of Modern Times and marked a great divide between the 'Edwardian Summer', when the sun always shone, and 'Between the Wars', when the weather was changeable. More soon about Dad's account of his own stirring times but first let me tell you about some other sources of information I excavated. There was another present I got at Christmas 1940. It was an illustrated book for boys about the history of flight and, like the stories from Greek mythology, came ostensibly from Uncle Leslie, who had come up to Southport for a seasonal break from the London blitz. He had joined the AFS [Auxiliary Fire Service] so after a hard day's work photographing bomb damage he nightly climbed ladders to fight fires. He must have been a hero. Anyway on Christmas Eve spoil-sport Dad persuaded him to leave the pub and spend what the next round would have cost on improving books for his bumptious nephew. I am glad he did because both those books, the first I could honestly say I had read as well as gazed at, marked me for life and the one about flight also gave me a lucky break that did a lot for my self-esteem. More later. Flight, I now learnt, began very suitably right at the start of Modern Times with the Wright Brothers in America. Then the Aces, some of whom were German, did daring deeds in the Great War. But it was after the war that the pace hotted up and a lot of Meccano was needed to keep pace with the story. Alcock and Brown conquered the Atlantic. The airship R34 followed suit. Then the Smith brothers made it to distant Australia. Intrepid Alan Cobb, returning from the Cape, landed his flying boat on the Thames right outside the Houses of Parliament. Wow! Intrepid Charles Lindbergh then flew his pug-nosed monoplane

Spirit of St Louis solo across the Atlantic. Then the even more intrepid and also female Amy Johnson, Australia bound, all alone and with a failing engine, spluttered across the foggy Timor Sea to make Darwen and also history. How brilliantly modern they all were, those magnificent men, and women too, in their flying machines. Some of the latter were truly beautiful. I loved the swept-back seaplanes, ancestors of the Spitfire that won the Schneider Trophy outright. But my favourite was the little red De Havilland Comet that in 1936 sped in a futuristic flash 'from Mildenhall to Melbourne', showing a clean tail fin to less advanced competitors. My new attachment to Victorian Glossop had not wiped out my earlier attachment to modern design.

Then there were the 'glorious years' books that both sets of grandparents possessed. They must have been published to celebrate the Silver Jubilee of George V – the event that coincided with Sambo's immolation – for both compilations, though different, covered the years 1910-1935. Both arranged striking news photographs in chronological order with a dozen or so pictures for every year. From them I acquired a firm chronology of Modern Times into which I also slotted the data I got from my aeroplane book and other sources yet to be identified. We began with Edwardians at the seaside and went on to the Delhi Durbar, with newly crowned King George, sumptuously installed, receiving the homage of his Indian subjects. Then images unfolded in rapid, almost cinematic, succession. Mrs Pankhurst in the grip of a burly bobby. Winston Churchill confronting anarchists in the East End. Captain Scott marooned snowbound in a hut. *Titanic* sinks. King and Kaiser ride together in Berlin, all unawares. Tommies in deep mud. German sailors going down with the upturned *Blücher*. Tanks on the Somme. Women driving trams. Crowds butchered in Petrograd. Trotsky speaks. German fleet scuttled at Scapa Flow. The Treaty signed at Versailles. The Cenotaph in Whitehall. Field guns in Dublin. 2LO goes on air. Royal weddings galore. Pitch invasion at Wembley. Suzanne Lenglen wins at Wimbledon. Steve Donahue wins the Derby. Tutankhamen strikes back. LNER Pacific *Papyrus* does 108 mph! Undergrads and Mr Baldwin defeat General Strike. Rudolf Valentino dead. Labour in power – but not for long. R101 crashes at Beauvais. Mickey Mouse arrives. *Queen Mary* launched. It all needed a lot of Meccano but everything as always found a place.

The 'glorious years' pictures were richly supplemented from a private source that gave yesterday's news a particular immediacy. A wooden box kept under the bookcase in the Study contained hundreds of actual photographs brought home by Grandpa London and Uncle Leslie from the papers they worked on and a selection is reproduced as *Plate 10*. They came in glossy or linen sepia finish, were usually stamped 'Sport and General', 'Northcliffe Newspapers' or 'Reynold's News', and sometimes had smudgy type-written labels stuck to their backs. Sometimes Dad and I looked through them together and he would tell me about the people in the pictures and categorise them as 'nasty piece of goods', 'brazen hussy', 'conshie' or, much worse, 'appeaser'. But I was free to rummage among them also on my own. I am not sure all the photos were the personal work of my relatives, and thus that they had actually met these famous people and got them to pose, like they got me to, but certainly that was the case with some of them. Grandpa himself told me he knew Lloyd George and had been to a posh house called Chequers where he had taken pictures of the then Prime Minister with his daughter Megan *[Plate 10 bottom, middle]*. He went back there ten years later to be entertained by another father-daughter duo for his socialist hero Ramsey Macdonald had also got to be PM and there he *was*, stretched out in a chintzy armchair by a roaring fire, his freckly young daughter lounging beside him in an unladylike pose, scowling at the camera. I knew just how she felt. The immediacy of the pictures was enhanced by some letters that accompanied them in the box. Philip Snowden, Chancellor of the Exchequer, wrote to say he liked Grandpa's pictures but his wife was less keen. Also von Ribbentrop's secretary conveyed how much Hitler's man in London *[Plate 10 top, middle]*, appreciated what Grandpa had done. Since they came in just the same format as our private pictures I began to look on these top people as part of the family. It seemed we revelled in an extended kinship network that included Chamberlain and Churchill, Bernard Shaw and H G Wells, comedians like Harry Lauder and George Formby *[Plate 10 top left]*, England cricketers like Hobbs and Sutcliffe, fascists like Oswald Mosely and King Edward VIII *[Plate 10 top right and bottom left]* and film stars like Mary Pickford. It seemed Grandpa was on nodding terms with all of those and many more. Lloyd George was my favourite 'uncle'. He looked in charge but took it lightly. He had a sparkle in his eye. I knew him in various situations. In one picture, taken in the garden at No 10, he dominated his cabinet and in another in the same location he upstaged foreign prime ministers, like snooty M Clemenceau and exuberant Signor Orlando. In another however he had lost his swank and looked uneasy at Paddington Station meeting a large lady which the label on the back said was his wife. I liked King Edward too. Grandpa snapped him riding in Hyde Park and also loping down a street in a top hat, with his hands in his pockets, apparently whistling, like a cheeky schoolboy up to no good. I had unfavourites as well, like smarmy Sir John Simon, fulsome Sir Samuel Hoare and gormless M Daladier, the French leader Hitler had danced rings round at Munich. So Dad said anyway.

But Dad's memory was my main source for Modern Times. He told me, for example, a lot about how it was when he himself was my age during the 1900s. He conjured village life at Poulton-le-Fylde in colourful detail, listing all the shops and telling me about 'characters', like a boisterous Boer War veteran called 'Modder River Joe'. Being smaller than other boys he seems to have been accident prone, forever falling off bikes and tumbling into ditches. He was great little reader though. It seems every week he devoured both the *Magnet* and the *Gem* quicker than Chris Gillings bolted down the *Hotspur*. He read books too, like *Tom Brown's Schooldays,* which he was sure I would enjoy too … if only. So come on in, the water's lovely! Yes, yes, I took the point and I enjoyed Dad's reminiscences but I could do without the heavy hints. He also told me about his own schooldays at Blackpool Grammar School and about days along the golden sands. At the Grand Theatre he and his mother saw Pavlova dance the dying swan. Then he filled me in about his later years in Rossendale, about student days and about holidays in Switzerland with Mum. His description of the soft rolls and cherry jam that came with their coffee at Basel, after a night on the train, made my mouth water.

But all that was just period background. Another set of Dad's reminiscences affected me more deeply. Indeed it ever afterwards dominated my view of the past and brought about major adjustments to my Meccano. I know exactly when I took up my screwdriver to bolt in this new element. It was on a rainy Saturday afternoon in July 1940, in the limbo between the fall of France and the start of the Battle of Britain. Invasion loomed. In a few weeks, Dad said, the panzers might be filing down the Snake, in which case he intended to take out the German revolver he kept in his bedroom drawer and dig in on Shire Hill. They shall not pass. In the meantime he sat on my bed and talked.

I had measles, lay in a darkened room with a bottle of Lucozade and was bored. Today was particularly hard because Mum and Helen had gone off to see the *Wizard of Oz* at the Ritz in Hyde and I was missing a long anticipated treat. So I was at a low ebb when Dad suddenly appeared and raised my spirits. He did it by talking about the Great War. I knew he had been in it but he had never before gone into much detail about his part in it. Now it all came tumbling out with the freshness that only an eye witness account can carry. To illustrate his story he went and got an exercise book and started to draw trench systems. You see, there usually wasn't just one line but two or three, one behind the other, although it varied from one sector to another. Between the front line and the others there were communication trenches at right angles to them. They were used for bringing up food, ammunition and all the other things you needed, often on the backs of mules. Fetching and carrying happened at night when the Boche was less likely to spot what was going on and send a whizz-bang or two. So bringing up supplies was dangerous. Sammy Holt had been on the mules so he was a brave man. Trenches were dug in zig zags, so if Jerry broke in he could not just rush you along hundreds of yards of straight line. He drew a plan so that I could see that made sense. There were dug outs cut into the trench walls but the deep ones were for officers. Privates like Dad and his mate Bill Gash had to make do with the shallow bivouacs they scraped out with their entrenching tools and reinforced with pieces of corrugated iron. It was usually muddy. You never took your clothes off and you had lice all over you. Lice came in stripes of different colours, which they said was because they supported different football teams – so there were Preston North End lice and Blackburn Rovers ones. You were always getting warm drinks from the field kitchen but tea and soup tasted much the same, petrol being a dominant flavour. You also got fresh white bread and Machonnochies' plum and apple jam to spread on it. Otherwise it was mostly bully beef in tins you opened with you bayonet. Shaving with a 'cut throat' was difficult but discipline demanded you did it daily. They envied American troops the new 'safety razors' they brought over with them. Shaving water came from shell holes and was green on account of poison gas and dead bodies but you got so you didn't much mind. There were bodies everywhere and bones sometimes projected from trench walls and, for a joke, soldiers hung their jackets on them. At the front of a trench, immediately behind the wire, was the fire-step you stood on twice a day to survey No Man's Land, between us and Jerry, whose front line might be as close as our Paddock but often it was further away. No Man's Land was full of craters with green slime and when you went over the top you had to dodge between them and also stumble over a lot of old iron and other obstacles. That made you a sitting duck for the Boche machine guns. Before an attack there would be an artillery bombardment. It was deafening but did not always work. The German wire was seldom cut and the machine gunners just hid in dugouts and then came up to mow you down. But you did not go over the top all that often or spend all your time in the front line. After about five days you went back to a reserve line and then had a spell in the rear. It was much nicer at the rear. There you were pretty safe and could relax. You had showers, improvised from perforated buckets – he made another sketch to illustrate that contraption – and slept in billets instead of bivouacs. And you went to the estaminet, for egg, chips and vin blink, played cards and had sing songs. He taught me 'Casey Jones' and 'I wanna go home' and we sang them together, despite my throat being croaky from the measles. There was much more too that I cannot recall and I cannot be sure all the above was related by Dad that very day in 1940, for henceforth he spoke about the trenches on many occasions. I admit also there may be the odd bit about trench life that may have come from other sources but I do not think much alien material has crept in and I swear Dad's account *felt* utterly authentic – he spoke with the conviction of somebody who had been there himself and his experience somehow got translated into my own consciousness. Indeed the impact of his remarks was life-changing. I still feel a special familiarity with the Western Front which to me seems almost like personal experience. Uncanny. I doubt if Dad and I were ever closer than on that day.

So I first heard about the First World War from the lips of an eye witness. I discovered the Industrial Revolution that way too, from a former child worker in a cotton factory. She was my Granny Southport and she began work in the mill in 1869, when she was seven. Her infancy thus coincided with the Cotton Famine consequent upon the American Civil War. I got to know about that catastrophe because it figured in a dialect poem Dad used to recite. He had researched the genre and his enthusiasm was infectious. It was by Edwin Waugh, the Shakespeare of the Lancashire lyric, whom Dad specially admired. A laid-off operative dandles a baby on his knee saying

Th'art welcome bony brid
But tha shouldna' coom just when tha did
Tha sees, times is bad …

That pretty bird could easily have been Granny Southport who was actually born during the Cotton Famine. Her stoical resilience in the face of the bad times she and her family must have endured, then and later, seems remarkable in retrospect. But she took hardship entirely for granted. Putting up with the rough along with the smooth was simply what you had to do, so 'think on'. So her sunny reminiscences were entirely lacking in whinge. Just as I came to realise that Dad had, at least in a certain sense, enjoyed the Great War, so also I picked up that when Granny was my age she was happy fettling at the mill. I wish I could remember actual reported incidents of factory life. Only impressions survive. They include however a strong sense that there were rewards as well as drawbacks in factory work. One was economic. She brought a wage in that the family relied on. Others were social. She was among family and friends. A mill was a close knit community. Also it offered job satisfaction. Being young you learnt fast and picked up skills quickly. Being small and nimble you could do things adults could not manage and that was a source of satisfaction. So she did not envy me a pampered childhood dominated by school. Not that she had missed out on schooling either. When she started at the mill she was a 'half-timer', alternating between mornings cleaning looms and afternoons learning the three Rs. School was not free. She had to take in twopence every Monday and nurtured no grudge about that either. Not to come up with the school pence was a disgrace in their street. Anyway you valued what you paid for.

Thus seventy years on Granny looked back on her early life at the mill, often with pride and never in anger. And thus an abiding impression was lodged in me, rendering me resistant to the propaganda of Charles Dickens and Karl Marx. They had not been there – or only fleetingly – but Granny had. Rather than the rhetoric of oppression I heeded on the spot reports and not just the ones Granny delivered. Here for example is Leonard Horner a factory inspector, active in the 1860s in a district that included Rossendale, 'happily' reporting a recent increase in the number of child workers.

I say 'happily' without hesitation, for now that children are restricted to half a day's work and are required to attend school, I know no description of work so advantageous to them as that in a factory.

Well, that was Granny's 'happy' situation. Although she said I should 'count my blessings' that I was living now and not then, you knew she didn't really mean it. I was growing up too soft, whereas the mill had toughened her. It had given her confidence in facing life and a standard against which to match her undoubted progress to prosperity. She spoke in similar vein about her home life. They were a big family in a small cottage but they made the best of it and looked after each other. 'Little birdies in their nests agree' she often assured me and I did not dare dispute the assertion on any grounds, pragmatic or scientific. And if you needed time on your own, to do a bit of crying perhaps, there was always the outside privy. Sure, she had once found a rat there but that did not too much put her off. Thus when she and Grandpa were in their eighties and housed in deserved luxury, they still preferred a distinctly smelly outside earth closet, furnished with carefully cut squares of newspaper – 'waste not, want not' was another of Granny's aphorisms – to upstairs arrangements acceptably sanitised to twentieth century standards. Avoiding the stairs? No, the precipitate unlit steps, descending without handrail from the back door, were a much greater challenge to arthritis. Rather the repeated trek was a sentimental journey back to an idyllic industrial childhood.

The mill shut at mid-day on Saturday. We should take with a grain of salt all those agonising accounts of unending labour in Victorian factories that you find in contemporary 'blue books' [government reports] and on TV today. So in the afternoon decent families did the housework, inevitably neglected during the working week. They took the furniture out and scrubbed it in the yard, while the flagged kitchen floor was drying off to a smooth cream patina, following its weekly application of donkey stone. Believe it or not, though, there were idle families where that practice was not unwaveringly observed. Which caused problems when she and Tom were courting. Scrubbing done and best bonnet on, Esther one Saturday called on Tom. But had they done their scrubbing? Had they heck! Instead they were sitting round the kitchen table while Tom read aloud from the *Weavers' Times*. Enough to end the romance? No, she had the measure of her man. Despite too much fondness for book learning and an excess of conviviality, he was doing well in his job. So on 30 May 1885 – was it a Whit wedding? – she married him. The night before he and his pals had been to Manchester. They went to a theatre – that anyway was their story – and had a group photograph taken. Granny liked a play herself and recalled weeping inconsolably when a troupe of travelling players performed melodrama at the fair. 'Nay lass, they're nobbut acting' they said to comfort her. She too sometimes went to Manchester, where at Lewis's they were trying to fob off a new sort of plum on a suspicious public. It was so bitter you had to put sugar and vinegar on it and eat it with a knife and fork. It was called a tomato. Trips to town, visits to theatres, sampling exotic fruits in department stores suggest a life-style above the poverty line. Which shows living standards for urban workers were going up. When I first got to know Granny and Grandpa Southport [Plate 2 top left] they had travelled a long way from their mill-side cottages, one scrubbed, the other un-scrubbed, but their lifestyle retained many of the habits and much of the outlook of their youth. So I found myself face to face with how folk had been in Victorian Lancashire when cotton was king and Gladstone was prime minister. It was communicated in gesture, in accent and in metaphor. They both had rich accents and used dialect dramatically. And they exhibited all unawares the customs of their lifetime together. It was not just preferring the outside loo but included touching daily rituals as well. Like the homecoming ceremony. As we have seen, Grandpa was still commuting in his eighties and had indeed been at work the day he had his fatal stroke in 1943. Leaving the cab that brought him from the station, he would hobble, stick in hand, up the garden path, negotiate the front door, hang his hat and coat on the stand beside his framed certificates, long ago obtained at the Haslingden Mechanics' Institute, and sink with a sigh onto the green velvet sofa in the living room, under a big photographic representation of 'Waterfoot from Rough Lea'. By which time Granny, despite a bad back – she was a martyr to lumbago – would have leapt from her chair with girlish agility to kneel at his outstretched feet and peel off his boots. They had been doing that, I guess, for half a century and more. Then there was the ritual of Sunday dinner. She of course had cooked it but it was J T Lord, master of his house, who presided at the head of the table. He would tuck his napkin under his chin and sharpen a long bone-handled knife with rapid strokes against a steel, before deftly dismantling the piece of seared flesh that had been put in front of him. Not that he really took precedence. He knew his place.

The chair Granny leapt from to greet her Lord was a horsehair rocker. It was the throne from which she dominated the living room. Behind her, above the wireless set, a high window commanded a view comprising the pear tree, an old bathtub [to collect rainwater] and a well-trimmed lawn [a gardener called weekly]. To her right was the big table which served as the hub of family intercourse. During the frequent, often overlapping, visitations of cohorts from the Lord tribe, not only were celebratory meals consumed there but conviviality waxed around it throughout the waking hours. Thus I encountered aunts and uncles, some of whose titles were honorary, and cousins some of them more than once removed. Eagerly I looked and listened but mercifully was not expected to perform. The table had mundane functions as well. Ironing was done upon it and female Lords gathered there for sewing, knitting and crocheting, the doing of 'work' being in our family as much a secondary sexual characteristic as it was in a Jane Austen household. The *News Chronicle* was read there and its contents discussed. Cards were played there. Patience was all but perpetual but games of whist, bezique and 'Beggar my Neighbour' were also much enjoyed. Not pontoon though. Granny's Nonconformity was both devout and strict and gambling was sinful. Drinking was scarcely acceptable either, not at the table anyway. Grandpa liked a whisky with his cigar but for both indulgences he was banished to the unfrequented dining room. When Dad and Leslie were in residence they took him to the Scarisbrick Arms and he liked that. The table coverings themselves provided innocent fun. At mealtimes a linen cloth was superimposed on the thick red velvet permanently draped over the mahogany and when somebody spilled something, commotion unfurled. Granny's strident expletives – 'Eeh! What's to do? Well, I never did!' – rang out over the operations of a prescribed rescue drill, which involved inserting a saucer under the linen so that the un-fast red dye of the velvet did not stain it. It did not always work, in which case that was an end to peace in our time, for that day anyway, demonstrating conclusively that little birdies in their nests did not invariably agree. I noted a curious fact. Even if it was me that upset the cup it was Dad that got the blame. It became increasingly clear that Granny disliked her son-in-law. When she shouted at him, as she often did, he was rendered dumb, or rather he emitted, not coherent speech, but little humping sounds. He had no response. I found that both shocking and reassuring.

Beyond Granny's feet, to her left, was the fire. Although it was later rebuilt in boring beige tiles, the hearth I first knew, Sambo's place of martyrdom, was a classic cast iron range with a projecting hood, swinging hobs and two ovens, the whole kept burnished bright in black lead. The cool oven was stuffed with orange peel, until the exigencies of war extracted the fruit concerned from English life, for dried peel made excellent kindling. Mum's profligacy in buying fire-lighters amazed and saddened Granny. Waste not want not! The imperative of that injunction probably also accounted for the sacks of discarded wooden bobbins – brought fifty miles from the Grandpa's slipper works at a cost surely greater than the retail price of firewood – that lay in the coal place next to the privy. The versatility of those bobbins as toys was remarkable. You could string them together to make a necklace for your mother, or use the loaded ligament open-ended as an offensive weapon. They made superb building blocks. Now I had added Ancient Times to my Meccano, temples and amphitheatres came to mind and the Coliseum frequently arose from the drawing room carpet. In the sandpit at the bottom of the garden, or on the beach, they could be used to mark out parallel lines – railway tracks along which they then ran as locomotives and rolling stock, ripe to be knocked satisfyingly but unpredictably askew when, with half a brick, you moved in to make a bombing attack. Thus the sandpit at 7 Cross Street became the marshalling yards at Ham or Gelsenkirchen after a visit from Bomber Command.

My grandparents' house was my Sutton Hoo. The regalia of an Anglo-Saxon king was unearthed at that site in Suffolk just before war broke out and its interpretation figured largely in academic discourse when I was a student. However I already knew the business of archaeology because at 7 Cross Street I had already excavated the regalia of a Victorian couple and subjected it endlessly to interpretation. Interesting objects abounded all over the house. The roll-top desk that stood in the living room, across the table from Granny's rocking throne was especially productive. It had pigeon holes and secret drawers and a shelf carrying domestic manuals, travel guides, a Baptist hymnal, two battered bibles and a couple of brochures, one announcing the attractions at the Bethel Jubilee Bazaar and the other celebrating the opening of Port Sunlight, a model village with attached soap factory. The well-thumbed bibles and hymn book were inter-leaved with letters, printed notices and press cuttings mostly relating to long ago funerals. I did my best to make sense of all those items and when stuck would ask around the table for guidance. As we shall see I discovered sex that way when I asked for elucidation on the function of a wet nurse – it seemed every home should have one for her duties were listed by Mrs Beeton – and then about the nature and purpose of Southalls' 'Compact Towels', as advertised in the Ward Lock *Guide to London*. In the bibles, between the testaments were blank pages ruled out for the recording of births marriages and deaths. They had been meticulously filled in so I discovered the names of my ancestors and their vital statistics. Some of them figured also in photographs lurking in the pigeon holes. One of them, surely taken in the early days of photography mounted on thick card, dimly showed a group of pale young men in moleskin trousers, one of whom was Granny's father. There were lots of holiday postcards as well, including several from France from 'Your loving son Albert', one of which showed a ruined church at a place called 'Albert, Somme'. I could not sort that one out. Granny and Grandpa got around themselves. I read Granny's notes for her talk to the Ladies Aid about their trip to Rome and there were photographs of their travels in Canada where they attended a world Baptist conference. There was a snap of Grandpa swimming in a steaming outdoor pool against a backdrop of the snowy Rockies. That seemed truly exotic. I read his 1913 diary too. It was in one of the secret drawers but it was not all that interesting. It recorded frequent stops at the Waterfoot Liberal Club on his way home from work and maybe that is why he would rather Granny did not see it.

The certificates in the hall intrigued me. Some were to do with the Masons. They were all red and gold, very fancy and referred mysteriously to lodges and grand masters. The ones from the Mechanics Institute were easier to fathom. I was told Grandpa used to hike there miles across the moor after a long day at the mill. It must have been worth it because he got 'First Class' in both hygiene and astronomy, although only a second in French. It occurred to me that those subjects seemed a bit remote from his job. I supposed he might have been sent to Paris with a suitcase full of samples but the vocational relevance of astronomy to a slipper maker escaped me for forty years, until I began to teach the Open University's Arts Foundation Course and had to grapple with instructional material compiled by Marxist academics peddling an ingenious theory. They said teaching astronomy to the proletariat reinforced the dominant ideology of bourgeois capitalism, because the workers, perceiving the unchanging natural order that holds the stars in their courses, will then be reconciled to the existing social order and eschew radical politics. Well, obviously, when you think about it ... The under-used reception rooms lay on either side of the hall. The big bookcase in the drawing room held the *Encyclopaedia Britannica* which I dipped into, especially the 'Maps' volume, and ditto a survey world geography but I left alone the collected works volumes, of which only those of Dickens seemed actually to have been read. His bust stood on the top of the bookcase, flanked by Gladstone and John Bright, twin pillars of the Victorian Liberal mentality. In the other corner was a tall wind-up gramophone with a limited collection of solid 78 inch records in its lower compartment. I ruined most of the records by failing to change the needle, something you were supposed to do after every playing. However I enjoyed pieces by Caruso and Dame Clara Butt as well as 'Tea for Two', one of the selections from 'No, No Nanette', a disc contributed, I think, by Mum and Dad in their dancing days. On the other side of the hall was the dining room. Nothing other than chocolate and Christmas cake was in my time ever eaten there and it was unfrequented except when Grandpa went there to smoke – beside his big chair was a cabinet holding cigar boxes and a terracotta tobacco jar – and when I used it for looking and thinking. The room exuded Edwardian grandeur with its contents all of dreadnought size. Enormous over-mantels, housing huge acreages of mirror, stood on the sideboard and above the fire. Thus the sunlight which filled this south-facing room was endlessly refracted to spotlight the paintings on the wall and the cut-glass decanters on the sideboard. In a cavity at the base of that monster piece was the object I liked best – a beautifully carpentered canteen of cutlery presented to Mr and Mrs J T Lord on the occasion of their silver wedding in 1910. The donors' names were recorded on little ivory plaques tacked between the recessed brass handles of the drawers. Among them were 'The Children', 'Mr and Mrs H O Ashworth' and 'The Foreman and Workpeople of Sir H W Trickett Ltd'. The affecting generosity of the latter ran to a set of soup ladles that surely only a pantomime giant could find a use for. An immense canvas of a racehorse in a stable filled half of one wall with lesser pictures, also in elaborate gilt frames, occupying most of the remaining space. A brass art nouveau fire screen stood on the hearth together with two extended lines of ebony elephants with ivory tusks, facing each other in descending order of size. Two mounted knights in bronze stood guard behind them.

It was in the dining room, at the age of eight, on a voluptuous sofa, bathed in the endless sunshine of the Battle of Britain summer, that I lost my virginity. My seducer was Rupert Bear and he taught me to read. I confess that, being vulnerable to ever growing adult pressure, I was a willing accomplice. Dad's anxiety about his son's intellectual capacity had become acute and I took pity on him. Perhaps I wanted to send him off up Shire Hill with his revolver to face the might of the invading Wehrmacht, knowing that after all his boy was normal. So I let Rupert have his way with me. I suppose really the credit must go to Rupert's creator, Mary Tourtel. Her accounts of the adventures of the amiable bear in checked trousers were published in a series of yellow-backed books available, price four pence, from Woolworths and I was addicted. Unlike my elders. I guess a further factor in my abdication of illiteracy was the increasing reluctance shown by grown-ups, compelled to read Rupert to me. So during the holidays I settled on the cushions of the sofa and taught myself the trick. The medium was just right. I could kid myself these were picture books. Certainly the story unfolded as a strip cartoon, with a single frame occupying the top half of every page. So I could work out what was happening pretty well, even without the words which filled in the bottom halves of the pages. They came in verse, a stanza or two per page, and that was just the job for me. I had developed an ear for words spoken metrically because reciting poetry had been part of my life for as long as I could remember. It will be recalled that my earliest firm memory was of standing on a stool declaiming Christopher Robin verses I had learned by heart. So in the end it was easy. Work out the action from the picture. Puzzle out how the words fitted the picture. Rhyme and metre afforded broad hints about what the words were. Then memorize the lot – a pleasant task because poetry was fun. Do that for every page and then go back to the beginning and, with the aid of the 'recording' now firmly lodged in my head, 'read' the book all the way through. To start with it was recitation rather than reading but gradually I recognised more and more words at a glance and began to pick up speed. Then I tried the technique on other Rupert books and sometimes got the drift of new material just by looking at the words without intensive contemplation of the pictures. Sometimes I dispensed even with memorization but not usually. For several years I learnt by heart a lot of what I read and hence a lucky break in the Scholarship exam, as we shall see. Thus, without totally exhausting all forty books in the series, and without quite exhausting my father's patience or his pocket – although he could not conceal doubts about the literary merit of the Tourtel oeuvre – I crossed a threshold. Henceforth a third element complicated my intellectual life and looking and thinking had to accommodate reading. It was progress I suppose and, as progress is said to be, inevitable. Still, I continue to regret a certain loss of innocence.

With which ambiguity let us conclude this account of learning without schooling. I am saying that during my 'primary' years I leant more out of school than from my teachers and that goes even for at least one of the three Rs – it was Rupert Bear, not Miss Little or even my Dad, who taught me to read. I did it my way. It also emerges that during those years I developed a particular attachment to history. Crucially I grasped that historical forces can be better understood if you arrange things in the order in which they happened. Chronology unlocks history. So in my head I built a 'Meccano' framework capable of infinite adaptation. It has served me ever since. At the same time I discovered that history was fun. Hence the huge pleasure I took in the Second World War.

Chapter 5

WAR

To a child never in danger but enjoying, for six whole years, an ever replenished feast of exciting events, the Second World War was a happy time and a learning experience of unrivalled efficacy. But although decades were to elapse before I recognised the damage, I was a victim of the war as well as a beneficiary and that in two ways. First, it made me a glutton and then it made me a socialist. We shall confront the first issue immediately and deal with the second in later chapters.

It was generally assumed that the day war broke out would be the day of Armageddon. Nobody who had seen *Things to Come* at the pictures or taken in newsreel footage of the Spanish Civil War was fooled by the cheery, 'carry on' tone of the government pamphlet about the coming 'emergency' that dropped through the nation's letterboxes during the expectant summer of 1939. An immediate maelstrom of bombs and gas would be followed by permanent famine. If my mother could not avert the former she could at least take steps against the latter, so while '*A tisket a tasket, I've lost my yellow basket*' tinkled out of the radio her larder shelves began to fill up. Tins of Libby's peaches and Del Monte pineapples were piled two and three high in the wall cupboards, leaving no room for the files of John West Red Salmon ['Middle Cut'] and Heinz Sandwich Spread which therefore had to colonise the stone slabs below, cheek by jowl with a sugar mountain, piled up blue bags of dried fruit, and a bucket of eggs preserved in Isinglass. Although both the government and the BBC said it was seriously wrong, Mum became a hoarder and persisted in that sinful state throughout long years of rationing. Furthermore, in order to feed her habit, she became a black marketeer. Her independent mind and nonconformist conscience, forged in the Bethel Baptist congregation at home in Waterfoot, Rossendale before the First World War, rendered her immune to propaganda. Duty to one's family outweighed even the moral authority of the wireless. Hence her sustained and massively productive campaign of preventive shopping. She kept it up long past the official end of the war, for the advent of post war austerity [socialism, that is] offered continuing incentives to militant housewifery.

I have already reported her rapport with high street traders. Well, following the commencement of hostilities, its warmth became tropical. Shopping with her in wartime was to join in a regal progress. With a cloth-covered basket slung over her arm, and a bulging oilcloth bag in the other hand, she sailed from admiring grocer to drooling butcher. We were as likely to enter a shop by the back door as the front. Alternatively a plain brown parcel would slide across the counter while money changed hands. What you picked up no longer seemed to coincide with the ostensible speciality of the shop. The demarcation lines noted earlier as a feature of the retail scene in pre-war Glossop, were now gaily crossed and re-crossed as a very free market established itself. Thus the butcher supplied butter, sugar and tomatoes. And chickens might be obtained from the tailor and bacon from the baker. It was all very cheerful. Every stop was a social occasion, like shopping today in France or Ireland, but with an extra thrill. For the delights of wartime retail intercourse were sweetened by their irregularity and my mother relished the illicit nature of this commerce. That surprised me. While my father, my teachers and the BBC were doing their best to make me law abiding, here was Mum gleefully embracing criminality. Perhaps moral confusion as well as chaotic eating was a legacy of my wartime childhood.

It certainly made me fat. Rationing and food subsidies are supposed to have been good for the nation's health. It seems the formerly poor now enjoyed an adequate and well balanced diet. I expect they did and you can't really quarrel with that. But what about the effect of rationing, and the compulsion to evade it, on the already over-stuffed? The high valuation placed by wartime culture on the acquisition of food certainly encouraged the Lord family to eat more ravenously than they had ever done before. I mean, it was wrong to waste good food wasn't it? It was unpatriotic. It was helping Hitler. There were posters proclaiming the wicked profligacy of leaving scraps on plates. Eating up helped the war effort. As Granny was fond of saying, 'Waste not, want not'. Indeed, as the war progressed, the values of grannies enjoyed an unexpected revival. Propaganda battened onto a widespread, homespun philosophy of frugality that, if past its Victorian prime, still had life in it. As well as eating up, we were urged to 'Make Do and Mend', to resist the wiles of the Squanderbug, and to heed the wise counsel of Mr Therm regarding the level of bath water – more than five inches was scarlet sin. Yet the cult of frugality went hand in hand with overeating. Not wasting food meant eating up, even if you did not need what was left on your plate, and constant eatings-up fed the appetite, thus constantly inflating the currency of need. As the old song put it, *'The more you have, the more you want.'* Certainly binges and blow-outs were endemic to life at our house during the war and in the subsequent age of austerity.

Take a typical Sunday. There was a cooked breakfast of fried eggs, bacon, sausages, kidneys, creamed mushrooms, tomatoes and fried bread, followed by ever replenished stacks of toast, ready 'buttered' by Mum with a spread she concocted according to a secret recipe, plus a choice of jam, marmalade or lemon cheese. A gargantuan roast lunch at one o'clock [prompt] was followed by a hot pudding, cheese with biscuits and celery, and then tea and biscuits. Tea proper at five brought plates of sandwiches spilling over with mayonnaise – cold meat, egg, salad and tinned salmon or 'Snoek' [a salmon substitute] – followed by scones and jam, followed by trifle with cream [probably mock], followed by wedges of fruit cake or coffee cake and a choice of iced buns and 'fancies'. Finally, at nine, a supper of Lancashire cheese, biscuits and apple pie was brought in. With touching Sabbath restraint Dad on Sundays usually missed out on the dish of tripe and onions that was a frequent late night snack on weekdays. In between times you kept the wolf from the door as best you could and here, I admit, we did feel the scourge of privation, sweets and chocolates being genuinely hard to come by, even at the Co-op butchers. At least they usually were. But when Dad went off with the Air Training Corps to bomber stations in Lincolnshire, where a discouraging expectation of life among the aircrew was sweetened by the authorities with generous applications of Dairy Milk, he came back staggering under bulk purchases of the stuff. I expect it was his answer to Mum's triumphs along High Street West. Also grown-ups were wont to give up their 'points' [sweet ration coupons] to children and substitutes were available, including homemade toffee and off-the-ration cough sweets [Victory Vs or Zubes] or pieces of liquorice root. If all else failed you could eat fruit but, unless it was tinned, fruit was considered a desperate expedient. Tinned peaches were something else you couldn't get, even at the Co-op butchers. The thing is, with me, all that face-stuffing acted on a genetic tendency to flabbiness. Thus by the time I was eleven I was seriously overweight. Not that Mum was at all concerned. Rather she seemed pleased. I was living proof of her triumphs over austerity. So it didn't bother me either and I even got my friends to call me 'Porky' and found their embarrassment puzzling *[Plate 11 bottom middle]*.

Thus war left me with a food problem that has never really gone away. A propensity to flab was intensified by the perverse effects of rationing, leaving me addicted to a high fat, high carbohydrate diet. Appetite having been divorced from biological need I was always 'hungry' – that is in a state of constant food arousal that in retrospect seems like the condition of perpetual sexual arousal that blighted my later adolescence. The latter was the most unpleasant thing that has ever happened to me but fortunately it went critical after the period of this memoir so you will be relieved to learn that I don't feel obliged to tell you about it. The point is that rationing did me harm but it was the only respect in which, during the war, I was exposed to physical peril. I always felt absolutely safe. Glossop was a 'reception area'. That is it was judged so uninteresting to the Luftwaffe that it was OK to send evacuees there from more vulnerable places. This official judgement was entirely sound. The only serious damage to property known in wartime Glossop resulted from the 1944 Great Flood and an occasion in 1941 when the 'Push and Pull' went through the station buffers and fetched up in Norfolk Street. Mrs Brown, our cleaning lady happened to be a passenger and received minor injuries but there were no other casualties, except the station lion, who temporarily had to leave his perch while the wall was rebuilt. Nor was I personally acquainted with any casualties of the war. Auntie Maud and my cousin Barbara retreated from Selsdon to Southport at the height of the Blitz, and again when the doodlebugs came in 1944, although Leslie, with a job and being a fireman, had to stay behind of course. The death on active service of an old boy was occasionally announced by Dad at morning assembly, but it happened less often than you might have expected, considering the rate at which the school ATC was turning out bomber fodder. So I was purely an observer of the war and not a participant one. I watched it only from the stands. The spectacle however was breath-taking and the experience compulsive.

To start with, everybody I knew was interested in the war. Everybody wanted to talk about it and never grew tired of it. It was a universal and overwhelmingly dominant topic of conversation. Life was an endless seminar. From 1939 to 1945, but not afterwards – after VJ Day talking about the war suddenly and strangely became taboo – I talked about it all day and every day. I discussed it with my parents and grandparents, with my sister and with aunts, uncles and cousins, with friends and schoolmates, with friends' parents and parents' friends, with teachers, with people who called at the house, with shopkeepers. I can remember the actual location of many lively analyses of the general situation – at mealtimes, in playgrounds, on bicycles, while train spotting, on the beach, while listening to the wireless, in classrooms, while walking to and from school, at the barber's, in cafés, while coming home from the pictures, while damming the Cowbrook in the Holt's garden or while studying *Aircraft of the Fighting Powers* in the Holts' kitchen. Indeed recollections of my life between the ages of seven and thirteen are inextricably intertwined with memories of how the story of the war was unfurling and what everybody thought about it. Indeed there was so much talk going on, some part of it studious, that we might almost think of British society during the war as a great big open university. Although people wore military uniforms or the overalls of workers, their daily experience often had much in common with that of a student. Like students do, they talked a lot. Most of the discourse was of course trivial and/or ribald but then so it is with students and, amid the buzz and the banter, serious appraisals of serious topics occurred often enough. For not only did the war give people plenty to talk about, it placed them in situations especially conducive to discussion. Millions had exchanged the taciturnity of family life for the incessant chatter of collective living. And many of those not called up to live communally in barracks, camps and hostels nevertheless sacrificed much of their spare time to the war effort and in the process exercised their jaws more than somewhat. My father, Flight Lieutenant Lord, chose the ATC *[Plate 11 bottom left]* but he might equally have done his bit with the Home Guard, become an Air Raid Warden, joined the Auxiliary Fire Service like his brother *[Plate 11 bottom right]* or served in another of the many patriotic organisations conjured into being by the war. In that he was not unusual. The scene of competitive local volunteering at Walmington-on-Sea, immortalised in *Dad's Army*, is profoundly true to life. They were all at it in wartime Glossop as well. And what did they do, before, during and after their shifts and parades? They talked and talked and then frequently adjourned to the pub to continue debate about the conduct of the war, the prospects for peace and even, from time to time, about the meaning of life. The ATC made my puritanical, anti-social Dad a regular at the Royal Oak.

Nor were students of the open university of war frequently distracted by fear or even by the imperatives of action. Immunity from the attentions of the enemy, such as we enjoyed in Glossop, was characteristic of much of the country during most of the war. Compared with, say, the Russians, Poles and Germans, and even with the French and Italians, we British had an easy war. We never suffered enemy occupation and we suffered less than is popularly supposed from aerial bombardment. Between the Blitz [in London and certain major cities 1940-1941] and the Doodlebugs [London only 1944-1945], there were hardly any air raids anywhere. Even our armed forces, between the Battle of Britain [1940] and D Day [1944], engaged with the enemy only sporadically – bombing German cities, sinking U-boats and defending the frontiers of Empire by keeping the Italians out of Egypt and the Japanese out of India – in operations involving, at the sharp end, only quite small elite companies of heroes. So even for men trained to fight [no women were permitted to engage in combat] the prospect of action was often distant and a great deal of time was devoted instead to waiting. That indeed became a big part of what people did and I carry in my mind an icon of waiting as central to the war effort. It was August 1945 and VJ Day, the official last day of the war. It was the middle of the summer holidays and we were staying at Selsdon and went up to London to see the sights. Dad walked straight through the barrier at Victoria Station without handing in his ticket and Leslie got drunk. But it was not the misbehaviour of my elders that I remember most, nor was it cheering crowds or Royals on the Palace balcony. Instead, memory is dominated by the sight of a long line of WAAFs queuing outside a public lavatory, singing '*Why are we waiting?*' The thing is, waiting is not time wasted. Perhaps like nothing else it gets you talking and talking, sometimes anyway, stimulates thinking and promotes intellectual growth.

I am suggesting a lot of that was going on in wartime Britain, a nurturing and convivial society that turned itself into a veritable open university of war.

Even children could join in. The debate was open to all and a well-stocked university library – a bank of learning resources – was accessible to kids equally with grown-ups. In it I browsed continually and contentedly. The war generated a dense crop of alien but interesting objects. I do not just mean the pill boxes and tank barriers that now enlivened car journeys, or the forest of iron stakes that sprang up overnight on Southport beach, but also new accessions to Mum's hoard, like dried eggs, Spam and Snoek, and all the important documents, like identity cards, ration books and savings certificates that were stashed in the bureau. Then there was the smart, modern range of 'Utility' furniture that, despite the war, refreshed my bedroom. Around Glossop exotic direction indicators replaced the road signs that were taken down to confuse invading Huns. 'EWS' plus a yellow arrow meant a static water tank [for fire hoses]. 'S' plus a white arrow meant an air raid shelter. The latter had the scary appeal of caves and came in various shapes and sizes. The flimsy brick structure with a concrete roof, opposite our house in Sheffield Road, was scarcely reassuring but in Cross Street Southport there was a proper grey bunker covered in creosoted sand bags. Beside it was a pig bin swarming with wasps which I sometimes had to brave with a bucket of kitchen scraps. The shelters I knew were never used for their designated purpose but they made good adventure play-grounds until they began to smell, due to multi-faceted misuse, and were locked. Who was supposed to unlock them if a wailing Stuka should happen to drop in, I do not know. ARP paraphernalia also gave scope for play. Stirrup pumps were fun, particularly in hot weather, and gas masks were always good for a laugh. In messing about with mine I cracked the eye piece and Mum had to write to Mr Fielding who, it will be recalled, was Chief Warden as well as Head of St Luke's. I was more frightened of him than of getting noxious fumes into my eyes and lungs but he was quite nice about it and got my mask fixed. Uniforms and insignia also had potent boy appeal. The smooth blue cloth of Dad's RAF officer's tunic and greatcoat was truly smart and occasionally Mum, his batman, let me polish the brasses, using an ingenious device called a 'button stick' to protect the material.

Dad had also kept his tin hat from the trenches and had it fitted with a new webbing liner. Less accessible, but scarcely secure, was the revolver in his bedroom drawer. It seems a German officer had surrendered it to Lance Corporal Lord after he and his mates, in 1918, broke through the Hindenburg Line and once and for all snuffed out 'Prussian militarism'. Or so they thought. Snuffing it out again was what Dad said we were fighting for. He had smuggled the Lüger home to show his mother but in 1940 he declared it to the police and, in view of the imminence of invasion, was rewarded with a supply of ammunition. So woe betide any Prussian intruder who rang our doorbell. He also gave me his old Border Regiment cap badge which I polished with genuine pride and refused to swap it in the cloakroom market place for militaria that flourished at the Grammar School. On that exchange, as well as badges and shoulder flashes, you could pick up a surprising assortment of weaponry and gadgetry, much of it harvested from the moors around Glossop. Do you fancy a compass? Or perhaps an altimeter? This one clearly had not done much for the crew who put their trust in it. For although the Luftwaffe never seemed to enter Glossop's air space it proved perilous to our own airmen and the numerous crash sites attracted swarms of schoolboy trophy hunters. Flying Fortresses seemed particularly vulnerable. Dad said it was because the Yanks were over-sexed but under-educated and if they had learnt navigation with the ATC they might have flown high enough to miss the Pennine peaks. Not that our boys seemed to do much better. A Fleet Air Arm Swordfish once crashed, not on the moors, but just behind Mr Goodwin's pie shop in High Street East. There was no damage and I think the pilot survived but we gawpers had a field day. Military vehicles were also part of the scene. Sometimes convoys of army trucks would thunder through the blackout escorted by despatch riders on motorbikes. During war savings efforts, like 'Salute the Soldier' week, tanks, guns, jeeps and even amphibious DUKWs might be demonstrated in the park or the market place. Thus the war constantly flaunted its delights before my eager eyes. But it changed my world by subtraction as well as addition. The things the war took away included, not only lemons, bananas, ice cream and the name 'Glossop' on the premises of the Glossop Carriage Company, but also garden gates and park railings, although not the splendid ironwork that gave distinction to the exterior of the Grammar School, the preservation of which from War Salvage was maybe the best thing Dad did in the war. *Plate 12 top* shows the gates and railings still resplendent seventy years later in in 2014.

Opportunities to explore this changed landscape were not restricted to Glossop. 'Is your journey really necessary?' it said over the booking office window. I often used to reflect that it was not but I was glad we were going nevertheless. And particularly by train. Rail travel was an exciting new experience for a car-bred boy. The sights and sounds left you in no doubt here was a war on, as the lines shuddered rhythmically under the weight of personnel and matériel. Trucks carrying tanks, guns and fuselages alternated with trainloads of gum-toting GIs. Carriages were full of uniforms in plumage as colourful as a wild fowl reserve. But the real bonus was the view from the window, long my favourite vantage point. From the faint blue light of the compartment, diffused by a single, painted, low watt bulb, I would peer through muddy condensation at the ghostly outline of blacked-out Manchester. Or, in bright sunlight, en route to Blackpool, I would gaze in awe at the bustling industrial city that was the Royal Ordnance factory at Chorley, urging the dawdling train forward before swooping Junkers, drawn to a prime target like wasps to a jam-pot, set off all that concentrated TNT and abruptly terminated my registration as a student at the open university of war. Things glimpsed in passing have left more of an impression than planned field trips to the battlefields but Dad sometimes laid these on for me. There was a tour of the ruins the week after the Manchester blitz at Christmas 1940. It was OK. The air smelt like bonfire night and there was indeed quite a lot of blown up buildings which, in the winter landscape, had a weird beauty. But what I recall most vividly was a slap-up, sit down pre-war lunch, complete with starched table cloths and black-coated waiters, under the dome of the Victoria Station Grill Room, right next to the twisted girders that had recently formed the roof over Platforms 11-16. They called that sort of thing 'Business as Usual'. Similarly a guided tour of the modifications to Liverpool docks is remembered by a jumbo-sized splinter, picked up while gormlessly running my fingers along newly-erected lengths of wooden fencing, intended presumably to keep looters off the bomb sites.

But my studies of the war were far from restricted to three dimensional artefacts. There was a wealth of printed materials as well. Because of the war I became a newspaper consumer before I could read. It was not so much the pictures. Even before the war the *Manchester Guardian* segregated them to a separate 'picture page' and they were largely dispensed with as the shortage of newsprint began to bite. It was the maps that grabbed me. I have already claimed that in infancy I mastered the topography of the Peloponnese and the Gulf of Bothnia but be aware that I am equally familiar with the sequence of Russian rivers running Dniester, Dnieper, Donetz, Don and Volga. Also I know my Skagerrak from my Kattegat and could locate the Lofoten Islands. I could, with my eyes closed, draw the coast of northern France [the Atlantic Wall] almost as accurately as I could delineate the sweep of the North African littoral from Alexandria to Casablanca, pinpointing not only Tunis, Tripoli and Benghazi but also El Agheila, Gazala and Mersa Matruh. In cartographical terms I could take you back to Bataan and point you towards the sands of Iwo Jima. If I had a Panzer division I would avoid the Pripet Marshes as well as the Qattara Depression. I know Antananarivo and Trincomalee. I know roughly how far it is from Lampedusa to Pantelleria and how Arnhem was a bridge too far. And, remembering the maps in the *Guardian*, I am prepared to believe that the old Moulmein pagoda did indeed stand beside the road to Mandalay.

So what? Well, nothing really. Except that it was and is immensely enjoyable. The pleasure embraces poetry and music, for they are beautiful names. Is it useful? Maybe, to some extent. Like well-bred Victorian girls, who included globe spotting among their 'accomplishments' along with singing, playing and embroidery, I acquired a world picture that was at least to scale. I built a sturdy geographical grid that nicely complemented my history Meccano. I came to realise that why things happen is intricately connected with where they happen. Also map mania confirmed my preference for non-verbal media. From a map you learn at a glance what pages of description would not convey. Or do you? Perhaps maps, particularly war maps, are traps for tidy minds. Those that so dramatically indicated the progress of the war showed coasts and rivers, lakes and mountains, roads and railways, bridges and frontiers. Towns and cities also appeared but usually as mere pinhead dots. But I do not remember them showing language and religion or even economic activity. They took no account of food and drink, customs and dress, art and music, sports and games, architectural styles or any of the other elements that determine cultural variety. So an assumption was created that the spaces being fought over were to all intents *uninhabited*. It was twenty years after the war, as Colonel Gadhafi hit the headlines, that I came to realise Libya was not simply a sandy playing field, empty until Rommel and Montgomery led out their respective teams, but the home of several million actual Libyans. I wonder what they did in the war? They were never in the news. So it was all too easy to forget that the direct route from A to B passed among the homes of real people, as did the arms of a pincer movement. The assumption of a cultural vacuum seems indeed to have conditioned the map reading of the supreme leaders of the Allied cause. Churchill boasted that he once pushed a map over to Stalin, with a line roughly separating Greece from the rest of the Balkans and the scribbled words 'Ours' and 'Yours'. And when Winston and Franklin D sat at that table in Yalta and examined the map with canny Joe, just like Jas and Alan and me in their kitchen, they seem to have picked out the wrong River Neisse, thus condemning several extra million Germans to ethnic cleansing from their ancestral homelands.

The point is that if you like maps too much you may fail to register people and that I think happened to me. I was crazy about maps. When I was not poring over the ones in the public prints, I was creating my own. Sometimes they were imaginary. I would delineate two or more countries at war, endowing them with physical features, towns, roads, railways and frontier defences. Then, with the aid of coloured crayons, I would mount an invasion by one power against the other and mark its progress, via pincer movements and daring landings by sea and air, until a strategic stranglehold was accomplished. Usually the invader won, partly because wartime erasers were no match for the thick imprint of 'copying' pencils and Tippex had not been invented. But sometimes my maps represented real places. I too, like the lads at Yalta, drew up my plans for the resettlement of Europe. I did it at the roll-top desk at 7 Cross Street with the aid of tracing paper, the *Penguin Atlas of Post War Problems* and the *Maps* volume of the *Encyclopaedia Britannica* [Ninth Edition 1903]. My solutions were sometimes radical. I considered letting the Germans have Alsace-Lorraine back to spite the Vichy French who had betrayed us. Map-making gave me a giddy conviction of infallibility. I knew best. Decisions, it seemed, were best left to informed experts, like me, having studied the maps. That way of thinking did not go away. It contributed to an exaggerated faith in planning that was later to plague my working life.

Towards 1945 my horizons were extended by a barrage of American magazines, not only *Life* and *Time* but also exotics like *Look*, *Colliers* and, most seductive of all, the sumptuous *Saturday Evening Post*. My Uncle

Leslie brought them to us from a treasure trove called the 'newsroom at Reuters' which yielded other strange fruits of war, including a swastika armband fresh from devastated Hamburg. But it was not just me. J G Ballard, another young boy fascinated by the war, but unlike me personally acquainted with its perils, describes in *Empire of the Sun* how Flying Fortresses dropped tons of magazines on Japan after the surrender, along with canisters of 'Lucky Strikes'. The American cultural offensive against Japan succeeded dramatically. So were the Yanks trying to colonise us as well? In Lord Street Southport, in the summer of '44, you might have thought so. It was lined at the kerb-sides with Studebakers, Oldsmobiles, Chryslers, Buicks, Dodges and Ford V8s and outside the Scarisbrick Arms I once spotted a Cadillac. They were driven by flyers catching some brief R and R at the Palace Hotel, requisitioned as a leave centre for aircrew engaged on hazardous daylight raids over Germany. At the time however I did not know that and acquiesced in Dad's traditional British disdain for bloody Yanks who were overpaid, over-indulged and over here. I recognised the cars on Lord Street from the ads in the mags but it was of course the images of food that stunned me from the pages of the *Saturday Evening Post*. There were unbelievable sundaes and monstrous hams dripping with honey and pineapple. Also there was a drink called 'Coca Cola' whose dazzling promise for after the war eclipsed the fading recollection of pre-war Dandelion and Burdock. Stateside it seemed you could still drop by the store and pick up just about anything consumable, including giant tins of Libby's peaches. These advertisements showed us what we were fighting for – big cars and fast foods. I suppose it is what we got. The gas guzzlers have gone from Lord Street but Big Macs can be had close by.

As well as magazines and newspapers I endlessly scrutinised books about the war. The Ministry of Information [propaganda, that is] did snazzy paperbacks loaded with pictures and that was just my ticket. I still have some of them. *Front Line* presented the Blitz appropriately like a series of stills from a film noir. *Eighth Army* came in sepia to go with the desert sand, but the pictures in *Fleet Air Arm* were in sharp focus and somehow breezy, like sailors are. There was also an MoI account of the Battle of Britain but I preferred the junior version put out by Puffin Picture Books. I began to collect these beautiful products when I was about ten and *The Battle of Britain* was my first purchase. Like the others in the series, it mobilised my favourite learning media in a collation of artist's impressions, cutaway drawings, maps, diagrams and bird's eye views, so how could I resist? The standard of production was very high despite the war. On thick, slightly lubricated paper, pages of coloured lithographs alternated with black and white illustrations. There was a text as well that was acceptable because brief and subordinate to the pictures. Thanks to Puffins, the Battle of Britain became the first historical event I ever studied in depth and analytically. As well as its story I learnt that the battle developed through distinct phases, triggered by significant decisions like the fateful German switch from attacking fighter bases to bombing London. At the same time I grasped something of the logistics underlying the conflict, identifying the different aircraft types, with their pros and cons, and noting Fighter Command's administrative machinery. Despite excellent maps the book did not eliminate people. The dog fights were populated and the consequences of losing were not shirked. I remember pondering the sun-drenched flight deck of a Heinkel 111. What a view for the crew, seen manning the controls. But I knew Heinkels were easy prey to Spitfires so I feared for those airmen, even though they were German. I was sorry that there were not more Puffins about the war but apart from not quite convincing accounts of happy childhoods in allied countries like the Soviet Union and nationalist China, the others mostly dealt with peacetime subjects like farming, natural history and architecture. The first two I greeted with modified rapture but the last enchanted me. As we shall see.

Apart from a single Biggles I do not remember reading story books about the war. Prose that was too continuous remained a challenge. Instead war fiction was lapped up at the pictures. Cinema then filled our lives like telly does today. Most weeks we went to the Empire, Glossop's premier rendezvous, usually on a Friday night. It was quite a social occasion. As well as local notables and people Mum knew from black marketeering and 'penny-a-week' collecting for the Red Cross, a large number of Dad's pupils would be upstairs in the 'one and nines'. If you went to the Grammar School you sat in the circle, leaving the supposedly verminous stalls ['one and three'], known to Chris Gillings as the 'spit and whistle', to the great unwashed who left school at fourteen. We always sat at the front, leaving a discreet distance between the Headmaster and out of school activities occurring on the back row. Sometimes however, on Saturday afternoons, we visited cinemas further afield, by bus to Hyde or by train to Guide Bridge or even Manchester, where we could choose between the Odeon and the Gaumont but avoided the now disreputable Gaiety, much declined, Dad said, from its fame as a 'legitimate' theatre before the Great War, under the direction of a mysterious lady called 'Miss Horniman.' At Southport, cinema going became orgiastic. There were no fewer than eight picture houses along Lord Street or just off it. Some of them were truly grand and had domed auditoria, illuminated organs that rose and fell during intervals, smart cafés serving various feasts with 'chips and TBB,' and deep-piled lounges with un-spillable ashtrays erect on chromium stalks.

Apart from their opening sequences, and the accents of the commentators, I remember little about the newsreels [Gaumont British, Pathé and British Movietone] or about documentary shorts like the American 'March of Time' series, or about all those white-with-a-touch-of-black polemics from the Russian Front with titles like *Forty Degrees Below Zero*. It was when the big picture itself was about the war that it came to life for me. What I really liked was a full length feature that stuck to the war but still had a story. Thus *Target for Tonight* was too documentary because you never got to know the pilot and his crew as real people. It lacked the human interest of say *One of Our Aircraft is Missing* or *Western Approaches*. However you could overdo the human interest and weepies like *Mrs Miniver* left me feeling cheated. I liked the Warsaw Concerto in *Dangerous Moonlight* and the bit where he did not desert his post at the grand piano even in the face of the Luftwaffe's ferocious assault, but the film contained too much of the irrelevance my parents encouraged me to despise as 'love stuff'. I do not remember seeing *Casablanca* first time round, although it seems unlikely we would have missed it, unless it was on Dad's index as 'sentimental Hollywood rubbish'. I would have enjoyed the fall of Paris and the bit in Rick's café where they sing the 'Marseillaise' in competition with 'Die Wacht am Rhein'. Otherwise however I would have found it too slow and carrying a heavy burden of love stuff. I liked best of all the sort of film where a diverse group of companions are bonded together in preparation for war and then go through its vicissitudes together and the survivors emerge as heroes. So *In Which We Serve*, *The Way Ahead*, *The Way to the Stars* and *Millions Like Us* all got five stars with me, despite a certain intrusion of love stuff in the last two. I also liked historical approaches to the war that set the present conflict in a longer perspective. So *The Life and Death of Colonel Blimp*, which began with the Boer war and took in the Kaiser's Germany and 1914-18 before coming up to date, was spot on. *The First of the Few* put the Spitfire into its place in the history of aviation and that worked for me as well. I seem to have fallen heavily for patriotism, camaraderie and heroism, particularly in the underplayed British manner, which was exactly the response the film makers usually wanted, although 'Blimp' made you think because it featured a good, brave German. Cinema-going powerfully reinforced in me a commitment to the allied cause that can only be described as passionate. We had to win because we were good and they were bad.

So what with all the talk, the exploration of artefacts, the map-work, the scrutiny of still pictures and surrender to the joy of moving ones, I had, as they say 'a good war'. I became immensely knowledgeable, holding the 'story so far' in a firm grip and aching to know what was going to happen next. For I did see it as an ongoing story and I had no doubt at all who the narrator was. He was called Alvar Liddell. Sure he did not always use his own voice, but sometimes adopted instead the warm tones of Stuart Hibbert, and occasionally teased us with the Yorkshire accent of Wilfred Pickles. But such variations notwithstanding, the voice I knew as Alvar Liddell had absolute authority, and the truth of what he said was incontestable. He told me the truth four times every day – at eight o'clock, one o'clock, six o'clock and, from 1941 onwards, bedtime having been put back for the purpose, at nine o'clock – prefacing the next instalment of unvarnished veracity with the spine-tingling incantation:

This is the BBC Home Service.
Here is the news and this is Alvar Liddell reading it.

The authority of Alvar Liddell exceeded even that of my father. Actually Dad had his doubts about Alvar. With a name like that he could be a bloody Jerry. Or maybe a damned Swede, neutrals – in effect, conshies dodging the column – being scarcely better than the enemy, who was at least prepared to stand up and fight. He considered complaining about suspect Alvar to the BBC. He harboured similar reservations about the appointment of General Eisenhower to command the Allied Expeditionary Force. It was an obviously Boche name and it was well known that millions of the bastards had hidden in the USA posing as immigrants. Did the President know about fifth columnists? But with a name like Roosevelt even Dad could see there was no point in communicating his qualms to the White House. They cut no ice even with me. They were almost blasphemous. If God and Alvar Liddell were distinguishable, the distinction to me was imperceptible. So let us conclude this account of how I learnt about the war with a celebration of the wireless, the heavenly habitation from which Alvar Liddell spoke the truth.

Although we had an extension speaker in the kitchen, our proper radio was in the 'Study'. The room was so-called because my parents thought 'lounge' vulgar, rejected 'drawing room' as too grand and 'sitting room' as too bleakly objective. Perhaps the name was appropriate enough. Although I generally preferred the kitchen table, I was supposed to do my homework there, at the 'bureau', a rickety drop-leaf faux Rococo escritoire that was too high and too small. Also I practised the piano there, an activity I did my best to avoid. Dad really did study in the Study. He did a lot of reading in a deep leather armchair by the fire and preferred that station also for marking sixth form essays and plotting the contribution of No 596 Squadron, ATC to the downfall of the Third Reich. The Study too was where Mum did knitting and mending. But what we mostly did there was listen to the wireless. The Murphy console stood under the side window, behind Mum's chair. It was big, standing about three feet high, like the shallow end at Woods' Baths. It was not one of your cheap and nasty Bakelite jobs but was made of wood, which came in two tastefully complementary veneers and in a style I later came to know as 'Art Deco', like the stand-up chromium ashtrays aforementioned at the Grand Cinema, Southport. It was bow-fronted and a very large speaker indeed took up most of the angular protrusion. This, together with the outside aerial, rigged from a soaring steel mast by the cherry tree in the Paddock, ensured a deep resonance that did no harm at all to Alvar Liddell's authority. The tuning dials were on the top and to work them you had to bend over the apparatus as though it was a wash basin. The two knobs, plastic but elegant with it, were shaped like chrysanthemums. When switched on, the set had a distinctive smell, like spiced electricity, that seemed to be associated with an occult green light that flashed when you explored the stations on short wave. And what a feast of stations were

131

there to be twiddled among. As well as different British transmitters, like Droitwich or Plymouth and Bournemouth, the whole of Europe was at your fingertips. You could tune to Luxembourg, Kalendborg, Frankfurt, Monte Carlo, Hilversum, Oslo and many more. Or you could try for real exotica on short wave. On that band you were usually only rewarded with crackles, or what sounded like Radio Babel, but sometimes Morse messages came across. Were they SOS calls? Had a British merchantman, homeward bound from Buenos Aires, spotted a pocket battleship?

The new set was delivered a month or two before war broke out so to start with we mostly took the National Programme from Droitwich, on long wave, but war wrought changes and henceforth our usual assignation was with the Home Service on medium wave. There was also the Forces Programme but that was mostly 'God-awful American crooners' or Sandy Macpherson at the Wurlitzer. Although Sandy's organ was acknowledged to be doing its bit for victory, Dad made it clear that the Forces Programme was only for 'B' formers and boys, like Chris Gillings, who 'slicked back' their hair. Music on the radio bothered Dad. He approved chapel favourites like Messiah at Christmas, preferably from Huddersfield, and also Gilbert and Sullivan – their story serialised on Sunday nights had us all in the Study on a three line whip – but classical music, even the 'light' sort as apparently played in palm courts, made him uneasy. He did not exactly warn his children off it, except on patriotic grounds – most of it was of Axis origin and its perpetrators had enemy names like 'Tauber' or 'Toscanini' – but he indicated that 'good' music was hard and not for a boy who disliked practising the piano. If cultivated Dad found classical music demanding then so of course must everybody else so he was scathing about certain announcers who appeared knowledgeable and enthusiastic. They were mincing posers and probably 'nancy-boys', a term he often used but never defined. You could tell that from their plummy voices and 'insipid' accents. They were dodging the column with a soft job at the BBC and should be sent up the line at the double. Most popular music also figured on Dad's index, although ballads that he had heard his mother sing, or soldiers' songs of the Great War, or numbers he had once danced to with Mum, before they were married, enjoyed partial exemption from the veto. It was however applied rigorously to 'cacophonous American jazz' and to that 'dreadful Vera Lynn'. Censorship of wireless programmes was not restricted to music. Dad's anti-clericalism has already been noted.

It was compounded by the 'constipated' voices of the 'bloody parsons' who conducted the Daily Service, another set of putative 'nancy-boys and conshies'. Thus religious broadcasts were always switched off promptly, unless perchance Granny Southport was around. Children's Hour, as we have seen, was also suspect. Larry the Lamb was slated for slaughter as was his shepherd, Uncle Mac, whose voice, as we know, consistently betrayed the compacted state of its owner's bowels.

'Variety' however was OK. Dad was an actual fan of some of the radio comedians and comedy shows regularly brought laughter to the Study. He and Sammy had been to see 'Bandwagon' live at the Palace in Manchester and for weeks afterwards went on in 'I wish you could have seen it' vein about the antics of Big Hearted Arthur Askey and Stinker Murdoch. He also enjoyed 'ITMA' and 'Mrs Handley's boy' enjoyed a standing invitation to bring Sam Ferfechan, Colonel Chinstrap, Mrs Mop and Funf, along to the Study. Meanwhile in the kitchen we listened to 'Workers' Playtime', beamed to us every dinnertime from a factory canteen 'somewhere in England' and on Saturday nights I was allowed to stay up for 'Garrison Theatre', which was soon renamed 'Music Hall'. First Jack 'Blue Pencil' Warner ['mind my bike'] would read out censored letters from his brother Syd, who was with the forces 'somewhere in France', or exchange banter with Charles Shadwell, conductor of the BBC Variety Orchestra [signature tune: 'The Spice of Life'] before introducing the artistes. Rob Wilton, Mum's favourite, might recall 'the day war broke out' and how, over a cup of tea, his missus asked 'what are you going to do about it?' He would have told us but 'they've been open five minutes' so he had to go. Sandy 'Can you hear me mother?' Powell and Two Ton Tessie O'Shea, who was rather vulgar, were also regulars and sometimes Norman Evans, talked to us from 'Over the Garden Wall'. We once saw him [or was it her?] live on one of the Blackpool piers. Then we might renew our acquaintance with Stainless ['Semi-Colon'] Stephen, or Cardew the Cad or Will Fyfe, to whom, on a Saturday night, Glasgow belonged, or Gilly Potter, reporting the response of Lord Marshmallow to the ongoing national emergency, or Jeanne de Casilis or the Western Brothers and many more, right through the bill down to Wilson, Keppel and Betty.

But enough of frivolity. Although after eight on Saturday evenings merriment filled the Study and, if Dad had recently been a guest of Bomber

Command, Malteesers and even Quality Street circulated like port in a common room, at nine Big Ben took over from Charles Shadwell and the Doric mood was re-established. Then Alvar Liddell might announce the fall of Smolensk, the capture of Fort Capuzzo or the mysterious arrival of Rudolf Hess in Scotland. But the Nine o'Clock News on Saturdays was not as solemn as it was on Sundays. Then Alvar was preceded by the National Anthems of the Allies – all of them, even the ones still squirming under the Nazi jackboot but pluckily resisting – and might be followed by Churchill himself or by J B Priestley, his great Yorkshire under-study, telling us what we were fighting for. Entertainment was all very well but the news was what the wireless was really for and, for six years, I soaked up the truth just as Alvar Liddell told it. It was so compelling that I have never since had to rack my brain about the sequence of events during the Second World War and often even remember, not only what I was told, but also just what I was doing at the time. Thus 1939-1945 is a long series of news-related happenings, like a progression of Kennedy assassinations. I remember, for example, lying on the Study floor, just after 'Music Hall' one Saturday in 1941, poring, as so often, over a map. Alvar Liddell had just said the German warships *Bismarck* and *Prinz Eugen*, in the Denmark Strait, off Greenland, had sunk the *Hood*, our biggest and most unsinkable battleship. Quick, get the atlas. Rummage, rummage, rummage. Crikey! However did they get as far as that? What about the British blockade? What about Coastal Command? Thus again it was seminar time at the open university of war. Or there was that Monday tea-time in the living room at 7 Cross Street. It was hot and we had just come in from the garden and switched on to get the score in the Victory Test Match, a scratch series between England and Australia, laid on after the end of the war in Europe. But instead of the match commentary we found that Alvar Liddell was speaking. He announced a totally new type of bomb, greatly more destructive than anything ever known before. We had just dropped one on a Japanese city that had never been in the news before and it looked as though the war was over. That was the end of Alvar's story. But let me try to retell it from the beginning, just as I remember it, with the news all mixed up with what we doing at the time and what Dad said about it.

When I was seven and a quarter, on Friday 1 September 1939, Germany invaded Poland. It was not a complete surprise for the wind recently had been full of straws. There had been trouble to do with Danzig and the

Corridor. Then Grandpa's friend Herr Ribbentrop had flown to Moscow to see a certain Mr Molotov. Dad was amazed and very excited by that news although I was not sure why. Also the Glossop Territorials in full kit had gone off to camp and a big crowd came to the station to wave them goodbye which seemed a bit excessive if they were only off for a couple of weeks. I went too with Mum and her best friend Mrs Marsland, whose eldest boy John was a Terrier. Then there had been that fantastic day-trip to the Isle of Man with Dad and Grandpa Southport. We went on a big ship and had a slap-up lunch in a posh restaurant on board and through a porthole I was sure I had seen the tail of huge fish diving into the waves. They said I was just imagining it but I wasn't and many years later I discovered I was right and that porpoises are commonly to be seen basking in the Irish Sea. At Douglas we rode on a horse-drawn tram and Dad sent a box of kippers by post to Granny and Grandpa London. The most exciting bit was leaning over the ship's rail coming back into Liverpool in the still evening sunshine and seeing a veritable armada of ships in the Mersey. Dad, no doubt by way of preparing his son for Armageddon, said they were bringing in munitions from America so we would be prepared if we had to fight the Germans again. Which, after the news about Poland, it now seemed we definitely would have to. So would the French because they were our allies and did what we said. But it was OK for them because they had the Maginot Line, which the Germans would never ever be able to cross, and furthermore France was a lot bigger than Britain and less densely populated so it was us that would get the brunt of the bombing. That seemed unfair.

We had just come back from London where Grandpa had taken a big photograph of all the Lords gathered around the bird-table in the garden at 47 Ena Road, Norbury. It is reproduced as *Plate 11 top*. That's me in the middle. Mum is holding Helen and Dad has taken up a position of uncharacteristic modesty behind his sister Adela [left] and Maud. You can tell Leslie is a socialist because he wears an open necked shirt and smokes a pipe but Auntie Marion, smiling through behind Mum and Granny London, conceals her left wing convictions under a chic jacket. Grandpa looks a bit startled because he had left the camera on a time switch before scrambling across to take up his pose next to Barbara. London was where the bombing was mostly going to happen. We had seen people digging trenches on the commons and in the sky there were barrage balloons, which Dad said were no use. We had also inspected an Anderson shelter that was being demonstrated just over the fence you can see in the picture. It looked very cosy to me but again Dad said it would not work. Grandpa meanwhile was sticking sticky paper on their windows and making the dining room gas-proof so Granny, who had blood pressure, need not go to the shelter. Bombing was also expected at Gorton and Openshaw, two inner Manchester suburbs, the child population of which was evacuated to Glossop, a few weeks after our family photo-session and just as the Germans invaded Poland. Gorton and Openshaw were 'slums' so the evacuees were 'alive' and also bed-wetters, and it was a good thing none of them was billeted on us. Considering the size of our house our immunity was surprising. It seemed to be to do with Dad's appointment as Chief Billeting Officer for the Borough of Glossop.

Sunday 3 September was clear and hot and that morning the news was so important that Mr Chamberlain himself took over from Alvar Liddell. At quarter past eleven the Prime Minister spoke to us in the Study. He said our man in Berlin had given Herr Hitler a note, to which the latter had failed to reply and even I could see that that was rude. Consequently he had to tell us that 'this country is at war with Germany'. I departed into the sunlit rose garden and there meditated, in a solemn if child-like way, upon the breaking of nations, half expecting the sky to be darkened that moment by German aircraft. Since the bombers had not arrived by teatime we all resorted to the aforesaid rose garden for an al fresco version of our usual set-to. The tablecloth had daisies in improbable colours embroidered by Mum, following a pattern. It was spread out on the cover of the old well, newly but ineffectually padlocked against the curiosity of 'the Holt boys'. There was conversation with the Hursts over the wall. The dilatoriness of the Luftwaffe was noted as was the excellent weather.

Next day Alvar Liddell said the Germans had sunk the *Athenia*, a passenger liner. Such un-gentlemanly behaviour, at so early a point in hostilities, scarcely boded well for the spirit in which the war was to be fought. The Germans were also found to be cheating through the use of magnetic mines. A cutaway drawing in the *Illustrated London News* [or was it *War Illustrated*?] showed how they worked. It was an ingenious device. You had to admit Jerry was clever. He seemed to be doing pretty well in Poland too, where the defenders' cavalry had no chance against the German tanks. Which was scarcely surprising and why did they even try?

The Poles it seemed were not very clever. Then suddenly the Russians joined in and even Dad was surprised. Next we knew, there was a picture in the paper of men in foreign uniforms confronting each other in what looked like a tram. It was a bit surprising, in view of their old fashioned way of conducting the war, that the Poles even had trams. Anyway they had surrendered and judging by the map in the *Manchester Guardian*, they must have been beaten all ends up, for the country was split down the middle and divided between Germany and Russia. It seemed unfair that the Russians, who only came in towards the end, got as much as the Germans.

In a way it was a relief to get Poland out of the way. It was a long way off and the names were quite hard to say, although 'Warsaw' had a nice sound and the thought of a River Bug was amusing. But it was hard to see how we could join in. You only had to look at the map to see that even the Royal Navy could not get there. Apparently the only way we could help the Poles was with 'leaflets'. We sent planes to drop them on the Germans, explaining why they did not ought to have invaded Poland and please not to do it again. You can imagine what Dad thought about that. Stainless Stephen was also sceptical. And rude too. He said he hoped the Jerries kept the leaflets because they would need them when the proper bombing started. With the German army busy in Poland why did we not just cross the unguarded Rhine and use the Siegfried Line for the purpose suggested in the song? Dad disapproved of that ditty. It was boastful and tempted fate. That however did not stop the Holts and me, at the kitchen table, playing the Siegfried Line game we got from Woolworths. It came with cut-out shirts, socks and bloomers to hang against a backdrop of guns, wire and pillboxes. Anyway, with Poland gone, and the bombers not come, and people stopping carrying their gas masks, and a lot of the evacuees trekking back to Gorton, thank goodness, there was time to take stock. The big question was why it was all so quiet on the Western Front, except for George Formby, Gracie Fields and Maurice Chevalier, all of whom were out there entertaining the troops. Dad did not approve of George because he was gormless and later, on account of their unsatisfactory war records, he withdrew his goodwill also from both Gracie and Maurice. But I worried about Hitler's plans now he had made short work of the Poles. I hoped that, while Gracie was waving good luck to our boys, our generals had stayed back at headquarters doing some map-reading. Had they noticed that the Maginot Line stopped a long way short of the English Channel? Surely the Germans would just march round that end. However it was the BEF, our army, which held the vulnerable bit along the Belgian frontier and Hitler, like me, would have noticed that. Which is probably why he held off. Well ...

If not much was happening in France, hostilities were in most satisfactory progress on the high seas. A sneaky U boat had trespassed into Scapa Flow and sunk the battleship *Royal Oak*. Alvar Liddell had not said much about that but I found out and thought about it quite a lot. It was not really cheating because we had carelessly left the net open, so it was not surprising a brave German commander had taken advantage of our sloppiness. You had to admire Jerry. It was only us and them in the running for top prizes in the war – i.e. crosses, Victoria and Iron. But not to worry, Dad said. Winston was back at the Admiralty and we could count on him. He was right. Towards Christmas three plucky British cruisers cleverly won the Battle of the River Plate, forcing the pocket battleship *Graf Spee* to scuttle herself with a great deal of smoke at Montevideo. Although the score was now one proper battleship against only a pocket one it was the style in which *Ajax*, *Achilles* and *Exeter* had fought that made all the difference. And, despite the decency shown by *Graf Spee's* captain in shooting himself, the Germans had again shown lamentable lapses in sportsmanship. *Graf Spee* had been sinking unarmed British merchant ships whose only offence was to bring cheap Argentine beef to succour the British poor – almost a charitable mission. So good for Winston when, in the New Year, he sent the navy into Norwegian waters where we captured the 'prison ship' *Altmark*, carrying survivors from *Graf Spee's* sinkings. To stave off boredom those incarcerated sea dogs had improvised Ludo sets out of cardboard boxes. That bulldog spirit would win the war.

Why was the *Altmark* in a Norwegian fjord? It was to do with Swedish iron ore, which was essential to a German war machine denied other sources of supply by the British blockade. But why not just ship it straight across the Baltic instead of going via Norway? That was puzzling. My map-reading had by now taken in the Baltic in a big way. That was because of the other compensation for the 'phoney war' in France. The rotten Russians had disgracefully flung their ill-trained hordes against little Finland. But the Finns were modern as well as plucky and they stopped the invaders on the Mannerheim Line, a Santa Claus version of the Maginot, immortalised in one of the Babar the Elephant books. When peace was made in the spring, and I entered the changes in copying pencil on the appropriate page of *Phillips' New School Atlas*, it was clear the Finns had got much better terms than the Poles had had to put up with. Which showed it paid to be modern. It also showed the Russians were not very good at war-making and that was a comfort because they were supposed to be allies of Germany. But were they really? One Saturday afternoon in February, while I was doing some painting at the kitchen table, Winston Churchill, from the Free Trade Hall in Manchester, addressed me and Dad on the extension speaker. He said the intentions of the Soviet Union were a riddle, wrapped in an enigma, contained in a conundrum and Dad was impressed. It was the way he said it. Dad was also much taken by a David Low cartoon in the *Manchester Guardian*. It showed a long train taking war supplies from Russia to Germany but the wagons contained nothing but portraits of Stalin. So maybe Stalin was not really friends with Hitler so I should not worry too much about the poster on the wall at Bradburys, the gents' barbers in the Market Arcade. It charted the military resources of the various powers and you could see the Russians had got many more troops and tanks than either us or the Germans and almost as many ships as us as well. So just suppose they got themselves properly organised ...

The phoney war ended just before the Easter holidays. By that time the snow had gone. On Sheffield Road the drifts in January had reached the bedroom windows. What happened was that the Germans invaded Denmark and Norway. What did I say? There had been something else going on in the Baltic. The Danes had no time to be plucky and that was bad news for the bacon ration. The Norwegians were plucky but it did them no more good than it did the Poles. We were not much help either. We sent troops to Narvik which I supposed was better than nothing but when you looked at the map you could see Narvik was a long way from anywhere much, except the North Pole. So Norway was a bad job and eventually, towards Whitsun, the House of Commons got to know about it and Mr Chamberlain had to go. Good riddance, said Dad, who said he was an 'appeaser,' which was as bad as being a Nazi or a nancy-boy. He did not like Lord Halifax either. Fortunately however Alvar Liddell did not give us Halifax but Winston instead. Oh happy day! That changed everything, said delighted Dad. Trust Churchill and we were bound to win. All criticism was now suspended for the duration. Bad news made no impact. France might fall. The bombers might come. So might the German army. But with Churchill at the helm everything would come right in the end. Dad was besotted, Winston's greatest fan. The more he was offered blood, sweat, toil and tears, the harder he laboured. The more he was invited to fight on the beaches, fields and landing grounds, the more blood-curdling became his opinions. The only good German, he began to say, was a dead German and I believed he meant it. He was not of course alone. Everybody was saying much the same. Unrestrained passion in our cause seemed universal. It was a cause in which fervent national unity was matched in fervent hatred of the enemy. Churchill one Sunday told us it was our finest hour. Although I was now eight – I had got to that age as the Germans marched into Paris – it was not for me to dispute it.

You will be relieved to learn that this ball by ball commentary on the war, as observed by a precocious if illiterate child, will now cease. I was thirteen when it ended and by then my knowledge of the conflict had inevitably lengthened and deepened but I doubt if it had gained much in sophistication. My interpretation remained the product of propaganda – of Alvar Liddell, aided and abetted by Churchill and distorted by Dad. It would have gone something like this. We had challenged and defeated a renewed German bid for world domination, an aspiration that was intolerable because justice and morality required that the world be dominated by Britain, perhaps with the USA as a junior partner. Securing Anglo-Saxon hegemony was known as the 'defence of freedom'. After the disgraceful defection of the French – I was right about that gap beyond the Maginot Line – defending freedom had been a close run thing. But, thanks to Churchill's speeches and 'the Few', the German advance had been checked. After two further years [1941-1942] of defiant vigilance, during which the USA and USSR had belatedly attached themselves to the British cause, General Montgomery's decisive victory at El Alamein had put Germany on a permanent defensive and determined her eventual defeat. After the enemy's economy and morale had been clinically disabled by Bomber Command, the march to victory had been inaugurated on the D Day beaches and had culminated on Luneburg Heath, with the surrender of the German army to Montgomery. In the later stages we were significantly helped by the Yanks who, despite inferior levels of education and culture, and some questionable social behaviour, had made an important material contribution to victory. The Russians had also been of some assistance. American help was appreciated also in the defeat of the barbaric Japanese, who had taken advantage of Britain's defence of freedom in Europe to fall upon our Empire in the east. The war against Japan had been brought to a timely conclusion by the invention of the atomic bomb, a product stemming from the symbiosis of British minds and US dollars.

The full absurdity of that adolescent interpretation, which perhaps does not deviate wildly from some standard British perceptions of 1939-1945, only became clear after decades in which studying the war, and passing on what I found out to students, were to be major preoccupations. Eventually I came to recognise that the contest between Britain and Germany was peripheral to World War Two, the centrepiece of which was the terrible confrontation between Nazi Germany and Soviet Russia, probably the bloodiest episode in human history. Thus I came to be profoundly appalled by the Holocaust and to be additionally stunned to discover that it occurred among other gargantuan, ideologically inspired liquidations of undesirables – like prisoners of war, 'intellectuals', 'partisans', 'class enemies' and tainted ethnic groups – facilitated by the war and perpetrated by both sets of belligerents. Most of that understanding came much later. Very little of it was transmitted by Alvar Liddell. He did not know much about what was happening to the Jews or, if he did, he was not allowed to say. Does that mean I regret sitting for so long at his feet? No. Like the author of the *Young Briton's History Reader* he offered a narrative that, although flawed, being both partial and partisan, was at the same time vigorous and clear and a firm account offers a starting point for revision, and revision is what history people delight in. In fact I have been revising Alvar with immense pleasure ever since that melancholy Monday in 1945 when he told us about Hiroshima and it became clear that story time had come to an end and I must put away childish things.

Chapter 6

RITUAL

It is time to tell you about the Grammar School. At St Luke's we had been subjected to the Three Rs, and I made adequate progress in two of them. At the Grammar School however we exchanged them for a different set of Three Rs. We were governed by Ritual, instructed by Rote and taught to revere Rhyme, by which I mean the glory of English Literature, than which history had known no comparable outpouring of sublimity. On the whole the Grammar School Three Rs were good for me but unfortunately they did not constitute the totality of my grammar school experience. While blossoming under their encouragement I was simultaneously poisoned by other influences, the fall-out from which proved long-lasting. Those tocsins will be addressed in Chapter Nine after the Three Rs have been celebrated.

The Scholarship results came out on 5 June 1942. It was about the time Tobruk fell and the news from the Russian front was soon to be dominated by the name of a city, not previously in the news, called Stalingrad. It was hot and Friday afternoon so Standard IV, the urgency of whose studies had flagged in the months since the Scholarship, set off in crocodile for North Road, where St Luke's enjoyed occasional use of the outfield at Glossop Cricket Club. We sat in the sun and Miss Max went through the motions. Suddenly Mr Fielding appeared, pivoting fast across the grass, looking more than ever like General De Gaulle. He had a piece of paper – the results! He told us that two of the eight County Minors allocated to Glossop schools had been awarded to St Luke's pupils. Pause to allow a swelling of corporate pride. Then he announced the names –

Lillian Webster and Richard Lord. Suddenly I was famous, and with fame came bounty. Jelly was produced and it seemed I was to have a bicycle. Next day, in dazzling summer light, Mum and I went to the parish church at Old Glossop where Miss Lee was getting married. There was applause and even cheering. It was the lovely bride of course they were acclaiming but I let myself toy with a fancy that the real focus of admiration was that infant prodigy Richard Lord. And him not yet quite ten! Congratulations certainly flowed. Even Dad went all unnecessary. See him grinning in *Plate 11 bottom right*. You would have thought that, being in the trade, he would have been more circumspect but perhaps it was relief, not pride, he was feeling. He may have been agonising more than I realised about late reading and careless counting. He would be worrying still if he knew the truth. For, inside, I knew I still could not properly read, not the way Jas and Chris Gillings could. They just scanned a page and it went in. Not so with me. I peered at the print, took it a line at a time and even then found it helpful to let my finger run under the words while, under my breath, I sounded each one, thus reading aloud on the quiet. Yet, for that bold piece of plagiarism about the Wright Brothers and the beginning of manned flight, I had won what seemed like the Nobel Prize for literacy, while Jas had failed the Scholarship and then done so badly at the Grammar School that they made him do the first year all over again. That was inexplicable. Not that I felt any pangs of conscience about my own shady trick. I had not broken any rules. Nor did I conceal what I had done. But nobody believed me. Even Dad preferred not to know.

At this middle point in my schooldays some indication of the state of play between me and Dad may be useful. Six years had elapsed since that great Oedipal explosion prompted by my sister's birth and, at least superficially, Dad and I seem to have made the accommodation Freud predicted. Dad agreed to tutor me in masculinity while I agreed to pretend to be a boy. The war was a big help in that department because a close interest in matters military was 'manly' and that above all seemed to be what Dad wanted me to be. So he and I, as we have seen, endlessly debated the progress of the war and that genuinely brought us together. We walked and talked together, pored over maps together, looked at newspapers together, listened to Alvar Liddell together and watched war films together. That way, one to one, he taught me a lot and not just about the war. He took me to interesting places. He got me to memorise a whole anthology of verses that stayed in my head ever after. He told me stories about famous men to supplement *The Young Briton's History Reader*. All that was very valuable and thanks, Dad. But it came at a price. I had to conform to Dad's idea of an ideal boy. A whole collection of tastes and interests, attitudes and assumptions, values and norms, mores and role models was thrust upon me. Some of them seemed OK but others felt uncomfortable and I lived in constant dread of being discovered in activities that offended against Dad's code of manliness. It was actually not a very coherent code and that was another problem. Identifying its rights and wrongs and goods and bads was not easy. Why, for example, did he ban the *Beano* but approve of the *Hotspur*? Presumably because the latter relied on words more than pictures, which was fine for Chris, who could read, but no use to an illiterate like me. Also wordy comics were manly because they carried school stories and tales of adventure, unlike the picture comics, like *Dandy, Beano* and *Radio Fun*, that I devoured furtively at Bradburys' the barbers. Then why was sticking pins in butterflies and aborting baby birds by blowing their eggs a manly activity, while stamp collecting and train-spotting were not? Keeping rabbits was also manly and patriotic too, so he installed a hutch on the veranda of the summer-house and then told me off for neglecting its furry inmates. Which would have been fair enough if I had wanted those quivering albinos, but I didn't. They won me a prize though. While we were away on holiday they came second in the 'Holidays at Home Week' rabbit show. Playing cricket of course would have been the acme of manliness but since, among the boyhood of Glossop, it was played in the streets or in Manor Park it attracted boys who, if manly, were also rough and thus not suitable companions for the headmaster's son. The alternative of playing with Dad at the stumps he set up in our Paddock was unsatisfactory because my bowling was wildly inaccurate and I had butterfingers. Jas was no more acceptable as a bowling machine because he was all too accurate and had adhesive palms, thus ensuring that Dad's innings would usually be short.

Then there was the abiding topic of what I was going to be when I grew up. My success in the Scholarship sent Dad into over-drive on that one and he eagerly plotted my progress through the great screening plant of life with ever escalating optimism. It seemed I was on the 'Arts Side' which was classier than Science. I was to proceed through successive jigglings and shakings and down various chutes to Oxford, and more specifically to

'Christ Church', the top college. Dad's choice surprised me. With a name like that it must be awash with 'bloody parsons' and perhaps 'nancy-boys' as well. There it seemed I would chum up with 'good fellows', much more suitable than the unspeakable 'Holt boy' or even Chris Gillings, who liked jazz and 'slicked back' his hair. The good fellows and I would 'knock spots off each other'. That sounded perilous but needs must, I supposed. Having 'taken a First' [Dad had one of those but only from Manchester] and won a 'blue' [what, unmanly me!] it would be off to one of the 'inns of court,' perhaps the 'Middle Temple,' before jiggling onto the 'King's Bench' and then shaking down onto the 'Woolsack', which apparently cuddled the bottom of the 'Lord Chancellor', top man in 'the Law'. Nothing was impossible for the holder of a County Minor Scholarship. Well, there was poetry in the names, I had to admit, even though I had little idea what they meant. But did I have to be a lawyer? Now that my favourite Puffin was *Village and Town* by S R Badmin, I would rather be an architect and on the sands at Southport I used to build model new towns, like the ones Badmin promised for after the war, fed by motorways with fly-over junctions constructed from driftwood. Wow! However Dad said architecture was on the Science Side, so it was a non-starter. I did not dare tell him what else was on my career wish list. Sometimes I dreamed of having a small shop, perhaps a newsagent and tobacconist. In an essay written in February 1945, while the RAF pulverised Dresden, I confessed that unworthy urge to Miss Hughes, our English teacher. It is Saturday night, the last customers have departed and my shopkeeper is able to 'refresh himself with a smoke' before he 'lifts out the till drawer, which to his joy is heavy', and having counted his takings, 'hums a tune as he washes himself in the little room at the back of the shop,' before locking up and going home in time to take his wife to the second house at the pictures, knowing that tomorrow, being Sunday, 'he can, if he wishes, do nothing but eat, sleep and smoke'. I call that job satisfaction. I had another ambition too, so unworthy I did not even dare confide it to Miss Hughes. I wanted to be teacher, like Dad, but of course I concealed that deeply shameful inclination. He was not a sadistic father but I guessed his self-control might snap if confronted by such blatant evidence of his son's deficiency in manliness. But maybe I took it all too seriously. Perhaps Dad's plans for me were just idle thoughts. Fantasising about the future was what people did in 1942 to take their minds off the present. 'Post war reconstruction' was, like aircraft recognition, a popular wartime hobby.

Not that Mum entertained post war fantasy. She was too busy with the here and now, in particular with foraging for items of school uniform. Shortages and rationing had caused the Grammar School to relax its erstwhile strict strictures in matters of dress. Even caps were no longer compulsory. But scarcity intensified rather than diminished parental pride and, one way or another, most of us in the 1942 intake arrived decked out in something like the accustomed manner. Mum's greatest triumph was acquisition of a second hand pre-war blazer. You can see it in the 'Scholarship Boy' photograph. It was dazzling. Its stripes alternated narrow lines with broad, and black ones with coloured ones. The vivid greens, yellows, reds and blues indicated the four 'houses' among which, for some arcane purpose, we were to be arbitrarily distributed. The breast pocket bore the crest of Lord Howard of Glossop, founder of the school *[Plate 12 bottom]*. It displayed a rose, a crown and three daggers above the motto 'Virtus, Veritas, Libertas'. Dad explained as well as translated. I do not remember his thoughts on truth and liberty, although he presumably was broadly in favour of both, but he expounded 'Virtus' at great length, defining it as 'all the manly qualities'. Well, he would wouldn't he? So the school, although co-educational, was as keen on manliness as Dad was and, since the uniforms of both sexes were identically emblazoned, it must be good for girls as well as boys.

I insisted on wearing my new school blazer *[Plate 9 bottom]* even on holiday. It was sported, rather suitably, along Blackpool promenade, where it stood out like an island in a sea of air force blue, its wearers distinguished only by shoulder flashes proclaiming 'Poland', 'Canada', 'Norway' and others of the Allied Nations. Mid-war Blackpool was animated and modern as well. The streamlined trams, still pre-war bright in green and cream, flitted across the majestic sunsets we enjoyed from the observation lounge of the Caledonian Hotel, itself so modern that they had both a potato peeling machine and a dishwasher. Low-flying gulls daringly intercepted low-flying Botha trainers, as they skimmed the forest of rusting stakes that continued to protect the Golden Sands from the field-grey hordes, whose arrival was still half expected, even though the bulk of the Wehrmacht, just then approaching the Volga, was massed all of four thousand miles away. The lights were dimmed but everything else sparkled. The Laughter Man roared from his glass case outside the Funhouse at the Pleasure Beach, while long queues snaked towards the adjoining booths of Fat Alice and her well-hung neighbour, Epstein's Adam. At that moment the Jews of Warsaw were also queuing – for the transports to Treblinka. But we knew nothing of that and nor did we let the bad news we did know about spoil the fun. The ungrateful Indians were revolting and the failure of a big raid on Dieppe showed invading France was not going to happen soon despite the popular demand 'Open the Second Front Now', scrawled on many walls that year. The Holt holidays coincided with ours, although they stayed in only a boarding house, not at a 'private hotel' like us, and they were not on the front. Nevertheless we fraternised enjoyably, there being a war on. I think Jas braved the Big Dipper whereas I conquered only the less precipitous Roller Coaster. But then he was older than me. All too soon, as they say, it was back home to retrieve the prize-winning rabbits, engage in 'back to school' rituals and cultivate Virtus.

Lord Howard's purpose in setting up 'Glossop Technical School' – its handsome exterior is celebrated as *Plate 12* – had been to prepare bright kids for good jobs in local factories and offices but in the wake of the 1902 Education Act, which in effect provided a grammar school in every town, it got diverted from a vocational to a liberal academic mission and duly changed its name to 'Glossop Grammar School'. That had already happened by the 1920s when the Howards, bowing to a silent revolution which dispossessed the English landed class, quitted Glossop Hall, leaving its grounds, renamed 'Manor Park', to the townsfolk as a parting gift. Of all that I was of course unaware in 1942 and I am not sure that Dad knew much about it either or felt that it mattered. As far as we were concerned the Grammar School was there in the beginning, was now and ever would be. Amen. We were wrong of course. It went in the 1960s, only five years after Dad himself went. But at least Lord Howard's impressive edifice still stands and thanks to the efforts of local activists has recently been 'listed' as of architectural merit. It is now an adult education centre and no doubt its noble proportions work their magic on its present clients the way, without my realising it, they did on me when I was young. For his lordship's architect did a smashing job, as did the Italian craftsmen who were brought in to embellish the structure. The choice of 'Queen Anne' baroque, combining rationality with theatricality, suited the grammar school ethos. It forms a simple rectangle, constructed throughout of finely dressed stone, with four great gables dominating the corners, like turrets on a castle keep. There are big sash windows, round-headed at first floor level, and an abundance of convoluted ironwork. Its most dramatic external feature is the curving sweep of an entrance staircase leaping a basement area that suggests a moat. There are high gates at the top and bottom of the site – the ones the war salvage people wanted to take away until Dad stopped them – and the stone piers that front the building are linked by heavy railings. Big, boxy iron drainpipes carry the date 1899. Indeed the stately pile much resembles an aristocratic residence. You might call it 'Castle Howard', suitably evoking the baroque. A bog standard comp it is not.

The grandest feature is still to come. Once swept across the entrance bridge you pass through oak doors into the School Hall. But forget the chipboard tattiness of school halls you may remember and behold the palace of Cinderella's prince. It is a cube accommodating lengths of spiralling stairs, tightly coiled. Think of Jack's box with the lid on, or imagine a baroque Roman fountain brought indoors, with streams of descending pupils standing in for flowing water. Not one but two grand staircases project themselves from a balustraded balcony above you. They are of stone with sinewy wooden handrails writhing on their iron supports like fibrous strands of jungle foliage. They turn precipitately, scorning the interruption of landings, and completely reverse direction, before tumbling their users into a 'basin' lined with green marble mosaic, whence smaller flights wind down into the basement and onto the drive. And all day long, across the mosaic and up and down the stairs the teachers and the pupils come and go, their movements transcending mere pedestrian progress. Using these stairs was never simply the means by which you changed levels. It was an event, a celebration – a ritual. It made what we did and what was happening to us important. It stamped schooling with significance. Wow! It all explodes in the memory seventy years later and in 2014 we tried to capture it photographically *[Plate 13]* and I even had the temerity to stand in my father's footsteps.

Not that Dad seemed to notice the grandeur of the Hall. To him it was just one of many pains in the posterior maliciously inflicted on him by 'County', a mean-minded tyrant with which he was in constant contention. The space was not only miserably restricted but the stairs were downright dangerous. You could see what he meant. At the points where they turned on their axes, the steps narrowed to a lethally acute angle. Thus it was decreed that the slower traffic, going up, must use this end of the step, leaving those hurrying down to manoeuvre at the broad end of the wedge. A sensible precaution, you might say. But why not altogether avoid the perils of two way circulation by designating one staircase 'Up' and the other 'Down'? Then upward toilers would no longer have to scale the north face in avoiding the avalanche of descending travellers. Here, as often at GGS, the shadow of sex obscured the light of reason. The indelicacy of a co-educational staircase was unthinkable. What fleeting visions might inflame and at what cost to life and limb? So we had a 'Boys' Staircase' and a 'Girls' Staircase'. This was only one page in a voluminous manual of movement control that Dad compiled, determining how we should route ourselves about the school, the satellite huts and the extra accommodation we made use of in adjacent buildings. He issued complex maps covered in dotted lines and coloured arrows, as *Plate 14* demonstrates. The required pathway varied according to whether the journey was outward or inward and of course according to the gender of the travellers. Single file was de rigeur, even when only two or three were voyaging together. Ike and Monty should have conscripted Dad when they were planning D Day. He would have answered the call with alacrity and without undue surprise.

Although Dad did not realise it, our baroque Hall was perfectly designed for the daily act of solemn ritual that new every morning reminded us, not only that we were a tight-knit community, but that our community was part of something bigger than itself. Although I could bore you with historical analysis, just what that something was still eludes me. At the time of course, although, as we shall see, my father's role in it confused me, I never questioned its necessity, its essential place in our lives. That's ritual. You do it and then you do it again and again and you feel better for it. You don't think about it. Assembly happened because it happened and a good thing too. Without it, going to grammar school would have had less point. Nor did I ever reflect that the architectural character of our place of assembly played a determining part in securing its emotional impact. For, although Dad would have indignantly rejected the thesis, it certainly did. In Dad's eyes, as I say, the Hall was blatantly unfit for purpose. He was wrong. Like the House of Commons the space was just about big enough to contain all those expected to assemble there – but only at a pinch. Which is the point. There is nothing like a pinch for bringing people into intimate communion. Thus every day at 8.45 all four hundred of us infiltrated ourselves among the cascading stairways and just about fitted in. Juniors filled the well of the Hall, the basin of the fountain, boys of course on the left and girls on the right, first years of course at the front and third years at the back. Senior forms thronged the balcony and over-spilled into adjacent classrooms.

I think I hear martial music from Miss Greenwood at the piano – unless it is Friday and Hamilton Harris, peruked maestro, is in attendance. As the music dies our Leader, canonically invested, makes a measured progress from his wolf's lair behind the Hall, mounts his improvised rostrum and, head bowed and hands clasped together across the front of his body, turns to face his expectant followers. The starting stance is exactly that of Hitler at Nuremberg. His asymmetrically positioned post is the third step up the Boys' staircase, just before it commences that spectacular axial pivoting by which it reverses direction. It is a happy choice because the dynamics of the baroque operate, not straight up and down, but in diagonals and ellipses. From a conventional platform a speaker can only hammer his audience but from his chosen spot my father could *skewer* his. An elaborate ritual now unfolds. Most of it, though I knew it not at the time, comes out of the *Book of Common Prayer*, its cadences, to my subsequent joy, thus finding permanent lodgement in my soul. So there are introits, collects and blessings. We begin with a hymn, perhaps No 43 'We build our school on thee O Lord'. Then a reading. Then a collective chanting of the Lord's Prayer, led by the Head Boy. This chief acolyte, assuming an angelic asexuality, takes up his position at the top of the *Girls'* Stairs, at the opposite and higher pole of the elliptical orbit he shares with the High Priest. Thus in the baroque tradition, which embraces contradiction and resolves it, the normal rules governing gender and hierarchy are transcended. Now our senior prefect leads us in prayer by firmly enunciating the first word of each phrase for completion by the congregation:

OUR	*Father*
WHICH	*art in Heaven*
HALLOWED	*be Thy Name.*

At the end there is space for a sermon but if it is Monday, and barring some malefactor having been discovered in gross iniquity, demanding instant public denunciation, it will give place to the ritual incantation of scores in last Saturday's matches. Football: First Eleven 3, Buxton College 1. House Football Under 14s: Flamsteed nil, Nightingale 2. Girls' Hockey: School 5, New Mills 2. It is just like Bolton Wanderers, Hamilton Academicals and all that on the wireless. On other days we attend respectfully to a homily. Cheating in exams is despicable. Culprits should expect exemplary punishment. Certain Fifth Formers in uniform have been detected eating in the street. Such conduct is unbecoming among grammar school pupils and will cease forthwith. The Field Club will meet at 4-15 today in Room 14. John Furniss, Head Boy 1942-1943, then of the RAF, has been killed in a flying accident. He was the brightest of the best. Thus from Monday to Thursday. Friday assembly is grander still. On that day the Lord's Prayer is sung in Hamilton Harris's own metrical version and is sometimes followed by Tallis's 'Te Deum'. Participating in that anthem, as a member of the Senior Choir, brought me as close to submission to whatever it was the school stood for as I ever got.

In brief Dad did Assembly remarkably well. *Yet he didn't mean it.* That he rejected its message with contempt I knew for sure. For at home his blasphemy was incessant, his scathing hostility to 'bloody parsons' was obsessive, and he consistently expressed deep scepticism about the validity of religious belief. He had denied his children Christian baptism and made it clear that any perverse attempt at church-going on their part would have dire consequences. All that confused me more than somewhat, although the hypocrisy of the celebrant did not, at the time, dull the impact of Assembly. Later however I took fervently against the legal obligation of state schools to engage in a 'daily act of worship'. Indeed throughout the thirty years war against the system that constituted my career in education I was the implacable enemy of everything ceremonial. I laboured with puritanical ferocity to liberate students and teachers from the gaudy trappings of corporate solidarity. So I derided assemblies along with speech-makings and prize-givings, cups and trophies, uniforms and badges, caps and gowns, receptions and presentations, parties and entertainments. When eventually the obligation to furnish a 'broadly Christian' act of worship fell upon me personally, I simply ignored it and nobody at 'County' protested, or even seemed to notice. That sad response, or lack of it, is as disconcerting in retrospect as my intemperate arrogance. Looking back I am chastened. Strangely, the urge to denounce a charade has gone away.

For special occasions, when it was necessary for Dad's congregation to be seated and formally drawn up at his feet, the Hall was not big enough, so we decamped to the 'Vic', the town's capacious assembly room, above the public library. Glossop's Victoria Hall had been erected in 1887 to commemorate Queen Victoria's Golden Jubilee. Its lofty eminence rose, conveniently close by, on an island site opposite the Gothic Unitarian Church. Both buildings, in tandem with the handsome Grammar School gave cobbled Talbot Street a graceful ambience. If our precinct was a touch less handsome than what they savoured at Eton, we nevertheless did OK. Not that Dad took that blessing on board either. Dependence on annexes – we used 'Fitzalan Street', the Unitarian Sunday School, as well as the Vic – was another of the crosses imposed upon his aching shoulders through the malice of County. Hence the coloured arrows on his movement control charts *[Plate 14]*. Crocodiles, segregated by gender, direction of travel or both, perpetually circulated in single file between the school and the two annexes, which served a variety of everyday purposes as well as housing special assemblies. Art and music happened there. Those subjects held lowly positions in the curriculum but a lodging of sorts had to be found for them so makeshift provision in the Lecture Room of the Vic and the ante rooms at Fitzalan Street was what they got. Also, in the absence of anything purpose built – yet another of Dad's crosses – the Vic had to make do as our gym. When the welfare state broke out, round about 1942, and schools suddenly had to provide dinners, Dad's overburdened shoulders almost gave way. Luckily he had Fitzalan Street and it became our canteen. Milk was dispensed there as well as midday messes. At 10.20 daily we all filed across four sets of cobbles, in the course of a return journey, to have the insanitary beakers we carried unwashed in our satchels, filled with lukewarm milk from battered aluminium pitchers, by prefects with dirty hands, posted at trestle tables. At dinner-time, two sittings at those wobbly table tops were necessary to accommodate the mass of unfortunates condemned by distance or parental intransigence to gristly mince and tapioca pudding. Thus Fitzalan Street acquired a distinctive smell, in which trace elements of overcooked plain fare, trapped between bare floor boards, combined with dust and spilled milk to produce something lingering and particularly nasty.

The ritual power of the daily and special assemblies was echoed in a series of festivals that punctuated the school year, unfurling according to an annual calendar which varied little from year to year. The cycle began in September with 'Lifeboat Week'. The collecting boxes, hawked from door to door, were actual model lifeboats and that was fun. Dad used to take me on the Saturday afternoon to the big count and I marvelled at the piles of copper, impregnated with silver nuggets, paraded on the lab benches of Room 8. Totals and targets were elaborately recorded and updated on the elevated blackboard, so it felt like the control room at Biggin Hill during the Battle of Britain, as seen in my Puffin Book, with WAAF plotters charting the fate of 'angels' and 'bandits'. When we passed last year's figure pride burst out all over and I was not immune to the warm glow. However the early part of the autumn term was otherwise unadorned. They used to say this was when the real work was done but I did not believe it. What counted was the intense swotting you did just before the exams. Towards the end of October however there was the Half Term Lecture. We broke up at dinner-time on the Friday and then had Monday and Tuesday off. After break on Friday morning we all filed along the imaginary dotted lines, in single file according to our allotted genders, and took our seats at the Vic for a lecture by a visiting academic, usually from Manchester University, which was where Dad went so, apart from Christ Church, it must be the best. Sometimes the discourse was illustrated on the epidiascope, a magic lantern otherwise reserved for sex education and aircraft recognition, so its deployment enhanced the atmosphere of festivity. Do I remember what we were told? More than you might think. One guy was an expert on accents. He listened to posh Miss Wanklin and pinpointed the very Birmingham suburb she came from. Somebody else told us what the Greeks meant by freedom but it went over our heads and he didn't use the epidiascope. A group of early music enthusiasts played the lute and the viola de gamba. But the lecture that most gripped me was delivered by a dazzling doctor of dentistry whose subject was simply 'Skulls'. He brought specimens, ranging from birds and mice to large zoo animals, all gleaming peroxide white. It was this display that launched Jas and me into that craze, already recorded, for boiling up putrefying animal heads in our washhouse.

When we came back from half term the ritual tempo accelerated in advance of a mighty explosion of pomp and circumstance called 'Speech Day', the highest festival in the liturgical year. S Day came in early December and was actually two days, or rather two nights. Because even the Vic could not accommodate the anticipated throng all at once, the Senior School greeted its loyal supporters on one evening while the Juniors welcomed theirs in somewhat lesser state on S Day Plus One. Rehearsals and preparation took up ever increasing swathes of after-school time during November and those of us with a personal stake in the action became psyched up like troops preparing for battle. Even in the middle of the war Speech Day remained a full-dress occasion, with invitations on thick card and a generously printed programme detailing the past year's triumphs. On the day itself we hardly knew each other. Teachers came in gowns with splashy hoods, girls sported coloured house sashes, and we all turned up well-scrubbed, and slippered in freshly blancoed pumps. After an exacting inspection in our own classrooms, at 7.20 exactly, we were marshalled by prefects through the black-out along the accustomed arrowed pathways to take our places at the Vic, girls on the left with boys on the right, lower forms to the fore with the sixth form at the rear, immediately in front of the 'Reserved Row', a sternly unyielding bench allotted to second class VIPs, like staff wives. Teachers below platform rank arranged their academicals on chairs flanking their own classes. Behind us a packed flush of parental pride is already mustered, for late comers know not to expect mercy. In front of us, on a still empty platform, two rows of labelled chairs, front rank armed, rear rank unsupported, lie behind a table piled high with books and scrolls. On the dot of 7.30 a door opens stage left, and a stately figure mounts a short flight of steps to extinguish the already subsiding hubbub. It is our own Mr Holt, but he is unfamiliar tonight, in a good grey suit, the remnants of a ginger mane oiled and combed to maximum effect and his gown embellished with an inverted cone of turquoise silk, rusted with age [MSc Liverpool]. He gives a curt command. 'School stand!' As we obey, the Platform Party files up the steps and arranges itself as appointed. There is the Chairman, his gubernatorial colleagues, the chained Mayor and his bedecked Mayoress, the attentive Headmaster and the suave Visiting Speaker, the Second Master and his Senior Mistress, the Head Boy and his Head Girl. My Mum is there too, in a hat and a flowered frock. It is not altogether clear why she is there but it suits her. Her smile outshines the fixed grins of the public people.

You see, even now, I cannot describe the scene without sending it up. Yet it all made perfectly good sense. Formality and schooling are inseparable. You cannot have a formal occasion without rules and protocol, including, I suppose, orders of precedence. And formality will be expressed in dress, and dress is an effective way to express things. Nor is it a bad thing to insist that young people on parade are properly turned out. Also the black-out *was* perilous so you couldn't responsibly let a horde of kids swarm unsupervised through the unlit streets between the school and the venue. So why the irresistible drift into satire? Because I belong to that bubble-pricking, myth-exploding generation that took the establishment apart in the sixties and has ever afterwards claimed a licence to mock. My own satire on speech day was less savage than Lindsay Anderson's in *If*, but it anticipated his by some twenty years. In 1947 for the Senior Party – yes, another dread item on the liturgical calendar – I wrote the script for a speech day skit. The idea hit me in bed one Saturday night and the gags kept coming long into the small hours. It was the first time I ever wrote anything untutored, unsponsored and on my own initiative and it was gloriously exciting. The flow of words and wit was unstoppable, as curiously was the outflow of my bladder, so that unaccustomed nocturnal trips to the bathroom not surprisingly brought my father onto the landing. Was I all right? I sure was. Never better! I did not reveal the plan but he took it, as they say, in good part when, a few days later, I borrowed his gown, stuck on a false moustache and delivered a 'Headmaster's Report.' They liked it a lot. They said it captured the style of the original with uncanny precision. Which is scarcely surprising. I had after all lived with the Gauleiter through all of my fifteen years.

There were two parts to the programme and speeches did indeed dominate Part One. After 'Lift up your hearts/We lift them Lord to thee' – that the supreme being addressed in the school hymn was an entity even higher than Dad was never made entirely clear – the Chairman delivered his 'Remarks'. They were inaudible but mercifully brief. Then Dad presented his 'Report.' I always enjoyed it. He went back over the past year like they did on the wireless on New Year's Eve, explaining how well we had done despite the ongoing emergency and the failure of County to render due assistance. It was good because thoroughly prepared. For weeks

I had watched him scribbling and rubbing out in his chair in the Study and then going upstairs to practice his delivery in front of the wardrobe mirror. But as for the visiting speakers, I can't remember who they were, let alone what they actually said, except that one, an old boy, came wrapped in bright red doctoral robes and urged us to make good like he had done. Then the Speaker, or perhaps it was the Mayoress, distributed the prizes and certificates. Those to be honoured had already been siphoned off onto a special row where we sat in the order in which we would be called. You shuffled along until it was your turn and then stepped out perkily and, to dutiful applause, went up the left hand stairs, crossed the stage, took the outstretched paw in one hand and your reward in the other, and went down the right hand stairs. A bit of an ordeal but worth it and not just for the book. I once got *The Observer's Book of British Birds* with a congratulatory label stuck inside *[Plate 12 bottom right]*, done in coloured inks in artistic writing. It was a useful manual and, it must be admitted, a source of pride. I used to flash it at Jas, who of course never won prizes. He was admirably unimpressed. Even people who left last summer came back to collect their school certificates. The girls in this group were objects of Dad's special scrutiny and every year, to his gratifying indignation, some 'Jezebel' came 'dressed to kill' and turned the platform into a cat walk. Most however, for one last time, put on the uniforms they had laid aside, and even donned ankle socks and white pumps.

At the interval the platform was cleared and for Part Two it was over to us, the town's young elite, parading the high culture the school had stuffed into us. There I go again and it is not fair. Sure on Speech Day, before a largely uninitiated audience, we dished out snippets of what Matthew Arnold – who arguably moulded the grammar school the way his father transformed the public school – called 'the best that is known and thought in the world'. But we ourselves were not uninitiated. The verses and dramatic excerpts we offered arose naturally out of the daily immersion in great literature that, as we shall soon see, occupied a great deal of our classroom energies. We were not just showing off but trying to communicate some things we really had come to value. The music master came only one morning a week so somebody else – I cannot remember who – must, out of school hours, have trained the choirs, whose robust performances filled the Vic on Speech Day. But whoever it was did it well and the performers genuinely relished what they did. We obliged with hymns and anthems, lullabies and barcarolles, operatic choruses and musical comedy favourites, folk songs and madrigals. Nymphs and shepherds were called away, Greensleeves provided every satisfaction, fetishists of smoothing irons and wooden clogs were gratified and a mountain maiden's dawn complaint was overheard. Furthermore we resolved to rejoice in our fleeting youth, lamented the departed brave, made an uncompromising commitment to our country and sought to rebuild a middle eastern city on a green site somewhere in England. Our finest feelings however were reserved for 'Creations Hymn' by Beethoven. Although unfortunately an enemy alien, he was long dead so he qualified as a good German.

But naturally it was the literary part of the programme that took precedence. Dad as we know had his reservations about music. Again much of it was done in unison. Collected treble voices piped Border ballads and the massed basses of the Science Sixth, a virtual girl free zone, came on strong with imperialist favourites like Kipling's 'Boots' and 'The Congo', by Nicholas Vachel Lindsay, a piece that sprang into life with racist expectoration and would probably be banned today. The Authorised Version, always so-called, was also in good standing – as literature of course, not for its superstitious message. David's Lament over Jonathon was also accessible to the Science Sixth. Then of course there was Shakespeare, top in literature just as Beethoven came first in music. The austere conditions – no costumes, make-up, lighting, scenery or props – favoured solos or duets, like Beatrice and Benedict or Oberon and Titania, rather than densely populated scenes. The quarrel between Brutus and Cassius was frequently re-enacted, on one occasion by me and Douglas Swallow. That must have been embarrassing for neither of us suited either of those manly parts and could scarcely between us summon an ounce of 'virtus'. My casting as Polonius, giving fatherly advice, seems similarly improbable but still they sent me on. Or rather he did, for this of course was Dad, still forcing his son into ill-fitting garments. Another year my command performance was Tennyson's poem about Ulysses contemplating early retirement and that role maybe came closer to the real me. This time I had 'chosen' the piece – would you rather be hanged or shot? – against something swashbuckling and Shakespearean. Other alternatives to Beethoven's literary opposite number included Dickens and Sheridan. The Turner twins did well as Sam Weller and his father. But why Sheridan? It worked though. Pam Butterworth and Geoff Darwent were convincing as Lord Peter and Lady Teazle, perhaps because they were an item in real life. And why Molière, another staple? Probably because, despite the disgrace of Vichy, French culture then retained a cachet it has now lost. Grammar schools, a genus established [1902] simultaneously with the Entente Cordiale [1904], felt obliged to promote it.

Perhaps I have singled out Speech Day as the climax of the annual programme because I sometimes got star billing something I never knew on the sports field, an arena from which I was permanently excluded, having been infallibly diagnosed as an uncoordinated wimp. But if urging the flying ball was your thing then opportunities for glory were plentiful at GGS, even in wartime, and they were ritually celebrated. What you did for the school on a Saturday afternoon, in the mud of winter, or in a breathless summer hush as shadows lengthened across the cricket field, was generously applauded and ceremonially commemorated. I wish that joy had sometimes been mine. But let us continue through the liturgical calendar. Christmas followed close on Speech Day but for a clumsy clot it was not a happy time. School parties were not for fun but were ritual exercises in correct social behaviour. 'All boys dancing!' my father once proudly recorded in his diary, on the morrow of a festive gathering. All but one actually. I was confused as well as inept. Except at Christmas the school seemed to disapprove of sexual attraction and erected formidable defences against its imperatives, like the segregated staircases and having boys and girls sit separately in class. Douglas Swallow's father said sex was only for after the School Certificate and the Swallow line roughly seemed to coincide with the school's policy. Except on this one night of abandon when the barriers were flung down. Just because it was Christmas you were required to work your way through a whole harem of provocatively clad girls, engaging each one in public copulatory gyrations, elaborately choreographed. I just could not do it. It paralysed my head as well as my feet. So I just sat miserably on the edges of the ritual debauch defying parental glares – Mum, a keen dancer, was always there as well as Dad – and regardless of the court martial I knew I would face when we got home.

Things looked up in January when it usually snowed and football was quite often cancelled. February however was the season of the 'Sixes', a mammoth six a side football tournament, from which exemption was all but impossible. I knew that from witnessing the agony of Douglas Swallow, who once boldly withheld his name from the entry forms posted outside one of the huts. Dad, inflamed by a glaring gap in the lists, dropped suddenly like a hawk into III Upper's Latin class, wearing his gown and perhaps his cap as well, for he used both those appurtenances as weapons against subversion. He hovered over Doug's desk, sizing up the affront to 'virtus' cowering beneath him. There was an entry fee of three pence, so Doug, clutching at a straw, pleaded poverty. Dad disdained to dispute this excuse, which he knew to be preposterous since Doug's father was a manager at Waterside Mills and no doubt enjoyed an inflated wartime salary. Instead he flung down a three-penny bit, added the vile boy's name to the list and duly retrieved the coin as entrance money. The game would be played. School spirit would be upheld. Dad was a master of classroom theatre who could work wonders for a Shakespeare text as well as demolish delinquents. So there was no way out of the Sixes and my best hope was that our team would lose in the first round. But one year the other five in Trevor Hewitt's six were so good they could safely hide me in the goal, where I suffered repeated icy sessions with fingers crossed lest the others carelessly let the ball trespass into the goal mouth. It hardly ever did.

Towards the end of the spring term came the house cross country runs. For the Seniors it meant a stiff five miles, up the Snake and back round Mossy Lea and I would have enjoyed it if I had known I was OK at running. But I only discovered that when it was too late to enter – I was forty seven when I took up jogging – so, since it was for some reason easier to evade the Cross Country than the Sixes, I chickened out. I enjoyed the spectacle though. Lessons finished early and everyone gathered around the great iron gates of the school which, marked the finishing line. The School Magazine also came out just before Easter and we were all compelled to make a voluntary purchase. It was a sort of printed version of Speech Day, part official record and part anthology of pupil contributions, massaged by Dad, the editor in chief. Eventually some of my stuff appeared. I wrote for example a piece called 'From a Window in the Huts' about daydreaming and looking outwards from Room 15. It was nice seeing my name in print but I was embarrassed by the editorial 'improvements' – literary quotations and Latin tags – added to my contributions by Dad. Although it had been in suspension during the war the annual school play reappeared in the calendar afterwards and it too happened just before we broke up for Easter. It was usually Shakespeare and that did not strike us as specially challenging because we all did one of his plays in class every term and were used to proclaiming blank verse, and enjoying it even though we did not always understand it. So although most of the cast were not sixth form Eng Lit specialists, and some were no older than fourteen, we revelled in doing the play. Rehearsals began in January and built up to a three night stand at the Vic, or some other outside venue, at the end of term. Hamming Shylock – dropping my knife so it quivered in the floorboards – in front of an awestruck audience in the galleried intimacy of Littlemoor Sunday School is a precious memory.

The summer term came without frills until after the exams which, as we shall see, were themselves conducted with considerable pomp. But in July, with the School Cert out of the way, the year ended with a feast of festivity at the centre of which was the Annual Inter-House Sports Day. The Lord Street field was kitted out with ropes, painted lines and seating for a considerable crowd. Shifting quantities of rigid classroom chairs, in single file of course, over to that somewhat distant arena was a menial chore rightly imposed upon wimps like me who failed to qualify as competitors. We feeble rejects were then cast as cheering spectators as more manly contemporaries engaged in an afternoon of muscular endeavour lubricated by house spirit. At the end, we all formed a hollow square to witness the distribution of trophies and to salute the 'Victor and Victrix Ludorum', the fastest boy and fleetest girl. I shaped a bit better at the Swimming Sports held at Woods Baths the Monday after Sports Day. I won nothing but did enjoy the privileged status of competitor, being part of the Flamsteed team for the Junior four by one length breast stroke relay. Flamsteed was a seventeenth century astronomer who happened to have been born in Derbyshire before making good in London. He was one of four notables of our county who gave their names to our houses. Nightingale was of course the Lady with the Lamp. Howard was presumably the local aristocrat who founded the school but who Spencer was nobody seemed to know and only I cared. Not that I thought the house system, then or at any subsequent point in my iconoclastic career, anything but a hollow sham uncritically promoting snooty values. For example the children of militant miners I later taught at a grammar school in south Yorkshire were dragooned into houses named after the coal owners their fathers ritually denounced. Any new found softness towards the ceremonial aspect of schooling discovered during the compiling of this memoir stops short at the absurdity of the house system. I am with Fletch, the self-styled 'recidivist' in *Porridge*, the TV prison comedy. When urged to go out and shout for A Wing against B Wing he asks why. 'Because it's your wing, Fletch.' Ronnie Barker's response is a look, more eloquent than many words. Me too. Not the others though. My contemporaries lapped it up and house competition was pervasive. There was an endless round of house matches. Houses ran and swam against each other, played each other at chess and competed against each other in prose and verse speaking contests. House points were even awarded for 'School Work' to identify the collective brain of the year. There were house parties [more dancing!] and house outings [Yippee!] to caves and circuses. Each house had its captain and supporting officers and these appointments – their holders were chosen by teachers not elected by peers – were recorded in the School Magazine and remorselessly trotted out in CVs. The sinecures granted to officers of clubs and societies like the Field Club [we hunted bugs, not foxes], the Stamp Club and the upmarket Literary and Debating Society were similarly recorded for posterity and used in evidence.

And so, in time for Glossop Wakes [the annual week-long closure of the mills], the school year came full circle and the joyful strains of 'Lord dismiss us with thy blessing' might be heard by passers-by in Talbot Street. But not before a final great ritual gathering. Constantly our achievements, or lack of them, in class-work and homework, were registered in the teachers' mark books, and three times a year were totted up and combined with the findings of formal examinations at Christmas and Midsummer or of briefer 'class tests' taken at Easter. From these computations a grand order of merit emerged which was solemnly promulgated at a special assembly on the last afternoon of term, held not in the baroque jewel case but in the baronial amplitude of the Gothic Victoria Hall. After, in our own classrooms, receiving our reports in sealed envelopes for delivery to our parents, we proceeded by the designated routes across the cobbles to the Vic and arranged ourselves, as always by age and gender, to confront the Gauleiter in Majesty. Today he was not, as on the same platform at Speech Day, attended by courtiers in sumptuous attire, but up there in splendid black-gowned isolation. He carried a sheaf of papers – the lists. As silence intensified he commenced a slow and long-sustained incantation. Every pupil in every form was solemnly categorised as 'A', 'B' or 'C'. Furthermore the top, second and third in each form were creamed off from mere run of the mill 'As'. The reading seemed endless, proceeding class by class and in order of seniority, with 'A' forms taking precedence always over 'B' forms, right through from the first year to the fifth, except that at Midsummer verdicts upon the fifth formers had been delegated to the School Certificate examiners and would be revealed only late in the holidays. The occasion was invested with awesome authority. It was a day of judgement.

Attached to the judgements were prophecies, self-fulfilling ones. Indeed at the end of the first year, after three terms of jiggling and shaking, a prophecy was made that marked many for life. For the chute down which you were now dispatched had a determining effect at least as powerful as the great screening associated with the Scholarship itself. This moment of truth for my year at Glossop Grammar School came rather suitably at the turning point of the Second World War, as in July 1943 the Red Army won the Battle of Kursk and with it a strategic initiative the Wehrmacht was helpless to reverse. Until now IIA and II Alpha – confusingly and inexplicably, the first year at GGS was called the Second Form – had been separated only by age. Next year however we were to be divided on merit and 'A' Form sheep would graze in strict segregation from 'B' Form goats. To be told you were a 'B' was bad news. It not only meant your future programme of studies would be different – only 'A' forms for example were thought fit to cope with Latin – but, worse, an adverse judgement, from which there was no appeal, had been passed on your intellectual capacity. You had been found wanting. You had proved too thick to pass through even the biggest holes in the jiggling plate. You were officially inferior. In due course you should expect employment only in humbler occupations. And good riddance really, for your heavy pedestrian presence would hold back your sleeker and faster contemporaries. Henceforth nothing much was expected of you. It was your turn to sit at the back and do basketwork because 'B' kids knew they were not much good and so did their teachers, so both sides lowered their sights and failure was expected. Only relative failure of course. This was after all a grammar school so you would be nudged towards an inferior School Certificate, almost certainly unadorned with 'distinctions' and maybe devoid even of

162

'credits'. At 16 you might hope to become a typist or a lab tech but forget the sixth form and tell your parents to wean themselves from pipe dreams about university. There would never be a doctor in your house. That was the stark truth. The exam results revealed it and you couldn't argue with results. Sure, the odd cussed 'B' former, like my friends Jas and Chris, occasionally did fight back and make good but contrary evidence seldom has much impact on received opinion. At the time it didn't much grab me either but I look back in indignation. At least half my contemporaries were found wanting on flimsier evidence than that of the carefully designed tests which, the previous year, had revealed them as suitable for an academic type of education. For compared with the Scholarship, the end of first year selection was crudely based. It relied, not on material scientifically designed to identify high intelligence, but on mere quizzes and drill tests. Factual recall was all. Reason and imagination played little part. If you had kept neat notebooks, or simply legible ones, and dutifully done your swotting, you did well. If not ... well, thank you and goodbye. Which was silly. Idleness can be rectified. The effects of rejection are harder to repair.

In 1943 the axe fell more cruelly than usual for, the exigencies of war notwithstanding, Dad had achieved a famous victory over County. He had won a new hut, containing two extra classrooms. It now squatted on a patch of playground between the Boys' Gate and St Luke's. To me it was a source of wonder, for it was constructed, like the penguin pool in my Puffin Book, from concrete, a glamorous material, redolent of modernity, that made even brick look old fashioned. Furthermore the 'composition' floors were not laboriously laid by carpenters but poured hot into their allotted spaces just like the toffee mixture Mum poured onto a baking tray to cool and set. They called it 'pre-fabricated' and, to an eleven year old modernist like me, that was a mind-exploding concept. Dad's triumph at Derby [home of County] however was bad luck for the likes of Chris Gillings for it allowed our cunning leader to divide our 'grossly congested' year group – the war had brought an upward leap in grammar school recruitment – into three forms instead of two. He did it by creaming off a 'Three Upper' which, when we came back from the holidays, would accommodate the elite of our intake leaving behind a skimmed mass, whose undistinguished attainments were not to be further discriminated amongst. Thus IIIA and III Alpha would be equal but inferior and two thirds would have been rejected after the first year exams instead of the usual half. About fifteen percent of the 1942 cohort of Glossop children moving into secondary schooling had been identified as suitable for the Grammar School but now only five percent survived to enjoy its full benefits. Not that we of the famous five percent, the pampered beneficiaries of selection, despite our manifest intellectual pre-eminence, questioned that judgement. We wouldn't would we? So when, a year later, continuing 'congestion' caused three forms to be merged once again into only two and a few survivors of the 1943 shipwreck were drafted into the conventional IVA, we felt a certain affront. They would not stand the pace and we would be held back. They did though and we were not. Which made you think. So did another development that came in the wake of R A Butler's 1944 Education Act. Certain thirteen year olds who had failed the Scholarship and were languishing at West End, now curiously designated a 'secondary modern' school, despite being built of stone not concrete, were allowed to come across to the Grammar School as 'late transfers'. Dad of course was apoplectic. He thumped the tea table and added 'bloody Butler' to his demonology alongside 'bloody parsons'. These officially diagnosed inadequates would never cope with the intellectual challenge of the School Certificate. They did though and, to be fair, Dad took the point. He did his sums and discovered that they tended to out-perform indigenous 'B' formers. Which made me do some more thinking, this time about self-fulfilling prophecies, although of course that is not what I called them. These West End kids had enjoyed belated success despite previous failure. Perhaps success was the key. Nothing succeeds like it.

But back to the Vic and the mark reading at the end of the summer term. Once it was over we could relax and anticipate six weeks of freedom. Even those who had received bad news need not think too much about it until after the holidays. So the next item on the agenda induced a special felicity. When, many years on, I have sometimes encountered GGS contemporaries it often figures in reminiscence. Those were the days and certain well remembered words in particular still bring a catch to the throat. What we recall with gratitude is a selection from the writings of St Paul which my father had, I think, personally compiled for use as a valediction at end of term assemblies. Snatches reverberate

Whatsoever things are true, whatsoever things are honest, whatsoever things are just, whatsoever things are pure, whatsoever things are lovely, whatsoever things are of good report; if there be any virtue, if there be any praise, think on these things. [Philippians 4:8]

It was so well done. What a surprising man my father was. So Lord dismiss us.

Chapter 7

ROTE

School life then revolved around rituals, a daily and annual pattern of formal corporate activity designed to make us feel part of something worthwhile. On the whole that objective was achieved. When I grew up and became a teacher myself I used to despise the rituals of schooling but probably I was wrong. We need routines to live by and also myths to give meaning to the routines. I was wrong also about the bread and butter part of school life – what went on day by day and term by term in the classrooms. Basically, we were told things and then we wrote down what we had been told and then we were tested to ensure that we had got hold of what we had been told. It was rote learning. We were *drilled* into academic proficiency. During most of my working life, although actually I often used to teach by rote and my students seemed to like it, I felt there must be a better way of doing it. But maybe there isn't. Rote learning works. Such anyway is the conclusion I draw from remembering how it was at the Gauleiter's academy.

Our teachers certainly felt no urge to apologise for the drills they put us through. 'We call it the mallet process', Mr Holt was fond of saying, and bang it in he did, all day and every day, with rapid staccato blows. Yet we didn't mind for he did it with style and gusto and leavened it with humour. He was probably our best classroom artiste. Again and again we fell about at the drop of a well-loved catchphrase:

You've made a Mrs Arabella Bloomer of it, Mister. Do you know who Mrs Arabella Bloomer was? She was an American lady. She invented an article of female clothing.

Mrs Bloomer was only one of an international cast of celebrities whose shades Sammy conjured for our delectation. Another was the seventeenth century founder of Cartesian theory, one 'Ray Nay Day Cart'. 'He was a Frenchman' he would add, by way of identifying the accent and perhaps introducing a note of incredulity that a nation well known for frivolity could nurture mathematical genius. He loved being the institution he knew he was.

You're not as good at Mathematics as your mother, Miss. She used to shape very well in my class. 'Muriel' wasn't it?

Pause for gale of laughter and/or stylised groaning. Thus the mallet process was relieved by the ritual drolleries of a proud and close knit community.

Unlike our baroque Hall, the classrooms and laboratories in which we submitted to the mallet process, lacked architectural distinction and even distinction one from another, except that some lay in the main building while others belonged to a hutted encampment erected after the 1914-18 war, on a piece of ground originally known as the 'Tennis Lawn'. The huts were a temporary expedient the termination of which, particularly now there was another war on, was not to be expected in the foreseeable future. Anyway what was wrong with them? They were rough but they were ready and there was a consensus that classrooms should be functional not decorative. Lessons were an exchange of words that ought not to be impeded by fancy architecture or, for that matter by images of any kind, other than what was fleetingly exhibited on the blackboard. In that Protestant ethic even art treasures were suspect and our exposure to such decadence was limited to a few hoary reproductions, faded almost to extinction and hanging in corridors, lopsided and disregarded, in thick black frames – the 'Laughing Cavalier', a Degas dancing girl and the inscrutable Mona Lisa. Nor, it was supposed, should our thoughts be lured away from the teacher's discourse by what we could see through the windows. Except in the huts, they were so high you only see sky, clouds and weather, which of course, in combination with the flaws in the glass, sometimes engendered a beauty that was irresistibly distracting. On the dungeon floors of our penitential classrooms a shrubbery of wooden desks and chairs sprouted from a soil of matt brown parquet [main building] or bare grey boards [huts]. The desks came in many varieties but shared common features – a tip-up top, sometimes padlocked to secure the personal belongings of the current tenant, a groove for pens and pencils, and a brass-covered inkwell, typically blocked with blotting-paper pellets. The ink supply being thus rendered uncertain, most of us carried a personal bottle of Quink and breakages were common. The chairs too varied in style but not in discomfort, so the audiences teachers addressed from their elevated lecterns, if captive, were never static. For five hours every day we wriggled and squirmed as we listened, chanted and scribbled.

That is mostly what we did also in the labs, except that there you shuffled your bottom on a high stool instead of a low chair. There, despite rigid insistence on aprons, home-made from off-the-ration blackout material, our protective clothing seldom served its intended purpose, because we were hardly ever allowed to remove a glass stopper, light a Bunsen burner or even turn on a tap. I suppose there was a war on. So although in our notebooks we had to write, 'we took a test-tube', it was not true. *He* took the test-tube, not us. Occasionally too he would make something turn blue or even burst into flame, but not often. Usually we just took down dictated notes or copied a diagram from the blackboard. It was good however to go to the Physics lab, the one room in the school that departed from the bare walls, high minds consensus. Although practical activity in Physics was as rare as it was in Biology and Chemistry, its genial proprietor, 'Waff' Hall – short for 'Waffle' *[Plate 14 second right]* – defied the unspoken ban on graven images. He covered the walls in charts and stacked the surfaces with assorted curiosities, including a miniscule aircraft carrier he had constructed himself, which came complete with little planes and decks that actually rose and fell. Exotic assemblages of apparatus, incorporating balloons, tin cans and a gramophone horn, lay beside an alarming collection of military hardware harvested by donors to Waff's museum from moorland plane crashes and the detritus left by paratroops who trained on our uplands before departing for 'Market Garden', Montgomery's ill-fated plan to seize a bridge too far, at Arnhem. 'Waff' of course indicated a readily activated predilection for digression. It might be a funny story to explain difficult distinctions, like that between mass and density. Or it might be a piece of local lore, like the saga of the Symondley Coal Mine Murder or a eulogy of Ginger Lee, the only true begetter of our huts. 'If you don't believe me, look outside Room

15'. We did and found a corroded plaque with the faint inscription 'Ginger Lee 1919.' That enterprising speculator, in the spirit of swords into ploughshares, must have converted soldiers' billets into children's classrooms. I liked the huts because you could look out of the windows and hence my school magazine article aforesaid. From Room 15 you could just about see the station and even do a bit of train spotting in a French lesson. But to Dad of course they were anathema, perhaps the heaviest of the crosses he was called upon by County to bear.

Room 14 was the twin of Room 15. It was in the same hut but lacked the panorama. In 1942-1943 it was the base of II Alpha, the class in which I was placed, and it was here, on our first day, that we met Miss Rhodes, who was to be our 'form mistress'. In a brief preliminary session before lessons started, she arranged us at desks, girls on the left, boys on the right, allocated pegs in the lobby, and gave us our timetable. We had not had one of those at St Luke's, where we almost always did the same things at the same times in the same place with the same teacher. Now it appeared we would be visited by different teachers for different subjects, and for some lessons we would ourselves travel, always in single file of course, to different classrooms. That meant we would only spend five 'periods' a week with Miss Rhodes because she was a French specialist and was thereby debarred from confusing us in Maths or English, for enlightenment in which fields we would be dependent upon, respectively, Mr Brown and Miss Norris. Miss Norris was bad news. Even new kids knew she was ratty so woe betide us in English. The week was divided into thirty five periods of forty or forty five minutes, four in the morning, two before break and two after, and three without interruption in the afternoon, during which more somnolent part of the day periods were made five minutes longer. Some subjects were obviously more important than others because they got more periods. English and Maths came equal top with six each. French and Science must matter quite a lot too because they got five apiece. Games/PT got three periods but Music and RI must be rubbish because they each got only one. That left two periods each for History, Geography, Art, Domestic Science [Girls] and Handicraft [Boys]. The latter should have been Woodwork but Mr Bell, who taught carpentry as well as art, was away bridge-building on the River Kwai. Also a Rolls Royce aero-engine, used by the ATC, occupied much of the floor space in the Woodwork Room. So instead we did cardboardwork with the temporary Mr Gooch, as we shall see. Some subjects were subdivided. Maths broke down into Arithmetic, Algebra and Geometry. I was bored by Arithmetic, mystified by Algebra but got to like Geometry a lot, once we got shut of Mr Brown who did nothing but make us draw triangles and circles with painstaking accuracy using 4H pencils kept rapier sharp. Painstaking I was not. Similarly Miss Norris did both English Language and English Literature. The latter to start with was not even English for we did the Greek myths I knew very well already, so I found Miss Norris, who never seemed quite well and often wore a muffler, boring as well as ratty. It was all a bit puzzling. Dividing knowledge into subjects and allowing children to make assumptions about their relative importance, although probably inevitable, invites misconceptions and crude judgements.

What did we actually do under the various subject names? It was no wonder our school was called 'grammar' because we engaged in that sobering activity for a very large part of every week. We got a load of it in Latin, as well as French, and Eng Lang was mostly grammar as well. We were forever doing declensions and conjugations, tenses and moods, cases and genders. And we learnt never to start a sentence with a conjunction or to use a preposition to end it with. We mastered the departures from regularity of certain Latin verbs and nouns and some French constructions as well, and discovered that irregularity was the hallmark of English, a robust language that disdained slavish orthodoxy. We also did a lot of translating. There was Latin into English, French into English and also 'proses' which were truly hard and involved converting an English text into compositions in those alien languages – enemy alien, I used to reflect, Latin being the ancestral tongue of Mussolini and French being what they spoke at vile Vichy. We translated in English as well, converting vulgar speech into 'Standard English'. But English as taught at the Gauleiter's academy is too big a topic to be dealt with along with bread and butter subjects like Maths or Chemistry. It was regarded more as a religion than as just a subject on the timetable. So it will be given the special treatment it warrants in the next chapter.

The soap opera of the Dupont family offered a little variation from grammatical grind in French but Latin was just grammar piled on grammar and thus particularly distasteful to me. The only pleasure I ever found in it was the chanting of war cries. Sometimes at break a band of 'A' formers [only 'A' forms did Latin] stomped around between the huts ferociously declining and conjugating in unison. It was blood curdling.

Is! Ea! Id!
Eum! Eam! Id!

Eius!!
Ei!!

Eo!!! Ea!!! Eo!!!

It mystified bull-headed 'B' formers, who normally enjoyed a certain muscular ascendancy in the playground. I was not however deceived by 'Latin Cricket', an end of term diversion invented by Miss Newton, our white-haired classicist and Senior Mistress, whom even Dad deferred to, perhaps because she looked a bit like an ungainly version of Granny Southport. Her unfortunate nickname was 'Bummy'. It was the way she walked. Latin Cricket was about as successful a gambit for turning pain into pleasure as my mother's identification of rice pudding with ice cream. In truth I found Latin very hard and infinitely boring and resented the unremitting toil its service imposed upon me.

French was not much better and I thought the way it was taught was stupid. It made no sense to start a new language with boring old grammar. The thing to do was to *use* French, not analyse it. I thought of driving as an analogy. Dad knew absolutely nothing about how a car works. He hardly knew how to open the bonnet let alone fix anything underneath it. Yet he frequently got us to Southport and back without much incident. Was not language learning something like that? When, at the maternal knee, you are learning your mother tongue, that lady does not say, 'Now dear, tomorrow you will be two, so we are going to start the pluperfect.' You got to be fluent by using a language not by learning its grammar. Instead of getting bogged down in possessive pronouns and past participles, we should just learn a multitude of French words, perhaps by looking at lots and lots of pictures, showing real life situations, with objects labelled in French and phonetic help to say the words right. Then it would be easy to puzzle out a piece of French writing and get the hang of the peculiar but admittedly picturesque ways the French expressed themselves. Using a foreign language called for exposure, not grammar. Look at the various refugees who lived in wartime Glossop. The Cohens for example had come from Germany and Mrs Swinburne was French. They had picked up quite good English very fast. They just had to since, despite all that grammar taught at the grammar school, there were only two, or perhaps three people in Glossop, who could string together half a dozen words in French. I meant Miss Wanklin and Miss Rhodes, our French teachers, and also Dad who sounded convincing when he declaimed the French text on the HP sauce bottle. None of them anyway had any German so they would have been useless to Mr Cohen. Not that Dad, even if able, would have been keen to help that 'Boche', who happened to be Jewish as well and was therefore doubly unwelcome. I am afraid he really did talk like that and worse, as I would tell you if, in a politically correct age I was brave enough to report his actual words. The point is that our intrepid refugees, without formal instruction, had learnt English simply by using it and now their enchanting accents, along with whiffs of perfume and cigars, brought continental sophistication to insular Glossop. I used to bang on like that quite often but nobody wanted to know. Debating the whys and wherefores of the curriculum was not a favourite playground pursuit. It was on the timetable wasn't it? If you want your School Cert then just do what they say. I tried out my arguments with Dad and Miss Newton as well but both were unimpressed. The 'direct method' was a lazy way. Nothing worthwhile was to be achieved without effort, so if grammar hurt it must be doing me good. So, in the end, I buckled down, did proses for homework, learned declensions for a test tomorrow, and eventually got School Cert 'credits' in both French and Latin. I took no pride in that empty achievement. It was certification without education, although I don't suppose I put it like that.

But I may have been wrong. In questioning the grammatical exercises that dominated our lives in class I had gone along with the general assumption that the purpose of education is to equip children with a body of knowledge, and a repertoire of skills, directly applicable to real situations they would encounter in adult life. If asked to justify the mallet process in respect of language learning, my friends, their parents and our teachers would all, I am fairly sure, have trotted out some version of that 'instrumental' view of what schools are for. You learnt maths so you could join the RAF and navigate a Lancaster. You learnt English because using it correctly, like not saying 'I' when it should be 'me', would help you get a good job. And you learnt French so you could, after the war, engage in sophisticated leisure pursuits, like ordering coffee and croissants straight off the boat at Boulogne. Finding instrumental justifications for Latin was harder. However it was rumoured to be the linqua franca of the medical profession so, if you wanted a doctor in the house ... It was rubbish of course. For instrumental purposes grammar is a waste of time. Rubbish however often prevails.

There is however another way of looking at it. Learning grammar may be worthwhile, even though, for practical purposes, it is useless. Knowing how to use the gerundive with 'est' will not, in itself, help you do brain surgery. But having patiently mastered one complex organism, like the Latin language, you are likely to acquire the confidence to scrutinise others, like the human body – or the British constitution or the market for Mars Bars. I am saying hard subjects induce mental toughness, a capacity for hard thinking that will help whenever you confront complexity. Also they develop moral fibre in the learner because they demand perseverance and demonstrate that patient, nit-picking hard work pays off. Traditional 'useless' subjects have another advantage. They never go out of date, while a curriculum that strives always to be topical will inevitably fall behind the times. It will almost always become outmoded before children have a chance to use the specifics they have picked up. Since relevance is a chimera, we may cheerfully embrace irrelevant subjects, using them, like pieces of gym equipment, to develop mental fitness.

The instrumental way of thinking about the curriculum that plagued me in the matter of grammar gave me bother also when I contemplated our daily ration of Maths. Why, like Eng Lang, was it 'basic'? Certainly counting and measuring figured significantly in daily life – more so then, in that pre-digital age, than they do now – but we had already, most of us, passed the Scholarship, which indicated a high level of competence in counting. Did we really need any more practice? Well, mine was not to reason why. We had two Maths teachers and their methods, though maybe equally valid, contrasted interestingly. Sammy Holt *[Plate 14 bottom, second left]* applied to Mathematics the direct method I craved in French. He never explained but just involved us in non-stop action. He roared in, pounding the floor, gown flapping over threadbare sports jacket, books and papers suspended about his person. He began a forty minute monologue, even before he pitched his belongings with impressive accuracy onto the sloping, polished surface of the compact teacher's desk, like a Swordfish fighter-bomber landing in a storm on the deck of an aircraft carrier.

Open your Dew Rell Page 56
[Durell's Algebra – he pronounced it 'Al Gebra' thus emphasising its fiendish Levantine origins]

WRITE!
[Taking up chalk and splattering board with opening proposition]

X squared + 2xy

We were expected, in our orange-backed, narrow-lined Maths books, to keep pace in mere pen and ink, with this human machine gun. We were not to interrupt. We were not to get flustered and never mind if we got stuck. With sufficient repetition the magic of the drill would make everything clear.

Looks over boy's shoulder at inky confusion.
You've made a Mrs Arabella Bloomer of it. What have you made?
A Mrs Arabella Bloomer, Sir.
Yes. So we shall have to rub your nose in it.
Conducts boy by ear to blackboard for prescribed treatment.

He often ran out of chalk and sent one of us to the Staff Room for more ammo. Even more often he ran out of blackboard and rubbed out the last ten minutes outpouring in a frenzy that precipitated a dust storm, the fall-out from which settled over his hair, his jacket and his glasses. The latter, like those famously worn by the late Jack Duckworth of *Coronation Street*, were held together by Elastoplast, the stickiness of which invaded the lenses, thus aiding the adhesion of chalk dust so that, in order to see at all he had to slide his specs down his nose and peer over the top like Mr Chad looking over his wall. Chad was a wartime folk icon often to be found on public walls with the legend 'Wot no ... ? [Something in short supply, like beer or the Second Front]. Eventually Harold Cottrell started hiding the board duster, leaving Sammy stomping helplessly. Then Harold learned how to play a tune on his teeth with a pencil, but a furious Sammy never swung round fast enough to catch him at it. 'Cott-rell, was that you?' Harold indignantly protested his outraged innocence. Later he discovered that if you banged on the pipes in Room 15 the reverberations were heard, not in that room, but next door in Room 14. So sometimes, in French or Eng Lit, as echoes of Sammy's familiar fusillade penetrated the party wall, we might notice a smile on Harold's face as his fist descended to the plumbing.

Our other Maths master was a forty-ish, Oxford trained, melancholy Welsh football player known as 'Bore Jones' *[Plate 14 bottom, first left]*. The name was most unfair. He did not bore me. For while Sammy drilled us like recruits on the square, Mr Jones treated us like fellow academicians. Sammy explained nothing but Bore explained everything and for me that worked much better. First he would establish the principle. Then we worked examples slowly together, every step scrupulously explored with elucidatory questions to the class and the chance for us to ask as well. Then a homework task, carefully marked and promptly returned. Yes, it might be boring if you did not listen, but if you did have the patience to follow what was being said it was rewarding. Also he seemed in touch with our situation as learners. The problems he set, although suitably taxing, tended to work out so you knew you had got it right even without looking up the answer at the back of the book. Since two sides of a triangle are necessarily greater than a third, it follows that AB + BC must be greater than AC. It was so sweetly reasonable. It was Bore who gave us Euclid, the Greek geometrician whose work I found so congenial. It seems Euclid had written six books of theorems and we referred to them by their original numbers, a notation I found romantic. Book One was all about triangles and included I.4 [congruency], I.5 ['pons assinorum'] and, most famous of all, I.47 as originally deduced by the great Pythagorus [the square on the hypotenuse]. We laid out the proofs in standard format under successive headings – 'Let' followed by 'It is required to prove' followed by 'Given' followed by 'Proof'. The last introduced a totally logical train of thought arriving at an incontrovertible conclusion. Wow! After we had mastered each theorem we did exercises called 'riders' in application of truths already established. I loved doing riders. Indeed finding an elegant solution induced profound satisfaction, something like the joy of harmony in music. Furthermore I really did seem better than the others at this particular numbers game and that felt good after years bobbing along, when we did Sums, in the wake of quick witted calculators. I also took satisfaction in the Greek-ness of Geometry. I did not receive a full blooded classical education but am struck in retrospect at the extent to which in childhood I was exposed to the heritage of Greece and Rome. The least nutritious element in that experience was the Latin I was taught. History delivered more, as did the bedside books previously identified. But the extent to which Science and Maths teachers contributed to my ever growing fund of classical lore is interesting. Waff Hall's evocation of Archimedes at bath-time was hilarious but it was the broad gateway to Greek thought opened up by Bore Jones that reverberates in recollection and makes me give thanks. Our clumsy gropings with the language of Caesar and Virgil never matured into an intellectual grasp of the content, let alone ignite any poetic response. But Euclid spoke to us loud and clear, in the original although not in words. Maybe it was something like reading Homer in Greek.

So much then for communication subjects, those dealing in the manipulation of words and figures. About half our time was given to grammar and sums so, when trivial pursuits like Music and RI were given their minimal due, some ten periods a week were available for the acquisition of what might be called 'mental furniture' – a broad selection of facts and concepts fit for a trained brain to sustain and contemplate. Some of them seemed to be useful, to have instrumental value, but most had no particular relevance to the situation of being English and about thirteen as the Second World War raged. Factual seeds were planted in our heads in the expectation that some of them would yield a harvest in thought. In the end, it was hoped, the habit of disciplined thinking – using evidence to arrive at valid opinions – would be established and I think it worked out that way as often as could reasonably be expected. The essential unity of these lessons in good thinking was however concealed behind subject barriers. Subjects were separate territories with defended frontiers, each nourishing distinctive habits and customs. The world of science was specially set apart. It seemed you had to be a different type of person to be a scientist, different in personality as well as in aptitude from a historian or an Eng Lit specialist. And science itself was subdivided into the autonomous republics of Physics, Chemistry and Biology. They existed more or less in that order of precedence although it was to be expected that Mr Casey would vigorously assert Chemistry's claims to equality of esteem with Physics. The lesser status of Biology however was not in dispute. It was a girls' subject.

In that hierarchical and partisan atmosphere it was difficult at the time to see the many characteristics that these descriptive subjects and their modes of operation had in common. It is only in retrospect that they seem of a piece. In these lessons we were told about nature, living and dead, with a certain preference for the latter, and about the behaviour and achievements of people, mostly male and mostly dead. The information had a random quality. It was never clear why some topics got into a syllabus when others did not. Why for example did we do the geography of Norway but not of Germany? Why learn the qualities of sodium rather than iron? Why did our teachers explain the surprising way in which fishes breathe but ignore the mechanics of human respiration? Why did we study the Second Burma War but not the First World War? It is probably because the selection of facts for retention seemed arbitrary that I appear to have forgotten a lot of what I was taught. But that might be a false impression. It may be that a substantial factual fall-out from a thousand mostly well conducted lessons has become inextricably mingled with that pot pourri known as 'general knowledge'. Anyway I often know the answers on 'University Challenge' and I am glad about that. I owe it in part to some good teaching when I was at the peak of my capacity to soak up facts. My schooling furnished my mind richly and I thank my teachers for that.

The methods by which knowledge was imparted in these descriptive areas proved a more important legacy even than the factual content. What we learnt was less important than what we learnt about how to learn. First, we were told. Alternatives to word of mouth instruction were occasionally employed. Now and again we were required to obtain information from a textbook and just once in a while he did something pretty with copper sulphate or something alarming with potassium. But what the teacher said was, far and away, the most important source of information. Secondly we wrote it down. Note making was central. Having received information it was a moral lapse not to record it. That sacred obligation was almost always discharged with pen or pencil in a bound book. When loose leaf filing was first offered us in the Sixth Form it came as a heady blast of post war modernity, as mind exploding as the Biro pen and the New Look, two other dividends of peace that made their debut in 1947. Before the Sixth Form we were not trusted to make notes for ourselves but instead they were devised by the teacher and passed down to us either by dictation or by having the class copy material chalked on the blackboard. Occasionally duplicated items were distributed and pasted it into our books. But opportunities to pass around the classroom bottle of Gloy were rare because reprographic technology was still primitive and the school had few resources. Dad's secretary had a Gestetner stencil duplicator and that was about it, except that Miss Sillito, our History teacher, sometimes brought along a set of rubber map rollers, loaded from an ink tray, which she deployed deftly across the pages of our stretched open exercise books. Miss Sillito personified the white heat of technology for it was in her fingers also that I first beheld the ball-point pen just mentioned. But such occasional treats notwithstanding, lessons normally revolved around note taking. We had distinctive notebooks for each subject. Science books came in shiny, semi-stiff, linen finish in bright colours and Geography, which claimed to be a science, got something similar. A dingy blue-black jotter however was good enough for mere History which was definitely on the Arts Side so not deserving of distinctive stationery. Because of the paper shortage we were pressurised to use every inch of our books so notes were too often cramped instead of being spaciously laid out and that made them harder to 'revise' from later. Saving paper cripples thought. A pity but there *was* a war on. Otherwise the method worked well. In effect each teacher, in instalments, provided us with a scheme or narrative he or she had personally constructed – a syllabus broken down into digestible pieces. It was delivered in a variety of formats, so as well as acquiring a coherent body of facts and ideas, we sampled different ways of recording information. Continuous prose often gave way to 'note form' in which the liberal use of abbreviations, sub-headings, under-linings, capitalisation and numbered points broke up the pages, giving each one a distinctive image that could itself be memorised. I found note form a great aid to absorbing information, particularly when it was supplemented by maps, graphs and diagrams, normally copied from the blackboard. Some teachers daily constructed chalk-work masterpieces only nonchalantly to rub them out at the end of the lesson, knowing they were preserved for posterity in our notebooks. If any copies survive of Miss Greenwood's intricately

Plate 1 THE GAULEITER

Cecil Lord, Senior English Master, Stretford Grammar School, Manchester 1935: caricature by the Art Master.

At the general election of that year, the last for a decade, the 'National Government' [a coalition led by the Conservatives] increased its majority. Dad's raised arm and Hitler hairstyle indicate robust right wing opinions. His black garb even suggests sympathy for Sir Oswald Moseley's British fascist movement. He grew out of those opinions, if he ever actually held them, and by the time I became aware of politics he had arrived at a Churchillian 'Stop Hitler Now!' position.

Plate 2 COUPLES

My grandparents
Tom and Esther at their Golden Wedding 1935.
Their Christmas card from the boss 1910

Wartime courtships
My parents, Nell and Cecil 1917. Dad as a recruit to the Border Regiment. Mum as 'Snowball'.
My Aunt Maud and Uncle Leslie c1918. Leslie as mechanic in the Royal Flying Corps.

Plate 3 WEDDINGS

In the garden at 7 Cross Street, Southport

Maud and Leslie 1919
Mum as bridesmaid. Esther in finery eclipses dowdy Ada [third from left]. The young men had all survived the war unscathed. Dick took the picture so is not shown.
Nell and Cecil 1926.
With best man and bridesmaids, my aunt Adela and cousin Barbara

Plate 4 1920s

Dick and Ada with their brood of bright young things.

Clapham Common? c1923. Haven't they done well? The togetherness of the couple looks contrived.

My parents postponing parenthood.

Mum pretending to drive the Austin Seven. Outside 7 Cross Street. Note Dad's uncanny resemblance to a fellow Great War veteran.

On holiday with my cousin Barbara

Plate 5 FIRST STEPS 1933

Southport and Norbury. With my cousin Barbara, Chum, [Aunt Marion's Airedale terrier] and of course Dad, seemingly his son's ever-present best playmate. NB slipper-maker's bobbins, a favourite and versatile that illuminated my childhood.

Plate 6 INFANCY 1934-1936

Clockwise from top left.

With usual playmates, Birchington, Kent 1934

'Shaving'. For Reynold's News. Selsdon 1935?.

With 'murder weapon' train-set. Selsdon 1935

Banished! For attempted murder of baby sister.

Selsdon January 1936. With snowman and
Margaret, from next door but one.

Patrolling Polruan Road, Chorlton 1935

Plate 7 UPWARD MOBILITY 1936-1937

Moving on. New house 1936.

At Stretford. NB capacious porch and leaded lights. There was also a brick garage and a dysfunctional immersion heater. I am four and aware of my seniority.

Moving further on. New Job, New Car 1937

Selsdon May 1937. We had been celebrating the coronation of King George VI and Dad's appointment as Headmaster, Glossop Grammar School. Left to right: Dad, Maud, Mum with Helen, Margaret, me, Barbara. Scratch on DND 838 is not visible but the self-inflicted damage to my fringe still shows.

Plate 8 GLOSSOP 1937

Holly Wood.
Our house 1937-1949
in 1937, Maud visiting.

As it is today [2014]

Mossy Lea.
A favourite walk. Substantially
unchanged since 1937

The Station Lion.
Erected by the Duke of Norfolk,
lord of the manor, 1847

Plate 9 ST LUKES 1937-1942

Former St Luke's C of E School [2014].

Here I was taught the Ten Commandments and suffered 'Mental'. Airy accommodation built 1897, the year of Queen Victoria's Diamond Jubilee. Re-housed in tatty modernity 1980s. Mrs Wood was the doyenne of the millocracy whose members competed in philanthropy with each other and Lord Howard of Glossop.

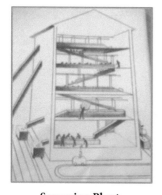

Screening Plant.
From The Magic of Coal [Puffin Picture Books 1944?]. The 'Scholarship' as an industrial process.

Scholarship Boy 1942.
Despite limited literacy I manipulated the screening plant and beat the system

Plate 10 SOME OF GRANDPA'S FRIENDS 1919-1939

Press photographs by R W Lord [bottom right]. A large box of Grandpa's 'snaps' was endlessly perused. That way I learnt about modern times.

Clockwise from top left

George Formby, entertainer, with his wife Beryl 1939

Joachim von Ribbentrop, Hitler's ambassador to London c1936

King Edward VIII 1936

Noel Coward, playwright and entertainer c1937

David Lloyd George, with daughter Megan at Chequers c1920

Sir Oswald Moseley, with his wife Cynthia c1920

Plate 11 A FAMILY AT WAR 1939-1945

The House of Lords, Norbury August 1939.
Left to right: Adela, Cecil, Maud, Helen, Richard, Nellie, Marion, Ada, Leslie, Barbara, Dick.

Flight Lieutenant C Lord, C/O No 597 [Glossop Grammar School] Squadron, Air Training Corps

'Porky' Digging for Victory, St Anne's 1943

Leslie in the uniform of the AFS [Auxiliary Fire Service]

Plate 12 NOBLESSE OBLIGE 1899

Technical college built by Lord Howard

It became Glossop Grammar School. Abandoned 1959, in favour of flimsy modernity but listed in the nick of time c2000. Photographed 2014. NB baroque ironwork successfully defended by Dad against the War Salvage people.

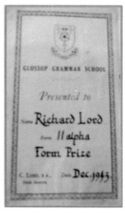

Howard Crest and Motto

In mosaic at Glossop Municipal Buildings [1923]
(left)

Adapted as school badge, as on prize label [1943]
(above)

Plate 13 THE HALL

The baroque jewel case, fashioned for Lord Howard by Italian craftsmen

Here my agnostic father presided daily over an 'act of collective worship', followed by a homily. He always stood on the third step of the Boys' Staircase, occupied in this 2014 photograph by the author. It was a tight fit for some four hundred acolytes of the Gauleiter but enclosure reinforced community. Always powerful.

Plate 14 THE SCHOOL PRECINCT.

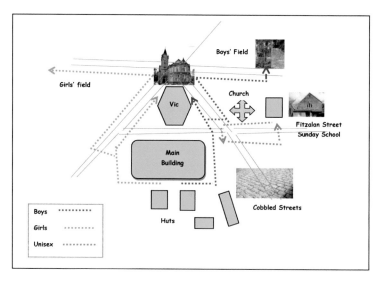

Showing Dad's dots.

We had to proceed always in single file along designated, gender-specific routes. Deviation delivered detention.

Some of our teachers [in ATC disguise] 1943.
Left to Right
Pilot Officer 'Bore' Jones [Maths]
Flying Officer 'Sammy' Holt [Adjutant] [Maths]
Flight Lieutenant 'Joe/Gau' Lord [CO] [English]
Pilot Officer 'Waff' Hall [Physics]
Pilot Officer 'Spell' Brown [General Subjects, PE]

Plate 15 EXERCISE BOOKS 1945-1947

History

Content by Miss Sillito.

Blots by me.

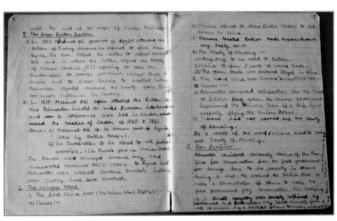

English

- Clause analysis 1945
- Decoration by Comrade Higginbottom of VA 1947

Plate 16 PROPAGANDA

The Gospel according to Puffin Picture books.

S R Badmin Village and Town
Bad Old Days
Industrial squalor, legacy of
Capitalism - and Appeasement.
The name on the front of the
factory is 'Chamber and Lains'

Brave New World
High rise living with a penguin
pool on every corner

Margaret and Alexander Potter The Building of London
Careers Education
When I grew up wanted to be a planner with an anglepoise

labelled sectional drawings of the amoeba they must now be collectors' items valued like the illustrations to seventeenth century treatises on horticulture. She was our best blackboard artist but most of the others also wielded a mean stick of chalk. Then there was tabulation. Information displayed in rows and columns somehow hits the brain [mine anyway] more rapidly than when it is rolled out in measured prose. Imagine a train timetable in continuous prose and the point is made. It seems to stick better that way as well, perhaps because you carry an image of the table itself as well as of the data it encapsulates. We used lots of tables in most subjects. It suited clause analysis as well as the properties of oxygen and the battles of the Napoleonic War. Since our notebooks were lined, the matrices were readily constructed although you needed a ruler to do the verticals and it was a pity we did not use graph paper in other subjects as well as Maths. White hot Miss Sillito was a mistress of tabulation as well as cartography. Through tables she made dates fascinating. When you saw all the different things that were happening in different places at the same moment in time and tried to make links between them, enlightenment was apt to strike. It was a like having a rider work out in geometry. Bliss! Rote learning can be exciting, not boring.

The third stage of the mallet process was recycling. Memorising notes for a test was a standard device and tests took several forms. Mass recitation was the simplest. 'State Boyle's Law' he might say, and in response the whole class would assert in unison that

For a given mass of gas
At a constant temperature
The product of pressure times volume is constant.

We remembered it like that – like lines of a poem we had been set to learn by heart, which we often were. Trouble arose if the unison broke down. If you had not done your homework, or if you did not get the point, if the penny had not yet dropped, you tried to blend into the obscurity of the general chant while he scanned thirty odd pairs of lips picking out defaulters. If detected you might be kept behind until you could give a satisfactory solo performance. You might call that attention to the special needs of slower learners but we just called it detention. More elaborate testing arrangements began with 'Take out your rough books. Question

1 ...' and culminated in 'Change books!', followed by 'Hands up those who got less than six'. As well as the shame of exposure members of this condemned group also faced detention. This form of testing was rapid, efficient and economical. It was particularly economical of teachers' labours because it generated entries in mark books without any physical inspection of pupils' notebooks. The drawback was the possibility of collusion so sometimes boys had to exchange books with girls, it being assumed that cross gender collusion was improbable because unnatural. Also rough book tests were interspersed with 'slip tests'. In that version we wrote answers to dictated questions on strips of paper which he or she had to take away and actually mark. The impact on the teacher's workload however was minimal because answers typically required only one-word, right or wrong responses that were readily ticked, crossed and totted up. As well as tests there was of course homework. I can remember a lot of grammatical exercises, French and Latin proses, English compositions and perpetual workings of mathematical examples but am hazier about what we did for homework in Science, History and Geography. Memorising for a test often figured, I think, but presumably we must also have been given written assignments. However, if you taught say Geography, and only got two periods a week for each of fifteen classes, you might find over 250 names in your mark book. So it was wise to go easy on setting work that had to be marked. Fair enough, I think, looking back.

It seems clear that saving teachers' energies was a major consideration. But why not? Tired teachers are no use to their charges and that is surely a major problem with 'activity learning'. Teachers scurrying between a clutch of individually programmed groups become exhausted, thus risking control and authority, indispensable attributes that, by contrast, the 'test on Tuesday' method automatically reinforces. Note also that, in wartime particularly, our teachers worked hard for their salaries and not just in the classroom. Out of school activities included an elaborate sporting programme that often had them turning out on Saturday afternoons and a whole detachment of our male staff were officers in the school squadron of the Air Training Corps. You can see them on parade in the photograph [Plate 14]. Not Lieutenant Casey however, who served instead in the town Home Guard, an act of mutiny that much irked my father – as it was meant to. It emerges then that there was much to be said for the mallet process. Yet ever since 1854, when Dickens lampooned Mr Gradgrind's school where some ingenious and economical arrangements for the mass propagation of factual knowledge were exhibited, the teaching methods just outlined have been mocked as 'rote learning'. In my own progressive days I once sang lustily in that chorus of derision. Yet despite virulent disdain the institution, though battered, survived in the classrooms I supervised. I used to wonder why. Had its recalcitrant practitioners not heard the good news? Or did they wickedly stop their ears to the progressive gospel? In evangelical fervour I missed the wood in preaching at the trees. For the truth is, rote learning works.

That being established let us review how it worked for me personally. My favourite subject was always History, with English Literature, which will be reserved for the next chapter, a close second. I also liked Geography and Biology. Unfortunately however, since to get a School Certificate you had to cover a prescribed breadth of studies, and not just concentrate on the subjects you found easiest, it was necessary in the fourth year to choose between History and Geography. Biology moreover was not considered important enough to be a School Cert subject at all and we all dropped it after the second year. I found Physics and Chemistry less appealing than the subjects just mentioned but still liked them better than Latin, French or the rest of Maths apart from Geometry. However, since the School Cert demanded a foreign language, we all had to do French and Dad said I had to keep on with Latin because I was on the Arts Side and a passage had been booked for me via Christ Church to the Middle Temple. It seemed therefore that Law too must be on the Arts Side but why, please, was that? Such philosophical wranglings exhausted me and I later discovered I was no good at Philosophy either. Anyway on the timetable Physics, essential for serious scientists, was set against Latin, without which no decent university Arts course would give you a place. So that was that. Thus the descriptive subjects I spent most time on were History and Chemistry but, before the great choosing and dropping that happened as you started the Remove [fourth] year, I picked up a smattering of others as well.

What Miss Greenwood offered II Alpha in her Geography lessons was a thorough survey of the physical features of the British Isles, together with some account also of economic activity. It was useful as well as interesting. Ever since I have known with considerable precision where I live and that is a comfort I would not like to do without. People with otherwise well stocked minds – like my wife who once assured me Blackpool was on the Yorkshire coast near Newcastle – sometimes reveal a chaotic sense of place and I am glad I am not like that. Inside a turbulent psyche there has, ever since II Alpha, been in me a still centre that includes the sure and certain knowledge that the Lammermoors lie south of Edinburgh and that the Quantocks are in Somerset. Or at least they were until the barbaric local government carve-up of 1974, a body blow to our heritage almost as devastating of the coincidental stifling of the railway system, the spoliation of the country houses and the liquidation of a thousand grammar schools. But if you superimpose the motorways and take account of deindustrialisation, Miss Greenwood's description of Britain still serves very nicely. For, as well as the ranges aforementioned, I can locate the Brecon Beacons and the Chilterns and when the southbound M5 leaps Shakespeare's Avon I know it is the Malverns on the right and the Cotswolds on the left. I can name most of the rivers that swell the Humber, including exotics like the Swale, the Ure and the Soar, as well as the Ouse and the Trent. I know roughly why it is wetter in the west and why in winter it is often colder in the south east than the north west. I know corn grows better in what used to be Rutland than in what used to be Westmorland. I know Nottingham, like Honiton is, or was, noted for lace, and that once upon a time Northampton manufactured boots and shoes, Paisley as well as Preston produced cottons, Sheffield ground out knives, Bury concocted black puddings and Doncaster made butterscotch as well as locomotives. Furthermore I know what an oast house is for and the difference between a trawler and a drifter. And I know you can, or could, get to Rosslare from Fishguard and to Stranraer from Larne. All this and much more Dolly Greenwood told us between the Siege of Stalingrad and the Battle of Kursk. I am so glad she did. But unfortunately after the first year we lost her and started to do Geography properly with a subject specialist, which apparently Miss Greenwood was not. Proper Geography seemed to concern itself exclusively with virtually uninhabited places. So we learned about the Amazon rain forests where he said the fug was too stifling to survive in, except at a city called Manaus, where the streets were paved with marble and they had an opera house, extravagances which seemed over the top to me. And we explored the tundra of Norway with a thoroughness exceeded only by our extended investigation of sheep farming in the Australian outback. Despite having argued above in favour of irrelevance as a curricular principle, I have to report that this fragmented and inhuman Geography put me off. Why not get real? Was there not a war on and were not geographical factors crucial to its outcome? Like how to get armies across deserts and steppes and seas and rivers, or how to transport bomb loads to deal death in Berlin. And like the environmental issues that would have to be addressed after the war when devastated cities came to be rebuilt and industries returned from munitions to civilian production. With such juicy problems to get our teeth into why dine out on salmon tinned in British Columbia? Perhaps because real life was too complicated to fit into a School Cert syllabus. People got in the way of Geography.

Although we lost Miss Greenwood for Geography we kept her for Biology, which was her proper trade. Because she was a woman, I supposed. Real men flexed their muscles on Physics and Chemistry, disdaining the life sciences. Which perhaps is why Darwin did not figure beside Archimedes, Newton and Lavoisier on the roll call of dead scientists we were called upon to revere. So we lost Miss Greenwood for good at the end of the second year and, although it was sad to say goodbye Dolly, I had to admit that Biology had been something of a disappointment. Being quite into nature – what with keeping frog spawn, sticklebacks and rabbits, losing hedgehogs, and examining the assorted corpses, including once a substantial rat, deposited by our cat behind Mum's sewing box, to be found in the environs of Holly Wood, I had been looking forward to the subject. The first blow was that it began with plants instead of animals. Lessons typically consisted of submitting various bits of vegetation to the mallet process. They had to be broken down into their component parts and also classified into species. So we brought in twigs and noted that, although sprigs of sycamore had basic features in common with their opposite numbers in the horse chestnut family, they were also distinctive in shape, texture and colour. We did similar exercises with conkers and acorns and with buttercups and daisies. Such guided observation was then of course carefully recorded in our notebooks, usually in the form of tables or as copies of drawings made from the blackboard. Dolly's exquisite board-craft has already been applauded. I suppose we must also have had tests on such things as the principal parts of a flower – calyx, stamens and pistol – or the life cycle of the pussy willow. Then a term of patient botanical endeavour was rewarded by entry into the animal kingdom but, if I had been expecting lions, elephants or even human beings, I had to lower my expectations. For, apart from the finny residents of a glass tank and the invertebrate population of a wormery, the animals we contemplated were not even visible. Not to the naked eye, that is. They were so small they could only be examined under a microscope. Which might have been fun if we had had enough microscopes to go round but, there being a war on, we didn't, so we had to queue to squint down this black tube with brass knobs and a little mirror. You were supposed to adjust the thing to suit your own eye but I, with my two left hands, never managed it properly, any more than I managed to focus the penny in the slot telescope on the front at St Anne's-on-Sea. All I picked up was a congestion of bug-like elements in kaleidoscopic motion. It was quite pretty but without obvious coherence, so after a moment of simulated awe I made way for the next young voyager towards the frontiers of knowledge. My delight in spotting the spirogyra was faked.

But again the satirical urge carries me too far. Miss Greenwood sometimes transcended the mallet process and raised issues in classroom debate that truly made you think. In particular she communicated the fascination of doubt, showing us that blurred lines can be more compelling than sharp ones. What, she asked, was life? What distinguished a living organism from an inanimate mass? It turned out not to be all that easy to put your finger on the difference. Similar difficulty emerged when we tried to distinguish animals from plants. Then it seemed that some creatures were asexual, they could not be described as either male or female, and others were sometimes male and sometimes female. Wow! *There* was food for thought. It must have been good science teaching. We got the same sort of dogged striving after wisdom from Mr Casey, our Chemistry master. Sometimes, after he had done what he had to do with a Bunsen and a bubbling flask, and we were recording its significance by copying from the blackboard, he was wont to wander round the lab engaging individuals and groups in conversation. I remember one such. He tapped the steel spatula he always carried, like a badge of his subject, in the top pocket of his brown tweed jacket:

Is this metal?
Yes, of course. [Anybody could see that]
How do you know?
Because it's hard.

Is this metal? [Knocking on the solid timber bench]
No, of course not.
How do you know?
Well ... metals are shiny as well as hard.
That test-tube is shiny and hard. So is it metal?

Obviously not. Then he got us to remember sodium, which was not shiny when he got it out of the jar and not even very hard either. It only began to shine when he cut it with his pen-knife. And what about mercury? It was shiny but liquid. The point was made. Things are not necessarily what they appear to be. If there is a grand design to the universe, an underlying pattern, then it can take a lot of unscrambling. And even after a lifetime of disciplined exploration you can expect to see it, if it is there at all, only through a glass darkly.

But if the struggle to understand nature was long and hard – a bit like Churchill's 'blood, sweat, toil and tears' evocation of Britain's task in the war – at least we could stand on the shoulders of those who had gone before. It became clear that in Physics as well as Chemistry a lot of ground work had already been done and its fruits had been condensed into a series of 'laws' and 'hypotheses' and of course we had to learn them by heart. I remember the names of their proposers, universally euphonious and usually foreign, better than their content. Thus home-grown Olympians like Newton and Boyle were joined in an international brotherhood by Archimedes and Ptolemy, Copernicus and Keppler, Galileo and Avogadro, Toricelli and Lavoisier, Dulong and Petit. But learning to state a law did not necessarily help me understand its meaning and significance. Nor did physical demonstrations of its operation. If we had ourselves carried out the experiments that proved the theories perhaps significance would have been more apparent. But, as already indicated, despite being surrounded in the labs by the paraphernalia of experiment, we hardly ever did any. When laboratory equipment was used it was almost always the teacher who used it. On the rare occasions when we did it ourselves, in relishing the novelty of the experience we missed the point of the experiment. So in grappling with scientific theory I needed more help that I got. On the eve of the School Cert Chemistry exam I remember telling myself all I had to do was memorise all this mumbo jumbo, give it a bed and breakfast lodging in my brain, and then, since I was on the Arts Side and about to say farewell to Science, just vomit it into the answer book and never let it trouble my gullet again. I regret a cynicism that permanently closed my mind to science but I do not blame my teachers. The notion that knowledge is divided into Arts and Science, that never the twain shall meet, was not personally invented by Messrs Hall and Casey. And my inhibiting clumsiness and chronic untidiness were not their fault either. Mr Casey, it will be recalled, said my heraldic device should be a 'blot rampant on a field of ink'. He thought neatness mattered. I thought it did not. But now I think he was right. It lubricates the mallet process.

To start with, History with Mr Brown *[Plate 14 bottom, far right]*, of whom we got something of a surfeit since he also taught us Maths, PT and Games, was disappointing. He started with the Old Stone Age where we had already been at St Luke's, at least once, and did not add much to what I already knew about the Greeks and Romans either. In fact it was three years or more before classroom history brought about much amendment to the History Meccano I had already constructed from *The Young Briton's History Reader* and the other bedside resources already identified. But what could poor Spell Brown do? He was 'Spell' because he was brilliant at extracting splinters picked up on the boarded the floor of the Vic, our pretend gym. He only got two periods a week to conduct II Alpha all the way from the woolly rhinoceros to the Norman Conquest. Not surprisingly he never arrived, having got stuck in the Dark Ages, and did not even have time to take us on the promised trip to Melandra Castle, the local Roman site. Thus in III Upper we began the Middle Ages in the middle of a story we did not know the beginning of. It did not matter too much because the Middle Ages mostly concerned, not a rolling narrative, but a static depiction of monasteries, castles and three field villages inhabited by peasants in skirts and pixy hoods. Those institutions apparently resisted change all the way from the Normans to the Tudors, when the first two fell victim to modernity in the form of gunpowder and Henry VIII. Again in retrospect the appeal of all three topics to hard pressed teachers becomes clear. They were eminently susceptible to easy-to-mark diagrammatic representation – a tick for each correct label plus maybe something for artistic impression. Being bogged down in crop rotation, we never got to the waning of the Middle Ages, so in IVA, when we were told we were going to start on Modern Times, we just had to take it on trust that that leap into enlightenment really did take off in 1485 [British] and 1492 [European]. So we learnt nothing about what happened between Magna Carta and the Wars of the Roses, apart from what we picked up in English, when we did *Richard II* and *Henry V*. Apart from me, that is. I was well OK, thanks to *The Young Briton's History Reader*. We gathered that the modern movement was mostly to do with the Voyages of Discovery, the Renaissance and the Reformation, all of which were highly commendable despite being much participated in by our enemies the Germans and Italians. True to pattern, IVA finished the Tudors but had scarcely got started on the Stuarts before the 1945 summer term ended, and with it the Second World War. I guess not getting to the Stuarts was an abiding problem in the teaching of history in the days before both chronology and kings [as opposed to queens] became ideologically discredited. I even missed out both the Civil Wars and the Glorious Revolution in both the undergraduate History courses I later embarked upon. Doing Whigs and Tories without some nodding familiarity with those mould breaking episodes is hard work. So when, in Remove A, Bonnie Prince Charlie suddenly turned up at Derby, the habitat of County, Dad's bogey, he came completely out of the blue, into which element fortunately he soon disappeared back into. But enough of satire. This stale imitation of *1066 and All That* is not meant too seriously. At least in History the past was given some scaffolding, even if the structure concerned was wonky with some of the girders missing. Few people under sixty today are lucky enough to include that handy bit of kit on the inventory of their mental furniture. The problem was the mad rush. Only two periods a week was daft. We were forever starting something new without digesting what we had previously learnt. Even for an enthusiast perpetual frenetic novelty was a turn-off.

Then at New Year 1946 – I was thirteen and unhappy, being troubled by secret guilt, threatened by puberty and missing the war that had just ended – everything about History changed for the better. Those of us who had chosen the subject instead of Geography now got four periods per week and furthermore we got Miss Sillito who announced that we were starting the School Certificate syllabus. Our lessons suddenly took on a new sense of purpose. The programme ran from 1783 to 1914 in English History and from 1789 to that same going out of the lamps in European. The Industrial and Agricultural Revolutions were also included although bits of them antedated 1783 and of course English History included the history of the British Empire. It was an edifice satisfying in scope and scale. The imperial dimension reflected how the British genuinely, if erroneously, viewed the world at the end of the war that signalled the end of Empire. The Labour government that withdrew from India retained a high imperial profile elsewhere and seemingly did not anticipate further decolonisation. The story of Empire furthermore ensured a world view and gave us heroic figures from other cultures. O'Connell and Parnell, Smuts and Botha, Tipu Sultan and Surajah Dowlah were presented by Miss Sillito as great men, or at least worthy adversaries, and if Chief Cetawayo was a savage he was cast, as in the film *Zulu*, as a noble one. But probably it was the attention to European History in equal proportion to English that made most impact. School Cert History combined with the teachings of Alvar Liddell to show me that, whatever her position as a world power, Britain was also part of Europe and I came to know the map of the continent after the Congress of Vienna as well as I knew the street plan of Glossop. I could distinguish Schleswig from Holstein, Parma from Piacenza and Bosnia from Herzegovina. Furthermore I knew the genealogy of the Hohenzollerns as well as my own family tree. Robespierre, Napoleon, Garibaldi and Bismarck fixed themselves in my consciousness alongside Wellington, Peel, Gladstone and Disraeli and I answered the Eastern Question with the same cockiness I brought to the Condition of England Question.

It is possible to scrutinise Miss Sillito's method of teaching in particular detail because, by a lucky chance, one of my notebooks has survived, latterly in a garden shed. It is not a beautiful object, as you can see from the examples reproduced as *Plate 15 top*. They reveal handwriting that is infantile as well as a pathetic incapacity to control the flow of ink through the nib of a fountain pen. This battered remnant however is instructive because it records exactly what we learnt, and it sheds light on the ways in which we were required to absorb it. I guess this notebook was one of four. It relates only to part of the English History syllabus, so there must have been another dealing with the rest, and probably I had two other books, similarly crammed with data about European History. The surviving notebook covers the sixteen topics listed below, and also contains the general time-line seen in the photograph, so probably the whole School Certificate course was broken down into at least fifty units, which Miss Sillito must have delivered at the rate of approximately one a week over eighteen months.

• Greek Independence	• Shipping
• Palmerston's Foreign Policy	• Trade Unions
• The Crimean War [+map]	• Disraeli's Foreign Policy [+map]
• Chartism	• Factory Legislation
• Canada [+map]	• South Africa [at great length] [+map]
• Banking	• [The Scramble for Africa [+2 maps]
• India [at great length] [+map]	• Ireland 1783-1914 [at great length]
• Railways	• The Liberal Ministry 1906-1914

The list may cause some elevation of eyebrows. Yes, 'drum and trumpet' history predominates and the emphasis is unapologetically imperial. Aspects of Victorian life and culture that might figure prominently in a modern survey are not here. There is not much social history. The subjection of women attracts no disdain. Nor does the arrogance of the elite. Darwin is absent and so are Pugin, Pusey and Ruskin. Religion figures only as an unfortunate obsession, afflicting 'natives' in India and Ireland and causing difficulties for their benevolent but hard-pressed rulers. So the Irish Famine appears as an administrative problem rather than a humanitarian disaster. Miss Sillito however had to teach what the examining board dictated. Its imperatives were beyond her control. Anyway wars and foreign policy happened and colonies required government, so they deserve scrutiny. They concentrated the energies of Victorian politicians and also provided popular entertainment before big time sport got fully organised. Imperial, military and diplomatic history is as much worth doing as any other type of delving into the past. All history is interesting if you do it right and the way Miss Sillito did it was very right.

This is how she operated. First she told us about this week's topic or that part of it that was the business of today's forty minute lesson. She was a good narrator establishing a firm story line relieved by dashes of local colour, so sometimes you could settle down and just drink it in. But it was usually more of a two way process than you might suppose. She interrogated us constantly to check that we had got the point she was making and she encouraged us to ask her questions as well. Sometimes such interchanges matured into full-blown discussion. She liked that, and enjoyed jokes as much as we did, but she was strict in the chair. It was good to have your own ideas but you must produce evidence to back them up, otherwise they didn't count. That firmness in the cause of reasoned debate is evident from her marking of the only one piece of homework, as opposed to dictated material, preserved in my notebook. It must have been a revision exercise for it is about eighteenth century agriculture, not the Second China War. She only gave me 6½ out of 10 which, by soft, twenty first century standards, seems truly mean. The reason however is obvious from a string of terse interjections in red crayon [this must have been before she got her Biro]. 'Why?' followed by 'How?' followed by 'Why not?' and then another 'Why?' Clearly my effort was a tissue of unsubstantiated assertion. Those are just the sort of queries, more politely formulated, with which I might, in my days as an Open University tutor, have decorated a student assignment. Yet I was only fourteen, not forty four. Surely adult rules did not apply? Oh yes, they did! Intellectually we grew up quicker in those days, or so it is tempting to assume.

That then was the talking part of the lesson. It may have occupied about half the forty minutes. The second part was writing. It was then that I took down the dictated discourse that fills the notebook. Getting it on paper was relaxing. Writing came as a relief after the hurly burly of debate. It was probably relaxing for her too. A teacher can't be always performing and a spell of dictation pacifies a classroom. The almost unbelievable range and density of the factual content is what first stands out from even a glance at these notes. Look at the lower of the two History samples on *Plate 15*. It shows part of a near exhaustive exposition of the foreign policy of Palmerston [Foreign Secretary 1830-41 and 1846-51]. Part of it concerned the Eastern Question. You will see from the left hand page that the Fifth Form History set was expected to absorb, digest and reproduce a complex mass of information about the machinations, during the 1830s, of the Sultan of Turkey, the Tsar of Russia, Mehemet Ali [autonomous Governor of Egypt] and Louis Philippe [King of France], all of whom, were in contention about the disposal of the apparently disintegrating Turkish Empire, with particular reference to the future of Egypt and Syria and to the passage of warships through the Dardanelles, the strait that links the Mediterranean to the Black Sea. We needed to get to know all those guys, to have at least a rough idea where they were all coming from, and to locate accurately the places in dispute. Above all we had to grasp how Palmerston – standing aloof from the fray, but properly concerned, in his typically

British way, that fair play should prevail – fixed up a London conference [1839-40] that effectively reversed the Treaty of Unkiar Skelessi [1833] that the uppity Tsar had imposed on the effete Sultan. But the Eastern Question was only one of the five sets of happenings poor Palmerston had to keep topside of. Two of the others figure on the right hand side of the illustrated pages. We had to plunge into the maelstrom of the 'Opium Wars' with China and then the exotic Don Pacifico demanded our attention, as did Palmerston's long speech on his behalf, culminating in his contention that, if you could say 'Civis Britannicus sum' then you need fear no enemy. That discourse constitutes a weighty mass of complex material. The brightest of modern undergraduates would not find mastering it a pushover. Yet it covers only three of the fifty or so topics that made up the School Certificate History syllabus. Yet I do not remember ever feeling defeated by the task of absorbing it. On the contrary it was invigorating, enjoyable and indeed fun. And, for better or worse, I have ever afterwards remembered a great deal of what I took in.

The other thing to note about the notebook is how it taught me how to learn. It demonstrates various ways of storing information other than in continuous prose, a mode scarcely ever employed anywhere in the book. Even when points are not numbered or the material is not otherwise broken into bite-sized pieces, 'note form' is standard. Grammatical rules are suspended. Stylistic niceties do not prevail. Abbreviation is encouraged. Subdivision of a topic is mandatory, otherwise it will not make sense and will defy memorisation. So numbering or otherwise indicating points and subordinate points is essential. Maps can help, even the grubby cartography issuing from a marriage of Miss Sillito's inky rollers and my own dysfunctional fountain pen. So too can tabulation. My teacher's master chronology for the period 1830 to 1870 is reproduced in the upper photograph [Plate 15]. It lets you see at a glance the order in which things happened, on whose watch as prime minister and sovereign, and how different things have a habit of happening all at the same time. Grasp those essentials and history becomes fascinating. Dates do not kill history, they bring it to life. Without them you get lost, then bored and then resentful. But put any topic into chronological order and light will usually dawn. I am saying the rote learning dispensed by Miss Sillito was wonderfully effective. I also want to champion the practice of dictating notes. They come straight from a teacher's lips and that gives them a lively quality a textbook can never possess. You can't interrogate the author of a textbook but, if we got stuck, Miss Sillito was there at our service. Service seems to be the word. She sorted out the Eastern Question, not for the world in general but with us, personally in mind. There was something endearing about that. Thank you, Miss Sillito. You changed my mind.

Chapter 8

RHYME

For 'Rhyme' read English, Lang and Lit. It had a special place at our school. But why? The question used to puzzle me and it still does. Practical necessity is one answer. A precise knowledge of the structure of the language we use helps us say what we mean. So anyway we were led to understand. Yet today we get by communication-wise despite the decline of formal instruction in grammar. I do not know what exactly modern fourteen year olds do in lessons called 'English Language', if that quaint appellation even survives, but I think I get the drift. I guess they do not parse or do clause analysis. Maybe they turn out the occasional précis and they are probably encouraged to punctuate, at least in a basic fashion that disdains the semi colon and indulges dashes. I fear they may suffer 'comprehension' – the disembowelling of disembodied extracts of superior writing anthologised in latter day equivalents of Clay's *School Certificate English Practice*, the rod that scourged VA in 1947. Certainly 'Standard English' has long since been dethroned and talking posh has become 'unacceptable' to the extent that posh kids in elite schools meticulously cultivate Estuary. And of course modern schoolchildren text and tweet with enviable fluency in accordance with a body of usage unfamiliar to Fowler but binding nevertheless.

I am saying again that the teaching of grammar, if its justification was instrumental – it provided valuable life skills – was grossly overdone at Glossop Grammar School, and no doubt in a thousand other such academies as well. We were all already effective communicators in English. That capacity was exhaustively tested in the entry process so we would not have got in otherwise. We were all also already proficient in Standard English, although most of my schoolmates had an advantage over me in that respect. They were bilingual. They could use SE at school while switching when appropriate to the patois of the streets. I could not do that and my deficiency left me isolated. My only compensation was an exceptional command of SE. I had learned it at my mother's knee and beside my father's chair so it was second nature. I never had to think about what was correct for it just came out naturally. I was all but faultless. Not only was my pronunciation impeccable but I spoke as grammatically as I wrote. Of that there is documentary proof in that cache of exercise books, already called upon in evidence, that miraculously survive from my schooldays. The English books show that Miss Hughes almost always gave me nine out of ten for grammatical exercises. Nine was de facto perfection, ten being unthinkable on the grounds that it would have implied an absolute immunity to flaw incompatible with the human condition. Thus my School Cert 'Distinction' in Eng Lang was almost as predictable as night following day. I took no pride in that success. It was too easy and I resented the classroom time wasted in teaching me idle tricks like clause analysis. We could have spent the time better for example by doing more History or doing Geography *as well as* History instead of as an alternative. Both those options would necessarily give practice in the use of English. The inanity of clause analysis was a particular grievance I used to put before Dad. He was not unsympathetic. He agreed I did not need it but the others, being less advantaged in their parentage, did. Thus I was to shut up and just do it. Which I did it for example, just as the Battle of the Bulge subsided, on 7 January 1945, as is clear from the page of my English exercise book illustrated in *Plate 15 lower left*. If you can make sense of the findings there tabulated, then good luck to you, because they now baffle me. Not then though, as the crop of ticks indicates. Note that Miss Hughes missed the misspelling of 'principal' so I hope Dad did not check her marking of this piece as he was wont to do. He monitored my homework to measure the competence of his staff. Comprehension tests also attracted my scorn. They made sense if the passage set for elucidation came from one of the texts we were doing in Eng Lit, as in the first example above, or if they were related to our studies in other subjects, like History or even Chemistry, but pompous acreages of disconnected prose from Clay were boring because they had no context. That text book also supplied lists of hard words we had to learn, like 'hypocrite' or 'valetudinarian' or 'malingerer'. And we punctuated until the cows came home and did that thing called 'parsing', the nature and purpose of which now quite eludes me. Well, it was nothing to do with me. There was nothing wrong with my powers of comprehension and I knew plenty of long words already. But if pressed I would carry out the party tricks prescribed and collect my due in top marks.

All that assumes an *instrumental* justification for teaching grammar. As we have seen in discussing French and Latin it is difficult to make that argument stick. Grammar is not actually very 'relevant' and hence the collapse of elaborate grammatical instruction that set in during the 1960s. If however you adopt the mental fitness approach to the curriculum – irrelevance is more useful than relevance because it does not go out of date – as pursued in Chapter Seven, then clause analysis, parsing, comprehension, précis writing and all the other apparatus in the Eng Lang gym acquire sterling value. Using them hurts so they must be good for us. They make you think and what better classroom outcome could there be? On that day towards the end of the war, when I tackled the above quotations from Shakespeare and Walter Scott and worked out how their clauses had been put together, doing it must have made my brain hurt. Sure, as a gifted verbal athlete I would have found it easier than most, but spotting that 'whose heart has ne'er within him burned' is an adjectival clause, qualifying the conjectural man with a dead soul in the principal clause, is not something you can trip upon without strenuous intellectual endeavour. And I was only twelve. That Miss Hughes expected a group of children to rise to such mental heights is remarkable. Particularly so since it must have been what English teachers throughout Britain expected of their pupils when every town had its grammar school. What a brainy country it must have been. No wonder we were about to achieve final victory. If the Battle of Waterloo was won on the playing fields of Eton, then the Second World War was won in the grammar school classrooms. Discuss! Could twelve year olds do it today? Yes of course some of them could. The distribution of native wit is not time specific. But are they required to? No, they are not, and there's the rub. In Chapter Seven I found myself amazed that Miss Sillito expected VA – when some of us were only fourteen – to master the details of the Eastern Question along with some fifty other History topics of comparable complexity. I stand in similar awe at the intellectual dexterity Miss Hughes demanded in clause analysis.

There was something else Miss Hughes had us do that commands profound admiration. Grammar was only one of the elements that made up Eng Lang. Another, believe it or not, was creative writing, an activity pedestalised during the progressive epoch when grammar and grammar schools were disparaged. At our supposedly repressive academy we did a piece of creative writing every week. We did not call it that of course. It was 'essay' writing. Free composition was as much part of the School Certificate exam as grammatical exercises and comprehension tests and it is clear from my surviving homework books that for practice we did an essay a week, more or less. The slim, inky cahiers cover the period November 1944 to May 1947, from when I was twelve to when I was pushing fifteen and about to take the School Cert, so they provide some measure of what bright kids in the best state schools were in those days expected to accomplish. It is impressive. During that time I favoured my English teacher with thirteen grammatical exercises, a tabulated analysis of two poems by Milton and no fewer than thirty one freely composed essays. The imbalance between grammar and creative writing in favour of the latter is notable.

Thus most Sunday mornings, after one of the mammoth post war breakfasts confessed to in Chapter Five, I retired to my room, not to sleep it off but in a free-ranging way to record personal experience and to address issues of the day. Week after week, for two to three hours, I let my mind wander freely over my life so far and let my leaky fountain pen do the talking. This is what I have done and heard, looked at or read about and this is what I think about it. It came out hot, strong and with no punches pulled. Although I knew that, before we sat down to roast pork with crackling, I might have to submit my work for Dad's appraisal and put up with some nit picking. However I knew it was only technical errors he would correct. He would not police the content. I do not remember feeling under any constraint, even from my father, to express correct opinions. Grammar was sacred but comment was free. There was no political censorship or even any holds barred about what aspects of life at Holly Wood were fit matters for my pen. Miss Hughes showed similar tolerance, encouraged perhaps by the juicy insights into her boss's domestic situation that must have enlivened many a marking session. Sure, in her comments, she nagged incessantly about untidiness, clumsy handwriting and poor spelling but it was the quality of the writing that drew her attention at least as much as matters grammatical and presentational. She acknowledged I had a way with words. 'VG' and 'Well expressed' or like commendations were standard and my average mark was eight out of ten. She was however determined to curb the 'exuberance' of my 'verbosity', a failing she attributed, wrongly I think, to Dr Johnson instead of Mr Gladstone. Not that I ever took a blind bit of notice. That is clear from the surviving texts. Despite much tut-tutting my work continued to be both untidy and wordy. It is striking however that Miss Hughes never took issue about the *content* of my diatribes. She never challenged unsubstantiated assertions. She never complained that my socialism was rubbish or that my views on the Germans were racist. Nor did she condemn me as a bumptious little snob or reject my character assassination of a neighbour as libellous as well as offensive. In those days political correctness had not been invented and opinion-wise anything went. It was a freer country than the one we inhabit today. They said freedom of speech was what we had been fighting for and perhaps they were right.

Let us linger longer on the essays I wrote for Miss Hughes, for they shed light both on how we were taught and on my own personal development during the years when war was succeeded by peace and childhood was threatened by adolescence. Five essays related to texts we were doing as Eng Lit and may be regarded as critical commentaries rather than as free compositions. Three others permitted a mere factual outpouring without demanding much in the way of discussion. Thus I once recycled yet again that memorised narrative about the early history of powered flight which I had already used fraudulently in the Scholarship exam. Two further titles invited us to put ourselves in the shoes of somebody else and it was then that I produced that sympathetic evocation of a small shopkeeper putting the shutters up on a Saturday night that has been discussed already. But essays titles usually took one of two standard forms. The first invited a subjective account. We were to choose some episode in our past lives and tell it, amusingly perhaps, how we remembered it. My essay books carry twelve such pieces. The second was different in that it called for a measure of objectivity. We were required to review some current public issue and adopt a debating position in regard to it. We had to construct an argument.

These are some of the happenings I recounted for Miss Hughes. Others have been cited in earlier chapters and another, a determined justification of train spotting as a hobby, will figure in a later one. A frank description of my dismay at my sister's birth, taken from a homework essay, was included in Chapter One, as were two sunnier pieces of pre-war recollection, about how my father gave me a whistle-stop tour of the London sights and about a family outing to Croydon Aerodrome, and in Chapter Two there is a description of my bedroom at Holly Wood. Here are some others. A trip to the theatre is described. It was the Garrick at Southport, a fine Art Deco house long since abandoned to bingo, where we saw Dorothy Squires, a principal boy Mum said was famous, playing Dick Whittington. It must have been quite late in the war, for ice cream, unobtainable for a long period, was on sale at the interval. I was excited by the building, appreciated the buzz of anticipation before the curtain went up and did justice to the balletic elements in the show as well as to the jokes and the slapstick. Some wry comments enliven the piece, such as the taxi driver being disappointed with his tip and all of us at the end saying how much we had enjoyed the performance, whether we had or not. I think the panto essay, which feels like an honest recapitulation of real experience, is better than my piece about a visit to the zoo, which seems contrived, clichéd and possibly fictitious. Miss Hughes begged to differ. She went nuts about my Blakean description of a burning bright tiger and lashed out a stratospheric nine out of ten, a rare accolade. Then there is a convincing account of a holiday train journey from Manchester Victoria to Blackpool Central. There was such a crush waiting on Platform Eleven when the train steamed in that, by the irresistible democratic will of passengers unable to find seats, 'the guard's van [was] taken by storm and the first class compartments carried by assault'. That is how it was travelling in wartime. A lyrical account follows of how the engine, after pulling away with 'a gigantic blast of steam, followed by a number of subsiding puffs', gradually ceased to emit sounds as it gathered speed 'till the only noise made by the train [was] the rhythmic rattling of the coach wheels'. That is how it was in the age of steam. An evocation follows of the Lowryesque landscape between Salford and Bolton, then the thrill of thundering through darkness broken only by the 'red glow of the engine's fire on the tunnel walls' is appreciated, as later is the River Ribble, seen from a bridge, as it 'sparkles in the morning sunlight'. In another essay I described a meal I claimed to have cooked and how the jacket potatoes exploded in the oven. Was that true? Mum's kitchen was undoubtedly a war zone but I guess some fictional content crept into that piece. But perhaps the genre permitted fantasy and even encouraged it. Certainly Miss Hughes approved the saga of the disintegrating tubers for again she gave it nine and slapped on a 'VG'. I am almost sure a breath-taking account of an illicit fishing trip interrupted by the police must be a product of the imagination for I was never a lovable rogue of the 'Just William' variety. However a depressing reference to the incarceration of assorted living creatures in 'about fifty' jam jars in our summer house rings true. I remember with contrition being commandant of that concentration camp for the local fauna.

I am further disconcerted by the libel already mentioned against 'A Character I Know'. It is worth quoting at greater length because it demonstrates the extreme freedom of expression permitted to us and also the extent to which left wing attitudes had already invaded my outlook. I could blame the zeitgeist I suppose. A left-leaning social narrative had captured the British people by the end of the war. Socialism, if not Communism, was no longer merely tolerated but had become, like political correctness today, almost compulsory. September 1945, the date of this piece, is significant. Two months earlier the Labour election landslide proved we had experienced, not just a world war but a social revolution as well. Here then is the indictment presented by Comrade Lord, aged 13¼, against a member of what the Bolsheviks called the 'former classes'. That he was the 'common enemy' of the people of Glossop did not need stating. I did state it though.

[He is] detestable as he represents one of the worst classes of English society, that of the lazy unoccupied landowner. He was ... educated at a well-known public school. After leaving school he lived at home doing nothing useful for anyone but himself, and enjoying an idle, worthless, comfortable life. He dodged the 1914-1918 war with ease and when his parents died he inherited a vast amount of property. He now lives with his housekeeper, dog and bicycle, to which he is greatly attached, in a semi-detached villa in Sheffield Road, Glossop.

As all men, and most sensible women abhor his company he spends his time chatting with the women of the supposedly fashionable gentry ... who appear to think of him as a kind, benevolent gentleman … in order to encourage this illusion [he] collects for and subscribes to the 'National Society for the Prevention of Cruelty to Animals' and other allied societies, and also enthusiastically attends all the whist drives he can, although he is nearly always the only man. In the mornings he goes shopping on his dearly beloved bicycle. In the afternoons he does nothing. In the evenings, if he has no appointment at a whist drive or a committee meeting of the knitting club, he goes for a stroll with his dog and tries to talk to people he sees, though he is seldom successful.

The essay ends with an actual encounter with this 'common enemy'. It seems Sammy Holt, whose hedge was causing an obstruction hazardous to pedestrians, had borrowed my father's shears and set Jas and Alan to subdue the rampant privet, while I stood watching. Along came CE, 'his dog at his heels'. He ventured jocular disparagement of the alignment of the trim, eliciting a response along the lines of, 'When did you last cut a hedge?' CE did not deny his lack of topiary experience but 'piped up in his unique squeaky voice, "Well, I don't think much of your shears"'. Outraged at this supposed slur upon the owner of the implement in question, I was 'unable to control my emotions' and uttered some unspecified insult, without waiting for CE to pass beyond earshot. I harboured no regrets. 'I sincerely hope he heard what I said'.

What are we to make of this abusive rant? First, it was not me talking but Dad. He loathed our dog-loving neighbour – Dad divided humanity into dog-lovers [bad] and non dog-lovers [good] – with the sort of black bile we shall encounter in a later chapter when we listen to Dad's 'table talk', the glut of outrageous sentiment nightly vomited at the tea table. His antagonism was multi-faceted. That CE was a rentier living on 'unearned income' was anathema. When Mum asked for a rise in her housekeeping money he was apt to make a similar charge against her, although he did not dare accuse her of the 'idleness' that characterised CE. In 1945 the deification of hard work was also part of the zeitgeist. 'Workers only!' censorious conductors used to shout at rush hour, barring the platforms of their buses to laden shoppers. Having received a privileged start in life at a public school was another offence against current propriety, one actually that embarrassed many of the new Labour ministers. In this respect Dad gave the case against CE an ingenious twist. Not only had he attended a public school but it had been only a 'minor' example of the type. The offence of posing as a public school man was however insignificant in comparison to his manifest deficiency in manliness. Note that he had not only 'dodged the 1914-1918 war' but had done so 'with ease'. He was not only a blubbering coward but a devious blubbering coward. He should have been shot at dawn. However he faced an even more serious indictment than cowardice. He enjoyed the company of women. Which merited being hung drawn and quartered before being shot. At this stage in the hatchet job I was however out of my depth. Although I parroted all that stuff about whist drives and the knitting club I did not yet understand what got Dad twitchy about 'effeminate' men. I knew the adjective because it figured on one of the lists of hard words in Clay but I did not yet know that it carried a sexual charge. Despite witnessing strange happenings in the bushes on the school field, I was still, at thirteen, quite unaware of homosexuality as a physical activity or of gayness as an outlook. So, since I too found female company more relaxing than forever striving to keep up with my own gender, I understood why the feminine ambience of a whist drive might be appealing. However I was not going to let Dad think me one of those 'nancy-boys', mysterious but despicable creatures routinely denounced at tea-time. Thus to show Dad I was manly I sneered at CE. That I think is probably how this torrent of libellous invective came to be compiled. Astonishingly, Miss Hughes awarded it yet another nine out of ten. Surely she should have challenged the character assassination of a mildly eccentric fellow citizen. She didn't though. Nothing at all is pencilled in the margins of this essay, not even a single 'S' for a spelling mistake. She just wrote '9'. At least she did not add 'VG'.

The other standard essay format was the construction of a debating position. Sometimes it related to personal taste. Thus in January 1945 I debated the question 'Is the wireless a good thing or a bad thing?', concluding that on balance it was good, despite the prevalence of American variety programmes, like the Jack Benny and Bob Hope shows, that were 'silly, stupid and not humorous'. I was an opinionated little prig. Or rather the cultural absolutism of my father had increased, was increasing and ought to have been diminished. A year later I/we returned to the issue, chastising the stars of a comedy show called 'The Merrymart' as 'the worst pair of arrogant and conceited lunatics that have ever disgraced' the BBC. In May 1946 I defended the seaside against the countryside as a holiday destination. Not that a sojourn at a watering place did not also have its down side. In particular resorts were prone to invasion by 'trippers', who polluted the 'thoroughfares' with litter and 'affronted' residents with their 'horrible voices and paper caps'. As well as rude postcards, saucy headbands were popular at the seaside just after the war. With invitations to 'Kiss me Quick' or even 'Get up them Stairs' they invited brief encounters. Dad was not amused. In November of the same year I favoured Miss Hughes with my 'Thoughts on the English Climate', using them as a platform from which to promote a fundamental restructuring of the calendar, so as to maximise the probability of seasonal weather at public holidays. It involved seeking white Christmases at the end of January and abandoning the 'monsoon' month of August in favour of holidays in sunny September. Those arguments still seem to have force and for once they were mine, not Dad's.

Another group of essay titles encouraged specifically political debate and my responses to that challenge were vigorous, opinionated and impassioned. By the age of fourteen I had learned how to pound a platform and thump a tub. But where did my fevered opinions come from? From Dad you might think. Did these essays, like the libel on CE, simply parrot the prejudices thundered out at teatime? One of them certainly did and its circumstances of production are interesting. It was February 1946, the winter was severe and the new Labour government, rather than ending food rationing, now the war was over, ratcheted up the system with ever greater ferocity. One reason for that was that Britain, as one of the four occupying powers, was responsible for feeding some twenty million inhabitants of the British Zone of Germany, who for the time being were quasi-colonial subjects dependent on the British taxpayer. They were starving. In the frozen, devastated Ruhr, even heavy manual workers were striving to stay alive on less than a thousand calories a day, so to help the Germans John Strachey, the Food Minister, cut our rations. You can imagine the outcry. Miss Hughes invited us to join the debate. 'Should our food ration be cut for the people of Europe?' was the title she gave us. I lashed out furiously.

For six years these people have fed upon the produce of the occupied countries of Europe ... [and] have built up constitutions well able to stand up to acute shortages of food for several years. This is being consistently proved by wireless reports which tell of rosy cheeked children and of healthy, arrogant men and women ... [So] although I am fully prepared for the British people to make sacrifices ... to help the really starving nations of Europe, such as Poland ... I think it would be a grave insult to reduce our rations to feed Germany.

The Gauleiter at the tea-table could not have put it better. However I do not hear my father's insistent voice in my other political essays, which are outspokenly left-wing. Dad was never left-wing. Although he voted Labour in 1945, he disliked the working class and was quick to find fault with the new Labour ministers, finding fault being a major part of his mission in life. He found them galore, for example, in 'constipated' Edith Summerskill, junior Food Minister, and in 'squeaky' Aneurin Bevan, Minister for Health, who attracted opprobrium also for being Welsh. His favourite Labour looney was however Emanuel Shinwell, a class warrior and former coal miner – the last sin being beyond absolution – who, as Minister for Fuel and Power, was hopelessly out-manoeuvred by General Winter during the big freeze of 1947. On all that, at last, I took a stand against Dad. I did not share his rubbishing of Labour and 'New Jerusalem', the emerging collectivist post war millennium, in the building of which teething troubles had to be expected. Thus in defiance of Dad I embraced the dominant socialism of the day. We were the masters now, 'we' being the informed intelligentsia, leading the proletariat towards its reward for winning the war. In that noble endeavour I did not need Dad.

What then were the sources of my adolescent militancy? One was the literature of post war planning. In my bedroom I harboured a library of brochures, paperbacks and pamphlets heralding a utopia of motorway interchanges, cities built on stilts, communal feeding centres and the concrete penguin pools without which peacetime felicity would apparently be unsustainable. There will be more about this exotic cultural conditioning in a later chapter but for now, please note a single insistent message gleaned from the planning texts. The principal source of happiness is the state, so it follows that the gentleman in Whitehall knows best. I was trying on the shoes of that benevolent functionary, for I expected to grow up and sit at his very desk, shuffling plans under the beacon light of an anglepoise lamp and issuing helpful decrees. The siren call of the Left was also crooned by fifth form opinion and particularly by Arthur Higginbottom, who sat next to me in Room 15. He wanted to be an architect and have his own anglepoise, so he was doing Art for School Cert. The stigma of Art – we have seen it was a soft option for those who struggled with proper subjects – condemned poor 'Tat' in Dad's eyes. He was not a suitable companion for a high flyer like me. Mum agreed that Tat was undesirable but on different grounds. The Higginbottoms kept a chip shop so they were not nice to know. But despite discouragement Tat and I struck up a friendship and, in a gesture of solidarity with Comrade Stalin, whose *History of the Communist Party of the Soviet Union* Tat kept in his desk, we used to go across to the public library to read the *Daily Worker*, organ of the Communist Party of Great Britain. Our hero was Harry Pollitt, General Secretary of that enlightened body. It was thus that Tat, who was handy with his pencil, came to decorate the back page of my essay book with the device reproduced on *Plate 15 bottom right*. It nicely encapsulates the ideological position just indicated. The future was socialist. The state will lead the people. And there will be blood. That you can't make omelettes without breaking eggs was axiomatic.

That was the background to the ongoing critique of capitalism I presented to Miss Hughes whenever she gave me an opportunity of raising her awareness. Thus in January 1947 I explained to her, in suitably simple terms, just why it was that 'The Time has come for the Railways to be Nationalised'. There was an overwhelming case, I began, for state control, not just of the railways but of 'all major industries'.

Under the present system the whole profits of a railway company, or for that matter any other industry, go into the pockets of a handful of wealthy shareholders [like CE, or my Uncle Albert, I might have added] … [whereas] under nationalisation the profits of the railways would go to the betterment of the community as a whole.

Well, that was obvious to 'any sane person free from vested interests'. 'QED', as we used to write at the end of a theorem in Geometry.

With nationalisation the present deficiencies of the railways such as slow, uncomfortable, unpunctual train services; bleak, drab uncomfortable stations and, not least important, the present comparatively poor conditions of railway employees, would almost automatically disappear.

Note the semi-colon and also the saving 'almost' qualifying 'automatically.' Dogmatic I was not. Just sane. And compassionate. Up the workers. The response of my reader was congratulatory not critical. '9' 'Good', was Miss Hughes's only comment. She was right, in a sense. It is an articulate piece, a succinct summation of Marxism-Leninism. You would scarcely argue with that in 1947 any more than today you would challenge the narrative of feminism, or subject the evidence for global warming to rigorous scrutiny. Pervasive leftism marks other political essays. A grim account of Victorian working class housing, supporting the contention that we were better off in the 1940s than the 1840s, might have come straight out of Engels. In another essay I argued that Glossop was unsuitable for expansion as a 'new town' because the valley being narrow, only 'ribbon development' would be possible and that, being a product of unbridled capitalism, was deeply and universally deplored by planners. In yet another burst of socialism, prompted by the proposition 'We must end War or War will end Us', I declared it 'painfully obvious' that the USA, then the only nuclear power, was bent on the destruction of the Soviet Union before the latter acquired an atomic bomb.

I am saying that although grammar took up a lot of our time in Eng Lang, essay writing was at least equally important and it called for very different mental qualities. I am also saying the opportunities it provided for creative writing were highly beneficial. I owe to the imperatives of the weekly essay the habit of frequently sitting down and ordering on paper my memories, feelings and thoughts. Like other good habits acquired at Glossop Grammar School – such as learning things by heart – it enriched my life and still does. It is why I am writing this memoir. Working on it always makes me feel much better, even in the knowledge that perhaps nobody except a few intimates will ever read it. Creative writing works a treat so it was great that our teachers, and indeed the examiners, made us do it. But I wonder how far encouragement of creativity was the object of the exercise. If it had been surely Miss Hughes would have entered into *dialogue* about the *content* of my essays. 'Did this really happen or are you making it up?' or 'What is your evidence for that sweeping statement?' or 'You have put only one side of the argument' or 'Have you ever heard about the law of libel?' As I say, she never did that. Her marking seems to have been wholly constrained by three objectives, all of them disciplinary. First, she was to correct spelling mistakes and grammatical blunders. She did that meticulously. Since every week, for our class alone, she similarly scrutinised thirty odd other packages of error, it must have been very boring and I suppose we must salute her dedication. At the same time she was to promote tidiness and good handwriting and in that, with me, she had her work cut out. I expect she passed with relief from the chaotic ink-field of my book to the orderly, orthographic orchards typically maintained by the girls in the class. Finally she was to encourage something called 'good' style. I never knew what it was and suspect it doesn't exist. Certainly her weekly plea for me to curb my 'verbosity' went studiously unheeded. I mean 'studiously'. My resistance to stylistic conditioning was deliberate. I liked words. I enjoyed experimenting with them. The more I played around with them the more they gave me a buzz. It seems then that the object of the marking was to find fault rather than commend creativity. That situation however had an unintended consequence that was as brilliant as the terms of assessment were dim. It gave us total freedom of speech. Since 'she' took no interest our opinions, we could entertain whatever thoughts and feelings were fermenting in our impressionable heads. It took the emergence of political correctness some thirty years later to alter that happy situation. By then Glossop Grammar School had gone, along with the School Certificate and homework essays too, I guess.

Which brings us to English Literature. It was raised up at our school above all other parts of the curriculum and presented with a reverence not attached to any other subject, not even to Maths or English Language. Communion with the immortals of Eng Lit gave us Rhyme, the third foundation 'R' that, along with Ritual and Rote, constituted the grammar school experience. If Rote brought us light, Rhyme provided sweetness to flavour it. Promotion of 'sweetness and light' was the objective of Matthew Arnold, the schools inspector whose proposal that the best that has ever been known and thought might be distilled into a hundred best books, had a lot to do with the emergence of English as an academic discipline. That happened about the turn of the twentieth century, and at provincial universities rather than at Oxford or Cambridge, at the very same time as the grammar school was invented. The two were made for each other. Literature in English was more accessible to scholarship children than the Greek and Latin classics, so in the new schools it usurped their pride of place and what Homer was to Eton, Shakespeare became to Milltown Grammar. His works demonstrated nobility in thought and feeling and at the same time showed you how to express yourself with wit and eloquence. Perhaps Eng Lit had another function also that stemmed from the age in which it entered the school curriculum. In the noontide of the British Empire it encapsulated British values. Rhyme then constituted a big part of what grammar schools were all about. Furthermore at Glossop in the 1940s it was dispensed with a special intensity under a headmaster, himself a man of letters, powerfully driven to communicate his passion. For by a process that will be explored in a later chapter, Eng Lit had become for Dad, more than just his own particular subject. It was rather the faith he lived by. In a burning revolt against his Nonconformist upbringing, fanned by his experience in the Great War, he had made Shakespeare his Jesus.

For all that, as we know, Eng Lit in the first year made little impact on me. What supercilious Miss Norris gave us was mostly Greek legends. I knew them already and was not keen on others getting the key to my secret garden, stealing friends like Odysseus or Hector, to say nothing of coming between me and fair Psyche. Also I disliked the grubby texts issued to us, defaced by the scribbles and doodles of previous users and a squalid contrast to my beautiful bedside volume. You could pick up something nasty. We also recited a lot of ballads. The doings of Sir Patrick Spens and his friends were unfamiliar but they seemed poor stuff compared with the deeds of Agamemnon and his companions. Perhaps it was because Miss Norris did nothing to induct us into the historical background, to unlock how it was in the Borders in the middle ages. The Greek legends worked for me because of the Greek history I had picked up from my bedside books and because from war maps I knew the geography of the Mediterranean. But I had no idea where Dunfermline town was and Miss Greenwood never told us what it was noted for. And why was the king sitting there and which king was he and what exactly was he king of? I gave up. When text and context were divorced I got lost and wished my English and History teachers would put their heads together and dove-tail their syllabuses. We have already noticed how despite spending so much time with Shakespeare's kings the Hundred Years War and the Wars of the Roses never cropped up in History. So one way and another my early exposure to 'rhyme' was disappointing. There was however one book Miss Norris gave us that worked for me. It was *The Wind in the Willows*. Not only were Ratty, Mole and Toad depicted warts and all, and thus convincingly, but the locations of their doings were carefully delineated by an author with affection for the places he described. Not that they were the sort of places I knew myself. The stately river on which they messed about was quite unlike the roaring Cowbrook messed about in by me and the Holt twins. But the 'foreign' character of the riverbank was appealing. Kenneth Grahame took me travelling through the south of England and it was an interesting trip.

It was in the second year when we were twelve – in III Upper as our class was confusingly known – that proper Eng Lit began. That is we met Shakespeare. Actually I knew him already. When I was three and still living in Chorlton I used to finger the red leather binding of four handsome volumes in the bookcase which Mum, with a surprising hint of reverence, said were 'Daddy's Shakespeares'. That was mysterious but so is much of life when you are three so, for the moment, I left it at that. These books however were obviously special. They exuded sanctity, like the big bibles at Southport, and I respected that. Then one Christmas, as literacy was at last dawning, I was given a children's book of 'Tales from Shakespeare'. It was not much cop. The stories carried mistaken identity to ridiculous extremes and anyway the characters were mostly Italians, which was a turn-off because they were enemy aliens and, unlike their fiendish German allies, were no good at fighting, as we had several times proved at Sidi Barani. However the 'tales from' book prompted another look at the leathery 'Collected Works' now ranged behind Dad's chair in the Study. Three of the volumes had long names. Dad had to help me with two of them – 'Comedies' and Tragedies' – but I recognised 'Histories' and that was encouraging. Those three books were all poetry, as far as I could tell when I flipped their pages, but the last in the series, called 'Life: Sydney Lee', being in ordinary writing and illustrated as well, was more accessible. The relationship between Shakespeare and Mr Lee eluded me but the pictures in Volume Four certainly did a lot for the great man. They showed what he actually looked like and, even more enticing, what sort of houses he lived in. These were heart-achingly modern, with timbered fronts and leaded windows, just like the semi we had lived in at Stretford, before our exile to Glossop, and the ones lucky relatives in London and at St Anne's-on-Sea still inhabited. Which put Shakespeare one up in my eyes. He was positively suburban. Nevertheless mystery still attached to him. Then one day in 1943 Dad swept into III Upper's classroom and all was light. First he cleared up the mystery of Volume Four 'Life', which turned out to be *about* Shakespeare, not *by* him. He told us all about that life because, unlike Miss Norris he believed in context. He went right through the Shakespeare CV from birth via Stratford Grammar School and the London stage to death back in Stratford. The first and last events both occurred on 23 April which was also St George's Day and that was scarcely coincidence. He threw in stuff about butchers and poaching and first folios and second best beds and rounded off a lively lecture with a powerful evocation of the 'wooden O' on Bankside. When we later saw the Globe itself in Lawrence Olivier's film of *Henry V* the details coincided uncannily with what Dad had told III Upper and that did a lot for Dad's cred too. However could one small head carry all he knew?

Then it was on with the motley or rather – parts in the cast having been allocated to class members, with Dad keeping the starring role for himself – 'Take out your *Merchant of Venices*, Act One, Scene One'. Lesson by lesson for a whole term we read the play like that, with each line recited, haltingly – unless Dad himself delivered it, doing full justice to its sonorities – until Act Five was completed. Next term we would do the same for say *Julius Caesar*, followed perhaps by *Twelfth Night* in the summer. Thus after three years we had nine complete plays under our belts and ringing in our ears. Then for School Cert we did *Macbeth* all over again in even greater detail. It was a version of the mallet process but, as so often with rote learning, it had much to be said for it. We did not of course just read parts. The meaning of every word and every line was teased out by question and answer followed, if necessary by an official ruling from Dad or, more probably from Miss Hughes, his understudy, who replaced Miss Norris when mercifully, in 1944, that lady went back to London where she had come from, placing on that long suffering city a burden additional to the doodlebugs. We were expected to make marginal notes, thus further disfiguring our tattered texts, and were given long passages to learn by heart ready for a test tomorrow. In the end of term examinations we did 'context' questions. Unfortunately those exercises did not, in the case of say *The Merchant of Venice*, call for a discussion of sixteenth century Mediterranean trade routes or of anti-Semitism in the early modern period, for even Dad did not mix History and Eng Lit with such boldness. You simply had to 'translate' each passage while showing where it came in the text and what happened next. Well … you may be appalled, dear modern reader, and I think I know what you mean. Where is the feeling, the passion, the ecstasy? Sure that desk top way of doing

Shakespeare was deficient in a crucial respect. It took the drama out of the play. In the theatre you get the whole thing in three tense hours but it took us three laborious months. So pace and tension were lost and compelling twists in the plot were missed. We did not notice, for example, how in the courtroom scene Portia, having tried and failed with a softly softly appeal to Shylock's better nature, then goes straight for the jugular with a hard line judgement. Wow! But all was not lost. We did spend several lessons on Portia's analysis of mercy and its uses. That involved a careful scrutiny of Shakespeare's famous word craft and was also a demanding exercise in philosophical enquiry. What is justice? Should it be seasoned with mercy? If so, when? Which is asking a lot of twelve year olds but it is nevertheless good for them to be challenged. I am saying we missed out on the drama but appreciated the poetry and tangled with some hard thought. I think Dad saw a Shakespeare play as a series of profound poems linked by a shallow plot. His business was with the poetry not the drama and yielded to none in his informed feeling for poetry. It abided in his soul. And he believed he had a solemn duty poetry-wise. Since the best that has been known and thought finds its finest expression in poetry, in teaching us Shakespeare, he was transmitting to the next generation what he believed was the best ever written. There was nobility in that task. I think he thought it was above all what his school was for. Did Shakespeare, Gauleiter-style work? It did for me and on occasions when I have compared notes in later years with fellow survivors of the Gauleiter's academy it seems to have done a lot for them as well. Certainly his charismatic teaching is recalled with great affection.

I think it worked like this. The grip of the Bard on the mind and spirit tightened in three distinct phases. Phase One was the immediate reward of learning him by heart. We had to memorise acres of the prescribed plays for homework and in addition Dad had me get up other speeches for domestic consumption. Once as a family treat, after Christmas dinner, he had me stand in Granny's drawing room and declaim Mark Antony's funeral oration over Caesar. He lost no opportunity, by the way, of telling me that, as my second name, I was given Antony – without the 'h' – in tribute to that flawed Roman, a whim that has caused me endless bother when engaging with officialdom. I liked memorising Shakespeare though. By the time I was fifteen I carried in my head an extensive collection of Shakespeare 'recordings' that I could play at will, something I did frequently and with great pleasure. Usually I just recited them silently but, if I was sure I was alone, I might give them voice. I remember turning up the volume on a darkening November afternoon, going home alone over the Royle, the cinder track past the chicken runs. An overwhelming torrent of words just cascaded from my mouth. It was gloriously enjoyable. It still is, for I retain remnants of the collection. So Phase One brought instant and abundant pleasure, a joyful response to the *sound* of Shakespeare. Phase Two only gradually took shape. It took me beyond sound towards *understanding*. Usually in the first instance I only dimly knew what the words and phrases meant, even those already explained in class, but as I rolled them around in my mind, meaning began to dawn. T S Eliot observed that poetry communicates before it is understood and that certainly was my experience. As I puzzled over a favourite passage intellectual curiosity followed on libidinal satisfaction. I began to see what Shakespeare meant. It was not just particular words but whole speeches that clicked. It seemed Shakespeare had an understanding of the human condition not bounded by the outlook of his own time. He was a man for all ages and remarkably open minded. He did not judge. Instead he looked at what life throws up, chewed it over, offered a range of possible explanations but arrived at no final conclusion. He laid out the options but did not come down on one side or the other. Thus Hamlet reviews the pros and cons of suicide – a matter of interest to a depressed adolescent – but does not settle the question of whether it is better to be or not to be. And Macbeth deliberates on how far you should go in ruthless pursuit of self-interest. 'If it were done when 'tis done' then fair enough, just get on with it. But would doing it be the end of the matter? Would you get away with it? Thus in contemplating the Shakespearian software, installed in my memory, I pursued wisdom my own way. Confidence in doing it my way was Phase Three, the ultimate benefit of memorising Shakespeare. I had puzzled out the sense of complex passages by my own unaided efforts and it followed that the complicated thoughts of other authors might similarly yield to dogged contemplation. So at last, from about the age of twelve, I began to read properly. Whenever I got interested in something I started to read about it, often buying books with my pocket money. I discovered architecture for example that way. That new departure began with a Puffin Picture Book by S R Badmin called *Village and Town*, a seemingly minor work which, as we shall see, had a determining effect on

211

my adult mind-set, but having swallowed Badmin I confidently plunged into the burgeoning grown-up literature on post war planning that made the shelves of W H Smith's groan under the weight of New Jerusalem expectation. What my youthful immersion in Shakespeare did not do however was make me a lifelong fan of the Bard. It had been good while it lasted but he and I later parted company. I cannot recall when I last read one of the plays. Too often at a performance I fall asleep. And for me Stratford is a nasty little town, pole-axed by tourism. Curious. That outcome however does not invalidate the learning. Shakespeare expanded my intellectual capacity and filled my head with beautiful words. Many thanks. To Dad as well as to his saviour.

Was there Eng Lit at Glossop Grammar School beyond Shakespeare? There was Milton, a distant runner-up in the Poetry Premiership, followed by Wordsworth and Chaucer, who occupied the remaining two places in the top four. Dad's plug for the author of *Milton's Minor Poems* – his major works being, like sex, reserved for after the School Cert – did not galvanise Remove A the way his introduction to Shakespeare had had III Upper 'straining at the slips', like Harry's lads at Honfleur. You sensed Dad did not really like Milton. Sure he acknowledged the guy had a way with words but there was something about him the Gauleiter definitely disapproved of. Being, unlike Shakespeare, seriously into religion he was ideologically unsound. Since religion in England when Milton was doing his minor poems was in a state of extraordinary flux you would have thought Dad would therefore have put us in the picture about puritans, presbyterians and papists. But, disdaining to pander to the concerns of 'bloody parsons', he tried to present young Milton instead as a role model for upwardly mobile swots. He got into Cambridge when he was only my age [13] and went on to get a top job in the civil service. So think on. He had bad luck later though. He went blind and nearly got put on trial as a war criminal, like the Nazi leaders at that very moment sitting in the dock at Nuremberg. But which war was it Milton had disgraced himself in? History lessons did not come to our aid either. As just observed English and History should have illuminated each other but did not because syllabuses were not co-ordinated and anyway each year the history narrative fell seriously short of its target date, which meant we lost the hundred years between James I and George I altogether. Civil War? What civil war? So when faced with Milton's sonnet 'On the New Forcers of Conscience under the Long Parliament' we were really stuck. Take the catchy phrase 'New presbyter is but old priest writ large'. It sounded convincing but what did it mean? And how come the proceedings of that parliament were protracted? As for the phrase 'Clip their phylacteries and balk their ears' well ... what was one of those and what do you clip it with? And how do you balk ears? Was it the same as boxing them? Making us learn stuff we could not possibly understand without assistance seemed unfair. I learnt the piece by heart however and after a few repetitions, as usual, got to glory in the sounds. It communicated despite not being understood one solitary jot. Decades later however, as at last I caught up on the Stuarts, pennies dropped. Again the mallet process paid off in the end. Dad could have done better though.

Like *Macbeth*, we came back to *Milton's Minor Poems* for the School Cert, this time under the guidance of Miss Hughes. Judging by the exercise reproduced below, she prepared us efficiently. In a table we had to break down the twin poems *L'Allegro* [celebrating jollity] and *Il Penseroso* [celebrating melancholy] to demonstrate a calculated similarity of format. Thus the pleasures of the sunlight, 'robed in flames and amber light', contrast with those of the shade amid 'shadows brown that Sylvan loved'. I found twelve such pairs. And I was only thirteen at the time. Again a sophisticated exercise testifies to the elevated intellectual level Remove A must have attained. Presumably we also puzzled out the classical references with which the 'minor' poems are studded and naturally we learned whole chunks of Milton's splendid verse by heart. That was always worthwhile. I remember, for example, one golden evening, a few weeks after the School Cert was over, watching seagulls at rest from a Cornish cliff. 'Birds of calm sit brooding on the charmèd wave,' I thought, idly quoting the 'Ode on the Morning of Christ's Nativity'. Poetry can grab you like that. It catches you unawares and that is nice.

We must have sampled other poets as well as Shakespeare and Milton but I have forgotten which ones, apart from Wordsworth on Westminster Bridge [subject of another homework exercise] and Keats on the nightingale. According to the *Observer's Book of British Birds*, nightingales were quite rare so had Keats really heard one or was he just making it up, like I sometimes did with homework essays? In time however I ceased to be dependent on Miss Hughes, or even Dad, for the fix of poetry I was starting to crave. Indeed, as I exercised that capacity for DIY learning that sprang from immersion in Shakespeare, poetry became a serious addiction. So I needed a pusher and found one in the form of a book on Dad's shelves in the Study which I purloined it and set beside *The Observer's Book of British Birds,* the *County of London Plan* and *Locomotives of the London and North Eastern Railway* in the old kitchen dresser, which served as my bedroom bookcase. It was a volume in the Everyman series [green and gilt with embossed stripes you could run your nails along] called *Palgrave's Golden Treasury* and it was full of poems arranged in chronological order, a feature I found particularly helpful. You could tell at a glance that Shakespeare came before Milton, who came before Keats, who came before Tennyson. Thus the poems fitted easily into my History Meccano and I knew where I was. I started bang in the middle of the eighteenth century because that was where School Cert History began. If my teachers would not make links between the subjects, then I must do it for myself. Thus Grey's elegy became the first poem I memorised on my own initiative. During the long, hot, School Cert summer of 1947, I used to broadcast it sonorities from the saddle during solitary bike rides around the moorland borders of Glossop that served as a break from swotting. 'The paths of glory lead but to the grave' I vouchsafed to grazing sheep and swooping swallows, warning them against the vanity of 'storied urn or animated bust'. Animated busts were on offer elsewhere in the *Golden Treasury*. Beneath Julia's silk gown Robert Herrick detected a 'brave vibration each way free.' 'Oh how that glittering taketh me,' he said. Yes, it took me too. Particularly when, bored by, say the French subjunctive, my wandering eye found 'sweet disorder in the dress' across the room, where the girls sat. There was actually quite a lot of sex in Palgrave when you worked it out. There was that 'lovely woman' for example who 'stoops to folly'. What exactly was Thomas Hood hinting at? But mostly it was the sound that took me. Like the cadences of a chap called Campbell, recalling some battle long ago that must have been fought out of season.

On Linden, when the sun was low,
All bloodless lay the untrodden snow,
And dark as winter was the flow
Of Iser rolling rapidly.

That river really does flow extra fast. I know because we once stayed at a camp site on its bank and watched beer-swilling Munichers in lederhosen shooting its rapids on rafts.

We did prose as well as verse but you knew prose didn't matter as much because we just read the texts for homework instead of analysing them in class. Every term a classic novel or some elevated work of non-fiction was issued for our edification. The earth only moved once. *Under the Greenwood Tree* must be Hardy's least compelling hymn to rural misery because, although slow moving, it is not all that miserable. *Lorna Doone* at least had pace. According to a dutiful account I put into essay form, the Exmoor torrent, in which plucky John Ridd stood thigh-deep throughout a February day, rolled as rapidly as the Iser. There's manliness for you. There was dyed in the wool pluck also in *A Shepherd's Life*, W H Hudson's long forgotten tribute to horny handed Wiltshire peasants. I was bold enough to declare Hudson's characterization 'unreal and exajerated' [sic] and was rewarded by Miss Hughes, not only with an 'S' in the margin, but also with 'Well expressed 8½'. I wearied of the locations of our prescribed texts as well as of their insistent muscularity. Literature seemed always to be set somewhere on the Great Western. It was a pity we never did anything closer to home, like the Brontes, Elizabeth Gaskell or *Hard Times*. But we did do *A Tale of Two Cities* which, although jam-packed with manliness, at least did not unfurl in the West Country. Here also Eng Lit and History for once were united, for the origins of the French Revolution as presented by Dickens – the foppish aristocrats had only themselves to blame – chimed in with one of the causal factors identified by Miss Sillito.

One piece of prose changed me however. It was our set book for the autumn term of 1945 and at first sight I could not have guessed the impact it would have, for neither the author nor the title gave grounds for hope. Surely Siegfried was a German name and what was coming out about the Hun, in the war crimes trials currently in the news, suggested Dad had a point when he said the only good German was a dead one. Also it seemed this book was about country sports so it promised yet another dollop of manliness somewhere down south. Yet after just a few pages Siegfried Sassoon, who turned out not to be German at all, had become a closer friend than any I had so far encountered on the pages of a book – closer even than Rupert Bear or Mole in *The Wind in the Willows*. That was amazing because we did not appear to have much in common. He came from Sussex and lived among orchards and rectories, amid the trappings of English pastoral felicity, whereas it was only me who found beauty in mills and moors. Also going to classical music concerts was to him as much a part of everyday life as going to the pictures was for me. It seemed they induced ecstasy and I was prepared to believe him although it was a scene beyond my personal experience. Most of all he was good at games and I was rubbish. He not only excelled at cricket but practically lived on horseback and hence the title, *Memoirs of a Fox Hunting Man*. It seemed riding to hounds across the uncluttered downs in winter brought a thrill that exceeded even that of shouting poetry across dry stone walls from the saddle of a bike. I envied Siegfried his pleasures and his physical vitality but there was more to our relationship than emulation. Despite our different backgrounds he seemed very like me. Although bursting with energy he took his time. He liked his own company. He balanced activity with contemplation. There was space in his life for looking and thinking. Indeed he seemed to enjoy unfettered leisure, being, as far as I could tell, unburdened with a job and not registered as a student. But he was the opposite of idle. He did his own thing with intense commitment and thus beautifully. Indeed he offered a model for a liberated but energetic way of life that attracted me strongly and which, I suppose, eventually, through the blessing of early retirement, I actually secured. There was something else about Siegfried that put me at my ease in a way I never felt with any real life acquaintances, except maybe for my friend Jas who, I realise in retrospect, had much in common with my new literary hero. The fox hunting man was bold, brave and physically accomplished *but he was not manly*. Indeed there was something about Siegfried that felt positively feminine. I felt I too had feminine feelings even though they were constrained in the masculine strait-jacket buckled around me by Dad and school and the prevailing culture. I do not mean I was gay. I have never ever known any such promptings and when, at the age of thirteen, I first read *Memoirs of a Fox Hunting Man* I did not know homosexuality even existed. Certainly I did not know Siegfried was gay – nor that, after being a fox hunting man, he became a war hero and a war poet and an anti-war protestor. I found all that out much later. I knew at once though that I had a friend for life.

Which concludes our survey of the grammar school version of the Three Rs. During the second half of the war and in the early years of peace I was, at the Gauleiter's well conducted drill hall, inducted by ritual, rote and rhyme into some of what Arnold conceived as the 'the best that has been known and said in the world'. It was not all plain sailing but then a few hitches were only to be expected in wartime travel. Contrary to what I expected to remember when I set out on this exploration of how and what long ago I learned at GGS, I gladly acknowledge that the Three Super-Rs did me a lot of good. I am convinced they did a lot of good also to my fellow pupils, who every morning gathered tightly together in their hundreds under Gau's scrutiny in our atmospheric assembly hall. He and his staff performed public duty of a high order and the folk of Glossop owed them many thanks. Or rather that minority of local families did, whose children were lucky enough to get 'jiggled and shaken' by the selection system through the iron gates of the school. May I anyway offer my own belated expression of gratitude to the ghosts of Dad and his team?

However it was not just the strengthening medicine of the Three Rs that was prescribed for me at school. Some other treatments I was there subjected to seem in retrospect to have been little less than toxic. They did me a lot of harm. Hence the title of the next chapter – 'Poison'.

Chapter 9

POISON

Lest 'Poison' seems too strong a title, let there be a final summation of the benign aspects of my schooling at Glossop Grammar School. I was ushered into an ordered community whose ritual observances were powerful and sometimes moving. I was introduced to a range of academic disciplines and given effective training in their various rigours. That is, I was filled up by rote with assorted facts and skills by capable teachers who sometimes also got me thinking. And, mostly through poetry, I was encouraged to have feelings and to express them. It was not a bad brew. Again, the mixture as recalled inspires more respect than at the start of this enquiry I would have expected. As an instrument for intellectual development, the state education system, as it then operated, served me well. I wish my daughter had been so lucky. She suffered schooling in the dark ages – the 1970s and 1980s.

My own education also had a darker side. There were malignant growths as well as benign influences, poison as well as wholesome sustenance. Malignancy was rooted partly in those 'non-academic' parts of the curriculum that lay outside our preparation for the School Certificate, that is Art and Craft, and Games and PE, areas in which my performance was consistently dismal. In those subjects I discovered what it feels like to be found lumpish to the extent that no amount of jiggling will get you through the shaking plates of the screening plant, leaving you fit only for a slag heap, reserved for over-weight, ham-fisted, butter-fingered, clumsy clots with two left feet. In Art and PE I suffered the torments of failure that those left out of Miss Max's Scholarship Class must have felt in Standard Four at St Luke's. What made it worse was that there was apparently no help for it. Determinism prevailed. You were what you were and that was that. The ethic was not just Protestant, it was *Calvinist*. Inadequacy was incurable. If at first you don't succeed, then you might as well pack it in. A single failure to catch a ball, run a fairly rapid hundred yards, draw a recognisable Spitfire or rig up a cardboard box, proved infallibly that you were not up to it and never would be. You were no good, so go away. Another malignancy stemmed from the virtual absence of moral education. All we got were homilies at Assembly and a period a week labelled 'RI' [Religious Instruction], the content of which I have entirely forgotten but not the contempt in which it was collusively held by teachers and pupils. As I lurched towards puberty I found myself plunged into depression – although of course I did not know that name for how I felt – and in desperate need of moral guidance. I give advance warning that a blow by blow account of my ordeal – it began without warning on Sports Day 1945 – will be provided below. I fear it may challenge your credulity but I assure you the things I shall recount really happened. I was besieged by tenacious guilt that resisted rational rebuttal. It has never since quite left me alone.

Compared with my struggles with a troubled soul, being no good at Art was, in the short term anyway, not so bad. Art was not important. It only got two periods a week and most of us dropped it after two years anyway. Also we had to trek over to makeshift quarters in the Lecture Room at the Vic, the proper function of which was to accommodate the bar at public dances. Such signals were very clear. Art was academically inferior and if you carried on with it and did it for School Cert that proved you were thick. It was occupational therapy for the intellectually disabled. The production line tasks Mr Gooch set us confirmed that impression. Mostly we made posters advertising 'Odol Toothpaste'. We did it by numbers in a production line process where accuracy was all and imagination came nowhere. It was worse than doing endless grammar in English. It ensured the suppression of spontaneity and the death of joy. This seemed to suit the likes of Chris Gillings, whose mother wanted him to be a 'commercial artist'. He found comfort in a mechanical task endlessly repeated, but it defeated my stiff fingers and restless brain. My letters turned out too spindly if they were not too thick and they could no more stand up than a drunken sailor. When I applied paint, they went blotchy and sprouted whiskers, as an unsteady hand trespassed beyond pencil lines already scarred by frequent erasure. My artwork too was unconvincing. I could not capture a tube of toothpaste or represent shining teeth. Also everything had to be confined within an exact quarter inch margin, even when, as an end of term treat, we were allowed a session of free composition from a list of options like 'A Country Walk' or 'The Sinking of the Bismarck'. Sometimes he brought his ruler over and checked my margins and I would have got them wrong.

Art and Woodwork went together. That was partly because we were a small school and, since there was not enough work for two teachers, the Art Master doubled as the Carpentry Instructor. Perhaps also the arrangement reflected the 'Arts and Crafts' thinking of John Ruskin and William Morris. The workman, if his employers allow him freedom of expression, experiences the joy of creativity just as the artist does and drawing a firm line between art and craft is unhelpful. Indeed making things by hand that are useful and therefore beautiful is good for all of us. I understand that now, as will be clear from earlier passages in this book. In Chapter One my mother's Ruskinian satisfaction in housework was recalled and in Chapter Four there is an appreciation of how making Spitfires out of firewood brought so much satisfaction to my friend Jas. But somehow I never got that buzz myself, inheriting instead my father's DIY incompetence and the contempt for manual labour with which he disguised his hang-ups. Unfortunately Mr Gooch the temporary Art master proved quite unable to unscramble all that – to communicate the Ruskinian outlook and show me that my ineptitude was all in the mind. Had I instead been taught by Mr Bell the permanent incumbent such a rescue act might well have taken place, with immense benefit to my adult outlook and experience. For Gordon Bell was a kindly and understanding man who had been nurtured in the attitudes of Ruskin and Morris. In my early years at the grammar school however he was suffering forced labour on the notorious jungle railway forged by the Japanese to link their conquests in Thailand and Burma. When he returned, blinking in disbelief at his survival, he and his wife bought Miss Leech's bungalow and he turned its commonplace garden – part of the territory over which the Holts and I enjoyed playing rights – into an earthly paradise. No doubt it was an affirmation of life, following a journey on the railway of death. To learn carpentry and drawing at his gentle hands might have banished from my poisoned head a whole squadron of demons.

There is touching testimony to what Mr Bell might have done for me in the memoir of our school's most famous ex-pupil. Vivienne Westwood arrived in 1952, two years after I left. She 'loved school, absolutely loved it'. Furthermore she beat me in History, getting 90% in 'O' Level whereas in School Cert I only got 87%. However, although she flourished under Mr Scott, a successor of Miss Sillito, it was Mr Bell, she says who set her on the path that made her famous. The serenity with which he survived horrific wartime experience made him, says Dame Vivienne, a 'dramatic presence' in the school and she tells how 'he lisped because he'd been tortured and had his tongue cut'. Just before she had to leave because her family were relocating to London:

Mr Bell told me there was this art gallery in Manchester and so I went. It changed my life really.

I think that might have been during the autumn of 1957 when the Manchester City Art Gallery held a special exhibition to mark the centenary of the massive 1857 'Art Treasures' display, which had been Manchester's answer to London's Great Exhibition of 1851. I remember the centenary show. It was a knock out. No wonder it blew young Vivienne's mind. Then Mr Bell showed her a book about the Impressionists and got her to imitate Seurat's stippling technique.

He said, 'Don't do it with a little brush, don't be safe' and so I did these landscapes and things with a large stencil brush. Free.

It seems he was amazed at the talent he confronted, which was not confined to copying the masters. For he also

... saw me drawing some fashion sketch ... and he was the first person to say that I had real skill.

Wow! So that is how a great career was ignited. It's wonderful, isn't it how a little encouragement can change lives. Next Mr Bell helped her put together a portfolio, on the strength of which she got into art school. She says he gave her 'courage' to entertain a future beyond the horizons set, not only by her home, but also it seems by Dad's school, for she is sharply critical of the careers advice provided. Nevertheless Mr Bell said, 'Go on, go' and she did. It seems saying it got him into a bit of bother with his wife who 'got fed up with him going on about me!' Well, yes … she would, wouldn't she?

That is a heart-warming tale of how much good good teachers can accomplish and it is good also to know that Art at GGS became inspirational when Gordon Bell came back from hell. Unfortunately however that was too late for me. By then I had reached Remove A and we had put away childish things like Art and Woodwork, along with other trivial pursuits like Music and Biology. So instead of encouraging Mr Bell, I got hysterical 'Daddy' Gooch. He never had a chance. He was a prissy southerner with a high-pitched voice, washed up in Glossop in 1940 when the child population of invasion-threatened Lowestoft was evacuated to safe Glossop. Mr Gooch must have been one of the accompanying teachers and somehow got transferred to our school when Mr Bell was called up. The Lowestoft evacuees were acknowledged to be more fragrant than their Manchester predecessors but better personal hygiene did not soften the barbaric East Anglian accents by which Glossopians were now daily affronted. Thus racial tension escalated and that did not help Mr Gooch keep order. Indeed in his lessons discipline disintegrated as it never did with any of our regular teachers. 'Big sam! Big sam!' he would screech in torment. The imposition of cubes [big sums] was a sensible sanction of some educational value much favoured at GGS where the penal code, let it be understood, was exceptionally mild for its time. Despite the maulings poor Daddy Gooch suffered in the bear pit that was the Art room, his chief molester was not 'Doc' Foster or 'Animal' Dewsnap, the Fourth Form Torquemadas, but my Dad. At teatime, as we know, Dad summoned spectres to the feast, by way of reminding his children, that it was not just the Germans we were fighting but a whole regiment of bad guys including, conshies, pansies, profiteers, parsons and those, typically from the south of England, possessed of 'constipated' accents. Well, poor effeminate, Mr Gooch from down south, with his strangulated voice, was not only flagrantly out of uniform while of military age, but had had the effrontery to take lodgings with the Rev Dawson-Bowling, Vicar of Dinting, who to the offence of his cloth added the provocation of a double-barrelled surname. Like I say, he stood not a chance.

To crown it all Daddy Gooch could not teach Woodwork. Instead he offered book-binding and box-making, in cardboard and cloth. Arts and Crafts, like Morris at Kelmscott, you may think. But you would be wrong. The Gooch operation was more like the one pioneered elsewhere in Oxfordshire by another William Morris, the founder of Morris Motors. The Gooch production line was set up in what was left the woodwork shop, after the Rolls Royce aero-engine – ATC cadets stripped it down under the supervision of Pilot Officer Hall – had been installed. Take up your rulers and Stanley knives. Measure, draw, cut, assemble, glue and press. Deft boys, when they tired of Daddy-baiting, did it well. Chris Gillings and Trevor Hewitt rapidly knocked up the sort of thing you can pay a lot for at Laura Ashley. A tall container for example that nowadays might be used for pens and things but which, during the war, was used to house 'spills' – thin fillets of wood or tightly rolled strips of waste paper that could be lit from a fire or gas jet and used to light cigarettes and pipes. Using spills, like smoking, was patriotic. It saved matches, thus releasing timber for shipbuilding or the repair of bomb damage. It was by such sacrifice that final victory would be ours. So I was willing to have a go but as usual was all fingers and thumbs. I got glue in my hair and ears and the resulting product looked like a souvenir of Pisa. Mr Gooch was cross. My incompetence was wilful, yet another flagrant breech of discipline. Even the Head's son was playing him up. I suppose he was mindful of his precarious tenure and would have dreaded the brooding presence of the leaning spill-holder on the Headmaster's hearth. Every time he lights his pipe he will think 'Gooch must go'. I knew that his suspicions were well founded.

The effect on my self-image was traumatic. It indicated that I was irretrievably inept and no good at art. Dad was unconcerned. Art did not matter and anyway Gooch was useless. But that judgement bothered me. Being no good at art did not fit what I knew about myself. As we know, looking and thinking had so rewarded me in my early years that I made little effort with reading. It was inconceivable that it could bring rewards greater that I got from staring, comparing, perceiving and conceiving – an effective thought process which survived the acquisition of a measure of literacy. My thinking remained essentially visual, as it still seems to be even today. I read and I forget. I look and I remember. Even in old age I retain a visual memory of uncanny accuracy and limitless duration. I can remember places, buildings particularly, that I have visited only once and that perhaps fifty years ago, so that I recognise quite obscure locations, as briefly flashed upon a screen, without the assistance of captions or commentary. I am not boasting, just reporting. I wish I had made more productive use of what may be an unusual gift. Like for example becoming an architect or an art historian, options I always rejected because at school my mind was poisoned by a persistent message – you are cack-handed and no good at art. I knew the message was false. I was never happier than when gazing out of a window, particularly a window in motion. I loved the stones of Glossop and the memory of Manchester light still made me cry. I delighted in townscapes, like Stockport in November rain; industrial installations, like the Glossop Gasworks; moving machines, like the Tiger tractors or an LMS 'streak' briefly glimpsed in transit through Wigan. At Southport I felt at home in the Atkinson Art Gallery and among Grandpa's gilt framed horse paintings. My favourite books were still picture books and I endlessly pored over the photographs my other grandfather had taken, not just the shots of film stars and fascists, but also his studies of evening. I had an instinctive sympathy with Grandpa as he got his bike out towards the close of a summer's day and pedalled off to the promenade sure that, the light being what it was just now, he would capture the image that would crown his life's work. What he felt about sunsets, I felt about water. In every form it fascinated – as sea, as rain, as a thundering brook, as condensation on a window, or as a sinkful of washing up. So the Gooch judgement was absurd. Of course I was good at art. All I needed was some technical help with drawing and some practice in brushwork like Vivienne Westwood got from Mr Bell. But daft as I knew it was, I believed the Gooch message. Not for the only time in a troubled adolescence, using reason to confront a demon brought no comfort. I knew the truth but believed a lie. Now there's a funny thing.

Much later – probably too much later – I was rescued by my girlfriend, later my wife. We were students. Her art education in the private sector had been the opposite of mine. She not only took her considerable practical ability for granted but nobody had ever told her art was inferior, a proposition she found, as my granny used to say, too silly to laugh at. She knew all about William Morris. At Clifton High School they revered his teaching and some of the classrooms were hung with his wallpaper – the real thing [c1880] not modern reproductions. Furthermore, although they had her down as ripe for Oxbridge, they let her do Art for 'A' Level. At our school, remember, only those not bright enough for proper subjects did that. I never found out what Dad thought about that blatant piece of highfalutin' southern nonsense, because by the time in question [1956] he was deeply disappointed in me and pinned his last hopes for my redemption on this bubbly, well-bred, impeccably spoken product of a ladies' college, who for some unfathomable reason had attached herself to his disappointing son. So when, at the tea table, she fell to talking of Michelangelo he held his tongue, something, I think, that had never happened before.

Anyway, one day Anne took me to the National Gallery and we found ourselves among the Claudes and Poussins, not perhaps the most likely location for a Damascene conversion. It happened though. I forgot I was no good at art and swallowed these pictures whole. They were enchanting, full of light and water and feathery trees and dreamy architecture, among which St Ursula was embarking a shipload of virgins and tall Greeks were worshipping Apollo. I got a commentary on Claude's circumstances and on what he was saying to us, his latter day beholders. It seemed this arcadia was the Roman Campania, the hill studded, ruin-encrusted countryside around the Eternal City that we had briefly explored by bus the previous summer. Thus the happiness of last year was brilliantly conjured. So also was something more profound than nostalgia. It was the culture of the Enlightenment. Claude, she said, was one of a group of ex pat French artists who obliged visiting grand tourists with vistas that not only reminded them of their travels but captured also the spirit of the classical world they revered and emulated. It seemed an infinity of content, a cornucopia of ideas, was distilled into these scenes. Love art and unlock the past. Wow! Thus joy in looking and thinking was restored in me. At that point I should have been bold and taken the new path suddenly revealed. I should have transferred my academic focus from the early middle ages to art history. My studies were stalling because, the texts being in Latin, I couldn't read them and that, it has to be acknowledged, is a handicap in research. I could read pictures, though – as fluently and as rapidly as Chris Gillings read the *Hotspur*. But I missed the moment, dropped out of my post graduate programme and became a teacher at a pioneer comprehensive school in Brixton. I thought it was New Jerusalem but actually it was the Tower of Babel. But that is another story so let us return to Daddy Gooch.

In the end I dismissed his lies about me and my capacity for art appreciation but never rebutted the other charge he laid against me – that I was manually incompetent and irredeemably so. Although in my time I have assembled van loads of flat-packed furniture, I have always wielded an Allen key with more anxiety than joy. I cannot confidently do it myself and, although other factors, like Dad's example, are no doubt involved, I fear Daddy Gooch deserves some of the blame. He undermined my confidence. However my grammar school training in practical skills was not entirely counter-productive. For believe it or not I was found to be a halfway decent cook. I even made better jam tarts than Chris Gillings, a scholastic triumph I recall with as much satisfaction as winning a scholarship to Oxford. It was not of course part of the normal order for boys to enter the Domestic Science room. That only women cook, clean and sew, and that the only tasks about the house suitable for men involve electricity, plumbing and carpentry, was scarcely more open to challenge than the law of gravity. Still the times were not normal. There was a war on, there was a determination that post war would be different from pre-war, and social experiment was in the air. So in a bold foray into the spirit of post war reconstruction, Dad decreed that, for a six weeks' spell, boys and girls would swap cookery and cardboardwork. So we made cheese dreams instead of spill holders and mine were not bad, as even Mum admitted. Then we did pastry. It calls for cool hands and a certain touch and she warned us it would not be easy. That sort of introduction to a task, if delivered by Mr Gooch, would have made me glue my dithering fingers to my quaking knee caps, but I received the news from 'Miss' with all the suavity of a bomber captain at a briefing – 'Berlin again tonight chaps' 'Good-o!' Hence my besting of Mrs Gillings's insufferably capable little lad. Culinary ambition did not stop short with shortcrust pastry for, if we are to believe one of the essays I wrote for Miss Hughes, I was, before the end of the war, capable of preparing a whole family meal. Mum being ill, so the story went, I did jacket potatoes, pre-stuffed with a cheesy confection and followed it with bread and butter pudding. I even saved the day when the spuds, insufficiently aerated, exploded in the oven. I liked washing up as well, which in those days – before grease-conquering detergent, power-packed in squirty plastic – involved coaxing a lather by swishing a long-handled wire cage packed with left-over scraps of soap. It was not for queasy stomachs but I loved water, even filthy water, perhaps filthy water particularly. Was the penchant for female roles perverted? The possibility, though not formally articulated, concerned me somewhat. But only somewhat. I liked housework and both Mum and Granny Southport seemed to welcome my help. So why not? Also I liked Angela Brazil school stories better than *Tom Brown's Schooldays* but I did not tell Dad.

But before we do sex let us turn out onto the sports field. I was of course no better at games than I was at cardboardwork and the two failures combined to construct a pitiful self-image. I was a butter-fingered, fat wimp as well as a cack-handed, clumsy clot. The harm that perception has done me has proved life-long. It is not just that in consequence I missed out in youth on opportunities for health promoting exercise. In middle age I tackled that deficiency, took up jogging and was duly amazed at the broad, life enhancing benefits of becoming fit. But being 'no good at games' hurts the mind as well as the body and it isolates you. Solidarity with Manchester City, a force which bonded GGS contemporaries not compromised by commitment to Manchester United – or in Jas's eccentric case, Blackpool – was not something I could aspire to. I wanted to belong to the club but knew I was unworthy. A band of brothers would not want a wimp. Unlike the one on taking exercise, that inhibition has never gone away. A taboo about even *talking* sport has set me apart. I am saying that being 'no good at games' is not a minor ailment but a major impediment to a good life. PE teachers should recognise that and give as much attention to nurturing rabbits as they do to training lions. Perhaps today they do, but I got no such help from my own teachers.

I suppose it was not their fault. They were creatures of the Calvinism that, as we have seen, corrupted the grammar school outlook. If you are good already, we will help you do even better. But if you are no good, then go away because there is nothing that can be done about it. In academic subjects that outlook worked to my advantage. My ability was recognised and effectively reinforced. But in physical education the boot was on the other foot – even though the boot in question was immaculate. For to my shame, the only boy in II Alpha who did not relish football had the only pair of proper pre-war football boots with real studs, my mother, exercising her well-honed high street charm, having persuaded the manager of the Co-op shoe shop to rummage in his back room. Although they dripped with Dubbin, they did not fool the two captains invited by Mr Brown to choose the teams that September Monday in 1942 – the IIs did games that day – when, for the first time, we were marched to the Lord Street field. The workings of predestination were promptly demonstrated. Most of the others had spent much of their spare time since infancy kicking miscellaneous objects, including footballs, up and down streets, back yards and public parks. I however had never intentionally kicked anything in my life, except perhaps my sister. To protect his son from plebeian mores, my father had emphatically kept me off the streets, so I had no experience, no skills and did not even know the rules. I think Mr Brown might have spotted my predicament and offered some coaching but he seemed unaware that footballing 'illiteracy' even existed. He assumed we had all played before, knew what was expected and would be eager to get on with it. Hence the weekly agony of games day. Every week on the Lord Street mud-bath I stood and shivered while teams were selected. Always I was the last to be chosen, standing alone and forlorn at the end, as even Douglas Swallow shuffled off into the camaraderie of Trevor Hewitt's team. Trevor was the Second Form's answer to Stanley Matthews. I stood alone, forlorn and frozen throughout the match as well, breaking into motion only when the ball seemed to be coming my way, at which point I would dart smartly in the opposite direction. The combination of fear, exposure, shame and boredom made time freeze as well as the insides of my thighs. But at last the 127 bus trundled down Norfolk Street so I knew it was quarter to four and in five minutes the blessed long whistle would end my suffering. But only until next week. Please let it rain, or preferably snow. The friendly Glossop weather, famous for bringing arctic winters, frequently obliged.

Cricket was better. If agonising memories of the summer game are less acute, it is partly because Glossop in that season gets marginally warmer, so in standing idle you do not usually risk hypothermia. However going in last and fielding in the deep were standard experiences and, in view of its greater velocity, the need to avoid the ball was even more urgent. Yet, when we were batting, at least until a moment or two of terror at the very end of the innings, I had nothing to do but sit and stare, a situation I always found congenial, discovering with surprise that I actually liked the cricketing scene. It looked good and, when newly mown, it smelt good. The tree-girt enclosure of the Lord Street ground, furnished with stone walls, iron gates and a scoreboard, up by the ATC's clapped out Biggles bi-plane [a Hawker Fury c1930], had a charm deeply rooted in something hard to put a finger on but associated with the outlook of my new friend, the Fox Hunting Man, who was into cricket as well as horses. The thing had class. It was not really a team game, a mere mêlée of masculinity, but rather an occasion for individual knightly combat, conducted, like a tournament, in elegant clothing and with ritual courtesy. In its most extended form – the test matches that once again graced historic grounds in the victory summer of 1945 – it lasted for days, not hours, involved strategy as well as tactics, and was played with mind as much as muscle. Furthermore the game had a long and fully recorded history and had inspired literature. I liked it a lot.

So when first class cricket came back after the war I let John Arlott, the BBC commentator, take over from Alvar Liddell and beguile me with regular reports on this appealing continuation of international combat by other means. Thrilling to the exploits of Hutton, Washbrook, Compton and Edrich who humbled the Indians in 1946 and the South Africans in 1947, was some compensation for losing the likes of Montgomery, Patton, Zhukov and Rokosovsky, each of whom completed his final innings in 1945. However, since a wimp was not entitled to follow sport, listening in to cricket was a secret passion, its service as shameful as masturbation. In front of Mum and Dad I had to affect the same indifference to John Arlott as I feigned about the startling bikinis that suddenly inflamed the covers of the post war *Picture Post*. At school it was unthinkable for a miserable specimen to share the natural desire of other boys to know the latest score from Trent Bridge. I knew my place and it was a lonely one. Except in 1948. Then, at England's darkest hour, confronted by Bradman's invincible Aussies, a Dunkirk spirit was engendered. In that fateful summer even girls, let alone wimps, were allowed in the dinner hour to gather around the wireless in Room 1, to catch from Lords the last overs before lunch. It was as exciting as the general election had been. And the outcome made you realise what it must have been like, in 1945, to be a Conservative – or a German.

Football for two terms, cricket for one. That, apart from brief excursions into athletics – the Cross Country before Easter and Sports Day in July – plus some attention to swimming, was all we got by way of Games. In swimming, as we have seen, I floated above wimp level and at one red letter Assembly actually received a bronze medallion for passing the life-saving exam. The latter had been touch and go because I had to grope blindly for the wrapped brick he threw into the deep end, because nobody had told me it was OK to open your eyes under water. The PE programme was completed by a single period a week of physical jerks. It happened at the Vic because the school had no gym, a deprivation that dominated Dad's bellicose dealings with County. It did not bother me. A boy who could not erect a spill holder could do without vaulting horses and wall bars. In the absence of torture equipment, PT – it only became PE as part of New Jerusalem – was just bending and stretching, interspersed with orthopedically threatening activities involving a 'medicine ball'. It was not clear why we did it. It was not strenuous enough to make us puff and we did not do it often enough, or for long enough, to get our muscles bulging. It was neither aerobic nor strengthening. And with only forty minutes allocated you were no sooner changed than you had to get dressed again, and all that fetching and carrying of kit was burdensome. Still, it was better than games or cardboardwork and there was always the chance of a laugh. Running on the spot caused the light fittings in the public library below us to swing merrily as snow-flakes of displaced plaster mingled with dandruff on the head and shoulders of the ratty librarian. Then there was the legend of Derek Moss. PT sessions often ended with a bout of boxing and Chris Gillings, you will not be surprised to learn, made my nose bleed. Once, it was said, Mr Brown, who affected a roll-top cream sweater, puffed out his chest, took guard and said, 'Go on, hit me!' Derek did – and knocked him cold.

It wasn't funny though. Being infallibly adjudged rubbish at games maimed me for life. As I say, it suppressed the natural appetite for exercise and contributed mightily to the depressing body image that plagued my social relationships. I thought I was a mess and I thought that was equally obvious to other people, including girls. You should not do that to a kid and I blame, if not individual teachers, then the grammar school system. If you lacked talent it rejected you. On the other hand if you were good at games laurels were lavishly proffered. As we have seen, even in the middle of the war, an impressive programme of Saturday afternoon matches was maintained and that said a lot for the commitment of teachers, none of whom were PE specialists. Do teachers still do that today? I doubt it. It was well into the peace before the Gauleiter so far dropped his standards as to permit inter-school matches on Saturday *mornings* instead of afternoons. But woe betide any First Eleven star who took advantage of the morning fixture to play again in the afternoon for Glossop FC, the Manchester League side, whose ethos was not just plebeian but quasi-professional. In his tea-table rants against such 'Quislings' [the name of Norway's wartime Nazi puppet] he called for capital punishment but, since we lacked an execution chamber as well as a gym, he had to be content with stripping them of their prefect badges. If they were to apply for university, they should not expect references. But back to rabbits like me and Doug Swallow. We should not have been allowed to slink away but should have been encouraged to get fit, remedy shortcomings in skill and to get stuck in like real boys. Or, alternatively and/or concurrently, we should have been encouraged in physical activity other than team games, particularly in sports you can carry on with in later life. Like tennis, for example, or golf or riding. Just before I left school for National Service I came under the wing of a more thoughtful games master with that sort of outlook. He took the sixth form Geography class on a field trip to the Lake District, threw in an ascent of Scafell Pike in a blizzard and let us go off to the pub to celebrate our survival. I came home aglow with unaccustomed pride. Then he chose me for the cross country team, persuading me I was not too bad a runner where the distance was long enough. So thanks to Mr Donaldson, I did not leave school before savouring the bliss of a post-match tea, set before us sporting heroes by the girls of Hyde Grammar School. Those young ladies of course also knew their place.

And so to sex, a topic that will prepare us for the discussion of moral education already announced and for the outpouring of guilt about which you have been forewarned. It may disappoint you that the confessions to be inflicted on you do not relate to sexual activity although, since sex as experienced by adolescents in post war Britain offered so many opportunities for shame, the habit of feeling guilty that engulfed me in 1945 soon got mixed up with sex as well. For Glossop Grammar School of course did not offer us an 'education in personal relationships'. It did not even provide us with a sure and certain knowledge of all the facts of life, although the special one-off double period, halfway through the First Year, devoted to basic enlightenment about the mechanics of heterosexual intercourse, was well conducted. I am not necessarily saying that was not enough. It might even have been too much. If every lobby calling for the inclusion in the curriculum of its own particular package of admonitory propaganda – don't smoke, don't drink, don't eat sweets, don't deny global warming, don't become a suicide bomber – then there would be no space left for mind-expanding irrelevances like Milton, Mathematics and Magna Carta. Also teachers are not parents and parents should not, in a cavalier fashion, simply abdicate their responsibilities to teachers. Anyway how come all teachers are supposed to know all about sex? Some of us may have led sheltered lives.

That said, a problem about learning the facts of life in wartime Glossop has to be acknowledged. The trouble was you did not know who and what to trust. Sex was unlike all the other foci of extra-curricular curiosity – like football or train spotting or bug hunting or what was happening in the war – in that reliable sources of information, instead of being super-abundant, were seriously hard to come by. Think of all the learning resources identified in Chapter Five as aiding study of the war. There were books, magazines and papers to read. There was the radio to listen to and films to be enjoyed. And there were squads of self-appointed grown up experts ever ready to favour you with interpretations of Hitler's intentions and Churchill's likely responses. Or take the situation of those of us into train spotting. One of our brotherhood had had this brilliant idea of listing all the numbers, with names where applicable, of all the locomotives of each of the four companies that then operated the railway system. So there was now a wholly reliable Ian Allan pocket-sized handbook for each of the LMS, LNER, GWR and Southern Railway and every time you 'copped' an engine you had never seen before you ticked or underlined the number on the appropriate page. Great. There was however no Ian Allan Sex Book, serving simultaneously as a reliable list of all possible options and a record of personal achievement. So how did you find out about sex?

Apart from a book Dad put in my hands, about which more in a moment, the only known printed resource touching on the matter in question was a paperback called *The Red Light: Things a Boy Should Know*. It could be purchased at the bookstall in the Market Hall but no boy questing after knowledge had to my knowledge been bold enough to offer his sixpence to the chap who ran the stall. Anyway having blued your pocket money where would you hide the filthy text afterwards? What if your mum found it under your bed or it got confiscated while being passed round the class? Which left personal enquiry. Why not just ask your dad? In those days you just couldn't. Asking your mum might be thought even less likely to elicit pukka gen, although in that respect it will be discovered that I was luckier than most. Attempting such initiatives was usually just too embarrassing. Whenever family conversation strayed near the ever interesting topic – that couple who had had to get married, that woman who was no better than she should be – shutters were put up quicker than the blackout at sunset. So what was a growing boy to do? The only resource remaining was the peer group. We simply misinformed each other. A potent brew of hard fact, half-truth, error, fantasy and wishful thinking constantly circulated, in two distinct vicious circles, among the pubescent of each sex. Apart from private communion with your own body, you hardly ever found out anything about sex otherwise than through discussion with friends of the same age and sex. That was just how it was. The peers had their way with me quite early and readers will not be astonished to discover that Chris Gillings, that smooth-tongued alternative communicator, was a prime mover in my initiation. It was in February 1943, when I was ten and two thirds, that he proposed this surprising but, I had to admit, plausible thesis about how sperm gets to be deposited where it can do what it has to do. By an odd coincidence he proposed it in Ellison Street, the very same thoroughfare in which, a year before, on the eve of the Scholarship Part One, he had taught me the most common name for the interaction he now described. Only this time it was opposite the Norfolk Laundry, not outside the Elim Tabernacle.

The seed Chris planted did not fall on stony ground for Mum and Dad had already taken certain initiatives by way of preparing my mind for revelation. Thus at the Christmas just past I had been given the book mentioned above. *Living Things for Lively Youngsters* was packed with truly amazing stuff. A lot of it concerned 'evolution', which was a theory about how life began, and how creatures got progressively more complicated. It was difficult to reconcile with the story of creation told us by Miss Little in Standard Two but on the whole I thought evolution more convincing than the bible. Wow! Dad of course reinforced what he took to be his son's wholesome revolt against the claptrap pedalled by 'bloody parsons'. He was himself a fan of the Huxley brothers, grandsons of Darwin's original champion. Julian was often on the Brains Trust, Dad's favourite wireless programme, and Aldous, a novelist he patronised, had so far persuaded him that short-sightedness is all in the mind that he tried to walk along St Anne's Pier without his glasses. Fortunately the tide was out. However, pleased as he was at his son's enlightenment, my pre-occupation during the Christmas holidays with decorating the kitchen walls with my own versions of the evolutionary lighthouse – a tower with us humans at the very top beaming light, amoebas at the bottom invisible in slime, and butterflies fluttering halfway up – must have been hugely frustrating for Dad. Whenever would the daft lad get further on in the book? Still such a slow reader! It must be Norris's fault. She would have to go. The section of *Living Things for Lively Youngsters* he hoped I would get to before the end of the holidays was a double spread on which the essential differences between men and women were graphically represented, with each part labelled in correct scientific terminology. He could not of course let it inspire further drawings. Our kitchen was not a public lavatory. But surely it would spark off that serious talk for which he was steeling himself. For it seems that, as the Second World War reached its turning point at Stalingrad, Dad determined that his son too experience a moment of transition. I was to learn the scientific truth about sex. Yet he chickened out of personally providing direct instruction. So, the *Living Things* book having failed in its mission, some other surrogate must be enlisted. Otherwise I would learn the facts of life exactly as, in the end, actually happened – on the street.

The first surrogate was my mother. She proved surprisingly informative when I tackled her on matters arising from the treasury of old manuals – guide books, cookery books, bazaar catalogues and so on – that survived on my grandparents' shelves. As we know, I liked them because they offered a quick trip into the past and also because they were often profusely illustrated and lively images, as we also know, had for me more appeal than boring words. One query related to Mrs Beeton who, in discussing the complement of a gentleman's household, referred to a 'wet nurse'. It seemed every home should have one. But would she not catch her death and the baby too? Mum explained. Emboldened by that prompt response I tackled her on another mystery lurking within Ward Lock's *Guide to London and the Franco-British Exhibition 1908*. There, among recommendations for Whelpton's Pills ['The Family Doctor in Your Pocket'], Dr J Collis Browne's Chlorodyne ['The Universal Remedy'] and Keatings's Powder ['Kills Bugs, Fleas, Moths, Beetles, Mosquitos'], what seemed like the best idea before sliced bread was announced. Southalls' 'Compressed Towels' were made for ladies on the go and one of them is seen held handily between a delicate finger and an elegant thumb. Full sized towels were 'scientifically packed' into the 'tiny silver packets' shown in the ad. Brilliant! – and not at all expensive, even allowing for subsequent inflation, for Size A cost only a penny and the largest size [bath?] was yours for a paltry twopence. Astonishing! Whatever would they think of next? Why had the idea not caught on and also why were they available only to ladies? Surely men too would be glad to lighten the load of their suitcases by leaving bulky bath wraps at home? As an outraged victim of sexism I appealed to Mum for explanation. Without fuss she duly explained about periods. They had another posher name that sounded like the chapter in Durell's *Arithmetic* dealing with rods, poles, perches and other units of mensuration. That was the trouble with words, they could sound the same, or nearly the same, and yet mean something entirely different. Anyway Mum's news was a big surprise. Had she really got it right? These days her lack of book learning was beginning to irk me. But being female she must surely, in this matter, know what she was talking about. She had apparently put up with nature's untidy arrangements, month after bloody month, for something like thirty years. While feeling sympathy for woman's lot, I realised there was after all something to be said for being male. There was disenchantment too. I had hitherto nurtured an ethereal view of womankind, as not only kinder and gentler but also possessing a certain inner cleanliness, available to rough men only through the agency of Andrews Liver Salts. So, while a woman was set to toil, and tears became her, I had wrongly assumed her to be immune to blood and sweat. Well, there you go.

Although intrigued by Mum's revelations I was not yet possessed of a full account of the facts of life, Dad's timetable for instruction by proxy being behind schedule. It was into that cognitive limbo that Chris hurled his bombshell and in exactly the circumstances Dad feared. Was Chris right? As in the face of Mum's plain speaking, I showed initial scepticism. My doubts were strengthened by Chris's insistence that the activity he described was normally confined to the bathroom. Surely not. It was well known that 'doing it' required a prone position. That was vouched for in a well-loved playground ditty that ended 'Mary said, 'Oh what a whopper'/Let's *lie down* and do it proper'. The italics are mine. The floor area of a typical bathroom was, I felt sure, too cramped to permit easeful congress and anyway why not use a bed, that being more comfortable as well as more spacious? Also if sex was specific to bathrooms then most Glossopians would have to do without it because 'slums' were not en suite. Was there even a Gillings bathroom? Another obstacle to the Gillings thesis was that sexual intercourse, as he described it, seemed too silly to laugh at. It was slapstick. Could normal sober grown-ups really take part in antics more zany than anything George Formby, the Three Stooges or Laurel and Hardy ever got up to? Could my parents engage, voluntarily and even eagerly, in the sort of ungainly – and, let's face it, rather disgusting contortions – implicit to Chris's theory? That was the crunch. Surely they would be risking their health as well as sacrificing their dignity, for the business apparently involved putting to alternative use organs hitherto assumed to be dedicated exclusively to excretion. Yet, if Chris was right, Mum and Dad must have 'done it' at least twice. And so must his parents, with or without a bathroom. So must Mr and Mrs Holt, and Mr and Mrs Swallow, despite being Particular Baptists. Indeed, if Chris was right, all married people must be assumed to be at least occasional participants in this crazy carnival of filth. Its celebrants must include all of the male teachers at our school and also the former Miss Lee and poor Miss Rhodes, who had just married a Free Frenchman, a category of performer said to be especially eager. Mr and Mrs Fielding must do it, with or without his wooden leg, and so must Mr and Mrs Churchill, when he was not speaking on the radio, Sir William and Lady Beveridge, when he was not writing his report, and also the King and Queen, his stammer notwithstanding. Also if the Gillings Thesis were to be aligned with national stereotypes then the De Gaulles, being French, must be up for it all the time, and the Chiang Kai-sheks, being Chinese and thus exceptionally fecund, must be assumed to do it at least twice nightly. It was easier to imagine the Axis leaders in play. They were ludicrous anyway and well known to be filthy swine. But in view of the girth of their spouses, you had to feel sorry for those hard-pressed ladies Frau Göring and Signora Mussolini. The Führer however emerged from this re-assessment of adult charisma with enhanced credibility. As a bachelor he was exempt from the romp, the idea of extra-marital sex being a leap too far for our stunned contemplation. Well, I didn't know what to think and needed to withdraw to one of my hideaways to do some pondering. The more I thought about what Chris had told me however, and related it to the diagrams in *Living Things for Lively Youngsters*, which I had at last discovered, the more I inclined towards accepting it. Except for the bit about bathrooms. I was not a complete mug. I think I checked it out with Alan Holt as well, Jas being preoccupied with modelling a Mosquito fighter-bomber. So Chris was probably right but I wished we knew for sure.

We did not have to wait much longer because Dad, unaware that the enemy had outflanked him, was about to launch his spring offensive on behalf of science against the smutty mythology of the streets. In fact Chris's revelations may actually have been prompted by Dad's opening move in the campaign. For Mrs Gillings had already had 'The Letter', a missive, it seemed, that had simultaneously been delivered to the houses of all my classmates. 'Have you had The Letter?' they were asking, all agog. I soon discovered that a communication from the Headmaster had been delivered to the parents of everyone in my class except me. Special lessons were scheduled on a basis of strict gender segregation with an opt-out facility. Reactions ranged from mystification, through anxiety to hilarity but speculation about 'The Letter' stifled all other conversation, the recent Russian victory at Stalingrad notwithstanding. There was electricity in the air but, since nothing had come to our house and nothing had been said to me, I felt left out. I could see there was something daft about Dad writing to himself, but should he not let Mum know? Anyway at the end of every term he wrote to report to himself that his son had done well despite being untidy so what was different now? Thus while, all over Glossop, cups and cutlery rattled as 'The Letter' unlocked tongues, at our house tea came only with the usual denunciations of the Boche, conshies, pie shop profiteers, bloody parsons and southerners with constipated accents. Why did he not even mention the special lessons? Why indeed?

Perhaps what happened went something like this. Although Mum had done well she had not managed the whole truth. So somebody else must. Enter Squire Roe BSc. Mr Roe had joined the staff only just after Christmas and he was a lucky chap. Although an old boy of the school he had languished for years at West End. Now however, fields of recruitment being attenuated on account of the war, he had made that crucial leap from the mass of mere teachers into the elite of schoolmasters. So he owed Dad one. Also sex education was in the air. In the wake of the Beveridge Report [November 1942] talk of how different things were going to be after the war had reached a crescendo. As well as pre-fabs for heroes, free false teeth and a penguin pool in every town, there would be lashings of hot and cold sex talks in schools and youth clubs. Dad was up with the zeitgeist. By his bed he had a book called *Sex Education* by Cyril Bibby, a Dickensian name combining moral probity with the faintly ridiculous. Which showed that, like the great and the good generally, he was all for it – except when it came to telling his own boy what he needed to know. Soon it emerged that Mr Roe was the man for the job. Maybe at interview, like you do, he had indicated commitment to a trendy cause, so what happened served him right. In a trice he was commissioned to tell all to the First Year boys, for the special benefit of the Head's son.

He did it remarkably well. With the aid of an epidiascope, and thus in blacked-out conditions that concealed blushes and made it easier to use your hands to stifle giggles, the Gillings Thesis was triumphantly upheld. The facts of life were now scientifically demonstrated in no-nonsense graphics. Some of them might even apply to me and, now that certain details had been sorted, that was not entirely unpalatable. It was a relief to know that, rather than excretory organs doubling up as reproductive ones, each sex, in its different way, was kitted out with two distinct sets of parts, disposed around the lower abdomen in a complex relationship. It was a bit like the various tubes, lift shafts, escalators, cables, sewers and water pipes that you saw, intermingled but segregated, in a cut-away drawing of Piccadilly Underground that I knew from the *Children's Encyclopaedia*. That was OK. You could get to live with the facts of life. In fact, when associated with some of the girls who were at that very moment also corralled in darkness, in another Fitzalan Street ante-room, learning from Miss Greenwood what was in store for them, the thing might begin to have a certain appeal. Thus a mood of cautious optimism developed. It was enhanced on the way home at dinner time when, as we were passing Corn Mill Bridge, Dad actually began to discuss the morning's events. In relief, I suppose, that the deed was done, inhibition was suspended. He was even forthcoming, declaring himself ready to answer further questions. So I tackled him on the last remaining mystery. As a veteran of life's factuality he must know the answer. Did the deed belong in the bedroom or the bathroom? He came down firmly on the side of bed and the verdict was gratifying. That Chris could sometimes be wrong was good news. I was asked if there was anything else I wanted to know. I had only to ask. Well, just at that moment, punch-drunk with new knowledge, curiosity was temporarily sated. Anyway by now we were almost in sniffing distance of Mum's chip pan and I had come to realise that sex and women do not mix. Still it was good to know the conversation might be reopened.

It never was though. Dad had done his duty, albeit mostly by proxy. The boy had been given an accurate account by a Chemistry graduate and that was that. In later years sometimes he told me dirty jokes but the rest was silence. So it was too as far as the school curriculum was concerned. Sex having been briefly flaunted in the classroom the topic was dropped. It should not henceforth get in the way of school work, at least not before the School Certificate. So the whole thing was handed back to the peer group, which continued to grind out its subversive mythology. Sex, it taught, was daft, dirty and dangerous. It was always good for a laugh but not something fit for your mother's ears. The chance of 'getting your leg over' was never to be neglected. You needed it but it was a pig pleasure, not one of life's higher satisfactions, like 're-reading Macbeth'. And if you were not careful you could pick up something nasty and it was never entirely clear whether or not the warnings in the public lavatories applied to masturbation – well, at least of the 'excessive' variety – as well as to infections associated with more sophisticated excursions into the forbidden city of lust. 'Delay is Dangerous' the posters insisted. So expect blindness next week and general paralysis of the insane before the end of the month. You had to laugh though. 'VD Can Be Cured' said one of the notices on the toilet walls. 'So can kippers' the graffiti artist responded. Leaving it to the peer group was not good enough, was it? But whether it had been the school's place to take on the heavy artillery of the counter-culture is another matter. Rightly or wrongly our school did not do moral education, sex-wise or otherwise. Neither did Mum and Dad. As I was to discover in July 1945, when I was just thirteen. In that month, in the very same week that the first atomic device was tested in New Mexico, another game-changing detonation occurred inside my head. Hitherto the knowledge that I lived in a state of snow white immunity to sin had buttressed even a self-image damaged by knowledge that I was clumsy clot and a fat wimp. At least I was a good boy. Not any more I wasn't. For on a summer afternoon I was suddenly pole-axed by the discovery that I so far lacked 'inner cleanliness' that even the largest dose of Andrews Liver Salts would not restore me.

Before I tell all, let me try to box the moral compass that then sustained me, or failed to sustain me. Let me explain how, in the course of my first thirteen years I had come to differentiate right from wrong. First, how far was moral education part of the school curriculum? Well, they had taken it seriously enough at St Luke's, a Church of England school where, as we know, Scripture came first on the agenda every day and sometimes they took us to church. There I had been taught the Ten Commandments and helped to understand some of them – although not of course the Seventh and I never twigged that 'false witness' was to do with lying. Also I was urged to love my neighbour by teachers who, I think, meant what they said. But such robust Anglican training ended when we went on to the non-denominational Grammar School. I guess Religious Education had never flourished in the grammar schools which, from the start, were state schools, not faith schools, and the 'broadly Christian' character of the RE prescribed by the new 1944 Education Act made little difference, despite much debate between the education minister and the church leaders. The thing was that RE – 'RI' [instruction] as we called it – failed the acid test for curricular seriousness. It was not a School Cert subject and that was that. So an aggressively secular headmaster like my father could safely shunt it into a siding. Certainly the content of RI lessons leaves no trace at all in my memory. Since we addressed religion only one a week what teachers prattled about on those peripheral occasions was obviously not important.

Not so the Gauleiter's homilies at Assembly. Through them, new every morning except Monday which, it will be recalled, was sacred to the incantation of last Saturday's inter-school football results, we were subjected to a moral mallet process. In the context of a solemn ritual that reinforced the authority of his instruction and gave it I suppose a 'broadly Christian' character, he preached a daily sermon. Before yet again drumming into his charges certain iron rules of correct behaviour, our leader would have beseeched the Almighty that 'all our doings' that day might be 'ordered by Thy governance'. It might seem therefore that those rules were handed down, not just on the Gauleiter's say-so, but with the imprimatur of the Almighty. Now that trick bothered me a lot. He may have deceived the others but I at least knew it was all a load of baloney. This guy putting it about was my Dad and he did not do God. Sure he worshipped a literary canon that included the Prayer Book as well as Shakespeare, but I knew his private views were closer to atheism than agnosticism. So his posture at Assembly was hypocritical. He was lying and, even though I did not know that bearing false witness was the same thing as telling porkies, I knew that lying was wrong. So come off it, Dad! Yet, even though I knew his position was deeply dishonest, I *believed* what the Gauleiter preached. Awareness of his hypocrisy weakened not one jot the power and authority of what he decreed. That was the rub. In a contest between reason and the rules the former came nowhere. What Dad pronounced ex cathedra from the third step of the Boys' Staircase was beyond refutation. That was the essence of the dilemma that was about to engulf me. What, you may ask, were these iron rules that held me captive? They can be condensed into a quartet in which the sublime rubs the shoulders of the ridiculous. First, to die for your country is the quintessence of manliness. Secondly, play up, play up and play the game. Thirdly, do not cheat in exams. Finally you must on no account eat ice cream at the bus stop. For ever and ever. Amen.

That then was the moral teaching I got at school. What about what I got at home? What did my parents teach me in the right v wrong department? I do not remember any philosophical discourse. If God does not exist, can his commandments still apply? They never directly tackled that rather fundamental question but you could tell a lot from what made them seriously cross and what they cheerfully indulged. If you did not believe in God – on the whole, Dad didn't and Mum was not all that bothered – then it did not matter whether there was only one god or a whole regiment of divinities. So the first four of the Ten Commandments did not apply to us. It would be OK to make a graven image on the kitchen table and as for Sunday being a day of rest, well some hopes because that was when I had to write my homework essays. The remaining six commandments however, with some amendment, did have force chez Lord. Mum and Dad were all for Number Five about honouring your father and your mother and, to be fair, they honoured and cherished their own parents, thus leading by example. The Sixth Commandment obviously did not apply to killing Germans but was otherwise mandatory. Dad seemed to imply that the Seventh, about adultery, the exact nature of which continued to elude me, did not apply to aircrew on ops but everybody else had better stick with it. Stealing [Number Eight] was certainly a 'No! No!' so the memory of infantile shoplifting at Woolworths troubled me somewhat as did that pinching of a tin of pineapples from Mum's larder that Eileen Hart had put me up to. It caused Dad to get crosser that he had ever been before and I certainly was not going to do that again. My problem about Commandment Number Nine has already been mentioned but I knew for sure that lying was bad. I was not sure what coveting was either but, despite their snobbery, my parents truly discouraged envy about other people's possessions, which perhaps was easy enough because we seldom met folk better equipped with material advantages. Finally there was that eleventh commandment that Moses had somehow failed to write down, which was surprising because it mattered such a lot. Thou shalt work hard. They taught that one by example too. Mum bustled for England and Dad was a martyr to the work ethic, beavering for most of his waking hours in the interests of Glossop Grammar School and No 596 Squadron, Air Training Corps, then digging for victory in the time left over. So I never questioned the work ethic. I took school work very seriously, did my homework conscientiously, helped a bit around the house and sometimes felt bad if I retired for too long to a hideaway. While aware of the charms of idleness, I tried to resist them.

But what about loving our neighbours? At St Luke's they said that was an omnibus commandment that subsumed all of Numbers Five to Ten. To be honest though, we didn't love our neighbours. Not much anyway. The thing was, we were better than most of them. Indeed belief in the innate superiority of the Lord family to the great bulk of humankind was fundamental to the moral conditioning I received at home. Since the attitudes of my parents were rooted in nonconformity it is tempting to relate the arrogant and unashamed snobbery, intellectual and social, which made the Lords tick, to the Calvinism noted above in relation to the grammar school outlook. All is pre-destined. Some are chosen, others are not. So if at first you err and stray, then you always will, because even a single sin proves you have not got what it takes. Certainly neighbour-wise there was us and them. We were intrinsically cleverer than them, more refined, better equipped to appreciate beauty and above all more virtuous. So since love has implications of mutuality, and thus of equality, and we were indisputably ranked above our neighbours, it was not easy to love them. But if we could not love them we could at least *serve* them. And we should. Improving the lot of the neighbours was what the Lords were for. It was our duty to get our inferiors to live better lives. That was why Dad was a headmaster. The grammar school promoted social mobility and Dad was a missionary in that cause. Lost among the working classes, of whom in general not much was to be expected, there were bright children fit to be shaped in the image of their betters. So as well as a dose of Calvinism there was an Evangelical streak in our make-up. When I grew up I would naturally become a missionary like Dad. He hoped I would serve as a lawyer but I was now rather set on becoming a post war planner instead – or even a teacher, though I kept quiet about that option. Despite being clumsy, no good at games and bothered by sex I was up to the task because I was clever and, above all, because I was virtuous. I possessed inner cleanliness. Until Sports Day 1945 that is. Then virtue suddenly evaporated.

What happened was this. The July sun was hot. I was of course a mere spectator, wriggling uncomfortably, remote from the finishing line under the far hedge, on one of the wooden classroom chairs lugged to the Lord Street field earlier in the day by the forced labour of us non-competitors, travelling in Indian file along the approved routes. I was bored. The house spirit, as we know, did not enliven me. My loyalty to Flamsteed was less than lukewarm and I could summon no pretend hatred for Howard, Nightingale or Spencer. So when the Senior Boys House Relay began [4 x 220 yards] I was stirred only by knowledge that reaching the relays on the programme meant the proceedings were nearly over and soon we could go home. But as sturdy thighs, threshing arms and coloured batons swung, a little unsteadily, round the sharp bend by the Hawker Fury, the pulse of spectator interest quickened. There were partisan shouts. A faint cheer was heard. Then somebody, somewhere let out a distinct 'Boo!' It was at that moment that my inner cleanliness departed. For I knew with icy certainty that, in some random access of contrived emotion, it was me that had booed. I had just broken Iron Rule Number Two and was revealed as lacking in sportsmanship. I had failed to play the game. I was a cad. That knowledge was intolerable and on the bright afternoon, darkness fell.

Calvin now played his cleverest trick. It was by your outward behaviour that inner corruption was revealed. Just one iniquity demonstrated a pervasive state of sin for which there was no remedy. Mere atonement was pointless. You were damned. So my situation was bad, very bad. I could be in no doubt about that. Sometimes on Monday mornings the Gauleiter demonstrated the absolute iniquity of the cad. The usually euphoric tones in which he reported Saturday's triumph over New Mills or Penistone were that day muted. For the happy occasion had been desecrated by louts among the Glossop supporters. Although it was hard to credit it, he had to report that, when the visitors scored, some of our boys had actually booed. Our Headmaster was astonished, affronted, chagrined. His distress remained unassuaged. How much happier for him if the school had lost the match honourably than that victory should be accompanied by so dismal a failure in sportsmanship. The offenders were unworthy of our company. Unfortunately his eyes had been less sharp than his ears and he had failed to identify the despicable cads. Had he done so, his vengeance would have been terrible indeed. However they themselves knew who they were. They stood amongst us, he was ashamed to say, that very morning. Let them ponder the monstrosity of their depravity and let their shame consume them. They were low. They were despicable. Let them hang down their heads.

Well, all that now applied to me. For an age to come my head never returned to the horizontal, although I would have done anything for permission to lift it up. If I had been old enough I would have immediately joined the army to catch what was left of the war – the going down of the rising Japanese sun – in the hope of dying for my country and achieving, after all, honourable mention at Assembly. But I was only thirteen and the atom bomb soon ended the war and put paid to that fantasy. So I glumly carried on. Despite inner anguish I went through the motions. Even in the immediate aftermath of being stung by sin I took part automatically in the complicated manoeuvres whereby Dad assembled the whole school into a hollow square to watch the captain of the winning house receive the colour-wrapped trophy from Mum in a floral frock. But the occasion was black edged. So too were all the other pleasures of that victory summer. Like the amazing election results. Winnie lost! Like the drive down to Selsdon the day before VJ Day. It was our first really long trip in DND 838 since 1939 and we all sang 'We were rolling along', as featured in 'Darryl F Zanuck's *Wilson*', the epic motion picture recently shown at the Empire. Like the trip into London on VJ Day itself and Dad not handing the tickets in at Victoria on the grounds that the war was over, and us kids having to wait a long time outside a pub, and then a trip on the river with my boozy Uncle Leslie taking the microphone from the official guide and having the passengers in stiches. And like the following Sunday, from Leslie's office in the Reuters' building, high up above a sanded Fleet Street, watching the King and Queen and the two princesses driving in an open carriage to give thanks at St Paul's. By then Leslie was sober enough to stop me saluting them from the open window with the swastika arm band he had just brought back as a souvenir from Hamburg. It seems he also brought back the tuberculosis that was to kill him three years later, just ahead of the arrival of antibiotics that might have cure him. It was the second early death in their family of three, for my cousin Barbara had died of cancer amid the doodlebugs in 1944.

Apart from news bulletins about war crimes trials, and also doing the life-saving bronze medallion, I have no recollections of the autumn term of 1945 until its final weeks, although I see from my English exercise book that I favoured Miss Hughes with recollections of holiday jaunts as well as the libel against our Sheffield Road neighbour discussed above. It seems it was also the term we read Siegfried Sassoon and perhaps my tortured conscience got some relief from exposure to his laidback attitude to conventional behaviour. Then, out of the blue once more and with even greater ferocity, Calvin struck again. It was a Monday morning, the Christmas exams were upon us and Room 2, Remove A's classroom, had been laid out with the desks strictly separated. The exam was Chemistry and Roy Read was sitting across the aisle from me. The separation of desks was formal rather than functional so, although I had no conscious intention of copying, a casual glance was enough to see what Roy had written. I had already, in my head, reached the same correct answer to the calculation in question but had not yet actually written it down. I confidently did so now, then handed in my sheets of foolscap and went home for dinner. It being Monday it would have been a 'broth' incorporating the remains of yesterday's roast and, it being washing day, the house would have been clammy with steam. Ugh!

Then I realised what I had done and fell deep into a fog of despair. The depravity of cheats exceeded even that of cads. Before the exams began we were always warned and Iron Rule Number Three was formally promulgated. Copying was unacceptably unacceptable and those apprehended were invariably named, shamed and ritually denounced at Assembly. Like cads they were unworthy our company and escaped expulsion only by the skin of their teeth. That fate however would not befall me. I was in no danger of being charged with plagiarism because what I accused myself of copying was a simple two digit figure, not a form of words, and furthermore it was the correct answer. That was confirmed at the start of the new term in January when Mr Casey gave us back our marked scripts to 'go over' and I found he had duly ticked the answer and awarded it two points. My outraged conscience expostulated anew. That scaly-tailed demon had already given me a miserable Christmas. Until that year the season had brought joy to me as to all mankind. Not anymore it didn't and actually it never has done ever since. Being bad at Christmas is one of my least appealing traits and maybe the trouble is rooted in what happened in 1945. Those two marks, the demon now declared, were the wages of sin. Which prompted a pathetic attempt at appeasement. Surreptitiously I scratched out the correct answer, substituted an incorrect one and presented it to Mr Casey so that my mark could be downwardly adjusted. For a worthless wimp that was a bold gesture because Mr Casey was formidable. He personified reason and wool could not easily be pulled over the piercing eyes that shone from under that bushy grey brow. The impromptu erasure would not have been convincing for my skills as a counterfeiter were inferior to what might have been expected of a well-trained chimpanzee, so this man of science would have been suspicious, to say the least. Anyway he did not co-operate in my secret penance but, while giving me a funny look, said something about a bit of luck doing nobody any harm now and again. Clearly he was disinclined to enquire further. If the boss's son was going dotty that was not his business. As we know, Mr Casey did not like Dad. Anyway he was a chemist not a counsellor.

That pathetic striving after absolution having failed, the ogre inside me continued for many months to twist the knife. Yes, I went through the motions. We have seen that I continued to get good marks in school, and outside it I pursued hobbies, like train spotting and planning New Jerusalem. The latter, which should have taken off immediately after VJ Day, had somehow got delayed and Dad, as we shall see, blamed the Labour government. But relish was gone. I no longer had fun. Frequently I hid away, engaging in gloomy reflections about my worth. A particularly depressing thing about those solitary sessions was that they demonstrated anew the poverty of reason. Logical argument made no impact on the demon. What had happened in the Chemistry exam was not cheating. My glimpse of Roy's script was accidental and anyway I had already arrived at the right answer. Excuses, excuses, said the demon, giving the knife a vicious extra twist. As for my breach of the honour code on Sports Day well it was merely an absent-minded lapse induced by boredom and was perhaps even intended satirically. Stuff Tom Brown! Why should modern boys follow the mores of Victorian toffs? Mere bluster, said demon. Guilt was impervious to reason. The more I argued the more demon stalked me. Time was scarcely more efficacious. If, in the course of 1946, I became gradually less obsessed by the two episodes, that simply meant that guilt about being a cad and a cheat merged into a wider conviction of impurity induced by the experience of puberty. To the delight of the demon that tormented me, in the course of that year I received incontrovertible orgasmic proof that I was infected by sexuality. So I had further, deeper, cause to loathe myself. Demon cheered almost audibly. Got you!

Do most people, with the onset of adolescence, suffer that sort of torment? I do not know for sure but I guess not. I guess instead that something unusual happened to me. It was very painful at the time and it left me permanently crippled. Indeed a poorly delineated but powerful conviction of guilt has, I confess, dogged my life. A deep conviction of unworthiness, upon which no amount of rationalisation seems to have any effect, has too often held me back from happiness and success. I am unfit, inept, unattractive, tainted with sin and deserve to be ostracised. Such a perception is a serious drag. The Dean of my college at Oxford – he too was a headmaster's son, the celebrated academy in question being on the Thames near Windsor – once told me I seemed to 'live with the brakes on'. That expresses my predicament rather well. That he said it, not about a schoolboy, but about an undergraduate, shows the long reach of the demonic rapist who had had his way with me almost a decade earlier. The metaphor of rape seems helpful in explaining what happened to me. Something leapt out of the bushes that sports day and violently possessed me. Like sexual abuse it was traumatic. And, like sexual abuse, it is not just appalling at the time but can stay with you and distort the way you live the rest of your life.

How did it happen? In this chapter I may seem to be blaming the school for not helping me to score goals and erect spill holders, and art education and games at Glossop Grammar School might indeed have been better adapted to the needs of those apparently less talented. Yet I sympathise with the supposed Casey view that it is not for school teachers to minister to the souls or psyches of their pupils. That, our Chemistry master would have said, was the business of religion and, as we have seen, not much religion was allowed to pass through the school gates. And being the child of lapsed Nonconformists, even less of it was given house room at Holly Wood. Perhaps that brings us nearer to the source of my problem. My parents had lost their faith but could not rid themselves of the ethic that had accompanied it. Perhaps in our house the Nonconformist conscience outlived belief in God and that is what screwed me up about right and wrong. In the next chapter, in which the focus shifts from school back to Mum and Dad, some light may be cast on that mystery. Did they really do to me what Philip Larkin says parents are apt to do? If so, could they help it?

Chapter 10

BREEDING

First let me give you Dad at full strength and then the iron brew can be subjected to analysis. Like Hitler he was apt to come on hot and strong at mealtimes. The Führer's 'Table Talk' has survived in book form, for his faithful secretaries, with whom he often shared his sparse refreshment, took down what he said and later typed it up. Unfortunately none of us in Mum's kitchen had shorthand so mostly I have to rely on memory, although some surviving fragments of my father's polemical writings can be called upon in confirmation of his outbursts. Here then is Dad's table talk. The scene is the quite small kitchen at Holly Wood and it is about six o'clock, sometime soon after the war, say in the winter of 1945-46. It is probably freezing outside and maybe the glare of standing snow lightens the gathering dusk and penetrates the steamy window. It is freezing in the rest of the house too but not where we sit for an open fire glows behind Dad's chair and the roaring gas under Mum's chip pan is extinguished only when the supply fails, which in the 'Age of Austerity' it sometimes did. Dad blamed the Labour Government and perhaps he was right. A cut in the rations has just been announced by the Food Minister – not that it applies to us, Mum being persona grata at the Co-op butcher's. Alvar Liddell is giving us the Six O'clock News but we are not really listening. It is no longer about pincer movements and amphibious landings in euphonious places but boring stuff about the United Nations and how many calories a day the defeated Germans are living on. Do we care? Stuff you Fritz, we're all right, thanks to Mr Gregory, the Co-op butcher.

The chairs we sit on – me, Dad and Helen that is, for bustling Mum hardly ever gets to use hers – are Victorian posh with green velvet seats, too grand for the plain deal table. Mum has just got them for a song from red-faced, well-heeled Wishy-Washy Walton, up Sheffield Road, who is de-cluttering, his wife having died. The modesty of the table is concealed under a linen cloth on which are spread a riot of comestibles. There are sauce and vinegar bottles, salt and pepper shakers, jars of jam, lemon cheese and bloater paste, plates of home-baked scones and tarts, and a cylindrical fruitcake for afters. The main course would be something and chips – fish maybe, sausages perhaps, a home-made meat pie, Spam fritters or occasionally dried egg omelettes, though Mum's allure along the High Street usually preserves us from that melancholy expedient. Whatever it was came with a big brown tea pot and an ever replenished plate stacked with grey bread. For this is the era of 'National Flour', not unpatriotically white but not properly brown either and gritty with it, so watch your teeth. Slices are cut frenetically, at an ever steepening angle from the horizontal, from a large crusty loaf. Yes, sliced bread *has* been invented but its image is proletarian and Mum disdains it. Each slice is generously smeared with a whipped up mixture of butter, margarine, milk and Ingredient X. Mum has to be resourceful for even in the back room at the Co-op, off the ration fat is hard to come by.

Dad has just finished his first helping. We eat communally but serially. That is Dad gets his first and tucks in without waiting for the rest of us. He has a tendency to grunt as he eats but whether by way of appreciation or complaint, or whether it indicates some oral impediment, is never quite clear. Now he thrusts his plate away to be replenished while he dabs at his moustache with a napkin – to be honest, we called them 'serviettes' – that has done well to survive the wash, for Mum's lusty hands incline to shredding rather than rubbing. Helen and I are still eating and Mum has given up her vain efforts to snatch a bite between firsts and seconds, while still keeping an eye on the fissile brew in the chip pan. It is at this point that the half sated oracle begins the pronouncements for tonight. He might begin with a de-briefing on the today's combat. An intruder from County shot down in flames. A disruptive parent seen off, smoke billowing from the starboard engine. Another slicked back B Form lout gone for a Burton. Yet another cringing colleague nailed as lacking in moral fibre. A maverick groundsman felled at his mower. A seditious footballer clapped in irons for desertion – playing for the town team instead of the School First Eleven. That's just for starters. Having disposed of a substantial second helping, and fortified by more Typhoo, he surveys the state of the world. Now hear this.

Science is inferior to Arts. Physics is harder than Chemistry, manlier and also useful for making atomic bombs. Biology is not a proper science although bug-hunting is a manly hobby. Geography is neither Arts nor Science so it is no use except for map-reading. American airmen were so dim they could not read maps so they used to bomb by day, following the railway lines to Berlin. Apart from L S Lowry modern art is rubbish and Art is not a proper academic subject. Only B Formers do Art and Picasso is obscene. Composers are also intellectually inferior apart from Handel and the Sullivan bit of 'Gilbert and'. People who claim to enjoy classical music are pretentious liars. 'Cacophonous Negro jazz' of course is not music at all, nor is the slush vomited by 'god-awful American crooners', like Bing Crosby. History is a soft option although inspiring in the hands of masters of English prose, like Gibbon, Macaulay and Winston Churchill. Latin is harder than History so more manly. English is both hard and manly as well as studded with master spirits. Shakespeare is the runaway top master spirit with Milton a poor second and Wordsworth third equal with Chaucer. Wordsworth, being a fell walker, was manly so boys should learn poetry and walk fells, or just moors if no fells are available. The best go to Eton, do Greats at Oxford and become judges. The next best go to Winchester, read PPE and become politicians. Oxford and Cambridge are better than the rest and Oxford is better than Cambridge which is coarsened by all that science. Manchester University [where Dad himself went] is the best of the rest and particularly better than London. Similarly the *Manchester Guardian* is better than the *Times*. Lancashire is better than Yorkshire but both are better than all the others. Hull, despite being in Yorkshire is not a proper university. It is fit only for B Formers like the Holt boys. Girls are more conscientious than boys but less brilliant. Girls' careers do not matter because, unless they are ugly, they will get married. Ugly girls should train as teachers or, in hopeless cases, librarians. It is OK for even pretty girls to go into the sixth form, because that will help them talk to their husbands and supervise their children's homework. They will go on the Arts Side of course because science is unfeminine. Women are difficult colleagues because they are mostly spinsters and therefore frustrated. So are bloody parsons. Just listen to their 'flatulent' accents. 'Yaa that has yaas to yaa, let him yaa.' Argh! They are nancy-boys to a man. Birds nesting and reading Jack London are manly. Collecting stamps, train-spotting, slicking back hair and reading comics indicate mental deficiency. Following American band leaders is especially deplorable. Being yellow they dodged the war. So did the nancy-boys and conshies. Ballroom dancing however is a 'desirable social accomplishment' – but only at school parties. Sex is relatively deplorable, even at school parties, except for war heroes and football captains but not if the former are American or the latter professionals. There is too much sex about, thanks to crooners, GIs and other 'unlovely' American imports. The Radio Doctor, who had a slot about 6-30, seemed to agree. A daily bowel movement is essential to good health and promotes the habit of contemplation. The Radio Doctor seemed to go along with that as well. 'How is your bile?' he used to ask. Grammar School children should shun working class attitudes. So they should avoid Sunday schools, youth clubs, the scouts and the army cadets and when called up for National Service they should choose the RAF or, better still, the Navy. The Army is just for the working class, like downstairs at the pictures. Miners come bottom of the working class. They dodged the war, are always on strike and a lot of them are Welsh. Working in the mills is not much better than mining. It is what louts from West End fetch up doing. Even managing a mill is not a suitable career for A Form boys. It is better to become a doctor but not a medical officer of health. All MOHs are interfering cranks who should be banned from grammar schools. Compared to headmasters assistant teachers are no good. Natural selection proves it. So they should be paid less or alternatively heads should be paid more. That is 'maintaining the differential' and ipso facto a good thing. Training teachers is a waste of time. It is those who can't teach who teach others how to teach. Higher degrees are also a waste of time. Educational research is claptrap of the first water. All education officers, like all American generals and all Labour ministers, are incompetent. All county contractors are corrupt as well as incompetent. So are all businessmen, like Uncle Albert, and they are also pig ignorant and have no manners. Again, all crooners are sick-making. There are two sorts of people – dog lovers and the rest of mankind. Sympathy for the defeated Hun is misplaced. Prussian militarism must be stamped out. All Germans are guilty. The only good German is a dead German. Italians are incompetent cowards and behave like nancy-boys. They should have stuck to ice-cream instead of going to war. You can't trust the French. All Japs are sadistic sub-humans. Just ask Mr Bell, only he won't tell you, silent hero that he is. Americans tend towards the sub-human but are not sadists. Russians are an enigma. Bloody Swedes are neutral and thus contemptible. Religion is the opium of the people. All parsons are pansies. All pansies are conshies. All opticians are profiteers as are proprietors of pie shops.

Thus the accumulated wisdom of the holder of a first class degree from, on his reckoning, the third best university in Britain, charged now with the moral and intellectual welfare of Glossop's golden youth. Did he really come on like that? Well among the considerable bulk of paper he left behind, I have found firm evidence that he did. Here he is for example in 1944, telling the sixth form Literary and Debating Society how the defeated Germans should be dealt with.

The German people have a national character which makes them the greatest menace to peace in Europe. The anti-intellectualism of the Nazis is merely the latest manifestation of the worship of brute force and passion for power that was in the earliest Huns. The Prussian typifies that spirit and the Prussian – the jack-booted uniformed conqueror – has never been seriously challenged by Germans as a whole. They are responsible as a nation and as a nation must be punished. The German must be given no say in the government of his country but must carry out the orders of his conquerors. A very big and non-fraternising army of occupation must take over so that he really knows what foreign occupation means and that he cannot again say he was not defeated.

And here are the same sentiments in verse, undated but probably also done towards the end of the war. The piece may have been intended for the New Statesman weekly competition, in which he took much delight.

I'm tired of hearing sermons on our economic sins
And how it's all because of trade a German war begins.
It wasn't economics started Bismarck on the prowl
And Kaiser William's followers were fat as any fowl.
The bug that's in the Prussian blood requires no common meal;
It lives on pride and pilfering, stupidity and steel.

He took to verse about crooners too, perhaps with the same readership in mind.

Shut up, shut up, you whining witch!
The wireless off I'll have to switch.
You love some lad. He is not true.
Well, I don't wonder much, do you?
I swear there is no love so strong
That it could stand that voice for long.

A few years later he returned to the theme in an address to the Glossop Townswomen's Guild, prefacing his remarks with an expressed wish to avoid 'pontifical ex cathedra judgements'. What the townswomen made of that we can only guess. You what?

Is there anything more 'sick-making' than the spectacle of a young man crooning
a love song, revolting in sentiment and appalling in its music, into a microphone
which is literally embraced as a substitute for the form of the beloved.

The point is the tea table tirade was not just for domestic consumption. He let it all hang out in public too. So perhaps, up to a point anyway, he really meant what he said. Certainly he broke almost all the rules of political correctness which govern public discourse in the twenty-first century and many readers will automatically dismiss him as a monster. He was an uncompromising sexist. He had no doubt that a woman's place was in the home. He was an outrageous snob and an unapologetic elitist. He was dictatorial and anti-democratic – a fascist perhaps. He knew that popular culture – not that he would have admitted the legitimacy of any such concept – was just plain inferior and it was his duty to protect his children and his pupils from infection by the virus that generated crooners. Like many contemporary intellectuals, he was a Social Darwinist, believing implicitly that good and bad cultural strains struggle always for supremacy. So he was perpetually into selection, compulsively sorting sheep from goats in a mass of supposed confrontations – male v female, intellectuals v philistines, Britons v 'less happier' breeds, the 'best people' v the working class, arts v science, English v inferior subjects, straights v gays [not of course that he ever learnt those terms], sublime poets v bloody parsons, William Shakespeare v Jesus Christ, dog lovers v normal folk. And so on and so on. In all that he was unrelievedly partisan – and permanently angry. Bellicosity was his default position, even in small matters. Although, in occasional serendipity, he might sometimes ask softly for 'a spot more char, Ma', usually, as he thrust the tepid dregs of his cup in the general direction of my quaking mother, his demand for a fresh brew was accompanied by the harsh expletive 'Not 'ot!'.

Dad's table talk then constitutes a monstrous affront to correct opinion as perceived today and, as I say, most readers will have recoiled in horror from the litany of offence. And yet ... well he was more than a bagful of egregious error. Paradoxically, as well as a ranting bigot he was a nice chap. In the classroom he was compelling. On holiday he was a great companion. When he stopped banging on he became a cool and rational observer of the world around him. And it certainly was a wonder that 'one small head could carry all he knew.' That comes from 'The Deserted Village' by Oliver Goldsmith, of whom maybe you have never heard, but it was a favourite of Dad's and one of the poems I used to declaim on those literary bike rides recalled above. Surely a chap who loved poetry as much as Dad did, and could so powerfully transmit its delights to the next generation, cannot have been be all bad? So how did he get to talk like that? Partly of course he didn't altogether mean it. He had had a hard day and was letting off steam. And sometimes maybe he was being deliberately provocative so that his children would challenge his arguments and start to think for themselves. In that he succeeded. My own mature views came to form an intellectual tissue sharply at odds with my father's mentality. Also we should take account not only of what he said but of the time in which he said it. This was immediate post war and minds had become warped in conflict. Take his views on defeated Germany. They were not his own but reflected a prevailing Allied consensus. The armies of occupation really were strictly forbidden to 'fraternise', although a conspiracy of GIs and frauleins mercifully ensured that the policy failed. And for a while it was official US policy systematically to de-industrialise Germany, reducing its guilty inhabitants to a race of impoverished peasants grubbing for subsistence. That was known as the 'Morgenthau Plan', after its author, Roosevelt's Treasury Secretary.

Nevertheless deeper cultural currents must surely have moulded Dad. Like all of us he was the creature of his upbringing and early experiences. By which of course it is not implied that the currents themselves were pernicious. It was just the way they flowed together and washed over him that induced the froth and frenzy inundating our tea table. I have identified five such currents sweeping through his formative first quarter century. They made him a lot of things we must admire, like an inspiring teacher, a loving father, an upright citizen and a sincere patriot. But they also made him angry, bitter and prone to mania. Let us look at them in turn. The first current was the Nonconformist inheritance that stayed with him for life, even after he let God go. Then there was his boyhood pursuit of manliness, spurred on by voracious reading but hampered by physical inadequacy, real or imagined. Next there was his grammar school education that made him both a scholar and a snob. Above all there was his war service on the Western Front. Its explosive impact made a man of Dad and brought him good feelings as well as bad thoughts. Finally there was his university training in literature. It showed him what he had been fighting for and it boxed his moral compass.

In childhood my father and mother were both deeply marinaded in Nonconformity, an experience that marked them indelibly. That statement may puzzle modern readers, for the idea of Nonconformity cuts little mustard today, when the long gone chapel way of life is no more than an arcane curiosity. But it once made Mum and Dad tick – she grew up a Baptist and he was trained in the Wesleyan strand of Methodism – so I need to tell you about it and hence a quick history lesson. Nonconformity is rooted in the doings of militant Puritans in the seventeenth century. Under Oliver Cromwell they won the Civil Wars, killed the King and abolished the Church of England, only to have victory snatched away when Charles II was restored in 1660. Those unwilling to 'conform' to the beliefs of the restored Church then went underground. But although legally excluded from public life they got on with their jobs and did very nicely economically. Original Nonconformists, like the Baptists, often took a stern view of 'salvation' – the way you get to go to heaven – claiming that only those *predetermined* by God will be let in. That was the tradition of John Calvin, the sixteenth century French Reformer. But during the 1700s Methodism, a new wave of Nonconformity associated with the 'evangelical' teachings of John Wesley, promoted a kinder view, preaching that all will be saved who experience 'conversion' – a sense of oneness with Christ, felt in the heart of the sinner – and most Nonconformists, including most Baptists, soon also became Evangelical. In the nineteenth century they recovered their civil rights and went into politics. By 1910 the Prime Minister, the Chancellor and most MPs of the governing Liberal party were Nonconformists. The excluded sheep had thus butted their way back into the fold. And they continued to get rich. A roll call of Victorian brand names – Cadburys and Rowntrees, Wills and Players, Tate and Lyle, Lloyds and Barclays – testifies to their commercial supremacy. My maternal grandfather, J T Lord the slipper manufacturer, owed his business success to membership of a Baptist congregation. He was a man of his times.

Thus the confident Nonconformity my parents were bred in sprang from a proudly nourished collective memory of persecution, triumphantly endured and reversed. That narrative generated a pervasive sense of 'us' versus 'them'. Dad's manic tea-table categorisations constitute a comic exaggeration of the sheep and goats mentality of Nonconformity and his menagerie of bêtes noires would have been recognised by many of his co-religionists. In it were corralled Anglicans [Dad's 'bloody parsons'] and the feckless – those undeserving sections of the working class that knew not they had bootstraps with which to elevate themselves – together with drunkards, gamblers and adulterers. At the heart of the matter of course was conversion, the life-changing experience that distinguished the saved – those born again into a purer life, lived in anticipation of eternal bliss – and the rest, from whom repentance was overdue and for whom, without it, if they could they but see it, the prospect was dire. Hence the supreme importance of respectability, the respectable and the saved being pretty much the same thing. A respectable life-style – temperate, honest, hardworking and self-sufficient – is itself proof of conversion. If you habitually behave yourself it follows you must be saved. If you transgress you will naturally try to conceal the lapse, even from yourself, because it casts doubt on your conversion. Thus the appearance of virtue matters almost as much as virtue itself.

Those then were some of the constituents of Nonconformity that engulfed both my parents as they grew up in the decade before the Great War. Its tenets were communicated, not just in the family, but in the busy congregational life of the chapels they attended. Dad recorded his deep involvement in chapel doings in a memoir he wrote in retirement. The premises of the Poulton-le-Fylde Wesleyans lay close to where they lived and it adjoined Tomlinsons' flour mills, the profits of which sustained the chapel.

We attended regularly each Sunday, dressed in our best clothes. After morning school from 9-15 to 10-15, we moved into the chapel for morning service ... From two to three in the afternoon was the second session of the Sunday school, and some children regularly accompanied their parents to the evening service beginning at six thirty.

Observance four times a day was quasi-monastic. And chapel was not just for Sundays. Much of the rest of the week, outside school and working hours, was also devoted to its activities, including

tea parties, potato-pie suppers, bazaars, jumble sales, literary and musical evenings, debates, lantern lectures, one act plays and dramatic readings, Band of Hope weekly meetings, art and craft classes etc etc

Except for the absence of sport, it mirrors the busy after school programme at Glossop Grammar School and probably the resemblance is not coincidental. For Dad thoroughly approved this 'amusement of the people, by the people and for the people'. From his Bournemouth redoubt, glaring at the ever rising waters of pop culture, he contrasted it grumpily with 'present day passive addiction to TV and radio and canned entertainment from the cinema and the gramophone'. He waxed especially lyrical about the annual Sunday school treat, which always seemed to happen on 'a warm day of early summer'. On wagonettes and Tomlinsons' flour lorries they went off to a farm where a picnic was spread out on trestle tables in a barn. Afterwards they had swings and games and races and paddled in a stream. Then came the idyllic ride home

through the leafy lanes in evening sunlight, while tired children listened to 'Now the day is over', 'Old folks at home', 'Sweet and low', 'Abide with me' sung with soothing harmony by parents and friends as the horses jogged steadily, along peaceful roads and the empty streets of our little town, to journey's end at the Chapel steps.

That reminds me of a famous evocation of summer in the English countryside. Just before the Great War broke out Edward Thomas was travelling on an express train that made an unscheduled stop at a wayside station called Adlestrop where the passengers were serenaded by 'all the birds of Oxfordshire and Gloucestershire'. Thomas was killed a few years later defending his pastoral vision of England. Dad was luckier and survived the Western Front. But as he stood to in his front line trench, I think he also remembered Adlestrop, or as he knew it, Poulton-le-Fylde. It was what he too was fighting for.

The Poulton Wesleyans did not need TV for they were living a soap. It brought scandals as well as treats and there were many opportunities for the wagging of tongues. A certain grocer, a 'pillar' of the congregation, suddenly 'left his home and family'. It was 'a mystery that excited our parents and their Chapel friends'. Well it would, wouldn't it? Was it sex or was it money? Alas, the Lord family itself was not immune to tongue wagging. Dick's wandering eye fell upon 'Mother's best friend' for whom he conceived 'a sincere affection, at times an infatuation'. That she happened to be the Chapel organist deepened the angst. Wow! An even worse menace to the family reputation was the state of Dick's photography business. He was not breaking even and in the end went cap in hand to 'Parky' Tomlinson. Young Parkinson was heir to the flour fortune. He was also something of a radical, indeed a future MP, so Red Dick believed he had a comrade in Parky. It was Parky who had encouraged him to deliver 'Why I am an atheist', his provocative address to the Welsey Guild. Perhaps he also encouraged Dick to join the local branch of the ILP, the Independent Labour Party, the doings of which further distracted him from the mundane pursuit of his calling. One red letter day Keir Hardie himself, the first ever Labour MP, had actually taken tea in their front room. Or so I used to be told, although some said the left wing luminary concerned might have been Ramsay Macdonald, the first ever Labour prime minister. Dick then was a citizen with connections. But when he asked his friend Parky for a little bit of help, Parky said 'No'. Even comrades must stand on their own two feet. If English socialism truly owed more to Methodism than to Marxism then class solidarity did not extend to bailing out bankrupts. God helped those who helped themselves, not those who failed that test. It was a bitter blow. Even after sixty years lingering hurt inflamed my father's recollections. The callous mill-owner had stuck to his 'unshakable business principles when he might, without much risk, have played the good Samaritan'. The episode surely contributed to Dad's disdain for business and businessmen which many years later exploded all over our tea table. At the time it almost destroyed the Lord family, for impending ruin, together with the matter of the lady organist, proved the last straw for Ada who, in the new year of 1913, decamped, taking the younger children back to Rossendale, leaving Dick in Poulton with his Jezebel and his creditors. How they eventually survived such a blow to their reputation I do not know but somehow appearances were kept up. Maintaining them, as we have seen, was a Nonconformist imperative.

The Lord brothers reacted differently to their parents' separation. Leslie stuck up for his dad while Cecil sided fiercely with his mother. That probably reflected an existing divide. Leslie, who was three years older, took after his father. He was tall and handsome, like Dick, and inherited also his father's practical skills and engaging affability. So Leslie left school when he was fourteen and became Dick's apprentice and also his political disciple. Together they fixed negatives and pursued positive thinking. Perhaps that timely injection of youthful energy kept the business going until the war broke out, bringing a buoyant market for studio portraits of young men in uniform, destined for sad parlours, in which they kept the home fires burning. Poor Cecil however felt excluded from the male bond. He was too young and looked even younger. He could not keep up and never acquired manual dexterity or developed the worldly capability Dick and Leslie took for granted. Perhaps that was Dick's fault. Maybe he neglected his younger son, failed to pass on masculine accomplishments and did not properly teach him how to be a man. If so it was lamentable for Cecil's shoulder, soon began to carry that king-sized chip about manliness that distorted my upbringing and still drove Dad to verbal excess at the tea table thirty odd years later. We know that few things mattered more to him in later life than playing the game, cutting a thrust and being ever ready for knightly combat.

Part of the problem was that Cecil was not equipped by nature with the sort of physique that being knightly calls for. In fact he was a little titch. When he joined the army at 18 he was still only five foot five and that was a real handicap. It was not that he lacked pluck. His memoir glows with feats of boyhood derring-do but his valour was not matched with discretion, so too often he fell flat on his face. Here are two distressing episodes:

... riding too fast on a cycle too big for me I was thrown by a dog ... unconscious ... severely concussed ... lump as big as a duck's egg

... with Leslie and some of his big boy friends ...wearing a brand new Sunday suit ... jumping water-filled ditches ... failed hopelessly ... fell into deep, muddy water ... [fears of] pneumonia and typhoid.

After he won a scholarship to Blackpool Grammar School he travelled daily on the train, at the mercy of 'Bully Jack', who mocked him when he had to collect a 'Shilling Parcel', of scraps and left-overs, from the local branch of Liptons, the grocery chain. That bargain helped his mother stretch the housekeeping money. Then, like Tom Brown confronting Flashman, Cecil one day flipped. He furiously let fly at Jack with both fists. But to no avail. 'Easily he held me off, and then delivered in my face a savage punch' which momentarily, so he says, knocked him out. Since sneaks are more despicable even than wimps he explained his 'prize shiner' as the result of hitting the swinging door when jumping off the train before it had stopped. It is a fair bet he usually performed that dashing manoeuvre with consummate incompetence, so questions were not asked and honour was satisfied.

Where did he learn the code? In the playground no doubt and among the fields and hedgerows of the Fylde, but the messages of the peer group grapevine seem to have been massively reinforced by what he read. He used to tell me about the stories he devoured, often by way of coaxing me from war maps and Rupert Bear onto real books for red blooded boys. In his memoir he celebrated his boyhood literary favourites. He tells us No 1 Chapel Street was a bookish home, in part because the bookcase filled up year by year with prizes for good work and exemplary attendance, collected from school and Sunday school by five bright children. Perhaps he over-eggs his claim that the literary character of their home was unusual, for in those days many families kept books. The years before 1914 were the high noon of the printed word as a mass medium. Educational reform had delivered universal literacy and rival media, either had not been invented or were still in their infancy. So they read, read and read again and, for better or worse, became what they read. In the endless debate about the origins of the First World War the belligerent impact of boys' reading is a neglected element.

The literary inheritance of our particular future warrior can be accurately reconstructed. Even the omissions are interesting. Dad hardly ever referred to any classic novels written after *Robinson Crusoe* [1719] and before *The Time Machine* [1895], the sci-fi fantasy of H G Wells. He was dismissive of Dickens and ominously silent on all female novelists except Louisa M Alcott. So when Mum took me to see *Pride and Prejudice* at the pictures he stayed at home and when we saw *Jane Eyre* at the Southport Palladium he just sneered and scoffed. Tales of heroism however enchanted the young reader. He absorbed the Greek myths. He loved Stevenson, Kipling and Conrad. He liked desert island sagas such as *Swiss Family Robinson* and *The Coral Island* by R M Ballantyne, and also the same author's *Martin Rattler*, set in the rain forests of Brazil. Then there were the naval yarns by Captain Maryatt – *Masterman Ready* and *Mr Midshipman Easy*. Arthur Conan Doyle was another constant companion. Most of all he rated the American authors Jack London and Mark Twain. London was a real life adventurer and gold miner who had climbed to success from the 'cellar of society'. As for Huckleberry Finn and Tom Sawyer, well they were in all respects what every boy should hope to be. When we saw *Tom Sawyer* immortalised in celluloid, also at the Palladium, it felt as though we were worshipping in chapel rather than just taking advantage of the 'sixpence in all parts' Saturday matinee offer. Young Cecil it seems could not get enough of true grit whatever the actual misadventures he suffered in its pursuit. The game boy got his kicks in verse as well as prose as the following eulogy demonstrates. It refers to *The Thousand Best Poems in the World*, 'a two volume Sunday school prize'.

This was an American anthology which incongruously combined corny and sentimental examples of American magazine verse with lengthy selections from Shakespeare and Milton and other classics. I make no claim that I rejected the pathos and melodrama and sob-stuff and steeped myself in the best of Shakespeare, Shelley etc. In fact I revelled in 'The Fireman's Wedding', 'Barbara Frietsche', 'The Old Armchair' and 'Curfew Shall Not Ring Tonight'. As one often called upon to recite, I drew uncritically from all parts of these volumes.

Decades later, whether 'called upon' or not, he was still reciting the listed poems, thus enlivening walks along the prom and journeys in the car. It was good. Although memory fades I think the heroine who silenced the curfew strapped herself to the clapper of the bell. That girl had guts like the venerable Barbara Frietsche. Even as Stonewall Jackson led his Confederate army into town, she hung out the forbidden Stars and Stripes, saying 'Shoot if you must this old grey head but spare your country's flag'. Stonewall relented.

"Who touches a hair of yon grey head
Dies like dog. March on!" he said.

Wow!

There was however one genre of boys' fiction that took possession of Cecil like nothing else. He was not alone. The run-up to World War One was not only the high noon of literacy it was also the golden mid-summer of the public school. Most boys of course never personally experienced the glowing buttocks endemic to that sado-masochistic, homo-erotic culture, yet a whole army of them felt part of the scene thanks to their eager consumption of school fiction. Dad never got nearer a real public school than a distant prospect of Rossall – Gothic mass visible from the window of the Blackpool to Fleetwood tram – but like millions of his fellows, and like 'Frank Richards', an author who, over 60 years, produced 60 million words of school story, he knew that world so well he almost felt he had been there. John Arlott, the cricket commentator, once interviewed Charles Hamilton [1875-1961], aka Frank Richards, and reported that although

like so many of his boyish admirers he had never been ... he wished he had and perhaps indeed really believed he had in his heart and mind.

I guess Dad enjoyed a similar illusion. He tried to think and act like he supposed the chaps did at Eton and Harrow and when he became a schoolmaster and then a father he felt an urge to pass on the values he extracted from the school stories he read as a boy. Among them *Tom Brown's Schooldays* naturally came top. Further down the league table came *The Fifth Form at St Dominics* by Talbot Baines Read and *Stalky and Co* by Kipling himself. In a monthly magazine called *The Captain* he spotted a rising star. He declared P G Wodehouse, who recounted the doings of Mike and his friends, 'the school story writer par excellence'. That judgement came despite the author's dodgy record in the Second World War which he spent in cahoots with 'Prussian militarism'. Dad was capable of generosity. *The Captain* was not the only boys' comic that stoked Cecil's passion. Nor were brief encounters with the upmarket *Boys Own Paper* or *Chums* enough to satisfy his raging appetite for the lore and language of school life. What really kept him on song were two weeklies that plopped onto the Chapel Street doormat as regularly as the *Clarion*, the seriously socialist journal that moulded Dick's opinions. The *Gem*, aimed at a mass readership of British boys, had been launched in 1907 while its stable mate *The Magnet* followed a year later. Cecil, being then just about ten, was ripe to be swept off his feet. Soon he needed both titles in a double fix. A soon as they were delivered he possessed them, reading them voraciously through the incidents of daily life – at meals, travelling to school, in the playground and lingering in the privy – until he had sucked them dry. Each comic was the home of a particular school. In the *Gem* 'Martin Clifford' reported from St Jim's the exploits of Tom Merry and the 'Terrible Three of the Shell', while the *Magnet* took you to Greyfriars where Harry Wharton and the 'Famous Five of the Remove', as narrated by 'Frank Richards', contended with an anarchical assemblage of avoirdupois called Billy Bunter. An appreciative article in the *Oxford Dictionary of National Biography* identifies both Martin Clifford and Frank Richards as pseudonyms of the aforementioned Charles Hamilton, an ebullient operator who once defended himself against George Orwell, no less, who had called him 'stupid' and berated his snobbery and his mocking racial stereotypes. Hamilton replied cheerfully that there was a lot to be said for aristocratic rule and foreigners were indeed funny. A pity he never came to tea at Holly Wood. He and Dad would have got on like the house on fire that Mum, with her cavalier deep frying, constantly threatened us with.

I have sampled Frank Richards. *The Banishing of Billy Bunter* was actually published as late as 1956 when the old boy was still churning it out but, except for fleeting references to cars and taxis, you might think it was set half a century before. I like it. It is funny. It has pace. The chaps are amiable. They bicker and pose but when the chips are down they stick up for each other. Even the 'beaks' exhibit a streak of humanity and wield their canes more in pantomime than in moral earnest. And Billy Bunter is a riot, a rich comic creation inviting us to cast a sceptical eye on the pomposities of life. Not that order and justice must not in the end prevail. The language is great fun. Sure it is polysyllabic and allusive. But Richards clearly loves the texts he hints at – the Greek and Latin classics and the bible – and he uses long words not to show off but 'for amusement only' [as it used to say on seaside slot machines]. But I wonder how many ten year olds today could cope with these word-rich sentences. Those Edwardian pals clearly knew their 'dics' from A to Z. It all reminds me, not of Thomas Hughes propounding Arnoldean virtues, but rather of Dad at his best. Not the ranting oracle of the tea table but the deft wordsmith, fund-holder of knowledge, anthologist of verses, spinner of yarns and teller of jokes who used to take me striding along the Marine Drive in autumn gales. Now I see where he got it from. Frank Richards unlocks Dad.

But back to the family split and coincidentally to the third cultural current that carried Dad through his formative years. It was the reformed grammar school, the remarkable national institution established under the 1902 Education Act. By 1914 every town had one, including smoke-stack boroughs like Glossop and Rossendale and bracing Blackpool too. By 1914 also a dispute about the grammar school curriculum had been settled. It was officially decreed that the humanities not technology should prevail and the model for the new academies would be the English public schools rather than the vocational colleges famously pioneered in Prussia. Sending Cecil to the grammar school at Blackpool seems to have been his mother's idea, encouraged by Miss Tebay, Head of Sheaf Street Elementary School. What that lady said made sense. Even if he was on the short side, Cecil was a clever boy who could go far, now they were living in the twentieth century and new opportunities had opened up. Did Mrs Lord know that, with a scholarship and a travel pass, it would not cost the earth to send her lad to Blackpool? Do well at grammar school and a good job would be his for the asking. Not just a job but a 'position'. That would really have tempted Ada as she looked a decade or two ahead. Cecil's bride would never know the insecurity of self-employment. With a monthly salary going into her husband's bank account she would never cower in anticipation of the bailiff's men on the doorstep or suffer cold shoulders at chapel. She would never have to scrimp and save and feed the family on Liptons' sweepings. Instead she would hold her head high as the wife of – well, a true gentleman. And just imagine being the mother of a gentleman. It would make up for everything she had put up with from that wandering wastrel, loud mouthed braggart and smooth talking philanderer she was yoked to. The sky was the limit. The boy might emulate his Uncle Arthur and become an optician. He might work at the town hall. He might even become a doctor or a lawyer – or at least a teacher. It was a dizzying prospect.

The project also did something to sort out Cecil's immediate problem, his perceived deficiency in manliness. It would not put six inches on his height but it would pitch him into an alternative field for knightly combat, one in which he was not vertically challenged. For he proved to be good at passing exams and that was most of what grammar schools were about. Competitive examination had been a great Victorian accomplishment fit to be ranked beside the railway system and parliamentary reform. The man chiefly responsible was Thomas Dyke Acland, heir to a large Devon estate and a lateral thinker. In the 1850s, following the end of the Corn Laws, he worried about the plight of farmers no longer protected against foreign competition. They needed to improve their yields, which meant adopting modern methods, which in turn demanded know-how and a spirit of get up and go. Acland thought such qualities could be injected, at least into the next generation, by reforming the slack 'middle class schools' fitfully attended by farmers' sons. He would galvanise the sleepy academies of rural Devon by giving them a target to aim at. So he established the Oxford Local Examining Board, its standards guaranteed by some of his university mates. It worked, similar bodies followed and young lives came to be forever dominated by exams. Without T D Acland, there would be no GCSE. Why he is not famous is a mystery. Anyway the new Edwardian grammar schools, finding examining boards already up and running, took them to their hearts. The challenge of the 'Matric' stiffened their sinews and summoned up the blood of inky contenders for honours. Thus swotting became manly. It was Cecil's salvation.

He duly won his place and with it a 'scholar's' contract with the Lancashire and Yorkshire Railway Company and in September 1911 set out on his way to the stars. At school in Blackpool he found reassuring echoes of Greyfriars and St Jim's. The school had an appropriate Latin motto, 'Meliora Sequamur' [we strive for better things] and Joseph Turral the headmaster was, according to my father

concerned to establish the social standing of his school as a place where his pupils might be shaped, in manners and 'superior attitude', into good imitations of the public school product.

266

He regarded with particular horror the cloth tabs provided by boot manufacturers, as an aid to dressing, inside the heels of their products. Hence a tirade frequently heard in the corridors

Boy, boy, tuck in those rabbit's ears protruding from your boots. Do you think we are a school for tradesmen's sons?

It was of course exactly that. By Dad's estimate three quarters of his fellow pupils came from the homes of 'tradesmen, shopkeepers and boarding house proprietors'. He himself offended against the Turral dress code. He had been correctly kitted out with cap and tie but the green Norfolk jacket with matching breeches, generously supplied by Aunt Gertie, the optician's wife who nurtured a touch of style, proved a barely tolerated aberration. However Cecil found himself thoroughly at home with the competitive swotting. His report book survives. It is spattered in the traditional manner with staccato commendations that seldom fall below 'Very Good' and sometimes rise to 'Excellent'. He was placed in the top class where at Christmas 1912 he came top and extracted the 'E' word even from Joe Turral himself, above a rubber stamp facsimile of his signature. That thoroughly modern headmaster seems to have been into technology for he also had a telephone installed in every classroom. Her boy's success must have been particularly sweet for Ada. At Speech Day in the pavilion on North Pier, the superior pier, she luxuriated in solitary state – Dick stayed away, as perhaps was now to be expected – on a front row reserved for the parents of prize-winners. The reward Cecil accepted from the hands of the Mayoress, was a deluxe edition of *The Adventures of Tom Sawyer*. It was an apt choice for, according to the *Oxford Companion to English Literature*, Tom is not only 'brave and generous' but also 'mischievous and ingenious'. That is, he used his head to think with rather than to butt with. Here surely was a role model for Cecil.

After Christmas though he had to move on, the trial separation, if such it was, having now become operational. He, his 'Ma' and his sisters scuttled back to Rossendale where he languished for a couple of terms at an unreconstructed academy, finding consolation in the stately reading room of the newly opened library at Rawtenstall. Public libraries were the siblings of the grammar schools, partners in an Edwardian educational revolution through which national brain power was engrossed. Then in

September 1913, at the time of his fifteenth birthday, Cecil was swept up again in the onward march of the grammar school which carried him forwards and upwards over the next three years. For in that month the Bacup and Rawtenstall Secondary School opened its handsome doors. It was sited, halfway between those two bastions of the cotton trade, at Waterfoot where, significantly for our story, cotton spinning had been displaced at Gaghills Mill, its principal place of employment, by the manufacture of casual footwear, as developed by the late, great Sir Henry Tricket, the 'Slipper King'. As we know Sir Henry was the patron of my grandfather, now a Tricket's director who had settled his family in affluence at a big house called Ross Mount, next door to a fellow board member. From their back windows they watched the erection of the new grammar school, only a couple of hundred yards away. When it opened Tom and Esther decided to entrust their youngest child Nellie to its care, thus letting her leave Ackworth, the Quaker boarding school in Yorkshire, where along with her brother Alan, she had been moulded hitherto. Alan stayed on at Ackworth preparing for medical school but pretty little Nellie was not going to need a career, so let her come home and keep her fond parents company. For they had just lost Maud, their other daughter, to teacher training in suffragette London and Albert also, as we shall see, had left home. Thus Nellie met Cecil. They contrived to stay together until death did them part, almost sixty years later.

The first thing they had in common, apart from a surname, was Nonconformity. Nellie's early immersion in chapel and its doings was literally total because they were Baptists. A letter she wrote from Ackworth at Easter 1913 survives and illuminates. In a breathless rush she chatters, not only about school, but also about the latest from Bethel, the Waterfoot congregation that was their extended family, as revealed by 'Darling Mother' in her last letter.

Esther had had a new dress for the Bazaar but at the special tea she had picked up something that did not agree with her. Nellie hoped she was all right now, as she was, despite the measles still lingering at Ackworth. All that is charming but anxiety is apparent between the lines. She has also had a letter from Albert. He being the oldest and she the youngest, they were especially fond of each other and she hopes to be allowed out from school to get her brother a twenty-first birthday present. But what he has just told her is a bombshell. He has a 'little baby' called Mary.

The truth is that Albert had had to get married and the female person concerned – well, a barmaid actually – was not joyfully welcomed into the family. Accommodation had been found for them in an unfamiliar and presumably ill-favoured part of Rossendale. 'I don't think I know where Gresham Street is,' Nellie wrote, perhaps with conscious irony. Albert however had written that 'they have a big garden at the front'. So it was not a standard two-up, two-down, opening straight onto the street, and you had to be thankful for small mercies. The point for our purposes is that even the Gaghills Lords, pillars of Bethel, were not immune to scandal, so whenever the teenagers with the identical surname became confidantes they had matters for mutual confession. They both knew what straying from the straight and narrow could do to family happiness. It must never ever happen to them and theirs. Their marriage, when in the fullness of time it came about, was to be founded in a fierce commitment to appearances. At all costs they must be kept up. So whenever tempers flared at our house, as they rather often did, Dad compulsively drew the curtains. And when, forty years on, widowed Maud, when nearly sixty, was discovered in adultery they were traumatised. Mum never really recovered.

Despite the commencement of hostilities in 1914 school life went on. Cecil got his Matric in1915 and stayed on for a year in the Sixth Form. I guess they let Nellie leave without bothering with the exam, it being different for girls. Soon she donned a nurse's uniform and helped out at New Hall Hey, a local manor house requisitioned as a military hospital. The lads called her 'Snowball' and you can see why from the photograph in *Plate 2 middle left*. Cecil too of course had heard the brave music of the guns and he too appears in *Plate 2* in uniform, that of a callow recruit of a callow recruit. By now that music had come very close to home for on 1 July 1916 a battalion of 'Pals' from nearby Accrington lost 500 men out of 700 on the terrible first day of the Somme offensive. But when Cecil left school a few weeks later he knew his duty. As soon as he reached eighteen in September, his patriotic eyes wide open, he volunteered for the East Lancs, the very regiment recently bereft of the Accrington Pals. I guess what happened to Dad over the next two years moulded him to a greater extent than any other adult experience.

He was not one of those stoical veterans who never talked about the war. Rather he talked about it eagerly whenever anybody would listen and that mostly meant me or Sammy Holt who had himself survived three years on the Western Front. So a lot of what follows comes from the horse's mouth. I have tried to supplement it from his official service book, available like millions of others online, but to say the least it is terse and only precariously legible. Name, number, regiment, date of enlistment, date of demobilisation, height [pathetic], military offences [none] and admissions to hospital [one – bad teeth after the armistice]. Much more useful has been *The Border Regiment in the Great War* by Colonel H C Wylly CB published 'For Private Circulation only' in 1924 but now available to all thanks to the miracle of Amazon. For in the event it seems there was no room for Dad in the East Lancs and he served instead with the Borders. Wylly is haughty – officer casualties are meticulously recorded by name but those of other ranks only as statistics – and clinical rather than elegiac. But he methodically plots the itinerary of every battalion from 1914 to 1919, recording each of its movements and naming hundreds of locations. Thus, through map-reading with the aid of Michelin and Google, it has been possible to trace the gyrations of 37822 Private Lord, C, 11th then 5th Battalion, The Border Regiment, from his arrival in France on 4 January 1918 until his departure on leave during the week of the armistice in November. Let us follow in his boot prints.

Although he volunteered in September 1916, his king and country, although desperately strapped for manpower in the third year of a war of attrition, for the next seven months appear to have spurned his gallant offer. One explanation may be his physical condition which was assessed on enlistment as no better than 'fair'. He was only five feet five, weighed eight stone four pounds and, with a deep breath, managed a chest expansion of only two and a half inches. That they took him at all is maybe an indication of how critical the general situation was in the spring of 1917. The 1916 big push on the Somme had failed. Unrestricted U boat warfare threatened to starve Britain into surrender. And the Eastern Front was wobbling terminally as revolution rocked Russia. Could an eight stone 'bantam' stop the rot? He would have been determined to do his best. He was eventually called up in May and sent to join the Border Regiment, based a hundred miles away at Carlisle. Under the pressure of a long war the policy of boosting morale by recruiting local lads to local regiments was clearly breaking down. Not that Dad reported any difficulty in bonding with 'foreigners' from Cumberland. The first eight

270

months of his service were spent training at Kinmel Park, near Rhyl. In later years he spoke derisively about the chapel-studded coast of North Wales, Rhyl being the pits, and no doubt that reflected dismal memories of square-bashing, kit inspections and weapon training at the double. I expect it was tough, but how else do you turn wimps into heroes? And it would have been physically good for him, what with the outdoor exercise and abundant plain fare at a time when getting enough to eat had become a problem in civilian life.

And so, in the new year of 1918, to France. Or rather Belgium, for he was sent to the Ypres Salient, the shell-blasted, blood-soaked remnant of that country saved from German occupation at the cost of becoming the second most notorious human abattoir on the Western Front. Two months before Dad's arrival, the terrible Third Battle of Ypres, had ended. It came to be known as 'Passchendaele' after the village that marked the final and negligible gain achieved by the BEF [British Expeditionary Force] in an offensive that in three months harvested nearly half a million casualties. 'I died in hell, they called it Passchendaele' sang a ghostly Tommy created by Siegfried Sassoon. During his training in North Wales Pte Lord would have heard much gossip about Passchendaele and could scarcely be unaware of what probably lay in store for him. He would also have read the newspapers in which he may even have seen some of Sassoon's poems which were published in the press before being collected as *Counter-Attack* in 1918. The bitter disenchantment of the heroic trench veteran, now a patient at a shell-shock hospital, could scarcely have reassured the thoughtful recruit. In November he would also have read about the Bolshevik Revolution, another event that would impact on his personal fortunes. In a coup Lenin had seized control of Russia – until now in alliance with Britain and France – and, to expedite revolution, immediately made peace, allowing the transfer of large German forces from the Eastern to the Western Front, where for the first time they established a numerical advantage. However because of the US entry into the war, just before Dad joined up, that asset was a waning one. Ludendorff, de facto supreme German commander, had to strike quickly to take advantage of his temporary superiority, before the arrival of American troops in overwhelming numbers made the Allies unbeatable. Thus when Dad arrived at Ypres the morale of the BEF, depleted after Passchendaele,

271

was at a low ebb. The memory of the late battle was traumatic. The certain prospect of a massive German offensive concentrated minds. Moreover it was deep midwinter and a dug-out with en suite icicles is not a romantic retreat.

Actually Dad spent his first month, not in the freezing trenches but at a probably wind-swept training camp where, out of immediate danger but serenaded constantly by the guns, he would have been taught some of the arts of trench warfare. Then on 7 February he went up the line to join the 11th Battalion and began to accustom himself to new routines. He would have experienced alternating spells in the front line, in reserve trenches and in further training at the rear. In the line he would be kept busy with the hard labour of trench housekeeping and tending the elaborate barbed-wire entanglement. Daily at dawn and sunset he would 'stand to' with rifle poised and eyes glued to the German positions opposite. Being constantly exhausted he would usually sleep soundly enough in a bivouac scraped from a trench wall and reinforced with corrugated iron. He would get to enjoy a diet of stews and bully beef enlivened by freshly-baked white bread laced with plum and apple jam. He would get not to mind the rats too much, even when he visited the latrines. He would learn to keep his head down against occasional artillery and machine gun fire and to be on his guard against snipers. But while Dad was with them, that winter in the Salient, the 11th Borders were not sent over the top in any major attack. However two raiding parties went out to bomb the German trenches and bag prisoners for interrogation. On the night of 20 March for example three junior officers led 60 other ranks into no-man's land. They got 'within bombing distance of the enemy, a few of whom were accounted for' but nine of the party failed to return. So although Dad's induction was 'quiet' it was punctuated by mortality. That was the norm. The day after the raid just described however, normality on the Western Front was dramatically suspended.

For on 21 March Ludendorff launched his expected offensive the initial effect of which was spectacular. It fell, not on the Ypres Salient where Dad was, but along the Somme further south, where the British line was broken wide open, allowing the Germans to advance fifty miles and take 75,000 prisoners. Such a shift from static to mobile warfare movement was unprecedented on the Western Front and it was feared that the German thrust would, as actually happened in 1940, divide the

French from the British and pack the latter back across the Channel. It was now up to Dad – and a couple of million or so his mates – to stop the rot. On 26 March the 11th Borders entrained for Arras whence, through two nights – daytime movement being too dangerous – they marched with full pack a further twenty odd miles under occasional aerial bombardment to take up positions along a new front line. Although we should not discount the pluck of the 11th Borders, that the German advance now came to a halt was mostly because the offensive had run out of steam.

The same thing happened to a whole series of German offensives that pounded the British and French lines through the spring and summer. After initial success each one stalled and meanwhile the build-up of American forces continued relentlessly. In mid-July the last German onslaught petered out and a devastating series Allied counter-offensives began. Meanwhile, in May, the 5th Battalion of the Border Regiment which had been mauled and depleted during the March retreat, joined the 11th in the Arras sector. The two were amalgamated and henceforth Pte Lord belonged to the 5th Borders. For a while they were lucky. Between April and July, as Colonel Wylly puts it with some disdain, in their quiet sector they were 'not very actively engaged'. The long respite however ended in August when the battalion was sent south to the Somme where, on 8 August in front of Amiens, Australian troops operating with massed tanks, had broken the German line, causing Ludendorff to declare it the 'black day of the German army'. It was the task of the 5th Borders to exploit the Australian success. They did not of course do it entirely on their own. The battalion belonged to the 97th Brigade, itself part of the 32nd Division, which belonged to IX Corps in General Rawlinson's Fourth Army, one of the four giant groups into which Field Marshall Haig's BEF was divided. Nevertheless Pte Lord was in at the kill. He took part in a series of successful Allied offensives the cumulative effect of which was the total defeat of the German Army on the Western Front. That fact is still too little noted. Instead, in the media and in the classroom, World War One is typically presented as a herding of lambs to the slaughter. Dad was no lamb. He thought he and his comrades had won the war and he was not wrong.

Between August and November 1918 he endured, and perhaps in a sense *enjoyed*, three months of intense excitement and extreme danger.

In a hundred days his battalion took part in five separate attacks across open ground, the most perilous manoeuvre infantry were called upon to perform. Trenches of course were life saving devices. It was coming out of them that was lethal. But as the 5th Borders faced death in the last months of the war they also in increasing measure breathed the oxygen of success and in the end knew the ecstasy of victory. Following an action on 10 August, along the road eastwards out of Amiens towards St Quentin, the 5th Borders advanced an unprecedented two miles in a day although, as a body of perhaps 600 men, they suffered 112 casualties in the process. The general came down to congratulate them. On 17 August they attacked again and in seven days advanced an astonishing twelve miles, reaching a place called Misery, which no doubt gave them a laugh over their char and bully. The Brigadier sent word to say he was proud of them, to wish them 'the very best of luck' and to express regret about their casualties, the extent of which unfortunately is not recorded by Colonel Wylly. After a brief spell in reserve the battalion, between 5 and 10 September, embarked on a further six day rush of fire-power and adrenalin. In a ten mile advance they crossed the Somme River and reached all their objectives – not only the 'green' and 'red' lines plotted at headquarters but the final 'blue' line as well. A somewhat longer respite followed during which they received tactical training for the coming assault on the long prepared 'Hindenburg Line', a formidable barrier in depth, scientifically designed with Prussian ingenuity and thoroughness to stop dead any further Allied advance.

The Hindenburg complex incorporated various waterways, in particular the Canal du Nord and, further east, the St Quentin Canal. 'Canal du Nord' is a name that resonates from my childhood because Dad often told me he and his mates had stormed it. Wylly's text however indicates that he got the name wrong, confusing it with the St Quentin Canal. But I do not suppose Dad and his best friend Bill Gash agonised too much over nomenclature. They just knew they faced a mighty challenge. The canal had steep, almost perpendicular, sides, its deep water was filled with barbed wire and beyond the opposite bank was an elaborate further array of trench defences. Although, north and south of the canal-side town of Bellenglise, there were two short tunnels, those obvious crossing points had been highly fortified, so it was daringly decided to attempt an amphibious operation as well, using collapsible boats and life belts taken from cross-Channel steamers. This may have been how Dad got across, although by 3 p.m. on 29 September, when the 5th Borders, as part of the second wave of that day's assault, reached Bellenglise, their predecessors, had already got across the canal and captured a bridge intact. That bridge became the scene of a famous photograph in which the general commanding the 46th Division is seen standing on it as he congratulates his victorious troops, massed on the vertiginous banks as thickly as a crowd on the terraces of a football stadium. Since he was not with the 46th Division, Dad's exultant face cannot be found among the Tommies in that picture but he was for sure there or thereabouts on the day it was taken. In fact by sunset the 5th Borders, with the 32nd Division, had leap-frogged the 46th and pressed on several miles eastwards, meeting declining resistance as the Germans in front of them fell back on a series of fortifications known as the Beaurevoir-Fronsomme Line, the last ditch of the Hindenburg system and in effect the final barrier between the BEF and the German frontier itself. On 3 October the Beaurevoir-Fronsomme Line was broken, the 5th Borders being among the units that captured Sequehart, its principal redoubt. They now took a deserved rest, marching to the rear on 5 October to live for a while in huts instead of bivouacs. In a week, in operations against the St Quentin Canal and the Beaurevoir-Fronsomme defences, the battalion sustained 120 casualties [including 21 dead] which perhaps represents one in five of their personnel. Dad, again was among the lucky ones.

When the 5th Borders went back into the action, later in October, they found themselves marching across green open country with the enemy in flight before them. But although the advance beyond the Hindenburg Line was a triumphant progress it was not a cake walk. As the sad case of Wilfred Owen shows – the telegram announcing his death came on Armistice Day itself – it was easy enough to get killed even with the finish in sight. But it must have been exhilarating. In last three weeks of the war, Wylly tells us, IX Corps, to which the 5th Borders belonged, 'marched 50 miles and captured 17,000 prisoners'. A dozen or so of the latter were bagged by Lance Corporal Lord – according to his own account he had received a promotion that the War Office mysteriously failed to acknowledge in his official service record. A German officer, followed by men with their hands up, formally surrendered his revolver. Were there heel clicks and an exchange of smart salutes? The diminutive, cack-handed little lad, who kept falling off his over-size bike trying to keep up with the bigger boys, had come a long way. And hence my discovery many years later of the phallic Lüger nuzzling Marie Stopes in Dad's bedroom drawer. When he went home on leave, early in November, he smuggled it through movement control, surely at considerable risk, and presented it to his mother along with another souvenir – a live louse, preserved in the seam of his trousers. He was at home on Armistice Day and when he went back the battalion had moved up into Belgium, to Yvoir on the Meuse between Dinant and Namur. To celebrate victory he and Bill Gash treated themselves to a cushy stay in hospital, having their teeth out, but they scarpered a bit smartish when victims of the Spanish Flu invaded the wards. In January 1919, since teachers were in demand, he qualified for early demob and in February sailed jubilantly from Dunkirk back to Blighty and Blackpool, where his mother had opened a boarding house. His father was once more an absentee – this time in London pursuing his new career as a press photographer. After Easter Cecil resumed his own career, becoming an uncertificated teacher in Rossendale and lodging with his Aunt Mary. He had exams to pass to qualify for university.

I believe the impact of the Great War on my father was overwhelmingly positive. He found true courage in facing great danger, particularly since he fought so much in the open as well as in the trenches. He passed the test, he survived – and he had won. His victory was not accompanied by magnanimity. Afterwards he continued to vilify 'the Boche' and had no doubt that, in helping to destroy 'Prussian militarism', he had helped make the world, and England in particular, a better place. He looked back with intense pride on experiences that were sometimes joyful. Above all the war made a man of him. The accident prone under-sized boy, his head spinning with tales of others' daring, but whose only previous prowess had been in swotting and pot-hunting, suddenly acquired a 24 carat war record and life membership of the fellowship of real men. At the age of 19 he even gained in stature and actually came home with his head held three inches higher. His status in the family was transformed. Sure Leslie returned as handsome as ever, in the cavalry breeches of the Royal Flying Corps, but he had spent his time, not storming the Hindenburg Line, but sitting in the Egyptian sun mending broken aeroplanes. Tables had been turned. Who was the big boy now? His courtship of my mother also surged forward, keeping pace with Leslie who married Maud in 1919. Those nuptials were celebrated with some pomp, as you can see from the wedding photograph reproduced on *Plate 3 top*. It is interesting that the four young men in that picture – Dad, Leslie and Mum's brothers Albert and Alan – had all come home from the Great War sound in wind and limb and they posed in their smart suits with a certain swagger. In the summer of 1920 Cecil and Nellie went to Switzerland as a fully-fledged couple, which was bold for children of the chapel. As the train passed along the former front line he claimed to recognise a bivouac he had once occupied but I don't suppose she was all that impressed. 'Very nice, dear'. He even triumphed in single knightly combat. At his village school in Rossendale, before he went off to university the headmaster was dying of cancer and his associated incontinence was mocked by the caretaker. Dad thumped him in the coke cellar and there was no more trouble. Quite right too.

The war brought him another bonus. He got an ex-serviceman's grant to do an English degree at Manchester University. He emerged with a first and might perhaps have embarked on an academic career. But he had acquired a taste for cut and thrust and that maybe made grammar school classrooms more appealing than lecture theatres. The study of literature nevertheless affected him deeply and is the final constituent in the moulding of his outlook. I think it taught him in retrospect what he had been fighting for. The thing that had been in peril from 'Prussian militarism', he concluded, was the spirit of England 'embalmed and treasured up', as Milton wrote, in 'good books' which constituted the 'precious life-blood of the master spirits' of English Literature. His mission was to pass on that heritage to future generations. Which is why English at Dad's school was more than a mere subject on the timetable. It was something like a religion. Embrace it and a sort of secular salvation was yours. That, it is suggested, was the effect on Dad of studying literature while absorbing the experience of war. I guess it was now that for him William Shakespeare replaced Jesus Christ. The god of the chapels anyway got his marching orders. Almost the only time after the war that chapel-bred Cecil went to chapel was when he married Nellie and that was surely done just to honour their parents *[Plate 3 bottom]*. For in the course of the conflict Mum too had apparently lost her faith, so it was not just being face to face with slaughter that engendered doubt in the Great War generation. Together then Cecil and Nellie bid God farewell but being a respectable couple they continued to keep his Commandments. They didn't need God to tell them what was right and wrong. Thus probably was born the atheist with the Nonconformist conscience that daily confused me at morning assembly when I was at school.

Chapter 11

PROPAGANDA

So, when you consider where he was coming from, it is possible to understand Dad and indeed to like him. He was brave, learned, articulate, well-meaning and sometimes fun. But much of what has just been related was unknown to me when I was thirteen and growing up with the Gauleiter was beginning to be a challenge. Getting him in double dose, both at home and at school, made it particularly hard work. Was he really, for example, the source of all wisdom? It is easy now, after seventy years, to see that his opinions were frequently flawed and that he often delivered them with all the subtlety of an artillery bombardment. When I was thirteen however and crippled mentally by the state of supposed sin that had descended upon me that terrible sports day, it was hard to query his prejudices, many of which, I fear, I simply took on board, at least for the time being. Liberating myself from them has been the work of a lifetime and, looking back near the end of that span, I cannot confidently say I have completed the task. Why else would I feel the need to write a memoir? Yet I was not entirely at his mercy. He could determine what I learnt in school and impose a strict domestic discipline but there remained a Dad-free zone. He couldn't stop me looking and thinking in the privacy of my own head. However as I look back I realise even that safe place was violated. Like a modern kid enticed into a digital chat room, I was seduced by strangers. The instrument of my downfall was not a grooming paedophile but the voice of wartime propaganda, a powerful influence on my developing mind-set which is the subject of this chapter. Its teachings were at least as perverse as the chaotic ideology dispensed by the tyrant of the tea table. Some of them indeed were scarcely less pernicious than the lies perpetrated by Dr Goebbels, the Nazi Propaganda Minister. You may find that hard to swallow so I had better set the scene with another quick history lesson.

When Winston Churchill became Prime Minister in 1940 he did a deal with his reluctant Labour coalition partners. He would win the war while they planned the peace. That way the welfare state, usually attributed to the Labour government elected in 1945, was actually planned and partly implemented under Churchill's auspices while the war was still going on. R A Butler's Education Act of 1944 for example was a hint to the electorate. After the war things were going to be different. It was the business of the Churchill government's own 'Ministry of Information' to amplify that message. Although the title implies free debate – here are the facts, it is for you to make up your minds – it was itself a piece of propaganda. Like Goebbels's outfit in Berlin, the title of which at least was honest, and like the 'Ministry of Truth' in George Orwell's *1984*, it was dedicated to indoctrination, to establishing a unified national state of mind conducive to total war. We have ways of correcting your thoughts. Very cleverly, the necessary national consensus was gathered in from two seemingly opposite directions. A left hook concentrated minds on the coming welfare state. That was Labour's contribution, supported by do-gooding Liberals like Sir William Beveridge and Tory 'wets' like Butler. Meanwhile a right hook reminded the British people of their heritage, the island nation's infinitely precious, deeply rooted way of life, now in dire peril. That was Churchill's speciality. His speeches united classes, ages and genders. 'Let us therefore gird ourselves'. The MoI co-ordinated consensus building by controlling the media through a strict rationing of scarce resources. Only agencies that were ideologically sound got the necessary newsprint or ciné film. That is how I, in my Dad-free zone, was snared into the consensus. For the recipients of MoI favour included certain organisations whose products I hungrily devoured. They included the BBC, Penguin Books with their children's 'Puffin' imprint, *Picture Post*, Gaumont British News and, believe it or not, Cadbury's Chocolates, which while going easy in wartime on the production of Dairy Milk, churned out a nice new line in creamy brochures about how, some sunny day when the grey skies turned to blue, we would all live in dinky cottages in airy garden suburbs, like the one they had built at Bourneville around their Birmingham factory. I thought these favourite mental companions were just giving me the facts, the raw material for looking and thinking. But actually they did my head in. As we already know from a glance at the essays I wrote for Miss Hughes, MoI approved products made me a fierce little socialist, who could not wait for the arrival of 'New Jerusalem', the collective paradise being planned for after the war by the Labour men in Churchill's coalition. Thus free learning was corrupted by propaganda. I didn't know I was being got at. And, as I say, it took me even longer to liberate myself from ingrained left-wing attitudes as it did to realise that Dad at the tea table sometimes laid it on a bit thick. There will be much more about New Jerusalem later in this chapter but first let me tell you about the other set of MoI approved attitudes, the conservative as opposed to the socialist vision of what we were fighting for. Let us call it 'Old England'. Tomorrow, sure, there will be the jam of New Jerusalem but in the meantime blood, sweat, toil and tears must be generously expended in defence Old England.

I can pinpoint the very moment I first grasped what it was Churchill said we must 'brace ourselves' to defend. It was July 1940 and I was just eight. France had fallen and I was still off school recovering from measles, which is probably why Mum had to take me with her when she visited Mrs Rowbottom, her hairdresser. The visit itself was not much fun. It was uncomfortable as well as boring because the cramped salon was actually the Rowbottoms' bathroom. A removable green plywood cover had been fitted across the bath itself and it supported an array of bottles, packets, copies of *Home Chat* and testimonials to the power of the Eugene perm. As scissors snipped and the drier whirred, they went on in hushed hints about a young woman whose downfall, it seemed, was only to be expected in wartime. However just as we were leaving Mrs Rowbottom brightened and, shifting the focus of her concern from domestic disgrace to the parlous situation of our country, observed that 'there'll always be an England'. Since a German invasion was presumed to be imminent and Dad was loading his Lüger to stem the advancing panzers, it seemed a rash prediction, but she said it with confidence and I wanted to believe her. A few days later I heard the plucky assertion again, this time on the wireless and set to sonorous music. Thus presented it banished all doubt. It exactly expressed what it was we were fighting for and, as the glorious Battle of Britain summer unfurled, the anthem reverberated in my head, bringing comfort and joy. The first verse said it all:

There'll always be an England
While there's a country lane.
Wherever there's a cottage small
Beside a field of grain.

I knew the very lane in question and the field of grain as well. They were in the picture behind the piano in the front room at Selsdon. It was called 'The Cornfield', which was odd because it was mostly the lane that you saw, with only a golden corny glimpse catching the eye at the very lane end, beyond the shady spring at which a boy in red trousers was quenching his thirst. It was obviously Battle of Britain weather. By recessing the cornfield, and showing only a corner of it, the painter made it more enchanting. What a clever trick. There was a smaller version of that favourite picture in a catalogue of old master reproductions available from the 'Medici' company, that Dad and I often scrutinised. Dad said the artist was Constable and he was joint top of the British School. Dad, as we know, habitually arranged things in order of merit. The name made me giggle for the association of a burly policeman with this sensitive evocation of Old England was amusing. The comedian Gillie Potter, creator of the delinquent Lord Marshmallow, saw the joke too. Once on 'Workers' Playtime', beamed to our kitchen from a factory canteen 'somewhere in England', he referred to two pictures in his lordship's collection – 'Lord Marshmallow after Constable' and 'Constable after Lord Marshmallow'. Well, you had to laugh. As Mona Lott put it on ITMA, 'It's being so cheerful that keeps us going'.

Once I had grasped the notion of Old England, I found symbols of what we were fighting for in many places. Anything rural and venerable began to arouse patriotic feelings. There were, for example, the gilt framed paintings in Grandpa's drawing room at Southport. Faithful horses stand patiently in their stable. Hay is gathered in. Sheep safely graze and the big soulful eyes of Highland cattle look trustingly at the beholder. Then there were all those tasteful lithographs that began to animate the walls of post offices, food offices and British Restaurants. They presented pebbly strands, wind-kissed copses, village festivals and scenes of agricultural life when horse power still resided in horseflesh. Also there was the cult of the invasion-threatened white cliffs of Dover, celebrated in best-selling poetry and populated by Vera Lynn with bluebirds. A spate of films bursting with vicars, post-mistresses and jodhpurred gentry, like *Tawney Pipit*, *Quiet Wedding* and *Went the Day Well*, swelled the chorus of praise for English country life. In the intervals of accumulating the credit of the many, 'the Few' who won the Battle of Britain relaxed at the Plough or the Waggon and Horses. Furthermore they took off from bases in the heart of the countryside, like real life Biggin Hill or the fictional Halfpenny Field, from which Michael Redgrave and John Mills found their *Way to the Stars*. Old England was to be found also at school in the texts we studied as literature. Although too many of Shakespeare's plays were ostensibly set in enemy Italy, and his characters had silly names like Bassanio and Antonio that sounded as daft as Mussolini, you knew that really the action was taking place somewhere just around the corner from Constable's 'Cornfield'. The Bard had this knack of making foreign fields forever England. Other 'master spirits' identified more directly with the English countryside, setting their works in villages or along river banks. That went particularly for my favourite set books – *The Wind in the Willows* and *Memoirs of a Fox-Hunting Man*. So, all in all, I had no difficulty at all in answering the essential question posed in 'There'll always be an England'.

Red, white and blue, what does it mean to you?

Well, obviously, the English countryside and the incomparable lifestyle it supported. It was our heritage and we were going to keep it. It was not for envious foreigners. Invaders would be prosecuted.

The temple to Old England at which I habitually worshipped as a schoolboy in wartime was provided by W H Smith and Sons. Sadly the premises of that now diminished cultural institution are not today easily distinguishable from other high street shops on the down side of upmarket, but in the 1940s the chain constituted a piece of heritage in its own right and the Southport branch in Lord Street was specially atmospheric. Beyond a sculpted façade you passed a well-stocked newsagent's counter, open to the street and thus reminiscent of the station bookstalls in which the company had its origins, before passing the portals of an antique hall, adorned with heraldic crests and lit through stained glass. It felt like the library of a country house or an Oxford college, although I did not know that at the time. Here a lavish buffet of heritage books was laid out on shelves and tables of solid oak. Paper shortage? What paper shortage? The MoI had bountifully endowed the consenting publishers who supplied the Smiths' chain. In that holy calm I used often to linger, having been released for a while from family collectively or given an hour of freedom while Dad, after our tramp along the beach, sneaked a pint at the Scarisbrick Hotel. What did I read? Or rather ogle, for at the age of ten, although now smitten with a taste for books, I remained barely literate and still preferred images to text. It was the Puffin Picture Books that first attracted me and led me to part with my pocket money. Part of my collection survives and the titles confirm Penguins' pact with the MoI to establish in British kids a ferocious attachment to their essentially rural heritage. It was through Puffins above all that I discovered Old England. Their titles evoke its rural essence:

Animals of the Countryside
Trees in Britain
British Butterflies
A History of the Countryside
Pond and River Life
On the Farm
Birds of the Village
Flowers of the Field and Hedgerow
Country Holiday

My favourite was *Village and Town* by S R Badmin. I see from the flysheet that I bought it in 1943, when I was eleven, and it is clear that by then I owned a dozen Puffins for I had ticked off my purchases on the list of titles. Stanley Badmin was a consummate illustrator, responsible for other Puffins as well, including the one about trees, who during the war [thus Wikipedia] was actually employed by the MoI, his task being to make, along with other artists, an official visual record of an English landscape that, being vulnerable to the ravages of war, might never be the same again. *Village and Town* is ecstatically beautiful. Sunlight glows on honey-coloured stone. The village street winds over the bridge, between russet pantiles and rose-tinted stucco, past a bow fronted shop, towards the big red house, above which the church tower stands perpendicular. It is always spring or summer and always afternoon.

There is always time. Work proceeds at the worker's natural, gentle pace and job satisfaction oozes from the farmer's ambling gait and the thatcher's communion with his tools. A carter and his dog approach the timbered pub, at the door of which the landlord stands in portly affability. Meanwhile children play by the stream. Wow! Yet there is something uncanny about the artist's vision. It did not properly strike me at the time – as I say, I did not know I was being got at – but on revisiting Badmin's homage to Old England forty years on it hit me hard. On the evidence of costume the above scene, which is a composite of several Badmin evocations of village England, seems to be set in the present day [the 1940s] but it is a present with an essential ingredient left out. S R Badmin seemed unaware that the Industrial Revolution had ever happened. He shows no power lines, no street lamps and not even a neo-Georgian telephone kiosk. And nowhere in his book is a motor vehicle to be glimpsed. Which is scarcely believable. Yet a similar lacuna typifies the whole Puffin oeuvre. Trains and boats, preferably in model form, were acceptable, and a place had to be found in the Puffin club for those war winning weapons the Spitfire and the tractor, but cars were consistently black-balled. They do feature, it is true, in *A History of the Countryside* but only as pantomime villains. They spawn 'garages and snack bars … covered with advertisement signs'. Which is 'untidy'. And they perpetrate 'ribbon development', which is 'neither town nor country' and 'is now being stopped'. Quite right too – the planners were about to inherit the earth. Furthermore cars transport vandals into the countryside, proletarian hordes of gormless dads, fat mums and cross grannies who bring their feral brats to engage in spectacular acts of environmental destruction.

Gradually I weaned myself from an exclusive diet of Puffins and tasted some of the other Old England treats proffered by W H Smith and Sons. These lay mostly out of the range of my pocket money and their adult sophistication was anyway inhibiting. But I browsed with increasing boldness and it says a lot for the public service ethic of the company that my prolonged grubby-fingered explorations of books I was obviously never going to buy was never censured or curtailed. Thus I found the Batsford series, the coloured covers of which carried Badmin-style pictures of rural England in the olden days, giving particular attention to the architectural types I had learnt about through poring over *Village and*

Town. There was for example a Batsford about cathedrals and others about parish churches, castles and country houses, all packed with superb black and white photographs. I still find black and white, with all its shades of grey, somehow more authentic than colour. There was another Batsford about something called the 'National Trust' which apparently looked after old buildings and natural habitats and that seemed a really good idea. With a name like that it must be part of the government and to an eager young socialist that did a lot for its credibility. It seemed too that every shire had its very own Batsford. I liked that too. I had learnt the shape of all the English and Welsh counties from my jigsaw and liked the idea that they were all different from one another and that their inhabitants played at hating each other and were perpetually locked in pretend combat. The return of county cricket after the war nicely irrigated that conceit. I was right to recognise the English shires as central to the notion of Old England. Alas they are not what they were. Their mauling at the hands of the Heath government in 1974 was one of the worst of many offences attributable to post war planning.

Another series I discovered was the slim, pocket-sized King Penguins. They were Puffins for grown-ups which meant most of the pictures were relegated to a special section at the back of the book. Before you got to the pictorial pudding you had to eat up your words, thus properly deferring gratification. The pictures were very interesting but what these books were about was not immediately clear from the titles. Here are some of them.

The Leaves of Southwell
Elizabethan Miniatures
Garden Birds
Caricature
Bewick's Swans
Edible Fungi
Misericords

There was much there to challenge my limited literacy. 'Garden birds' was OK but was 'Bewick' a place or a bloke or a species and how anyway did you pronounce it? To be honest, as a work of reference it told you less about swans than my *Observer's Book of British Birds* but the engravings were somehow rather exciting. You may remember they once excited young Jane Eyre as she pored over them surreptitiously behind the curtains.

And what, who or where was Southwell? And again how was it pronounced? That volume was full of plant life done long ago and very vividly – in stone, would you believe it – and you had to admire whoever did it even through you could not work out why it was done. 'Elizabethan miniatures' also defeated me. It was obviously nothing to do with narrow gauge railways because it was full of little portraits of people in ruffs wearing lots of jewels. Nor, if out mushrooming, would I trust the edibility of the gaudy fungi illustrated in that other King Penguin. And I gave up on both 'caricature' and 'misericords', although the pictures in both were amusing. All those mysteries however were enticing rather than off-putting. Someday pennies would no doubt drop and that was something to look forward to. Meanwhile I just liked looking at these pictures. Like the 'Cornfield' and the Badmin images they were icons of Old England. They represented what we were fighting for – something very old as well as truly rural.

So too did the volumes in Collins' 'Britain in Pictures' series. They were ideal for battling Britons on the move because, being slim quarto hardbacks, they would slip into even a stuffed suitcase and might serve very nicely, instead of a piece of cardboard, in a squared-off pack. There was a whole regiment of them and, as lined up at Smiths in 1945, they looked like a victory parade for, although their covers came in rainbow colours, they were of uniform design. They covered an increasingly familiar range of national treasures. British dogs, horses, postage stamps, trees, wild flowers, marine life, seamen, soldiers and boy scouts were all there. As were English inns, gardens, watercolours, sporting pictures, gentlemen's clubs, farming, cricket, pottery and china, and rivers and canals. The adjectives 'English' and 'British' seemed to be used interchangeably but the weather, of course, arguably the most cherished of the heirlooms we were defending, could only be 'English'. Even a few minority groups were daringly given a moment of glory. Thus *Life Among the Scots* was briefly noticed as were *English Children* and even *English Women*. Homage to the gentle sex was entrusted to the severe and aristocratic Edith Sitwell, one of a whole posse of the great and the good entrusted with raising ever higher the standard of Old England. Other knightly champions included

Lord David Cecil on English Poets
Rex Warner on English Public Schools
Edmund Blunden on English Villages
John Betjeman on English Cities and Small Towns
Vita Sackville West on English Country Houses
Cecil Beaton on British Photographers

We can only bow our heads. Cultural icons are not to be despised and perhaps some of the constituents of Old England were indeed in danger during the war, although less so, as it turned out, than at the hands of post war planners who inter much alia wrecked our town centres and closed our branch lines. Again however a yawning gap confronted me when, forty years later, I came to review the titles in the 'Britain in Pictures' series. A roll call of those *not* on parade will make the point. The absentees included

Artisans' Dwellings
The English Poor Law
British Grammar Schools and Public Libraries
Gasworks and Power Stations
English Suburban Semis
British Mills and Mines
English Football
Victorian Town Halls
Welsh Chapels
The British Motor Industry
British Film Stars

The hidden message of the heritage books displayed in the great hall at W H Smith's is more important than what it openly trumpeted. Old England was to be found down south and in the countryside. Furthermore its upper class patrons believed in yesterday.

At the time however I was unaware of that distortion. It was not just because of my innocence but also because during 1944 I came to be driven by an even more powerful engine of Old England propaganda. I became a train spotter. For the next three years, right up to the School Cert and beyond, 'copping' locomotives, along with burgeoning lust and the perpetual pricks of a bad conscience, joined together in a trinity of compelling forces to dominate my inner life. My conversion to train spotting was sudden. It occurred during a trip to the Manchester Museum, kindly arranged for III Upper by Miss Greenwood. But it was not the worthy accumulation of seashells and geological specimens – supplemented by a nice line in Egyptian antiquities – that blew my mind. Instead it was what happened on the way there on the train when so many of my classmates dug out of their pockets dog-eared slim booklets which they consulted urgently at specific points along the line and particularly as we passed the 'running sheds' [locomotive depot] at Gorton. From time to time they made pencil entries in their books, thereby inducing ecstasy. I was shown a copy of this 'Ian Allan ABC' and saw that it was full of lists, comprising all the engines owned by our local train operator, the LNER, whose network stretched all the way from London to the far north of Scotland. The several thousand locomotives in question were classified by what seemed an odd criterion, the arrangement of their wheels, whether of the 'driving' variety, linked directly to the business part of the locomotive, or mere 'bogies', fore and aft, that simply allowed the length of the ensemble to be extended so as to carry a greater weight of power-generating gear. Thus you might have a titchy 0-4-0 with only two driving wheels on each side and no bogies, fit for shunting trucks but not much more, or a mighty 4-6-2, capable of hauling a dozen luxurious carriages non-stop from Kings Cross to Edinburgh. I saw too that, within each wheel arrangement listed by the omniscient Ian Allan, the engines were subdivided into classes, like the 'Sandringham' 4-6-0s or the 'Directors' 4-4-0s, and that the locomotives of certain privileged classes were accorded, not just numbers but also a name, often a hauntingly poetic ones, which you could find on the plate prominently attached to the engines, typically as a crescent surmounting a wheel guard. Well, I was instantly smitten. I had always liked trains. We have seen how, when I was only three, Dad had taken me to admire the engines at London Road and then, on a memorable winter night, had wafted me straight down the line to Euston. Also, having been well trained at school in the arts of classification and tabulation, I had acquired a taste for organised information. Dad sneered at train spotters but had he thought about it he would have linked the intellectual habits the hobby reinforced to some useful classroom practices. Soon I had acquired my first Ian Allan, the ABC of the *Locomotives of the London and North Eastern*

Railway. Allan, whom we have already met, was a remarkable chap, as his entry in Wikipedia shows. While working as a clerk at Waterloo station, set to deal with requests from the public for information about engines and rolling stock, he hit on the idea of a comprehensive printed list and thus in 1942 published an *ABC of Locomotives of the Southern Railway.* Its success prompted corresponding ABCs for the other three companies, the LMS [London, Midland and Scottish], LNER and GWR [Great Western]. That way, almost single-handedly, Ian Allan created the cultural phenomenon of trainspotting. He deserves a book in tribute.

During that D Day summer, admitted to the fraternity and with my Ian Allan always in my pocket, I pedalled almost nightly to Dinting, the main line station from which the Glossop branch diverged, in time to observe the 7-20 to Sheffield – oh no, not *Lord Roberts of Kandahar* yet again! – and typically stuck it out ['Double Summer Time' meant it did not get dark until at least 10-30] until the sleek 9-03 express to Marylebone silently, announced only by a discreet trail of smoke, and with the motions of a race horse rather than a machine, made its rapid transit of Dinting Arches. On the station approach a gathering of up to fifty spotters, mostly grammar school boys, would be encamped, pencils poised, their bikes leaning drunkenly against the fences and strewed across the verges. What I copped at Dinting was soon augmented during holiday train trips to grandparents' homes at Southport and St Anne's. That took me into the territory of the LMS [London, Midland and Scottish] and called for a different manual in the Ian Allan series. In it I recorded exotic cops like 'Scots' – the 'Royal Scot' class of 4-6-0s which honoured the regiments of the British Army – as well as 'Jubilees' and 'Patriots' and once even observed a 'streak' [a streamlined locomotive] roaring at speed through Wigan [North Western] with a Glasgow to Euston express, while our Southport [Chapel Street] to Manchester [Victoria] stopping train was halted at a signal outside Wigan [Wallgate]. Bliss! Soon I began to embark on specific train spotting pilgrimages, first to Manchester [London Road], then to Preston, along the rural 'Cabbage Line' from Southport, and before long to distant Doncaster and even Crewe. After VE Day we started going to London again and henceforth no holiday there was complete without at least one circuit of the mainline termini, so conveniently linked by the Circle Line. Which meant I now needed Ian Allan's Southern Railway and Great Western ABCs as well. Meanwhile, the LNER manual having fallen apart from intensive use, I treated myself to a new copy, proudly transcribing the red underlings that indicated my haul of cops to date.

Those distant wanderings were rewarding but I think none of the happy experiences they brought quite matched two trainspotting epiphanies experienced along our very own tracks through Dinting. The first occurred soon after D Day and was probably to do with demands on the system imposed by the Allied invasion of the continent. One Friday evening the 7-20 had just departed when a cry went up among the throng on the bridge. A light engine, unfamiliar and extra-large, had just pulled up on the down line. Was it a Green Arrow? – a class of mixed traffic 2-6-2s, mostly un-named, that were elegant but not uncommon. No, it looked bigger than that. Wow! Suddenly the signal changed and we watched enchanted as 4471 *Great Northern* exhaled a puff of steam and made a stately progress, along the platform edge and out over the viaduct. *Great Northern* was a Gresley Pacific, no less. Between the wars Sir Nigel Gresley of the LNER had revolutionised steam traction by introducing locomotives with the 4-6-2 wheel arrangement, known, I know not why, as 'Pacifics' – six driving wheels supported by four bogies at the front and two at the rear. On the east coast main line these sleek creatures achieved speeds in excess of 100 mph and drastically reduced journey times. We knew all about them but never dreamed any would ever patronise our humble Great Central route through Dinting. Now you won't believe what happened next, the very next day in fact. That rainy Saturday – it was the Gamesley Rose Queen and at the nearby recreation ground ladies participated in a beautiful ankles competition – another distinguished stranger graced Dinting Arches. Guess who! Yes, it was! 4472 *Flying Scotsman*, foremost among the Gresley Pacifics was, with only one exception, the most famous railway engine in the world. Yet during that wonderful summer *Flying Scotsman* became almost as familiar to the Dinting fraternity as *Lord Roberts of Kandahar*, not that its glamour was thereby diminished. Better still, it and *Great Northern* were joined on our route by a dozen or more other Pacifics. Sometimes they hauled troop trains packed with GIs. When one halted at a signal we all sang out the ritual greeting of British kids to their hunky deliverers – 'Got any gum, chum?' We were rewarded with a shower of candy.

The exception to *Flying Scotsman's* absolute pre-eminence was another Gresley masterpiece. It belonged to his A4 class of streamlined Pacifics introduced in 1935 and its name was *Mallard*. I had memorised *Mallard's* supreme achievement from the *Meccano Magazine*. 'Between Little Bytham and Essendine on 3 July 1938' she had achieved a speed of 126 mph, never afterwards equalled by a steam locomotive. *Mallard* had majestic beauty as well as incomparable speed and to meet her was the ultimate trainspotting achievement. Cop *Mallard* and die. One day in the autumn of 1944 that consummation was nearly mine. A rumour rocked the school. The royal train was to pass through Dinting about 4-30 that day and it would be hauled by an A4 streak. It turned out to be true, so as soon as the bell sounded the school emptied faster than the pictures before the national anthem and a bicycle army set out for the embankment at Gamesley, selected by fourth form opinion as a better vantage point for an A4 in motion than Dinting itself. Did we crave a glimpse of King George's gracious lady pouring tea in the Victorian saloon you can now inspect in the museum, at York? No, not on your nelly. What we craved was the prospect of *Mallard* at speed. What we got was not quite that but it took us most of the way there. The royal train *did* speed past us. It *was* hauled by a streak. Its name however was not *Mallard* but *Sir Ralph Wedgwood*. Sir Ralph who? Well, you can't win 'em all. We had copped our A4 and that was wonder enough. It was a great day.

What, you may ask, has all that nostalgia about a puerile obsession – Dad was withering in his contempt for train spotting – got to do with Old England? The answer is that it blew my mind by a complex process that needs to be explained. The thing was that, unlike most brother spotters, I specialised in 'namers', that is in copping only that elite of locomotives distinguished by names as well as numbers. As I say there was poetry in the names. They were sonorous and memorable and since the habit of memorisation had become virtually instinctive, I learnt by heart many of Ian Allan's beautiful lists. Like this one.

… *Galtee More, Persimmon, Blink Bonny, Blair Atholl, Papyrus, St Simon, Sansovino, The Tetrarch, Captain Cuttle, Isinglas, Minoru* …

They are the names of classic-winning race horses and they adorned the wheel-guards of the Gresley Pacifics that galloped through Dinting in the last summer of the war. There is however more to the names than even poetry. They were not just euphonious but had profound associations.

They carried a message. When I was twelve of course, I was no more than dimly aware of that, yet by a sort of osmosis what the names represented became fixed in my mind so that when I look back I detect a grand unifying theme. As surely as S R Badmin and the heritage books at W H Smith's the lists recorded by Ian Allan celebrated Old England. In particular they did homage to the landed, 'feudal' ruling class that had created that beloved entity in the first place. The people, locations and institutions commemorated on the name-plates constituted an inventory of feudalism, laying out the elements of an established governmental structure, associated with a web of privilege. The system was headed by the crowned monarch and operated by the noblemen and gentlemen of Old England. Thus the Turf, as evoked by the Gresley Pacifics, was part of Allan's complete guide to the feudal system – a who's who of its protagonists, gazetteer of their habitats and compendium of the schools, clubs, regiments and other organisations which bonded them into a band of brothers. Scarcely a personage honoured on the name-plates, was not dignified by a title. Scarcely a place so commemorated was not the seat of a noble family. For the rest the lists celebrated the military and sporting glory, intrinsic to feudalism, and the imperial endeavour through which Old England had cloned itself across the globe. Through the practice of trainspotting, without knowing it, I deferred to all that.

Let us start at the top. The railways loved the royals. The pride of the GWR was the 'Kings' class, the names of which provided a complete roll-call of male monarchs from *King William I* to *King George V*. Kings having been monopolised by God's Wonderful Railway, the other companies had to improvise in their obeisance to royalty. The Southern embraced mythology for its 'King Arthur' class, while the LMS, when it belatedly launched its own Pacifics, had to make do with female royals, sometimes grovelling in desperation to elderly Victorian ladies like *Princess Beatrice*, *Princess Maud* and the seemingly hermaphrodite *Princess Arthur of Connaught*. When the company ran out of princesses it took up duchesses. Thus their graces of, inter alia, *Norfolk, Devonshire, Rutland, Hamilton* and *Buccleuch* greeted spotters along the west coast main line. In a big way too the LMS honoured the army and the Empire. Over seventy 'Royal Scots' hailed historic regiments, their badges resplendent above the name plates, and tongue-in-cheek admitted a few supernumeraries into the ranks. Thus *The Boy Scout* and even *The Girl Guide* might be seen preening themselves on parade at Crewe beside *The Coldstream Guardsman, The Lancashire Fusilier* and the *Argyll and Sutherland Highlander.* The Scots were supported by nearly two hundred locomotives in the 'Jubilee Class', the names of which extolled the Empire. They celebrated not only dominions like *Australia* and *South Africa* but autonomous Indian princely states like *Hyderabad* and *Mysore,* along with an archipelago of outposts like the *Falkland Islands,* the *Windward Islands* and the *Gilbert and Ellice Islands.* The 'Jubilees' also chronicled naval history, evoking warships like *Bellerophon* and *Warspite,* battles at sea like *Trafalgar* and *Camperdown* and salty admirals down the ages from *Drake* to *Jellicoe.* The Southern Railway too, whose lines served three historic naval bases, did homage in its 'Lord Nelson Class' to the sea dogs who had set Britannia to rule the waves.

Other classes delineated the life-style of feudalism, celebrating stately homes, public schools and the traditional sports of the landed class. Maybe the Great Western carried idolatry to excess. It listed comprehensively the names of the gentlemen's seats that graced its own lines – everything from palaces to mere expanded farmhouses – and laid claim also to mansions outside its territory. This magnificent tribute required the launching of some fifty 'Castles' – *Caerphilly Castle, Powis Castle, Cardiff Castle, Powderham Castle* and so on – followed, in descending order of motive power, and also roughly in the esteem of the houses concerned, by more than two hundred more modest but still stately 'Halls', and a smaller number of 'Granges'. Although the first names in these near interminable lists had resonance the sameness of the second deadened the romance. The LNER 'Sandringham' class better caught the poetry of feudalism by mixing country houses with football teams. Thus *Audley End* rubbed shoulders with *Doncaster Rovers,* thereby asserting a supposed solidarity between the rich man in his castle and the poor man at his gate. But principally that company celebrated the sporting life that lubricated feudalism. Having done homage to horse racing in the naming of its Pacifics, it introduced the 'Hunt' class of Gresley 4-4-0s. Each of those stocky little engines sported a fox over its name-plates and I was enchanted. I remember the *Quorn* and the *Pytchely,* the *Belvoir* and the *Grafton.* Perhaps my friend Siegfried Sassoon went out with them, that winter he spent in the midland shires. The charm of the scene was all but irresistible and disconcertingly, as I urged myself into the socialism apparent in my English essays, I found myself in thrall to feudalism. What a mixed-up kid I must have been.

Perhaps, after all, I should have taken up Dad's offer to send me away to one of the schools commemorated in the Southern Railway 'Schools Class' 4-4-0s. *Christ's Hospital*, Dad's preferred seminary, was among them along with *Eton, Harrow, Rugby* and so on, as were a few oddballs with puzzling names, like *Haileybury and ICS*, which turned out to be Mr Attlee's old school. So you could lead the Labour Party and still be posh. That message went to the heart of the matter. As the war ended and New Jerusalem beckoned it was still where you went to school that mostly mattered. In the post war struggle between Old England and New Jerusalem the railway companies were backing the former.

Their outlook was unashamedly feudal. To clinch the point, let us conjecture some locomotives that never figured in Ian Allan's lists. Since the railways represented the finest flowering of the Industrial Revolution, you might have expected them, in the naming of trains, to salute its heroic age. You might expect a roll-call of the great engineers and radical thinkers who forged modernity. Not so. I never copped the *Richard Arkwright* or the *Thomas Telford* nor even the *George Stephenson* or the *I K Brunel*. I saw no engines in the 'Revolution' class of regime changing 4-8-2s. I missed the *Karl Marx* at Euston, near his library seat at the British Museum, and the *Friedrich Engels* at London Road, near his Manchester counting house. Ian Allan unaccountably omitted both the *Adam Smith* and the *Rev Thomas Malthus* and I never saw the *Jeremy Bentham* carrying the greatest number out of Victoria, past his 'panopticon' prison, en route to Happiness-on-Sea. Was there even a *John Wesley* to be copped at Bristol [Temple Meads]? Certainly there was no 'Trade Union' class of heavy freight locomotives and no 'Board School' class of 0-6-0 tanks. And I failed to cop the *Self Help*, the *Work Ethic* or the *Temperance*. For, the railway companies spurned the industrial spirit. Like Dad they seemingly despised business and businessmen. The only partial exception was the Great Central 'Directors Class' which honoured its own top men and the Southern Railway 'Merchant Navy Class' which carried the names of shipping lines, like *Union Castle* and *Cunard White Star*. Otherwise the railway companies bowed to feudalism. Which is very odd because feudalism was just then in deep trouble. Note that most of the locomotives mentioned above were not built in Victorian times when the feudal landed class remained the richest element in society and dominated local and national government. Instead they were modern machines constructed between the wars when feudalism in reality was on its uppers. The collapse of farm prices due to the mass import of cheap food from overseas had slashed the rent rolls of belted earls and fox-hunting squires, while the onslaught of democracy on privilege had brought in punitive death duties. Consequently titled paupers in their hundreds were decamping from their estates and abandoning the country houses given star billing by the GWR. How interesting. However this is a memoir not a history book so we much leave the tantalising mystery identified but unexplored.

Thus Old England, if in dire straits economically, ran harmoniously along the lines. And so did I as, in search of cops, I undertook ever more ambitious train trips. Were my journeys really necessary? No, but they were thought provoking. My parents, who must have funded them, allowed me, at a still tender age, remarkable freedom to go off and explore that extended Victorian railway system that remained intact when I was young. Thanks, Mum and Dad. I tried for example four different ways of getting from Glossop to London, in each case arriving at a different terminus – Marylebone, Euston, St Pancras and King's Cross. The last was a tortuous improvisation but the ticket inspector accepted it as valid. Increasingly too I read about railways and their history. In a club chair at Southport's Atkinson Library, a temple of peace rivalling the nearby serene cloister provided by W H Smith and Sons, I discovered the *Railway Magazine*, which took me on mental excursions all over Old England at no cost to my parents. Eventually of course I found Betjeman, stopped at Adlestrop and came to realise there was poetry in trainspotting. There was a whole enchanted scene. In simply buying a ticket you became an integral part of Old England. In awe beholding a viaduct, or holding fast as an express roared by, or listening in bed to a distant, panting goods train slogging through the night, you felt content and peculiarly English. Through the railways something wholesome, venerable and truly rural circulated through the land like blood around the body. They pumped the invigorating air of the shires to refresh the industrial districts, before pumping it back again to the heart of Old England, somewhere on the Great Western, where it was itself renewed. We were all connected to Adlestrop until Dr Beeching closed the branch lines and constricted the blood vessels. My personal Adlestrop memory is of waiting at Kemble for the main line connexion. We had spent the afternoon rubbing church brasses in the Cotswolds and the August evening was golden. Beside us

Thomas the Tank Engine and his twin brother, fizzed contentedly, waiting in due course to go west to Tetbury or east to Cirencester, delivering city-stained travellers to rural regeneration.

Yes ... but. The transcendent beauty of Old England is undeniable but as a representation of where we were really at as a nation in 1945, at the end of the war, it was a travesty – at best a highly distorted picture, at worst a lie perpetrated by wartime propaganda. Not only did it gloss over the clapped out condition of our industrial system, including a Victorian railway system in urgent need of modernisation, but it wilfully ignored what S R Badmin, my bedside mentor, dismissed with disdain as 'The Other England', a monstrosity obnoxious to partisans of Old England. He meant the whole industrial scene and the attitudes it had engendered, a dwelling place and a culture which harboured more than half the population and not just those of us based north of the Trent. The above list of the namers never copped because they did not exist makes the point succinctly. The railways, once at the cutting edge of industrialisation, had espoused Old England. Their values were southern and anti-industrial. They wanted no truck with the 'Other England' and its satanic mills. Industrial revolution? What industrial revolution?

In the course of my trainspotting rambles around the Victorian network I became aware of that fascinating contradiction. The pilgrim route from Dinting to the shrines at Doncaster – station, sheds and locomotive plant – was particularly instructive so let us briefly follow that trail through the 'Other England' at its moment of exhaustion as the war ended. The sparkling Longdendale reservoirs, built by Victorian engineers to flush the cavernous sewers they excavated under Manchester, were quickly followed by the old Woodhead Tunnel, soon to be replaced but not just yet. It took twelve minutes of rattling and pounding to get through, while acrid smoke filled the carriages until vision was impaired. Nevertheless we opened the windows, leaning out to imbibe the sulphurous soup and feel the devil's breath on our cheeks as we invaded his domain. Our passage was punctuated halfway through by the tolling of a doleful bell that might have commemorated the hundreds of navvies who perished in the tunnel's construction. After Sheffield and through Rotherham, steel works lined the tracks and with luck the usually dim scene might be suddenly illuminated as a crucible was poured and in a big, black shed you caught glimpses of white hot snakes of metal. At Mexborough, where the stygian Don was presided over by white-capped cooling towers, blast furnaces gave way to coal mines and slag heaps lent pollution an alpine character. As we neared Doncaster disconcerting flashes of Old England lit up the wasted landscape. Conisbrough Castle, which featured in Scott's *Ivanhoe*, confronted the winding gear of Cadeby Main, while heavy laden coal barges on the South Yorkshire Navigation could be seen negotiating a wooded gorge below the medieval church at Sprotborough. Thus to a prolonged signal stop, amid acres of colliery wagons, before being admitted to the Great Northern main line to behold the solid mass of the locomotive works and the station platform that would be our vantage point for the next six hours. Then, after a day of steam, smoke, fire, poundings, pumpings, whistles, screeches and corrosive smells, with grimy faces and soiled collars, we took the route of desolation home again, and for days afterwards spat black and dug grit from our eyes. It was OK for us. We merely took a day return to hell. Some people however actually lived there. At Doncaster station you could watch a parade of Satan's slaves along a footbridge, spanning the platforms but inaccessible to those still in the land of the living. Over it the tramp of doomed shift workers, trudging to and from the locomotive plant, was continuous. They wore a penal uniform of blue overalls, flat cap and muffler and each toiler pushed a personal treadmill, a battered bike with a snap tin slung from the cross bar.

The thing is I *liked* it. Whatever S R Badmin taught, I found polluted south Yorkshire as beautiful as Constable's corny Suffolk. In L S Lowry I had already discovered the 'Other England' counterpart of the Old England landscapist and found his vision equally engaging. It was Dad who showed me Lowry. This was long before the painter became a national treasure but occasionally had his work reproduced in the *Manchester Guardian*. Dad liked what he saw and passed on his enthusiasm to me. I found nothing surprising about Lowry who, as far as I could see, just expressed in paint the beauty of a familiar townscape. But although its beauty was incontestable, industrial Britain at the end of the war disconcerted me. To start with, although the war had turned them into heroes – 'Workers only' the militant conductress would screech at rush hour – the workers seemed such a rough lot. Salt of the earth they may have been, but the penal battalion on the bridge at Doncaster, and the raucous flocks of fluff-covered, clog-clattering mill girls marching four abreast up High Street

East at tea-time, singing 'Don't fence me in', scared me, the way the 'scum' he commanded scared the Duke of Wellington. Fear was compounded by snobbery. My mother had taught me the workers were dirty and at teatime Dad dismissed the lumpenproletariat, which by definition had not passed the Scholarship, as collectively unintelligent and thus of no great importance. I was growing up though, and bold enough, at least in my head, to question parental stereotypes. We have seen that visiting Doug Swallow's house had already invalidated the automatic identification of terraced cottage with 'slum'. Now other heretical thoughts came in the train of that revelation. Despite their allegedly restricted intelligence, many workers could grow tomatoes, fix bikes and fence hen runs far better than anybody in our family. Did chip shop chips really differ essentially from those Mum fried? Why was it OK to eat tripe but not black pudding? Why was boring Standard English preferable to poetic dialect? And why should I shun catchy tunes on 'Music while you Work'? I was taking a few halting steps towards the ideas of popular culture and cultural relativism. Perhaps the workers were not inferior, just different. That possibility bugged me for decades.

The other problem about the 'Other England' I loved was its technology. Although beautiful, it was clapped out. The war had been won by sleek modern devices, like the Spitfire and radar, while British scientists had rolled out modern wonders like penicillin, jet propulsion and now, with a little bit of help from American dollars, the atomic bomb. Yet, despite all that, so much outmoded Victorian contrivance remained in use and, raddled with age and deprived by wartime pressures of proper maintenance, it functioned less efficiently now than it had done when it was new. In the age of steel too much was made of wood. In the motor age too much was driven by steam, or even pulled by horses. In the age of electricity too much was lit by gas. In the age of concrete too much was still built of timber and stone. Some of the locomotives I copped – hilarious with their tall chimneys, bulbous steam domes and exposed footplates – had been built when my grandparents were young. They were magnificent but anachronistic. I had to admit that steam traction of any sort was no way to run a modern railway and that the future was electric. I knew also that the unreconstructed mill girls who shunted me into the gutter had just done long shifts on jerky Victorian looms that had actually worked more smoothly when Granny Southport minded their like. Creaking locomotives and unreliable textile machinery were of a piece with other Victorian survivals that thrilled me yet disturbed me, like wooden coal trucks, narrow-boats, bottle ovens, steam tractors, mill chimneys, smoky tunnels and pungent gas works. I loved them but they would have to go. 'You been a good old waggon/But honey you done broke down' as Bessie Smith had put it. However the Victorian trappings of a dysfunctional post war economy did not go, not at least until much too long after the war. Instead picturesque contraptions were patched up ad hoc during the conflict, with the aid of generous government contracts, and after the war were left in place in deference to a near sacred, bi-partisan policy of full employment. The workers must have jobs, even squalid ones and even at the price of low productivity. For three decades after 1945 the British showed too much enthusiasm for social engineering and too little for real engineering.

Which brings us to 'New Jerusalem' the other of the two arms – the left one, matching the 'Old England' right one – within which Churchill's government held the British people in a tight wartime embrace. The phrase is biblical and involves three successive visions. In ancient times St John, as he recorded in the Book of Revelation, had had a vision in which our imperfect world had passed away, to be replaced by a perfect successor.

And I saw a new heaven and a new earth; for the first heaven and the first earth were passed away; and there was no more sea. And I John saw the holy city, New Jerusalem, coming down from God out of heaven, prepared as a bride adorned for her husband.

William Blake, early in the nineteenth century, had a similar vision. The Devil had besmirched England by perpetrating the industrial revolution but Blake had faith that Christ would come again, clear up the mess and 'among those dark satanic mills' build New Jerusalem, thus restoring a 'green and pleasant land', very like the Old England illustrated by S R Badmin in *Village and Town*. Then, during World War Two another vision was granted to Clement Attlee, Churchill's Labour deputy, who used the term 'New Jerusalem' to describe the plans for 'post war reconstruction' being drawn up by his party comrades within the wartime coalition. The Christian roots of the term should be borne in mind, for wartime culture was not, like ours, aggressively post Christian. The spiritual vision had however become deeply tinged with socialism, particularly with 'Christian Socialism', a persistent strain in English philanthropy and politics.

In which light we may re-read the vision of St John. The 'sea', the 'passing away' of which John had witnessed, may be equated with the war, an epoch making cataclysm, like the biblical Flood, after which things will never be the same again. It had washed away the corrupt old social order, in which the rich oppressed the poor, clearing a construction site on which God's gift, the 'holy city' of 'New Jerusalem', might, as Blake puts it, be 'builded here'. For 'God' read the wartime 'State', a mighty but compassionate engine, terrible to its enemies but exuding loving kindness towards its children, its faithful citizens. God has taken up residence in Downing Street. The flowing white locks of a venerable, wispy presence in the clouds had been exchanged for a substantial bald pate wreathed in cigar smoke. For 'heaven' read 'Whitehall' – a company of angels, a bevy of government ministers, served by an elite corps of cherubs known as 'planners', omniscient experts who have studied the problems and arrived a set of infallible solutions. Meanwhile an archangel styled 'Minister of Information', is attending, in holy places like Harmsworth [headquarters of Penguin Books] and Bourneville [citadel of Cadburys' Chocolates], to the gorgeous adornment of New Jerusalem, so that she may be delivered as a 'bride' to comfort and delight the troops and workers, coming home after their wartime ardours. Like Danny Boyle at the opening ceremony of the 2012 Olympics I am trying to capture the *poetry* of New Jerusalem – the 'welfare state' as it came to be less ethereally known. When I was ten or twelve I absorbed the New Jerusalem dream. It found a lodgement in my childish head and stayed there to constrain my adult judgement. I knew for sure there would be jam tomorrow even though, in the event, tomorrow kept getting delayed.

The idea of New Jerusalem may be given substance by looking at a piece of adornment devised by *Picture Post*, a magazine which, as already reported, contributed much to my cultural conditioning. I do not however remember the special issue of 4 January 1941 which anyway would have been too sophisticated for my eight year old head. I have in front of me however a facsimile reprint. It hit the rubble-strewn streets at a bleak midwinter moment in the war. Britain 'stood alone', the Blitz was at its most intense, and there was not much to look forward to in the spring, except renewal of the invasion threat. Nevertheless here was a 'Plan for Britain', something to salivate over in the shelters. This is how it is going to be, folks, after they sound the last all-clear. The cover shows some sturdy toddlers, stark naked apart from their Startrite sandals, on a slide at their state-run nursery. It symbolises a new start and evokes a promise of cradle to grave welfare. The table of contents puts New Jerusalem in a nutshell. You could copy it and pop it in your gas-mask case to study amid the drone of the Heinkels.

Work for All
Social Security
The New Britain must be Planned [architecture and town planning]
Plan the Home
The Land for All
A Plan for Education
Health for All
A Real Medical Service
When Work is Over [a plan for leisure]

Some of the authors were famous. J B Priestley wrote the last chapter. It will be recalled that he worked for the BBC, alternating with Churchill himself in Sunday night fireside chats with the nation. He wanted to liberate the workers from 'passive, mechanical enjoyment', like frequenting 'pin table establishments' and watching 'idiotic films', and go swimming and hiking instead. Julian Huxley, of the 'Brains Trust', wanted birth control and 'communal feeding' centres, since people left to themselves could not be trusted to eat balanced meals and get their vitamins. Other contributors were equally sure what was best for the workers. An educational guru from Oxford wanted to close the gap between state and private schools and seemed equally keen on outdoor classrooms. A modernist architect wanted high rise flats and clover leaf junctions and more about that shortly. A 'consultant' specialising in 'planning working class homes' wanted fitted kitchens, 'municipal hot water' and 'scientific refuse disposal'. All most admirable no doubt but it was left to three key contributors to identify the essential features of the New Jerusalem package. First, the post war state must retain its commanding wartime powers and use them to ensure full employment. Secondly, a universal social security system, including family allowances, must be established. Finally, a national health service was needed. Two years after *Picture Post* so confidently set out its stall, Sir William Beveridge, another Oxford academic, having chaired a government committee on social security, published his famous report, now regarded as the blueprint for New Jerusalem. It echoed the *Picture Post* manifesto.

We met Sir William one Friday night at the Empire just before Christmas 1942. I was ten and in my first term at the grammar school and I knew we were living in stirring times. For the Beveridge Report came out just after General Montgomery won the war. Well, more or less. Sure Churchill said the desert victory at El Alamein was not the end, nor even the beginning of the end, but he did think it was the end of the beginning. Which was very clever but I guessed the PM was just being modest for Alvar Liddell's account of this latest shuttle along the coast of Egypt and Libya had a quite different tone. The enemy he said was 'in full retreat' and he had never used words like that before. We were at Mersa Matruh before you could whistle 'Lilli Marlene', failed to stop, like we always had done before, when just past Benghazi, and come January we saw Winston himself on Gaumont British News taking the salute as kilted Scotties, to the swirl of pipes and with bags of swank, paraded through Tripoli itself. Wow! Peace could not now be long delayed, particularly as the Russians also seemed to be winning at Stalingrad. Which is perhaps what got me to take an interest in Beveridge. With the war ending quicker than we had thought, preparing for peace had become urgent and everybody said this chap's plan was just the ticket. I didn't like him much. He had prototype 'National Health' glasses and spoke posh with a squeaky voice. However I tried to be fair and get hold of his obviously important message.

In that endeavour I was helped by Cadburys' Chocolates which, soon after Sir William published his report, put out their own New Jerusalem picture book, subsidised no doubt by the MoI. A copy had been sent to our school but rather than let it clutter a classroom Dad brought it home for me to keep in my bedroom. His brief case on a Friday night quite often yielded treats like that, including posters about New Jerusalem put out by ABCA [the Army Bureau of Current Affairs] which stuck-in-the-mud 'Colonel Blimps', perhaps not erroneously, said was run by left leaning officers whose hair needed cutting and who were lining up our boys for Communism after the war. Those posters did not do much harm to the youth of Glossop except for the Head's son because mostly they fetched

303

up on my bedroom wall and nobody else saw them. As well as telling us what schools were going to be like after the war – as in *Picture Post* lessons would happen out of doors, like they already did that at Bourneville, where Cadburys already had New Jerusalem up and running – the brochure had a section about Beveridge. It seems he had found Five Giants lurking in England's green and pleasant land. They were called Poverty, Disease, Squalor, Want and Ignorance and they were in urgent need of slaying. Well you couldn't argue with that. Cadburys' showed all five of them sitting on what looked like wobbly lab stools. They were wobbly because the legs of the stools had already been eroded by a series of 'Social Reforms' – factory acts for example and public health acts – that had been going on for yonks, so a few good pushes now ought to do the trick. 'Ignorance' seemed an especially vulnerable giant. When all those outdoor classrooms became operational he would surely die of frostbite, like the Germans were doing at Stalingrad. However what Beveridge mostly wanted was 'Social Security', which would surely see off both 'Want' and 'Poverty' and good riddance. Mum and Dad seemed less convinced. It seemed we would have to get stamps like the ones Mum got at the Post Office for Olive and Mrs Brown. That was OK for them because they were working class. But it would be humiliating if we despite being middle class also had to have stamps and claim benefits. Ought not people stand on their own two feet instead of taking hand-outs from the state? The same sort of thing bothered Dad a few years later when another of Beveridges's ideas was being debated in parliament. If Labour's proposed National Health Service went through – which it obviously would because they had a massive majority – the Headmaster of Glossop Grammar School and his family would have to sit in the waiting room with the hoi polio, where we could easily pick up something nasty, whereas at present we went through Doctor McShannon's front door directly into his consulting room. .

To be honest I was beginning to find Mum and Dad a bit small minded, although I knew Social Security did not apply to us and Dad was never going to be out of work. And the details certainly seemed very dense and boring. But why could my parents not just rejoice in the glittering adornments of New Jerusalem, like I did? For there was a lot more to it than all that stuff about Full Employment and Social Security and some of it was truly brilliant. The bits about town and country planning exercised a peculiar fascination and for me modern architecture came to have a glamour akin to

Gresley Pacifics. It will be recalled that even as a small child I had recognised modernity, which I associated with the new, broad East Lancs Road, along which we sped towards Southport, and the 'Bauhaus' electric fire that warmed me at bedtime. Well, what with the move to Glossop and then the war and DND 838 being laid up for the duration, I had not had much in the way of modernity since those dear dead days. Then along came New Jerusalem adorned for my delight and flashed to me by Cadburys, ABCA and other organs of wartime propaganda although I course I did not know that was what they were. I loved the clean-lined buildings, interspersed with trees and parks, and those amazing road junctions that really did look like clover leaves. They would be made from 'reinforced concrete', a magic new medium that was going to bring sunshine to former slum dwellers, now elevated into cloud-capped vertical living, and hurtle us all from A to B at the speed of a Spitfire. Wow! At super-sandy Southport I used to build my own New Jerusalem on the beach. The sand had a firm consistency not unlike concrete and the sea in the approaches to Liverpool yielded abundant flotsam. Thus a piece of driftwood would serve first as modelling tool and then as the fly-over section of a motorway junction. Then at home time you could bomb your creation with half a brick. My urges were never wholly constructive.

Building New Jerusalem was far from just a game. Although quite unaware that that is what was happening I absorbed a whole social philosophy, practicals on the beach being part of a socialist conditioning that moulded me as firmly as the training in Marxism-Leninism a future Soviet apparatchik might have received at High School 999 under the kindly gaze of Comrade Stalin. My first and best tutor, believe it or not, was Comrade Badmin, he who in *Village and Town* had already inducted me into the worship of Old England. His over-arching *thesis* – although of course I did not know that that is what it was – was propounded, in mercifully few words but with incandescent images, in that same slim tract. Sure most of my favourite Puffin told a happy story about the unfurling of beautiful English architecture, right from the middle ages up to the eighteenth century, when it achieved twin pinnacled perfection in the Cotswold village and the classical terraces of Georgian Bath. Then there came an abrupt change of tone and tempo. Just after the building of Bath catastrophe struck. It was called the Industrial Revolution and it spawned 'hundreds' of smoke-blackened urban jungles, lacking in

305

'proper drains', its mean houses entangled around ugly factories. That scene, known as the 'Other England' was graphically depicted on Page 26 in black and white, colour being reserved for the Cotswolds and the Royal Crescent. The obscenity that was the 'Other England' – it is reproduced as *Plate 16 top left* – grabbed me firmly. Indeed it penetrated my brain and stayed lodged there for forty years so let us pause over the image.

At the apex mill chimneys, pithead gear and a gasworks contest the skyline. Black smoke unfurls among narrow lines of slum dwellings, the massed chimneys of which make their own contribution to the choking smog. Shirts are hung out in foetid yards to collect the soot. Only the poison dispensed at ubiquitous utilitarian pubs offers a brief respite from misery. These 'dark satanic mills' and their attendant hovels – Badmin's vision is a mirror image of Blake's – were perpetrated by 'rich men' who shamefully 'made money in trade' but themselves lived on hillsides far above the squalor they had devised, in 'fancy dress houses' that caricatured the architectural styles of the past. We may call these ogres 'Capitalists', although Badmin did not use that word. Perhaps he thought it had too many syllables for his young readers, and in my case probably he was right. The wicked Capitalists cared nothing for their workers, thinking only of 'how to manufacture more things cheaply and make more profit'. In the rest of the book we learn what happened next. 'Many other Englishmen' – led, it should be understood, by John Ruskin and William Morris, although Badmin, their 'Arts and Crafts' disciple, did not name his masters – 'hated the ugliness of their cities and tried to get back to a better way of living'. Bravo for them. They tried out 'garden cities', which were a good idea, but for a long time the Arts and Crafts men did not cut much ice with the wicked Capitalists. Then three pieces of great good luck happened in quick succession.

First, reinforced concrete, a wonder medium, was invented. Architects could now design very tall buildings and also penguin pools which, like outdoor classrooms, were icons of New Jerusalem. Every garden city should have one. Badmin's own evocation of Antarctica even had two separate gawping levels, so that grown-ups and children might study bird life from different but adjacent levels *[Plate 16 bottom left]*. The real revolution however would be in housing *[Plate 16 bottom centre]*. Apartments would have 'long sliding windows' opening onto 'wide balconies', on which, as well as on flat roofs, residents might 'grow things or sunbathe', the latter occupation being, like observing penguins and outdoor schooling, intrinsic to New Jerusalem. Even better, the new blocks of flats would be vertiginously tall, thus delivering therapeutic 'light and air' to the dim eyes and desiccated lungs of liberated slum dwellers. Also they could be raised on stilts, 'allowing garden or road underneath'. Miraculous! Furthermore living together in these commodious blocks would liberate residents from close confinement within their separate domestic circles, offering instead a 'communal restaurant, nursery, club rooms, and sports facilities', the use of which would so much 'make daily life pleasanter and easier'. Let's face it, the nuclear family is a bourgeois aberration. Under New Jerusalem – aka 'the Dictatorship of the Planetariat' – it would have to go.

The second piece of good luck was the war, and in particular the Blitz. It had done more for slum clearance than a whole vault full of well-intentioned acts of parliament. 'Come friendly bombs and fall on Slough', John Betjeman had sung. Whether the future Laureate had his wish I do not know, but Goering's Luftwaffe certainly obliged by lancing plenty of other urban carbuncles. Not that we should rest on Goering's laurels. According to another Penguin author, Ralph Tubbs, in *Living in Cities*, post war reconstruction would have to be preceded by *'re-destruction'*, by the systematic demolition of what the Germans had left untouched. Demobilised tank crews would be recruited as bulldozer drivers. Swords into ploughshares.

The war brought a third stroke of luck and this one was crucial to the Badmin thesis. If we look again at his picture of 'The Other England', reproduced above, an apparent detail will be recognised as the very punch-line of the argument for New Jerusalem. Observe the factory in the middle of the picture and read the company name, emblazoned beneath a pinchbeck pediment on the front of the building. It is 'Chamber and Lains'. Wow! In 1942, when *Village and Town* was published, the reputation of the late Neville Chamberlain, Prime Minister when the war broke out, had sunk to a level scarcely higher than that of Hitler himself. Not only was he a Capitalist – his family had been in trade in Birmingham – but he had tried to prevent the war by 'appeasing' the Führer. So in 1940 Parliament on behalf of the abused people of England kicked him out. By the end of the year he was dead and good riddance. However before then he had been anonymously denounced – along with his predecessor Stanley Baldwin, who was also in trade somewhere else

307

in the 'Other England', and a whole gang of Tory businessmen – in a vitriolic book called *Guilty Men* put out by Gollancz, publishers to the Left Book Club. It captured the mood of a nation intoxicated with 'Dunkirk spirit' and inflamed by Churchillian rhetoric. I think I remember a copy, in its distinctive yellow dust jacket, lying beside Dad's chair. It explained how these Appeasers who had befriended Hitler were not just guilty of treason. They were Capitalists as well. They belonged to that evil clique of rich men condemned by Badmin for thinking only of how to increase their profits, while grinding the faces of 'Other England' slave labourers. The equation was simple. Capitalism = Appeasement = Fascism and the point of the war became blindingly apparent. We were not just fighting to liberate the French, Poles et al, languishing under the Nazi jackboot. At the same time we were fighting to liberate the workers of the 'Other England', groaning under the lash of Capitalist-Appeasers. They were 'fifth columnists', the enemy within, and their time was up as surely as that of their hero Adolf Hitler. I absorbed the gist of the 'Guilty Men' sermon from a few well-thumbed pages of S R Badmin. Capitalist wealth creation was morally tainted and we were fighting to liberate its victims, the workers. Dad, when denouncing my Uncle Albert, the footwear manufacturer, was saying something similar. Thus was I got at.

The last page of *Village and Town* completed my surrender to New Jerusalem thinking. It was entitled 'The Future' and it insisted that the great opportunity set up by the arrival of reinforced concrete, the war and the exposure of the 'Guilty Men' would be lost if individual choice was not subordinated to collective planning. Without planning people would be able to 'build more or less what they fancy whether it is ugly or not'. Clearly that would never do. At my mother's knee I had learnt not only that the working classes smell but that they had no taste either. Not that Mum's own chaotic sub-Victorian taste would have got many marks from Badmin. However it was indisputable that it was the duty of those of us who knew better to give the workers fragrant homes with fitted kitchens whether they wanted them or not and the name of that public service was planning. 'The New Britain must be PLANNED', Maxwell Fry had screamed in *Picture Post*. He and his wife Jane were also admitted to my bedroom, for they had written an architecture book for children that I frequently savoured. It featured a modern house complete with wall to wall windows and sunbathing patios, just like the ones in Badmin.

Whether it had a penguin pool in the garden I do not remember. Ralph Tubbs agreed about the necessity for planning and so did Cadburys and a chap amusingly called Goldfinger who drew up the *County of London Plan*. Penguins published that as well and I bought it at W H Smith's which went in for New Jerusalem as well as Old England. Goldfinger was harder to understand than Badmin but I got the message because this glossy also relied more on images than text. Anyway there was a junior version in the form of another Puffin called *The Building of London* by another couple of New Jerusalem missionaries called Margaret and Alexander Potter. At the end of their book there was a knock-out picture *[Plate 16 bottom right]* that seemed to solve the problem of what I was going to be when I grew up. Here was a group of planners caught in the very act of planning. Surely it was a snapshot of me, say ten years on, building New Jerusalem. Wow! Meet three tweedy planners. The thoughtful one on the left seems to have strayed from the BBC 'Brains Trust', while the other two come by courtesy of Disney, the woman resembling Mini-Mouse, while the man looks like Goofy. They sit in their cut-away reinforced concrete kremlin, looking through a trade-mark picture window at an heroic bulldozer driver blithely engaged in 're-destruction'. 'Many buildings must be pulled down', we are told, 'before the new plan takes shape'. Hence the ruins of a mock-classical building labelled 'Profit'. Wow again! Clearly the tyranny of the 'Guilty Men' has been brought crashing down and it is now the planners' sacred task to rehouse the liberated slaves of capitalism. To this end they study a 'New Plan of London' lit by an anglepoise lamp which, as we know, was another icon of modernity. The planners' resources are ranged around them. Reports of government commissions line the shelves cheek by jowl with the works of the architect Corbusier, tsar of modernity. Rolled-up drawings lie beside a bottle of glue. There is a bank of drawers stuffed with benefits the planners are about to bestow upon their clients, the people of London. They include 'bathrooms', 'playgrounds' and 'flowers' as well as 'good things for housewives'. Meanwhile our benefactors reach out for further goodies. At Goofy's elbow there are gas cylinders labelled 'Fresh Air for London' and from what looks like a bag of sweets he extracts 'Fine Houses for All'. Brainbox similarly scatters trees from a can while Mini-Mouse, blowing bubbles, endows the city with 'sunshine'. Capitalism is dead, long live planning. I had a mission. My future was settled.

Chapter 12

POST WAR

So as the war ended, when I was pushing thirteen, I thrilled to the New Jerusalem vision dispensed by S R Badmin and the planetariat. I was ravenous for modernity. My hunger was prompted not just by images of penguin pools, tower blocks and motorway junctions but by still vivid memories of how life had been long, long ago, before I had been torn away from modern Manchester and imprisoned in a Victorian mill town apparently in terminal decay. It will be recalled that in infancy, whether or not I actually knew the word, I had already identified a style of life I recognised as 'modern'. It went with suburban semis, domestic gadgetry, 'Stop-Me-and-Buy-One' ice cream trikes and art deco cinemas. I still got fixes of art deco because Southport abounded in examples of the style – not just cinemas and the Garrick Theatre but a spectacular lido as well – but such brief tastes only intensified the longing. Particularly as during the war, when the supply even of rationed petrol dried up, the joy of speeding along the East Lancs Road, another icon of modernity, was taken away. Worse still, those invigorating holidays with smart-living aunts and uncles in super-modern London had long ago been suspended for the duration. They began again however, seemingly on a whim, less than three weeks after VE Day. For on Whit Sunday we got the train to Manchester, crossed over to the LMS platforms at London Road, and in great excitement set off for Euston and my first sight of London since the time, just before war broke out, when that family photograph was taken at Norbury and we had all played that new game 'Monopoly' in the front room at Selsdon. It was the train-spotting opportunities the holiday presented that first blew my mind. Not only did we go past the running sheds at Crewe South but in the afternoon, as we neared the end of our pilgrimage, I first clapped eyes on the roundhouse [locomotive depot] at Camden. Outside it streaks and Scots galore basked in post war, spring sunshine. Ecstasy!

Yet Camden proved a watershed, an end as well as a beginning – the last bastion of steam age Old England but also the checkpoint through which we were inducted into the modern world. It was the Underground at Euston that convinced me I had arrived in the future. There were these astonishing machines. All the stations you could go to for twopence were listed on an illuminated screen and, if you put sixpence in, you got fourpence change as well as your ticket. How about that? Phew! No wonder British invention had won the war. Then it was so easy to find your way with all those elegant squared off maps and those rows of coloured lights directing you to the main line stations – blue for King's Cross, brown for Paddington, green for Waterloo. Unbelievable! I sure had exchanged the dark ages for the age of reason. And the lift! It was enormous and resounded to an automatic Alvar Liddell who for our own good urged us to 'Stand clear of the gates'. The future was humane as well as efficient. Then a red bullet train glided along the platform with no visible means of propulsion except that shiny middle rail, exciting in its potency. At London Bridge the disembodied Alvar helped us regain the surface and we exchanged the red train for a green one, also self-propelled. The lack of steam was disappointing, because electric trains did not have names, but the indisputable modernity of the Southern Railway made up for it. Perhaps anonymity and modernity went hand in hand. And thus through a colourful landscape of back gardens to East Croydon. Not that you could see much through the windows because they retained the shatter-proof adhesive netting with which they had defied the doodlebugs, leaving just a diamond of clear glass to look through. Now there's progress. Glossop was addicted to lacy drapes but no cottage window had ever sported a stick-on curtain.

It was the same throughout the next seminal week during which I quaffed ever more intoxicating draughts of modernity. It is a cliché of post war reminiscence that London in 1945 was grey and shabby. Not to me it wasn't. I found novelty everywhere, much of it the direct consequence of bombing, which as Badmin and Ralph Tubbs had pointed out, had been a mercy in a way. Clear out the old to bring in the new. It was my Aunt

Maud's black plastic loo seat that particularly wowed me. Could anything be more modern than plastic or more stuffily antique than mahogany? So light and so hygienic. It came by courtesy of the War Damage Commission which had transformed 32 Littleheath Road into a veritable machine for living in. It was a gift from the government and that was how it was going to be now the war was over. The men from the ministry, who obviously knew best because they listened to the planners, would show us all how to live better. The black plastic seat matched the telephone which was forever ringing and usually it was a boyfriend wanting Mavis next door, where they did not have a phone. That was something else about the future. People would be always nattering over the air waves. Folk in Selsdon were doing that already, perpetually ringing each other up, even though they lived in the next street and could easily just walk round and knock on the door. Another piece of science fiction could be experienced down in Croydon. It was a modern house. You could tell that because it was made of concrete and plastic, had a flat roof and the sort of kitchen called 'fitted'. But the amazing thing about it was that it had not been built where we saw it, at the back of Kennards' store, but had been 'pre-fabricated' in a factory and then delivered in sections on a lorry. It seemed that, as well as tanks and aircraft, assembly lines could now turn out whole kitchens, bathrooms, sitting rooms and bedrooms, all with 'built-in' furnishings. Then they put them on lorries, took them where they had to go and rapidly bolted together the components of the required house, before getting a kiss from the ecstatic housewife, granted a dream house by the government as a post war gratuity, a reward for all that war work. Wow! and Wow again! What a brave new world we were heading towards. I supposed that if the happy family later experienced a happy event and needed an extra bedroom all they had to do was ring the ministry and hey presto! Magic but modern.

Then there were Lyons' Corner Houses. I remembered Dad taking me to one before the war and it was full of dancing black and white waitresses. Those girls were long gone into war work and the resulting labour problem had been solved with the devastating logic that post war was going to brim over with. Instead of serving the customers let the customers serve themselves, thus saving on wages as well as releasing labour to the war effort. It was win-win. Yet another Wow! Actually I was not technically a cafeteria virgin. They had introduced the system also at the British Restaurant in Manchester but the food there was so nauseating I scarcely took in the revolutionary delivery system. Not so the food at Lyons. There was this section called the 'Salad Bowl' and it was fabulous. Forget Mum's idea of a salad – dry lettuce with egg, tomato, salt and pepper – and feast on this burgeoning banquet of goodies all drenched in mayonnaise. And you could stuff yourself with just as much as your plate could hold. Furthermore the salad was only one element in the feast. You also got soup and a roll and not only a choice of succulent gateaux and flans but an ice cream as well. Plus coffee served in a scientifically designed cup that retained both heat and aroma. Austerity? What austerity? But it was how you served yourself that truly grabbed me. You paid your one and six in advance, thus cutting out all that eye-catching at the end which got Dad tensed up when we went to a café. Then you pushed a tray along a length of rails, like marshalling trucks in a goods yard, meanwhile scooping dollops of deliciousness with long handled spoons made of – guess what – transparent plastic, just like the cockpit of a Spitfire. Talk about swords and ploughshares! Amazing and remarkable! How wonderfully well the future was going to work. There would even be a place for old world charm for you took your groaning tray to a table with a chequered cloth and soft lights while somebody played 'La Vie en Rose' at a grand piano. You had to feel sorry for the Germans. Instead of a well filled post war they were getting 'Occupation' and starvation. On a bomb site there was an exhibition about their fate called 'Germany under Control'. Well, it was their own fault, I supposed.

Of course I did some trainspotting that wonderful week as well, making my first ever circuit of the Circle Line, thereby exploring some of the stations of the Monopoly board, and visiting Paddington as well. What a roof! The ironwork was so much higher and longer than even that at the Manchester stations and it had these cross pieces that made it seem like a big fancy church, particularly when smoke from the engines curled like incense around the girders. I knew Badmin would not approve because Paddington was Victorian and probably put up by rich men who cared only for profit and would have appeased Hitler if he had been around at the time. But bloody hell! – as I was beginning to say, being nearly thirteen – I didn't care … it was beautiful. Then, having with considerable satisfaction copped a couple of 'Kings' and some 'Castles', with which to open my account in my new Great Western Ian Allan, I continued along the Circle Line to Euston Square, and after a short walk through some surprisingly mean streets – to find them in streamlined London was a bit disappointing – to Euston itself. In front of the station entrance there was this huge arch made of massive Greek columns. It was certainly impressive but it seemed to be just for show. So it was not 'functional' and I was pretty sure the planners would not like that. There was also a plush booking hall that S R Badmin certainly would not have liked, but I had to admit I did a bit because in spirit it reminded me of Grandpa Southport's drawing room. The everlasting tension between progress and nostalgia already beset me. I certainly liked the veteran 'Prince of Wales' class 4-6-0 I found idling at one of the platforms. When Grandpa came to London, if he ever did, when he was young, this locomotive might have pulled his train. Now there were not many Prince of Waleses left so I was lucky to spot one. Just then I noticed a news-seller's placard with a strange device. 'PM Calls General Election', it said. Whatever was one of those? Stung by curiosity I bought my first evening paper and sat on a luggage trolley to investigate the phenomenon further. I had a rough idea what an election was of course. Having them, along with getting rid of rich men who thought of nothing but profit and appeasing Hitler, was what we had been fighting for. But there had never been one that I could remember. In fact the last one had happened in 1935 – it was what made the art master draw that cartoon of Dad looking like Hitler – and then I was only three. That was one of the things about growing up during the war. Certain news events, like elections and the Olympics and test matches, recurrent in peacetime, were in suspension for the duration. Democracy itself was to me, when I was thirteen, quite a strange idea. Churchill and the clever men around him, like ministers and generals and planners, knew what was best for us. They did very well as winning the war had proved so was consulting the rest of us really necessary? Did we anyway know enough to have a valid opinion? Were elections perhaps a bit like bananas, a luxury we could do without? Having grown up while democratic processes were in suspension, the disconcerting idea that government can be carried on quite nicely without them has always lurked somewhere in my political outlook.

It was not good news that I read while perched on that LMS luggage trolley. Indeed, if I had not been so excited about Paddington, and then copping a 'Prince of Wales', it would have made me distinctly sad. For here was a list of Churchill's 'Caretaker Government' – it would keep us going until the election results came out at the end of July – and a lot of Winston's chums had got left out. Big Ernie Bevin was not there and neither was mop-haired Herbert Morrison. The shadowy Mr Attlee had also gone and so had both the Arthurs [Greenwood and Henderson] to be replaced by a couple of Olivers [Stanley and Lyttleton] who sounded a bit posh. Even Sir Archibald Sinclair had flown the Air Ministry nest to be replaced by a cuckoo called Harold Macmillan. It was quite upsetting. Churchill's ministers had seemed such a happy family, pulling together smoothly under his benign direction and now suddenly they had fallen out. During the next few weeks the truth gradually emerged. It was not exactly a divorce that had happened because the members of the wartime coalition had never pledged themselves to a permanent accord. Indeed it turned out they were not really even friends but actually rivals who had just agreed to hold their tongues until the war was won. Which it wasn't really. The stubborn Japs still needed sorting and probably a lot of them would commit hara kiri rather than surrender, taking plenty of our boys with them. However the pent-up animosity to Uncle Winnie of his Labour nephews was such that they started slagging him off almost before the VE Day bonfires were out, ignoring his plea for them 'to finish the job' together. You could understand why he felt hurt. However there was no holding the snarling impetuosity of pugnacious Clem Attlee, hitherto so meek and mild. You never can tell, can you? Thus I discovered the existence of competing political parties, something else I had not much come across during the long wartime holiday from democracy.

There was going to be a 'polling day' before the end of term but then it would take three weeks to collect in the 'ballot boxes' of the forces overseas, so they could not count the votes until then. Which was frustrating because once you got the hang of an election it was exciting and the wait would be agonising. As it happened those three weeks were to be truly agonising for me personally because, between the voting and the counting, I behaved like a cad at sports day and lost my inner cleanliness. But you know that story already. Before my fall I had much enjoyed the election, which was a sort of continuation of the festivities of VE Day, when Glossop got covered in all those flags, among which Mr Hall had spotted both a Japanese ensign and the eagle of Tsarist Russia, both left over from World War One. Banners and colours were an essential part of the electoral junketings too and there was bother in that respect between Labour and the Liberals. Brian Leatherbarrow's dad who, despite running his own business, emerged as Labour to the core – as I say, you never could tell about anybody any more – said the Liberals ought to let Labour be red because Labour's anthem was 'The Red Flag' but the Liberals said they didn't want to be yellow, because it stood for cowardice and anyway they had been red long before Labour was invented. Which was true, as I knew from one of the New Jerusalem booklets from Cadburys which listed the various Victorian ministries, so surely the Libs had a point. Anyway, as the summer unfurled and the campaign hotted up, folk all over Glossop came out in the true colours they, like Mr Attlee and Sir Archibald, had camouflaged during the war. Despite the number of cars with blue posters in their windows and loudspeakers on the roof it was surprising how much support there seemed to be for Labour. Perhaps it was because you could never make out the words coming from the loudspeakers. So, although everybody said Winnie was bound to win, plenty of people seemed to favour the disloyal ministers who had stabbed him in the back before he had finished the job. Alderman Doyle, despite being an alderman, manager of a shoe shop and author of the 'Watchman' column in the *Glossop Chronicle and Advertiser*, was about the most Labour chap in town, closely follow by dark-suited, briefcase-carrying Sam Burgess, father of Anne Burgess, my sister's best friend, who spoke with a lisp and went to Kingsmoor private school. I envied them their red brick suburban semi further up Sheffield Road from our Victorian barn. Even Mum said Anne Burgess was 'affected' so how could they be truly Labour? However the most astonishing defector was Winston's erstwhile greatest fan who, despite being Headmaster of the Grammar School, and while coyly insisting that 'the ballot is secret', in the privacy of his own home indicated his scarcely credible voting intentions. Which settled it for me. Dad's authority remained hard to resist, particularly when endorsed by Alderman Doyle, the wisest sage in Glossop. Not that their sagacity cut any ice with Mum who, it now appeared, was a lifelong Liberal who, even at this momentous juncture in our island story, saw no reason to desert the path once trodden by Mr Bright and Mr Gladstone, the household gods whose busts stood on top of Grandpa's mahogany bookcase. Well, that my mother had ever cared a jot about politics was news to me. I was learning something fresh every day that summer – particularly that day at the beginning of the long holidays when the results came out and Labour had won.

Dad and I were of course ecstatic about the 'Labour landslide' as well as astonished. Astonishment indeed was general and even Alvar Liddell momentarily seemed to lose his iron composure, when early in the day – counting had begun first thing in the morning – he announced that the interloping Harold Macmillan had lost at Stockton, a place I had heard of because it figured in railway history. Amazing! It couldn't last surely? It did though. It was all so exciting that for a day or two even my recent loss of inner cleanliness got pushed towards the back of my mind. It was a precious time too in another sense. In retrospect it emerges as the last time the close father-son relationship, initiated almost ten years before when my sister was born and the King died, functioned in proper working order. For the moment anyway, as the election results gave us plenty to get our teeth into, our old cognitive companionship flourished at full strength. We spent hours that day in the Study, ears glued to Alvar Liddell, feverishly ticking off lists of constituencies, printed in the *Manchester Guardian* and *Radio Times*, just like lists of namers in the Ian Allan books. Sometimes he would explain and sometimes I would ask questions and sometimes we looked things up together. What he told me was interesting and he seemed interested also in my views on the big surprise. Sometimes too he would react to something I said with a kind of pride and I would feel good. Here was my favourite Dad, the prince among tutors. The Gauleiter was not present that day in the Study, and neither was the demagogue of the tea table. He was just my Dad and I liked him.

When the overall result could no longer be in doubt we took a trip into town in the evening sunshine just in time to see Hugh Molson's blue motorcade, hotfoot from Buxton, sweep across the traffic lights with horns blaring. It screeched to a victorious halt in Norfolk Street, outside the Conservative Club which was plastered in portraits of Winston, asking the voters to give him the tools to finish the job. So despite the best efforts of Alderman Doyle and Messrs Burgess and Leatherbarrow, the High Peak had bucked the national trend. Dad blamed our Labour candidate and perhaps he was right. It did not matter really in view of the general picture and Mum was pleased because posh Mr Molson had once come to tea at our house and been gracious about her fruitcake. Next day Alvar Liddell had further amazing happenings to relate. Churchill's

Daimler was at the Palace and the King had sent for Mr Attlee who had duly obliged in their Morris Minor with his wife at the wheel. Did that really happen or have I imagined it? Even now the excitement was not over because we needed to know who the new ministers would be. Dad bright-eyed and even mischievous in his euphoria, sitting in his deep leather armchair scribbling down the names of the Labour cabinet, is one of the happiest memories I have of him.

Euphoria does not often last, does it? Certainly Dad and I in our different ways soon fell out of love with Labour. For Dad, and Mum too I guess, it was the working class character of the new government that proved troublesome. As well as 'champagne socialists' there were rough diamonds among the new men and some of them even had accents. 'That Shinwell', a new recruit to the menagerie of tea-time bêtes noires, even spoke Geordie and, worse still, Aneurin Bevan, as well as threatening a headmaster's family with the communality of the doctor's waiting room, had the bad taste to be Welsh. Then there was the way Attlee had disposed of the Foreign Office, for so long the preserve of tall, dark Anthony Eden, a gentleman to the tips of his well-manicured fingers. That was something you could never accuse Ernie Bevin of being, for not only did he have an accent but he was a trade union leader. Dad had predicted the FO would go to young Richard Crossman who had been to Winchester, which meant he was even brighter than Eden, who had only been to Eton. By contrast, had Mr Bevin even passed the Scholarship? You could not count on it and was it a good idea for the country to be run by 'B' form types and worse? The end for Dad Labourwise came when 'that Shinwell', who held the portfolio for Fuel and Power, conspired with General Winter in the early months of 1947 to let the Lord family feel cold, a condition we had never endured during the late conflict with Nazi Germany. In fact we had almost exhausted our last remaining bag of coal, which I had personally hauled on my sledge from the Station Yard, and sat huddled around an oil heater in the kitchen, hoping there would be paraffin at the stores tomorrow, and listening to grounded journalists on the wireless telling us what would have been in their magazines that week if the government had given their publishers enough newsprint to print them. It was interesting though that, although Dad, flapping his arms for warmth, denounced Shinwell for gross incompetence and for waging class war – the year before he had annihilated the park at stately

Wentworth Woodhouse to dig for coal – his abuse was not tinged with anti-Semitism. Perhaps he was unaware of the minister's ethnicity. Jews usually had German accents, not Northumbrian ones. Or had evidence about the Holocaust, recently revealed at the Nuremberg Trials, brought about a change of heart in Dad? It would be good to think so.

My disenchantment was of a quite different character. I had no problem with accents and would not mind sitting in Dr McShannon's waiting room provided I had an Ian Allan book to keep me company. My complaint was that Labour never got anything done, at least not anything interesting. Sure there was going to be Social Security but that was no use to us because we had plenty of it already. And there was to be a National Health Service with free specs and false teeth, neither of which applied to me either. All that was boring. So, if I was honest, was the compulsive nationalisation that was going on, although I tried not to admit it because by 1947 I called myself a communist and was in favour of the state running everything and also punishing capitalists and appeasers. Dad disagreed. He disliked miners, particularly if they were Geordies or Welsh and he pointed out that nationalising the pits had not stopped coal strikes in the bleak midwinter. I argued also in favour of nationalising the railways although for a train spotter that had a flip side. I became sharply aware of that one sunny afternoon in 1946 when, fizzing stationary at East Croydon station, I suddenly beheld a brand new West Country Pacific, straight out of Brighton works and not yet fitted with a name plate. It was painted green. Not just green but 'Malachite' Green. Wow! I had never seen a coloured engine before, except for a vague infant memory of steamy red monsters at Manchester London Road. Malachite Green was the distinctive livery of the Southern Railway. Similarly the LNER had once used Duck Egg Blue for express locomotives and the LMS a shade of crimson. What a post war treat might thus be in store. But would company colours survive nationalisation of the railways? I thought probably not and it turned out I was right. With British Railways you could have any colour so long as it was black. Competition between railway companies, and the distinctive look that gave, not only to their engines but also to of the likes of carriages, stations, viaducts and lineside features, endowed the landscape with variety. I realised suddenly that a rich Old England texture was under threat and found my heart and head in a conflict that was to become familiar. Progress and nostalgia, innovation and conservation – are they compatible?

I was irritated too by the way Labour kept changing the names of things without achieving changes of substance. We now for example had 'secondary education for all', which might sound good in parliament but looked at on the ground it was ... well, 'bullshit'. That was another urbane expression that, having become what was now, to Dad's disgust, called a 'teenager', I permitted myself. I got it, not as per usual in verbal growth spurts, from Chris Gillings, but from Jas who like me was getting cynical about post war and had a nose for a waste product increasingly thick on the ground. Thus although the 'Scholarship' was now the 'Eleven Plus' it continued to sort sheep from goats in the same old way and a better class of person was still to be found at the Grammar School. They had also changed the name of the local transit camp for goats, turning 'West End Central School' into 'West End Secondary Modern School'. That was just daft. 'West End Peripheral School' would have made sense because, as you know, it was situated a long way from the Town Hall. But the chosen name was absurd because the building was not modern and how could they claim to be 'secondary' when they did not do French, let alone Latin, and their First Eleven regularly got stuffed by our Under 14s. All in all, despite changes of name, nothing changed.

Nominal massage was apparent in other aspects of the Glossop scene after the war. The Workhouse became the 'Shire Hill Hospital' which was also daft. Its actual address was 'Shire Hill *View*' which necessarily implied a certain distance from the topographical feature cited. I did not like it either when the showroom of the 'Stalybridge, Hyde, Mossley and Dukinfield' electricity company, next door to Finlay Mackinley MPS ['By Appointment to His Grace the Duke of Norfolk'] became just an office of the North West Electricity Board. It implied erosion of that local autonomy which, it will be recalled, had hitherto distinguished Glossop. I mourned the passing also of the Glossop Gas Company and of the School Board Man and the Sanitary Inspector. Before long even the Chief Constable went the way of all flesh. Would the Borough Surveyor be next for the chop? No doubt the functions of those estimable public servants continued to be discharged but too often by faceless ones based somewhere else.

However none of that was the prime reason why I gave up on the government of Mr Attlee. He and his ministers had failed in what to my mind was their principal duty – the prompt delivery of a concrete New

Jerusalem, as so helpfully delineated in *Village and Town*, S R Badmin's elegant and eloquent manifesto. I really had expected that, on the morrow of victory, demobilised tank crews would mount their bulldozers and the great 're-destruction', planned by the planners by the light of their anglepoise lamps, would everywhere commence. Even Glossop would echo to the crash of pompous masonry, music that, because the Luftwaffe never paid us any attention, we had been deprived of throughout the war. Then, in the twinkling of an eye, dispossessed profiteers, complicit in the appeasement of Hitler, would be marched off, tower blocks would outreach the mill chimneys, and at Woolley Bridge a clover leaf junction would smoothly segregate Hadfield-bound traffic from a stream of jet-propelled vehicles speeding towards the penguin pool in Norfolk Square, in front of a brand new concrete town hall on stilts. And pigs might fly. Glossop looked almost exactly the same five years after the war as it had done in 1945, which actually was not much different from how it had looked ten years earlier. It was desperately disappointing. It was true that a cluster of pre-fabs could now be found among some amalgamated backyards at Whitfield. Also the railway was going to be electrified, if and when, but not yet. Otherwise that glorious outbreak of modernity, prophesied by Badmin and presaged for me by Lyons' Salad Bowls, was not yet even around the corner. In fact the only construction project I can remember happening in post war Glossop involved the draining of a pond rich in frog spawn to permit a modest development of council houses on the Pyegrove. They had only two storeys, were not on stilts and did not have access to a penguin pool. It was however a start, I told myself, and they did have modern plumbing and it was right, I supposed, that slum dwellers should be rehoused. They deserved bathrooms as a reward for all that war work. But guess who moved in. It was not the less than fragrant Stanley, the ritual muncher of Swedish sandwiches, whose family surely deserved rehousing. Instead it was Chris Gillings! He was no slum dweller and they already had a bathroom, as his account of his parents' conjugal relations clearly indicated. If New Jerusalem meant fair shares as well as penguin pools this was a rum start.

As far as I could tell, on quite frequent further trips to the capital, it did not take off even in London. There, it is true, there were plenty of pre-fabs but along with the Salad Bowls and the ticket machines on the underground, and an actual if solitary penguin pool we saw at the Regent's

Park zoo, they remained the only really modern things in town. Until 1951 that is, when the Festival of Britain showed that New Jerusalem had not been entirely forgotten. I liked the Skylon, a sort of V2 rocket in suspended animation, and the Festival Hall was exciting – an essay in glass and concrete, its cavernous interior spaces ringed like a penguin pool with projecting balconies. To be fair, it was Labour that had done it. Soon however Attlee and Co were gone and Churchill was back and it seemed New Jerusalem was gone for good. By then though I was at Oxford and, as the Dean said, 'living with the brakes on', too depressed to care about anything much except sex which, in that then all but all-male citadel, seemed as much a broken promise as New Jerusalem. When I tentatively lifted my foot from the brake pedal, in the mid-1950s, nothing much had changed. The tower blocks had still not come, the slums still awaited their coup de grace, and a grid-locked road system remained entirely innocent of clover leaf junctions. Indeed it was not until 1958, thirteen years after the war ended, that an abbreviated stretch of British motorway at last caused an epidemic of over-heating among Ford Prefects and Hillman Huskies unaccustomed to the pace of modern living. So post war was a big let-down. And the swinging sixties arrived rather late for me.

The trouble with Labour was its timidity. Churchill is supposed to have called Attlee 'a modest man who indeed has much to be modest about'. Just so. Instead I wanted a leader with oomph who would not flinch as he put dynamite under rich men's palaces and, on newly erected concrete units of habitation, flew red flags to celebrate victory in the class struggle. For as we have seen by 1947 I was in thrall to Comrade Stalin as well as to Comrade Badmin. Good old Uncle Joe, our old wartime best mate, was now inventing the future fast, not only in the Soviet Union, but also the Soviet Zone of Germany and in the east European countries the Red Army had liberated from fascism. He was doing it moreover despite the atomic blackmail of Harry S Truman who also, through the bait of Marshall Aid, was trying to pollute with capitalism those west European countries not yet rescued and brought under Soviet protection. No, I am not making it up. For a while in early adolescence I really did spout meretricious rubbish of that ilk. There is abundant evidence of it in the homework essays discussed in Chapter Eight. My weekly correspondence with Miss Hughes, it will be recalled, resounded with left wing polemic. We must nationalise the means of production, distribution and exchange, an imperative that particularly applies to the railways. Towns must be planned, 'ribbon development' being a particular abomination. Private landowning is deplorable, property being theft. Christmas must be abolished or at least shifted to January. We should rejoice at our deliverance from Victorian capitalism, which had brutalised the proletariat but be on our guard against the new challenge of capitalist America. So raise the scarlet standard high. We know also that this naïve attachment to Comrade Stalin blossomed with my friendship with Tat Higginbottom, creator of the hammer and sickle device illustrated in Chapter Eight. It was inscribed in my English exercise book without attracting any rebuke from my teacher. Was she too was a 'fellow traveller'? On our trips to the public library to read the *Daily Worker* Tat and I discovered another hero. Harry Pollitt General Secretary of the Communist Party of Great Britain and thus Stalin's opposite number in this country. 'Harry was a Bolshie/One of Lenin's lads' went a popular ditty. He urged us to work for workers' unity, tell Truman what he could do with his Marshall Aid, and also send a contribution to the *Daily Worker* fighting fund.

I don't think we ever did subscribe and perhaps we were not entirely serious. Perhaps it was just my age. Perplexed by puberty, I embraced what I took to be grown-up ideas while clinging still to childhood simplicities. For truth to tell, I had another equally urgent gripe against Labour, as well as its failure to bring about New Jerusalem. It failed also to deliver the Great Rock Candy Mountain. During the war, although our family endured very little in the way of doing without, there was one aspect of austerity that could not simply be assuaged by a trip to the Co-op Butcher's. It was sweet rationing. By 1945 I was fed up with it and assumed that with victory it would stop. In a flash, as the lights went on again, I had supposed the jars standing empty and forlorn on the sweetshop shelves, would be recharged with humbugs, mint imperials, bon bons and Dainty Dinahs, while a miraculous draught of Dairy Milk and Aero, Sandwich Bars and Five Boys spilled across the counter. On the morrow of VJ Day, just as the bulldozers commenced re-destruction, I had no doubt the slot machines now rusting on station platforms would again, at the slide of a penny, discharge a bar of Nestlés. As the church bells rang out anew I expected simultaneous tinklings as a platoon of demobilised Stop-Me-And-Buy-One men pedalled gaily back into Civvy Street. As the bluebirds homed in on the White Cliffs of Dover I imagined convoys of banana boats bob,

bob, bobbing in their wake. Mountains of best butter would be restored to their marble plinths at the Maypole and aromatic sides of bacon would swing again from the ceiling hooks at Callaghans. Shelves everywhere would proffer Libby's peaches and Del Monte pineapples. The return of snappy Rice Krispies would end the monopoly of droopy Wheat Flakes. Addicted though I was to Heinz Potato Soup I looked forward to varying it with Kidney, Ox Tail or even exotic Mock Turtle. There would be an explosion of colour as dress materials cascaded over Edwin Bailey's counter and female legs would be swathed in silk or even nylon. Wow! Fireworks would be back and cigarette cards and Dinky Toys. So would Sarsaparilla and Dandelion and Burdock. We might even taste a novel nectar, denied even to pre-war generations and known thus far only to the GIs and their followers. 'Coca Cola for all' would better express our hopes of a better world than 'Secondary Education for All'. When that came about the sacrifice of war would not have been in vain.

Hardly any of that came to pass however, not anyway on the right side of the Festival of Britain or even of the Coronation [1953]. Sweet coupons survived until rationing itself was wound up in 1954. At Oxford in 1952 I received an exiguous weekly dole of butter, dripping through a nasty little screw of paper I was expected to store between meals in a college room I shared with mice. It was 1950 before I saw bananas freely on sale and that was not in England. When Dior's fabric-guzzling 'New Look' conquered Paris in 1947, Labour made strenuous efforts to stop it invading Britain and sabotaging the 'Export Drive'. That struggle marked the finest hour of Stafford Cripps's our austere Chancellor. Although fireworks did make an early come-back – all that war surplus TNT presumably – it was 1948 before Dinky Toys again tempted schoolboy shoplifters at Woolworths. Cigarette cards never came back and neither, I guess, did Sarsaparilla.

Eventually, when I was seventeen and again not in Glossop, I did at last taste Coca Cola, just as Stella Artois simultaneously flirted with my taste buds. Mr Hall's hope was that the novelty of the former elixir would moderate the appeal of the latter, despite the intense lager-friendly heat of the week in 1949 that a school party spent in Brussels. The hope was not entirely pious for Coke was truly different and we were amazed. Among my souvenirs is a ubiquitous jingle, inscribed on café frontages and the kiosks of street vendors:

Buvez Coca Cole glacée
Chacque bouteille est sterilisée

And what an interesting bottle it was that the stuff came fizzing out of, directed by a waiter's deft fingers into a tall glass charged with ice and lemon. No wonder that shapely vessel later became an icon of Pop Art. It was also apparent that in sophisticated Belgium both refrigeration and sterilisation came as standard. How unlike workaday Glossop where airs were not to be put on and a bit of honest muck never did nobody no harm. Iced drinks? Nay lad, don't be daft! You'll catch your death, like as not. That holiday was my introduction to foreign travel, an experience, like democracy, denied to war children, and as well as Coke it brought other heart-stopping firsts eagerly consumed. It was then that I first encountered filter coffee, chips with mayonnaise and dark cigarettes [sniffed but not inhaled]. It also brought me a first taste of love requited and of an intoxicating togetherness that transcended humdrum living the way Coca Cola glacée eclipsed tepid Tizer.

Then there were the lights. In austerity Glossop although the street lamps had been lit again after a fashion, power cuts permitting, shop windows were seldom illuminated and although 'Put that light out!', the wartime cry of the air raid warden, was no longer heard in the land, the feel of the blackout persisted. Not so in Brussels. Shop windows were everywhere ablaze and cinemas and café terraces cast an enticing glow. Furthermore a vast acreage of city wall was covered in intricate tubular patterns of light, some of which flashed and twinkled rhythmically, or progressed through intricate cycles of colour change. They proclaimed ways of pampering the body with products to imbibe, ingest, inhale or sensuously apply to yielding flesh. And they indicated ways of travelling at maximum speed with minimum effort. In Brussels that week Shell, Chanel, Citroen and Cinzano, the brands names of an age of affluence, already flourishing across the Channel but painfully slow to reach our shores, tantalised us urchins of austerity. Could High Street West ever emulate the Boulevard Adolphe Max? It seemed most unlikely. And you should have seen the food shops. You could get just anything and we took much of it home to amaze our loved ones. Sure, cheese, ham, sausages and patisserie did not travel well and the weight of a suitcase loaded with tinned fruit all but yanked my arm from its socket. But when I presented

Granny Southport – in this, her last year, she had come to live with us in Glossop – with a gargantuan block of Suchard milk her response made the effort worthwhile. That proud Victorian, a veteran of two post wars, whose upper lip was as stiff as her poker back, was openly emotional and the giant bar lay beside her bed, unopened but adored, more an object of veneration than a mere item of confectionary. When she died a few weeks later the chocolate was still unopened. I expect we scoffed it, telling ourselves it would have been what she would have wanted. But perhaps it would have been better to send it off with her when we took her to join her Tom in the graveyard at Newchurch-in-Rossendale. Frugal she may have been but she was no kill-joy, like astringent Stafford Cripps. Gratification ought not to be mischievously delayed. That was a big part of what put me off Labour.

An account of that memorable trip abroad has carried this narrative two years beyond the point at which it was supposed to stop. For a series of happenings between July and September 1947 seems in retrospect to divide childhood from the rest of my life. I do not of course mean I grew up in 1947 and put away childish things. On the contrary plenty of apparently childish things stayed with me for life. As already observed, the mind-set that has emerged from all this recollection, is very familiar and coincides to an uncanny extent with how I feel and think today. The child was indeed father to the man. The least important event of 1947 was the School Certificate exam itself. VA was expected to take it in its stride and we duly obliged. I remember taking pride in not being nervous. Less phlegm was expected of V Alpha who of course were less equal than us but no doubt they too did their best to keep calm and carry on, a task facilitated by the atmosphere of ritual calm established in a cool Victoria Hall, dressed overall in special exam desks, arranged regimentally under high windows and lofty beams. The calm of the exam room was matched by the calm of mind we brought to the occasion. For we came chock a block with data. From the saddle of my bike during the long evenings of a long hot summer that had followed an infamous winter, I reviewed a prodigious store of curricular knowledge safely stowed in a bulging brain. Great chunks of *Macbeth* and big dollops of *Milton's Minor Poems* rolled around my head, as lungs and legs tried to get me to the top of Symondley New Road without getting off. By now it was not just poetry I recited to an unresponsive ovine audience. All the seven subjects I was entered for contributed arias to enchant them and also the swallows which swooped on regardless. Definitions, dates, theorems, properties, conjugations and formulae provoked only the silent dust. But no matter, recapitulating them gave me strength for the morrow.

Which shows that rote learning works. I guess we are endowed by our creator with a capacity to learn things by heart and that it peaks round about the age of the School Cert, although in my case it had brought a jackpot win much earlier, when a piece of memorised pomposity brought me a Scholarship before I had properly learnt to read. The grammar school as an institution effectively harnessed the absorbent youthful memories of its clients. Getting things by heart is a cheap way of learning that makes life easier for both pupils and teachers. It relieves the latter of too much lesson preparation and helps them keep order. And the kids love it. Remember those Yorkshire fifth formers whose feats of memory were commended in Chapter Seven. Through a two hour coach trip they chanted the contents of their 'O' Level syllabuses, non-stop and without repeating themselves. Actually we all like it, don't we? Why else does the popularity of TV game shows never wane and why do pub quizzes sell beer? Yet during that unfortunate progressive era, when most grammar schools were extinguished, 'factual recall' was derided and the tide turned against memorisation. That was very silly. I know that now. But it eluded me in my own progressive days when I trampled tradition like Attila the Hun. We favoured 'discussion' over 'exposition' but you can't usefully debate issues unless you know some appropriate facts. When relevant data has been instilled by rote, valid argument will explode all over a lively classroom but all you can do with ignorance is turn it into flannel.

We had no need to flannel our way through the School Cert because we brought minds as well filled as our fountain pens to the Vic that Monday morning in mid-July when our confrontation with the Joint Matriculation Board examiners began. That was another advantage we enjoyed. The exams came right at the end of the school year, so we crammed in an extra two months of instruction beyond what is possible today, when they begin soon after Easter. All that accumulated knowledge brought confidence. Barring catastrophic bad luck we knew we would pass. Extra luck and/or extra dexterity should yield 'credits' and 'distinctions'. It all took about ten days. Usually there was a paper in the morning and another in the afternoon. Sessions varied in length but two hours was typical. A paper was often divided into Part A and Part B, the former requiring simple factual recall while the latter called for problem solving, although along predictable lines which we had been trained to recognise and respond to. Eng Lit came first, suitably to the aura of sanctity attaching, at the Gauleiter's academy, to that sacred field of knowledge. As well as requiring proof of familiarity with the aforementioned texts by Shakespeare and Milton, the Board in 1947, had us contemplate some journalistic jottings collected as *More Essays by Modern Masters*. It was fun in its way but it denied us engagement with a big novel by some major 'master spirit' like Jane Austen or Thomas Hardy and maybe it foreshadowed the great dumbing down that came later in the post war epoch when Eng Lit, like classical music, had to do homage to pop culture. Still, ours was not to reason why so, taking a refill of Quink, I duly demonstrated familiarity with J B Priestley as well as Shakespeare before emerging into the glare of a sub-tropical noonday and beating a well-trodden path across the Royle to Mum's soothing chip pan. I felt I could have done better but was not seriously disconcerted. It was early days. The School Cert was a marathon not a sprint.

Arithmetic on Monday afternoon went as well as could be expected. Being notoriously 'careless' I was vulnerable in that field, which anyway I dismissed as a Cinderella discipline, an attitude unlikely to generate careful calculation. But judging from notes I compared with others afterwards I seemed to have done OK and looked forward cockily to Tuesday morning's paper, which was Geometry, my best numerical subject, in which I counted on a high score to compensate for carelessness in Arithmetic and mystification over Algebra. But the Geometry paper was by general agreement a 'stinker'. Instead of encouraging a display of the formal Greek logic I enjoyed it called for algebraic short-cuts. I thought that unfair and my spirits sagged. But only until Tuesday afternoon when, fortified by my daily fix out of the chip pan, I hit the History paper like the dam busters' bouncing bomb. In a mighty outpouring of hard facts, political, social and economic, relating to Britain, Europe and the British Empire 1783-1914, I emptied the reservoir in my head to fill not only a twelve page answer book but a flutter of supplementary sheets as well. Now I was into my stride and the rest of the circus ran its course without much incident. Algebra on Wednesday perplexed me less that I had feared and Thursday was practically a day off, for getting a distinction in Eng Lang was no problem to a native speaker of Standard English. My Standard French, as tested on Friday, was a soupçon more precarious but not more than somewhat. So I duly translated from French into English and vice versa, showing an adequate command of the pluperfect and of irregular past participles, before getting the drift of Miss Wanklin's mercifully measured 'dictée'. That was the first week over. It was easy – even easy peasy. Only Latin and Chemistry were left for after the weekend. Not having completely mastered either valency or the gerundive, I did feel obliged to spend an hour with my Chemistry exercise books and another consulting North and Hillard's manual of *Latin Prose Composition*, but there was still time to bike over to Dinting for some therapeutic trainspotting. Then by four thirty on the second Tuesday it was all over. A piece of cake, as Battle of Britain pilots used to say. They did in films anyway. It had been oddly relaxing as well as stimulating. I got to like luxuriating on a summer's afternoon in the big space of the Vic, silent except for a pianissimo puttering of purposeful pens, with the windows open, the curtains ruffled by a balmy breeze, and a smell of fresh-cut grass wafting from the nearby cricket field to mingle with whiffs of surgical spirit from the first aid table, which introduced a hint of peril into the exam experience. There could be casualties. Not me, though. However it showed our teachers cared and wanted us to do well.

So the School Certificate was not hard if you were well prepared. When I thought about it afterwards I concluded that more or less anybody could handle it, given the necessary training and commitment. When the results came out they showed that that applied to the duffers of V Alpha as well as to us brain-boxes in VA. Could it be that even those drafted onto sorry transports of Scholarship 'failures' and despatched to West End all those years ago, would have proved quite capable of picking up School Certs, if they had been gently reassured about their abilities and given the disciplined training we had received? Well, next year that question would be answered, for the first group of 'late transfers' rescued from West End was due to take the exam. You will not be surprised to learn that they did very well – better actually than many indigenous 'B' formers and that will not surprise you either. Dogs they say behave in conformity to the names we give them. Thus I began to challenge the efficacy of the screening plant. I became increasingly convinced that the system that established it was rotten. That conviction became part of a complex of progressive attitudes to education that came to possess me. It included an enthusiasm for comprehensive schooling, the purpose of which, I naively supposed, was to provide a grammar school education for all. I was wrong of course. Going comprehensive imposed a secondary modern education on all but the children of the rich. But my insight about the School Cert was sounder. I still think success in a school leaving exam, demanding a quantity of factual recall plus a dash of good thinking, is no more beyond the capability of the average citizen than is the Driving Test. Sure, some of us need more than one go at the latter but in the end we duly get our licences, and having succeeded become confident road users. Success in itself builds confidence, which is why nothing succeeds quite like it. That goes for the School Cert as well. I did not get one because I was highly intelligent or unusually industrious, or even because I was middle class. Like everyone else I succeeded because I was well drilled. I had responded sufficiently to the 'mallet process'.

Chapter 13

COLD WAR

Despite having taken it in my stride I was glad the School Cert was over and that relaxation beckoned. The weekend after the exams finished I lay in the sun on Granny Southport's lawn, between the apple trees and the red hot pokers, reading a Penguin greenback ['Crime and Mystery'] called *The Public School Murder*. The memory of that golden afternoon has prompted one of those speculative visits to Google that have taken the back-ache out of research. It has yielded the blog of Martin Edwards, a crime writer who knows and likes this 'forgotten book' the way I once did.

FRIDAY, 6 JULY 2012

Forgotten Book – The Public School Murder

R.C. Woodthorpe was a pretty successful author in the 1930s, and his best known novel, which I have in a green Penguin edition, is my Forgotten Book for today. This is *The Public School Murder*, and its school setting, Polchester, is evidently based on Christ's Hospital, where Woodthorpe taught in the Twenties before going into journalism. ... The story is agreeably written, and it makes a virtue of the public school ethos, about which views are probably as divided today as they were in the Golden Age. ... I've never read anything else by Woodthorpe, but I would like to do so. The trouble is that his books are now rather elusive – it would be good if someone could bring them back into print. However, very little information seems to be available about Woodthorpe, and such detection work as I've been able to do has been rather poignant. ... His full name was Ralph Carter Woodthorpe, and he lived until 1971...

That account reawakens the pleasure, particularly as Martin Edwards has read exactly the same Penguin edition I devoured long ago. Furthermore it emerges that 'Polchester' was actually Christ's Hospital, the academy that, a few years earlier, Dad, in his quixotic way, had fixed on for his son. That scheme had foundered but, although I did not yet know it, he had not given up the idea of translating me from his humble school to a superior education elsewhere. Unconsciously I was perhaps not entirely averse to some such plan. I was aware of an educational firmament set high above the grammar schools, which were mere earthly reflections of a heavenly glory incandescent at those private schools which were oddly known as 'public'. I knew about Rugby because Dad had force fed me *Tom Brown's Schooldays*, adding a top dressing derived from his own virtual attendance at Greyfriars and St Jim's. Also I knew the names of a lot of other public schools, including Eton, Harrow and indeed Christ's Hospital, from copping locomotives of the Southern Railway's 'Schools' Class of 4-4-0s. That such institutions were a central part of the Old England I had discovered in the oaky ambience of the Southport branch of W H Smith's was very clear. I had also been deliberately confronted with private education as a political issue by my progressive Aunt Marion, who occasionally took it upon herself to wrench me from the reactionary grip of her stolid brother. She and her new partner David, whom she had met in the blitz adrift from his wife, had taken me to the Criterion Theatre. It was my first taste of a West End stage and I was impressed, somewhat against my great northern will, by the compelling intimacy of the auditorium, as well as by its plush luxury. The play was a New Jerusalem piece by William Douglas Home called *The Guinea Pig*. It took up an idea, recently floated in a government report, about the possible integration of the public schools into the state system. It was about a shopkeeper's bright son leap-frogging his local grammar to be drafted experimentally into a public school, complete with fagging, flogging and a wounded war hero to model himself upon. I much enjoyed the evening. Dad's aborted Christ's Hospital project made the action on stage seem close to home. Had I had a lucky escape or missed an opportunity? The answer eluded me and it still does. As a young socialist it was easy to be affronted by privileged schooling. It was unfair that most of us should be excluded from a head start amid the sort of architecture I only knew from S R Badmin's illustrations. But at least at Glossop Grammar School we were spared the sado-masochistic flip side of the experience. After seeing *The Guinea Pig* it struck me as dodgy that in Britain we trained our future leaders by getting them to beat each other up in cloistered detention centres. It seemed a perverted practice, not that I was sure what a 'pervert' was. It was a word you came across, loaded with dark hints, in the Sunday papers. Corporal punishment bothered me. I had not seen any since St Luke's but Mr Fielding's performances as public executioner had not been forgotten. The Gauleiter did not do that sort of thing and good for him. As a headmaster he had his merits. A lot of them actually.

The fact that I awarded myself *The Public School Murder* as a reward for finishing the exams demonstrates that at last, at the age of fifteen, I had reached a level of literacy adequate to full length works in continuous prose. I could now read, if not as fast as Chris or Jas or Doug Swallow – or that lad who could seemingly swallow a whole Dickens novel between breakfast and tea – then fluently enough to get through a story before I had forgotten what happened in Chapter One. Henceforth my thoughts were influenced by what I read as well as by what I saw and listened to and that seems to mark a watershed between childhood and the less innocent condition that followed it. When I trawl my memory for books conquered at this time [say 1946-1948] the resulting list is surprisingly long. Mostly they were non-fiction and that was due to practice at the public library as well as to Dad's censorship. You got four black non-fiction tickets but only two for fiction which, lest you missed the point, came in red for shame. Thus a title like 'Teach yourself Plumbing' was judged uplifting, while the works of Dickens and Hardy were pilloried as trivial if not salacious. Shakespeare escaped disgrace because drama counted as non-fiction. I thought it a daft system. Surely fiction as well as non-fiction sometimes made you think, *The Public School Murder* being a case in point. Also novels transported you mentally to interesting places at particular times. Other crime writers as well as R C Woodthorpe took me on rewarding journeys like that. With Dorothy L Sayers I enjoyed the company of fly-fishermen in Scotland and bell-ringers in Suffolk. It was exciting how a clever author could enliven apparently obscure places and practices. Sayers was evocative also about Oxford, alma mater of Harriet Vane, surely the author's alter ego, who was rescued from the hangman's noose only by the aristocratic genius of Lord Peter Wimsey. Reader, she married him. Then there was Georges Simenon who really was salacious.

He not only led me willingly beside foggy Flemish canals but also took me to places in Paris awash with forbidden pleasure. If travel broadened the mind, as everybody said it did, then so too did reading detective fiction.

I read proper novels as well as supposed pulp. The prolixity of Dickens defeated me. Also although we had seen both *Pride and Prejudice* and *Jane Eyre* at the pictures, I assumed those were girls' books and Dad would go berserk if he found any such reading matter in the hands of a son whose deficiencies in manliness already troubled him. However Dad hyped what he called 'the moderns', by which he meant the golden trio of H G Wells, Arnold Bennett and John Galsworthy. They all worked for me because their novels were like film scripts. Having dealt in images for so long the *documentary* quality of these 'modern' novels made them highly congenial. Like Sayers and Simenon these writers took me directly into distinctive locales. I enjoyed high tea above the shop in Burslem [Bennett], love among the lab stools in South Kensington [Wells] and the District Line in a pea-souper during the days of steam haulage [Galsworthy]. That the latter episode in *The Man of Property* occurred on the morrow of a notorious marital rape escaped me at the time. Trainspotting still eclipsed sex. Not for long though. There was another 'modern' on Dad's 'must read' list who like Shakespeare came on a black ticket since he gave his fiction dramatic form. I liked reading plays, perhaps because the text came in short speeches instead of extended paragraphs and that, for a reader who had only recently acquired fluency, was relaxing. The Irish playwright Dad urged upon me was not Oscar Wilde, whose works were proscribed at our school and I was at Oxford before I discovered the charge against him. There was apparently nothing like that about Bernard Shaw who furthermore was truly modern because still alive. He seemed to live a garden shed in Hertfordshire, from which he emerged on newsreels to wag his wise beard at the audience. His works figured prominently on the socialist shelves at Selsdon and Norbury, so I knew his ideas must be right – or rather left. Not that he thrust his philosophy at you too vehemently and sometimes, as in *Pygmalion*, he made you laugh.

That was more than could be said about some other black ticket books Dad brought home for me as supplementary 'set books'. They were about manly pursuits like mountaineering and archaeology and were deeply boring. In front of them despite trying to stiffen the mental sinews I seldom experienced comprehension let alone fulfilment. The failed 1933 Everest expedition had found an ice axe. Big deal! Could it be Mallory's? Did I care? I did not care either about the doings of Sumerians and Beaker People, or at least not as painstakingly deduced at tedious length from flints and bits of pottery. In plugging such dense tomes Dad put me off archaeology and mountaineering for life. He almost put me off 'civilisation' as well, when he had me tackle a book of that name by a certain Clive Bell. Although it was hard work, this time I *did* understand what the author was getting at – and rejected it as rubbish. What he did was pick out four western cultures – ancient Athens, Renaissance Florence, Elizabethan England and eighteenth century France – and then, simply *on his own arrogant say-so*, sanctified them as the most civilised ever known. He went on to declare that what they had in common – a high valuation on reason and beauty – were the essential characteristics of 'civilisation'. It did not stand up. The characteristics you fetched up with depended on your choice of top cultures and that was a matter of *opinion* – the opinion it seemed simply of Bell and his best mates. Why was the cultural superiority of Renaissance Florence beyond dispute? Bell never said. Without knocking Florence could you not make out a case for say Victorian Manchester or even Victorian Glossop? By the application of reason to wealth creation Mancunians and Glossopians had taken great leaps forward which made millions richer and thus better able to afford beauty and that was surely a civilised thing to do. The rich lives of my grandparents seemed to prove the point. With help from their betters they had bettered themselves. But I sensed there was no point in arguing with Bell and Co. I did not know they were a clique with clout, based in Bloomsbury, but I knew they shared S R Badmin's negative view of the Industrial Revolution, so they would never vote for Manchester. Indeed I began to be irritated by bossy Bell so Dad did me a favour in prescribing *Civilisation* as a holiday task. Spotting the author's parade of prejudice masquerading as reason made me tougher in mind. Watch it, Dad!

Now that I could tackle grown-up novels and non-fiction, non-picture books I danced more nimbly around my thought policeman. Not only did I taunt him with monthly purchases of *Trains Illustrated* but every month too at W H Smith's I scanned the new batch of Penguins and Pelicans, particularly the latter, the blue-banded non-fiction imprint. *Civilisation* was a blue band but it was Dad who paid for that. With my own pocket money however I gambled recklessly. There was a Pelican about opera by a bloke called Dent that I found compelling, even though I had never heard any operatic music apart from scratched Carusos played with blunt needles on the museum-piece gramophone at Southport. Systematically I attached what Dent taught me to my now elaborate History Meccano and got that familiar buzz. Whenever I put something into chronological order it started to make sense like it did in Miss Sillito's tables. Thus Gluck got screwed into the Meccano before Mozart, who preceded Rossini, who was followed by Wagner and Verdi, who were contemporary but represented different traditions. Opera, it further emerged, was mostly the business of Germans and Italians. A year or two earlier that would have put me off but now the war was over prejudice was in retreat. Well, up to a point. I kept *Opera* under the bed because Dad was as funny about posh music as he was about 'cacophonous American jazz'. It did not do to trail your coat. I did not flash Roger Manvell either. His Pelican was called *Film* and was another speculative buy stowed under the blankets on account of a message I was pretty sure Dad would denounce as heresy. Manvell not only provided a chronological list of classic films – always black and white, mostly silent and usually French – but he claimed that film-making was an art form. He meant not just *Le Jour se Lève* and *The Cabinet of Doctor Caligari* but some British films we had recently seen at the Empire, like *Odd Man Out* and even *Great Expectations*. I didn't think Dad would wear that and also I did not want to spoil his fun. He liked going to the pictures. It was time out from his arduous vocation. But if he felt he had to exercise his formidable critical faculties in the One and Nines as well as in Room 1, it would put him off. There was a case for entertainment pure and simple. 'People must be amused, Squire' as Dickens put it. Even headmasters.

One book above all that I read in 1947 changed my mind. It was John Hersey's *Hiroshima*. I bought it as it first appeared among the new Penguins at W H Smith's. It had grey bands which signified 'Current Affairs' but it was distinguished from ordinary grey bands by having the title printed in red. Not even the one about the Nuremberg Trials that I read simultaneously had been highlighted in the colour of blood but it too made a powerful impact. For it was in 1947 that I discovered the holocaust of the Jews as well as that of the Japanese. I did not conceal *Hiroshima* from Dad but neither did he show any inclination to discuss it. I guess he thought the 'Japs' deserved all they got after what they had done to Mr Bell and all the other POWs. But this book was not only about the travails of victims, it was also about how the character of war had become suddenly altered beyond recognition. Dad was not alone in his apparent indifference to all that. Nobody wanted to know. Despite the emergence of the Cold War in 1946-1947 I can recall among my classmates none of that fixation – part political commitment, part cold fear – on the eschatological potential of nuclear weapons that gripped my daughter and her friends as the confrontation of the super-powers reached its culmination when she was about fifteen. In recognising, thanks to Hersey, how the atom bomb had changed things utterly I felt alone. It seemed a collective amnesia, in the immediate aftermath of the war, generated such a rush to get 'back to normal' that it killed the appetite to analyse the terrible things that had happened. It was only in the 1960s, amid events like the Cuba missile crisis and the Eichmann trial, that the clatter of scales falling from eyes began to be frequently heard.

If I reached that point earlier than most, it was thanks to John Hersey. He told a terrible tale. It grabbed you like a novel and then you realised with a shock that these things had really happened and only two years before. The story emerged through the experience of a group of survivors. They were people you quickly got to know, like you did characters in a novel. You got to like them too because they were leading believable, respectable lives in a community that, despite being in Japan during the war, and thus in enemy territory, was remarkably like home ground. Hiroshima was bigger than Glossop – more the size of Stockport or indeed Southport – but the lives its inhabitants were living, attending schools or working in offices, factories and hospitals and riding bikes and catching trams, were very familiar. Here were people like us. Before he described the flash that came out of the blue, Hersey lovingly established his subjects so that they stopped being 'Japs', alien stereotypes, and became neighbours and friends. So their narratives were convincing and devastating. This is exactly what each of them was doing on the morning of 6 August 1945 and this is what then happened to each of them next. The contrast between the normality of their waking-up and the package of horror delivered, like the post, just after breakfast by an American bomber, was too obscene to be accepted. If it was a good world, things like that ought not to happen.

And how could *our* side have done this terrible thing? Reading *Hiroshima* dissolved my naïve 'Alvar Liddell' version of World War Two, as parodied above in Chapter Five. In rejecting it I really was putting away childish things. 'Sides' did not make sense any more. I had lost belief in the innate wickedness of all Japanese. Suddenly they stopped being vicious, yellow, slit-eyed, sadistic bastards and became just people. By extension I came to doubt the inalienable iniquity of all Germans. They too were just people and did not have to be dead before being declared good. But lest all that assertion of born again goodwill towards the human race, stemming from some holiday reading, seems too good to be true, let me confess that it was accompanied, in the heat of my adolescent brain, by an alternative negative stereotype. I came to hate Americans. It was the Yanks that had nuked Hiroshima. For by now I had shed another illusion – the Alvar Liddell propaganda that the atomic bomb was the achievement of brilliant British scientists assisted by plodding American technicians. The bomb was an all-American product so I was free to blame Harry S Truman, the nice guy in the rimless glasses who had stepped into Roosevelt's shoes and ordered the bombing of Hiroshima. Not only that but, *only three days later*, before the bewildered Japanese had had time to surrender, he had ordered a repeat performance at Nagasaki. Even if, by some specious body count the taking out of Hiroshima could be set against the cost of conquering Japan by conventional means, there could be no conceivable justification for an immediate second holocaust. The charge against Truman in respect of Nagasaki was unanswerable. Its gravity appalled me in 1947 and it still worries me. The unnecessary destruction of that city was as bad as any of the multiplicity of massacres the appalling Second World War engendered.

I was of course as wrong to hate Truman as I was to love Stalin. During my last years at school, through the benevolence of the Marshall Plan and the Berlin Airlift, as well as by firm use of the nuclear deterrent, he remodelled both Germany and Japan as prosperous free market democracies and saved western Europe from the slavery imposed by Stalin on those parts of the continent the Red Army conquered. That scenario seems obvious now but for decades I was blinded to it by the pervasive leftism of intellectual communities I frequented. I became the prisoner of simple minded formula – 'capitalism = America = wicked = capitalism'. Light eventually dawned in Berlin in 1985, in the queue at the Friedrichstrasse checkpoint. As the Stasi man scrutinised my face in conjunction with the image on my passport, I knew at last that west was best. Four years later, that truth having become universally acknowledged, the Wall came tumbling down.

So now that I could at last read there was plenty going on in my head. However in the halcyon days following the School Cert I discovered a pleasure that exceeded even curling up with a good book. It was talking to girls. That happened in the course of an unaccustomed coming together among members of VA. It was induced not only by post exam euphoria but also by the prospect of farewells. Staying on into the sixth form was far from automatic, even for 'A' formers, and those that did stay would hereafter find themselves divided by the 'sides' for Sixth Science and Sixth Modern inhabited different territories, physically as well as culturally. Unlike the Boys and Girls sides of Room 15, which now suddenly ceased to divide us as conversational intercourse leapt a barrier hitherto insuperable despite being invisible. With formal lessons abandoned and the end of term approaching, I was amazed to find myself crossing the room to chat with Margaret, Mary, Pamela, Lavinia, Helen, Lilian and other remote beings with whom for five years we boys had shared a classroom but not a network. Soon I found myself included in social activities that were truly coeducational. We took photographs of each other and signed the backs of the prints, adding 'SC' to our names as though the School Certificate was a degree or a decoration. I even lingered in Norfolk Square after school, leaning nonchalantly on my bike and coming on in blatant disregard of one of the Gauleiter's Commandments – thou shalt not engage in public chattings up at the bus stop. Best of all were coeducational bicycle rides to the moorland Broombank Reservoir where wild swimming was to be enjoyed in deep, cool, clear yet peaty-black waters. It was an enchanted place surrounded by heather and bracken and dry stone walls and it was supplied with little sandy beaches on which, in that fabled summer, a tropical sun every day beat down. The absence of changing facilities further lowered some erstwhile barriers.

To say I liked girls' bodies would of course be an understatement. Now we had reached fifteen or sixteen the bloom of youth was incandescent. Even girls previously categorised as plain blossomed into dazzling assemblages of sleek hair, bright eyes, inviting lips and vibrant skin moulded into exciting shapes. Even porky lads like me stretched out, substituting muscle for fat. My 85 year old Granny noticed the change when she caressed my firm shoulders with gratifying awe. And so she should have because, disdaining DND 838, I had just pedalled the sixty miles from Glossop to Southport. So sure, in at last encountering my female classmates, not as an alien species, but as living, breathing fellow beings, there was fire in the loins. But there was something else as well. There was delight in the heart and the head. For as well as breathing and heaving they did talking as well. They were actually easier to talk to than boys usually were. They did not show off like most boys habitually did. They seemed ready to talk about *feelings* instead of pretending they had not got any. They were less into sport and hobbies and not necessarily averse to discussing school work, provided it was on the Arts side, like I was. So I could confess a taste for poetry without being ridiculed. They even laughed at my jokes, particularly, I began to notice, when I laughed at myself. With girls you did not have to keep up that exhausting front all the time. Did I also find them, nurturing and sympathetic? Yes, probably. This was 1947, when the women of England, having tasted war work, to say nothing of the Yanks, had bolted back to the kitchen and the cradle, cheered all the way to the sink by their returning heroes. That quintessential post war year lay deep in the trough between the original 'votes for women' wave of feminism and the newer and mightier one that broke in the 1960s. So the girls I now met had been brought up to cultivate gentleness, gentility – and femininity. But that did not make them soppy. I encountered among them a mental toughness that matched my own. In those days to acknowledge that male and female were different, and that the difference deserved celebration, was not offensive. That did not mean that the difference was hierarchical, not at my father's school anyway. Boys and girls were intellectual equals. That was not in doubt. The probability that motherhood would interrupt the careers of most girls was not seen as a reason why they should not, on the same terms as boys, enter the sixth form and go on to higher education. A university training was valuable in its own right. That I think was Dad's relatively progressive position.

My coming out culminated on the last day of term. On that exhilarating afternoon my bike and I and nobody else, walked all the way home with Sylvia Hurst. She was probably not going into the Sixth, so maybe this would be her very last day of all. Thus it was sad as well as sweet. And I fell in love. We know that this was not the last time in my school career that I was stunned by Cupid's dart. Actually it was not the first either. Just before Christmas 1942, when I was ten and the war was turning on its axis at Stalingrad, I had fallen in love with Pamela Butterworth who, sad to say, had eyes only for Ben Garlick. For a week I suffered bewildering pangs but then the amazing preoccupation just vanished, as quickly as it had struck, and for another five years, although increasingly aroused by sex, I remained a stranger to love. Not any more though. This was the most real of real things. Henceforth Sylvia possessed me – a *mental* Sylvia that is. The idea of Sylvia and images of my beloved filled my consciousness and colonised my mind. So the mental Sylvia came with us on holiday to Cornwall. It was physically and culturally a formidable trek. In those days when the old Roman road system was about all we had, it took Dad three long days of hard driving. And he with his piles, for which he found fleeting relief in an air cushion. In the course of that odyssey I was introduced to exotic regions served by the Great Western, in which it was surprising that the natives actually spoke a guttural form of English and even seemed broadly familiar with modern technology. Actually these far flung locations were not as exotic as I had expected since their appearance coincided closely with the images in S R Badmin. We – the mental Sylvia and I – had to admit that Old England in the flesh was as pretty as Badmin insisted. So at Broadway and Painswick we surrendered unconditionally to the Cotswolds. We lingered in honey-coloured tea shops and sauntered along an avenue of venerable yews among the resting places of village ancestors. Next day, with Dad clinging to the wheel and clenching his buttocks, we caught a glimpse of Badmin's Elysian terraces as DND 838 made a transit of Bath. Then, at blissful Wells and blitzed Exeter, we were awestruck in our first encounters with the Gothic cathedral. The much-thumbed Badmin cut-away was now set before us, resplendent in 3D. For the next fortnight the mental Sylvia was my adored and faithful companion. We plunged together into Atlantic surf, recited Milton together at sunset on serene cliffs, and queued companionably to see James Mason in *The Upturned Glass*. During our virtual honeymoon she left my side only once, declining the offer of an afternoon of trainspotting at Exeter St David's, where in the last summer before nationalisation, the Southern Railway's upstart 'Atlantic Coast Express', flaunting an observation car to delight passengers speeding from Waterloo to Padstow, crossed the very path of its regal elder, the GWR's 'Cornish Riviera Limited' [Paddington to Penzance].

Twice Dad trespassed on the idyll. First, in the car between Falmouth and Truro, he suddenly burst out singing, his choice being 'Who is Sylvia?' a love song from *The Two Gentlemen of Verona*. It could have been coincidence. He head was full of Shakespeare, baritone solos from the 'Complete Works' not infrequently sweetened our car journeys, and the summer of '47 was succulent enough to move anyone to song. Nevertheless I was visibly confused, particularly when I thought I saw a smile on the singer's lips and suspected that Mum on the back seat was suppressing a giggle. The second intrusion however was vastly more momentous. Indeed for both of us it was life-changing. It signalled a calamity, the outcome of which was that, although Sylvia did after all join Sixth Modern at the start of the autumn term, I did not. Out of the blue – literally, the afternoon was drenched in the azure brilliance that pulls artists to St Ives – by the harbour wall of that iconic Old England fishing port, as I took the first lick of an ice-cream, and without the balm of any preliminary except maybe a 'by the way', I was abruptly informed that my education at Glossop Grammar School was now complete. In September I was to join the sixth form of the Manchester Grammar School. Just like that. No ifs or buts and not even the semblance of debate. Dad had spoken. It was, he announced, exactly what I needed, the perfect solution to a problem it seems he had been wrestling with quite without my knowledge. At this new school I would unquestionably do well, move on in due course to Oxford and inevitably become famous, thereby warming the cockles of my proud parents' hearts. Let the trumpet sound and the bells ring out. I would have the best possible teachers, dripping to a man with academic distinction and metropolitan sophistication, dwarfing the ruck of provincial plodders he had to make do with at benighted Glossop. Then of course there would the other boys, all those 'good fellows' with whom I would engage in that festival of spot-knocking-off he had been promising me ever since the days of that Christ Church/Woolsack fantasy he had conceived in the aftermath of my winning a Scholarship without actually cheating. Anyway it was fixed. My future was at 'MGS' – he had already taken possession of the initials, perhaps in token of the cosy hobnobbing he had engaged in with a certain Eric James. That personage it turned out was the '*High* Master' – nothing so mundane as a mere 'head' – of the great and famous school for which I was destined. In retrospect Dad's coup seems bold. Manchester Grammar School was hard to get into. Boys of eleven had to pass a test much stiffer than the Scholarship and even at sixth form level we might expect that the calibre of candidates would have been formally assessed. Not so in my case. A letter and/or a few words, perhaps confined to the telephone – plus no doubt a bill for the fees since Mum and Dad were too well off for a free place – seems to have done the trick and the magnanimous James had graciously acceded to Dad's request without requiring any evidence beyond a father's say-so of the intellectual prowess he claimed for his son. In the club of headmasters, it would seem, a nod was as good as a wink. Anyway I was in, sight unseen. Had Dad not done well? He indicated that some expression of gratitude might be in order. I failed to produce it. Instead I finished my ice cream, while appropriately a boat came in.

My initial reaction was not to question, still less to resist. I simply refused to acknowledge Dad's 'Declaration of St Ives'. I recall no further discussion then or during the rest of the holiday. The matter was closed. I remembered that the route back to our hotel ran briefly alongside the GWR main line, so for the moment the prospect of copping a 'King', or at least a 'Castle', concentrated my mind. It turned out to be a bad day in that respect as well and I had no such luck. I did not even discuss Dad's bombshell with mental Sylvia. While the sun shone let our happiness not to be besmirched. Which resolution insulated me from reality all the way back to Glossop via London. Dad's piles had also responded to sea and sun so he piloted DND 838 in a single long hop along the A30, stopping only for lunch at Crewkerne, a feast of succulent gammon and fresh-picked peas, the best meal, said my parents, since before the war. In London we stayed at Norbury instead of Selsdon, where Leslie was now sick unto death. I enjoyed Marion and David's house. It had records and pictures as well as books and the furniture reminded me of my post war planning books, although it was a pity they did not have an anglepoise. Students kept ringing up to enquire about courses at the Bec Literary Institute, of which David was the Principal and which Dad consequently disparaged. David was Welsh as well as full of himself. Mum did not like him either. She said he patronised her and maybe he did. But I enjoyed listening to the grown-up conversation that circulated around politics, the arts, religion and the effect on public morality of the 'use of rubber'.

Back in Glossop the shores of the heather-girt reservoir remained as inviting as any Cornish beach and mental Sylvia and I accepted their invitation. But, now we were back, why not a moorland tryst with the actual flesh and blood Sylvia? That was the rub. It rubbed so hard it inflamed the acne on my neck. Butterflies over a reunion with Sylvia at least kept the big issue at bay a little longer. It supressed anticipation of the daily trek to Eric James's quasi-monastic swot-shop to endure mutual spot-knocking among cocky males untamed by any civilising female presence. The thing was I wanted Sylvia – but I was scared. It was agony, this thing called love. It was all the things songs said it was. So there I was, bewitched, bothered and bewildered. A month of romantic longing had transformed a likely lass into a goddess on a pedestal. By mid-August the smooth-tongued chatterer of July had become fair Sylvia's tongue-tied swain. How anyway would I make contact? Remember this was 1947 and, except it seemed in London, hardly anybody was on the phone. It was only very recently that one had appeared in the draughty hall at Holly Wood. Without going so far as to knock on Sylvia's door and ask her out, I did often try to contrive a meeting. I wandered the streets and park hoping for a chance encounter, while at the same time dreading it. With increasing frequency I pedalled up Victoria Street to survey a usually blank facade, next door to the Nag's Head, which concealed my beloved. That it was almost always blank was a relief as well as a disappointment. Eventually however I was rewarded – and terrified – by a glimpse of my lady by an upper window binding her hair, but unaware of my gaze. Then I realised I was a Peeping Tom and felt ashamed. Today I suppose I would have also have accused myself of stalking. Remember too that accusing myself had become a way of life. The new post-School Cert me who read books, talked to girls and went swimming in wild waters had still not recovered the inner cleanliness lost that Sports Day two years before. I remained a heap of corruption, unworthy to grace Sylvia's divine presence. Was she not, in the words of the song, 'holy, fair and wise'? Maybe it was self-loathing that transformed the spot on my neck into a vicious carbuncle that had me at the doctor's the night before the School Cert results came out. Or maybe what that eruption truly betokened was the stress of perpetually denying the onward march of the future. MGS was going to happen. It was no good pretending.

I was dreading the results. Not that I had any worries about my own marks. I knew they would be outstanding. What I feared was meeting Sylvia, for nearly everybody came in to school that morning to collect their 'letters of success', so it was a big social occasion as well as a day of judgement. The outcome was a big surprise. For some reason Sylvia did not turn up and relief at her non-appearance made more impact than disappointment at my own grades. Quite a few of VA, like brainy Margaret Daniels, genius Bob Williamson and beautiful Pam Butterworth, collected 'distinctions' straight across the board. Not me though. I only got two of them, although my mark in History was stratospheric. I knew that because in those days actual marks as well as overall grades were published. I was not too bothered about my unexciting string of 'credits'. Miserable sinner that I was, I had few doubts about my intellectual calibre. The examiners must have made a mistake and also the Geometry paper had been unfair. Could my undistinguished School Cert even prove a blessing in disguise? Would it perhaps be insufficient to satisfy Eric James? Unfortunately his eyelids batted not. Members of the headmasters' club could fix a snowstorm in the Sahara. Dad even fixed it for me to get a prize next speech day. By increasing the number of prizes available and by totting up aggregate marks, instead of simply the number of distinctions won, he managed to include me among the top performers.

Thus following the Declaration of St Ives, as distraction was piled on distraction, the rest of the holiday was passed in silence on the big issue. Which was very silly because there were many things to be said on several sides of the MGS question and you would hope that, in any halfway happy family, some of them at least might have got calmly debated, preferably before any decision was made, but if necessary afterwards, with a view to making the best of it. Dad's position was undoubtedly valid. First, he was embarrassed by his son's presence in his school and anticipated an intensification of awkwardness in the more liberal conditions of the sixth form, particularly as he would then actually teach me. I think he feared for his authority and dignity and fair enough. Authority and dignity were basic tools of his trade. Secondly, he wanted me to have the best possible chance of academic success and a flying start to a career – a project that has been unfairly dubbed the 'Christ Church/Woolsack syndrome'. I do not doubt he wanted those things because he loved his son and wanted him to relish the pleasures of the mind and also to enjoy future job satisfaction and not just because, like his old mum, he was a dedicated social climber and looked forward to basking in the glory of my achievements. Very reasonably – at that time Manchester Grammar School headed the league tables for Oxbridge scholarships with some forty per year – he judged the teaching, the ethos, the peer group values and the Oxbridge connexions available there more likely to bring home the academic bacon than the facilities, human and material, available at his own modest little academy. Finally, for both the above reasons, unless he could have sent me away to a boarding school, he would have preferred me to have gone to MGS right at the start of my secondary education. However there had been a problem at that time, over and above the matter of submitting an only quasi-literate lad to an entrance test scarcely less demanding than that for the imperial civil service in Mandarin China. It was that there was a war on. He and Mum hesitated to submit their boy to a daily thirty mile round trip to and from a destination already several times favoured by the Luftwaffe and maybe slated by Marshall Goering for some happy returns. So was my journey really necessary? In the circumstances, they decided, perhaps it was not. That showed understandable parental prudence. However after the war, and after the School Cert, a quite different situation prevailed. Again, that was fair enough.

But so too was my case. Despite being the Gauleiter's son, a position that was not invariably unenviable, and despite imperfections exhaustively rehearsed in earlier chapters, I liked the place and objected to being arbitrarily uprooted, particularly since there had been absolutely no consultation and, what is more, the radical plan was to be implemented yesterday if not before. What did he take me for? Was I his son or his slave? Was it not human nature to prefer the familiar to the unfamiliar, unless and until the former became intolerable, which in this case it certainly was not? Anyway I was sceptical about the big push for academic laurels. I was not against them. Although not as exciting as looking and thinking – and now reading as well – getting some would be nice and sooner or later, I appreciated, I would have to collect enough of them to get a licence to switch on my anglepoise. But why couldn't I just swot at Glossop? People from our school *did* sometimes get into Oxford, despite what Dad dismissed as the Neanderthal teaching of his glum, narrow-minded colleagues. Which was an outrageous slur anyway. He did not quite put it like that but the drift of the tea table rant was generally in that direction. Sure nobody on the staff delivered the charismatic lessons he sometimes managed but, as earlier pages have amply demonstrated, the level of pedagogic competence at GGS was high and Miss Sillito in particular had inspired me. What a pity she had got another job and was leaving. She had shown me that, provided that your learning was well organised, it was what you worked out for yourself rather than what you were told that really counted. That was what made learning enjoyable. At MGS however I guessed, perhaps wrongly, that regurgitating what some clever dick in a gown dished out would be the standard requirement. Would they ever let me try out my own ideas, the way Miss Sillito did? I was coming to think highly of my own ideas. Had I not sussed out the character of the class struggle? Had I not seen off the posturing Clive Bell and, with John Hersey's help, passed judgement on President Truman? So although MGS might be a fine place in its way, did I really *need* to go there? I was not given a chance even to raise the question. The Declaration was final. Without a why or a wherefore the Gauleiter – didn't the nickname fit? – just expected me to bow to his will. To satisfy it I was to go off, on my own, into a totally strange environment where I knew nobody and all the others were long since firmly bonded. It would hurt. It wasn't fair.

These were reasonable doubts and fears. If, over a period of time, they had been talked through in a relaxed way they might have been overcome and I might in the end have gone along with Dad's basically sensible prescription for my future schooling. If for example they had been thrashed out during the few days we had recently spent with Marion and David enjoying rational debates about politics and such, then maybe Dad and I would have fetched up in something like accord. There was however another argument, one that for me was crucial, that would not have been put on the table even if open debate had been permitted. It did not even figure in the hysterical explosion of conflicting attitudes that was the eventual outcome of the Declaration of St Ives. For my chief difficulty with the MGS project, one which eclipsed all the above arguments, was simply inadmissible. It was about *girls*. I liked them. I desired them. Above all I enjoyed talking to them. Doing so had changed the quality of my life. At last, during those exhilarating post exam weeks, I had discovered the value of something about our school that until then I had scarcely noticed. It was *coeducational*. That gave it an ethos that, without being soft, was both more natural and gentler than could be expected to flourish at a boys-only school. For me that was decisive. There were no girls at Manchester Grammar School so I did not want to go there. Its wholly masculine character, I believed, must impoverish it. It was not of course alone in that deprivation. Many grammar schools, together with nearly all independent schools and all the colleges at Oxford and Cambridge, existed in a similar divorce from what was normal and natural. But although 'girls' was the decisive factor in my position I could never have discussed with my parents what I saw as the critical deficiency of MGS vis à vis Glossop Grammar School. Why? Because it touched on sex and talking about sex was taboo in our family, and probably in most families at the time. It was just not a fact of life parents and children could contemplate. Which placed us in a cruel dilemma because what I wanted to say was actually more about gender than sex. That however was a distinction that had not yet entered the culture. Remember this was 1947, two years before *The Second Sex*, Simone de Beauvoir's pioneering assertion of a new feminism, took its place beside *The Red Light: Things a Boy Should Know* on the dirty books stall on Glossop market. You couldn't miss it for there was a provocative nude on the cover. Thus, living as we did in post war darkness, my principal objection to Manchester Grammar School never got a hearing.

It was the very last day of the holidays before anything happened in the matter. On that Monday afternoon both my parents took me to Manchester for what, I suppose, was some sort of confirmatory interview. Anyway I was introduced to Eric James. He seemed OK, I had to admit. He was quite young [38 actually] and had the tweedy relaxed style of the nice master in *The Guinea Pig* and that made him easy to talk to. From Wikipedia I learn he had taught at Winchester but had himself been educated at a grammar school and maybe that had made him adept at crossing social barriers. The charm of the High Master surprised me because Dad said he was on the Science Side so I was expecting him to be gruffly interrogative like Mr Casey. Anyway he made Dad seem like a stuffed old shirt and Mum too seemed out of her depth, like she was with David, who was also a touch tweedy. With the holidays still going on and no boys about, the general look of the school, which we were allowed to explore unsupervised, also seemed OK. Dad got a fit of the Greyfriars when we came across a statue of a chap in Tudor dress but otherwise the buildings were refreshingly modern. They were red brick and reminded me of Dad's old school at Stretford. They were surrounded by a vast ocean of playing field and that was alarming. Avoiding flying balls amid those multitudinous green seas was going to be problematic.

However the scene reminded me powerfully of suburban Manchester, the paradise I had loved and lost the last time Dad had taken my life by the scruff of the neck. Which, considering that we were standing in the middle of suburban Manchester, was scarcely surprising. So was paradise about to be regained? Maybe, because it was all fixed that I would start in the History Sixth on Thursday. I was to report to Eric James's office at 9-15 that day. However I was not told where my cloakroom peg would be and that worry niggled as we sped homeward to something and chips. But the day had not gone too badly. Perhaps I could hack it after all.

Next day I realised I probably couldn't. That Tuesday term began at Glossop Grammar School and I imagined the survivors of VA, now promoted to the Sixth Form, warbling 'Lord behold us with thy blessing' in the baroque Assembly Hall. Sylvia, I was told, would after all be among 'those returning' and a reunion in the safety of a classroom seemed less daunting than a free encounter on the street. The chance would have been a fine thing. For I would not be there. Instead I had two days to kill before joining MGS. What was I to do with myself? In a daze I wandered through the empty park and found my steps taking the familiar path over the Royle towards school. At the top of Fitzalan Street I halted and, at the far end, glimpsed files of pupils ritually following the prescribed routes among the school buildings. What happy captivity. How achingly I longed for its gentle fetters. The sense of exclusion was overwhelming. Overwhelmed by great sobs I retraced my steps.

I cannot remember Tuesday afternoon or Wednesday nor do I remember much about getting myself to Rusholme that Thursday morning. I must have got the 8-09 to 'Ashburys for Belle Vue' and en route, from ingrained habit, no doubt scanned the sheds at Gorton for a lurking Pacific. At Ashburys I would have caught the 53 Bus. Now I was grown up, instead of my satchel, I had been supplied with a battered leather container, something between an attaché case and a cabin trunk, still adorned with the luggage label of a shipping line. Austerity ruled and making do was de rigeur. By 9-15 I was sitting as instructed in Eric James's outer office as gowned and tweedy figures swept in and out. One sang 'We plough the fields and scatter' as he swept and that right lustily. Others toted sets of text books which bore no resemblance to the mouldy green slabs of congealed blotting paper I knew from the big cupboard in Room 2 of blessed memory. Instead they were mostly brand new and some were actually Penguins. How very modern and how boldly un-austere. Though miserable I was trying to be fair. I sportingly scored one up to MGS.

The next episode made it two up. I was taken to meet Mr Bunn who was to be my form master. He was not effusive. Indeed he appeared not want me around at all. Come back at two o'clock, he said. In the meantime a walk was suggested, or perhaps ordered. There were some excellent water colours at the Whitworth and I could do worse than go there. He supplied minimal navigational assistance and omitted to mention what the Whitworth was. Yet I negotiated the sea of pitches and struck out in the direction of the city centre, half relieved to be given a temporary reprieve and half fearful of the demands of what I took to be a first assignment. I did not know a watercolour from a coat of whitewash although I did know I was no good at art because Mr Gooch had many times indicated as much. However there would be a test at two so I had better start learning fast. I pounded the pavements of a busy bus route, lined with flea-pit cinemas, used car lots and a violin emporium. The curry houses and sari boutiques of a later Rusholme had not yet opened their doors. Behind a scruffy patch of withered grass opposite a large hospital I found the gloomy bulk of the Whitworth Art Gallery. It was brick but too grimy to look modern. I slipped past a suspicious attendant to confront glass cases full of what looked like old clothes and second hand furnishing fabrics. Then I found an inner sanctum lined with pictures, just like Grandpa Southport's dining room, only in pale light not bright sunshine. They were beautiful. These painters liked the same things as I did, like weather and rocks and trees and torrents and the occasional Gothic cathedral. One of them was called Turner, it said on the frame. He had a lot of initials and I remembered him from the prints catalogue Dad and I used to pore over. He had this remarkable knack of communicating feelings, as well as places and objects, in what really did seem to be nothing more substantial than coloured water washed over a sheet of paper that was then hung out to dry. Despite being congested with misery, I was moved. It was a turning point. I began to reconsider the judgement about me and art.

As recollected in tranquillity and from a great distance in time, I regret what happened over the next twenty four hours. This new school was on the ball. Not only was the atmosphere youthful, brisk and modern and tuned to some radical ideas about learning – like it is fun and borders

350

between subjects are there to be crossed – but the men in charge knew a thing or two about how to motivate screwed-up adolescents, without either smothering them or antagonising them. Note that Mr Bunn had not told me to wait in the corridor, or even in the library, but instead to quit the premises – at ten o'clock on a school day! – and wander off into town. But note also that he made no compromise with rigour. He did not tell me to kill time but instead told me to do something useful. He set a task although he paid me the compliment of not spelling it out in patronising detail. He was getting me to find out in a grown-up way but equally he made it clear that in a grown-up way I was accountable.

However registering appreciation of how they did things at MGS emerged only over time. The imperative present was less serene. I had to be back at school for dinner. That deadline was not set by Mr Bunn, who had specified two o'clock, not twelve thirty, but by Mum, whose conviction that the human frame requires a substantial fix of fat and carbohydrate at least every four hours, was beyond challenge. So I trekked back across the playing steppes and sought out the canteen, clutching a ticket I had somehow acquired. It seemed additionally unfair that, even while beyond my comfort zone in so many other respects, I was now expected, instead of my usual mid-day pie and chip sandwiches, to retch daily on a penitential plateful of gristle and custard. The maelstrom of the canteen was every bit as bad as I feared. It was not just the mince and stewed apple but sitting silent among a chattering company of friends reunited. However yet another tweedy figure spotted me, sat next to me and did his best to engage me in adult conversation, while actually sharing the common mess. It was truly a republic of learning I had been projected into. Masters and boys sitting informally together was another first. That made it three up to MGS.

And so to the Library – it seemed surprisingly short on books – and the expected eyeball to eyeball about the Turners and Cotmans. It never happened. Instead the place gradually filled up with other boys who studiously ignored me, the way ins gathered together customarily ignore outs. Enter Mr Bunn without ceremony. Announcing the timetable was a chore rapidly accomplished and he proceeded within minutes to serious business. History. What is it and how do historians do it? His discourse was fascinating. Four up and counting. At three it was time for French which was to happen upstairs, so I kept the others in sight as they navigated the corridors. This new chap was even brisker. We were about to study the Romantic period in French literature. It had two founding fathers. Chateaubriand was one but the other sounded German and surely should have been a founding mother, since her name was Madame de Stael. Those luminaries were followed by four other perpetrators of Romance, namely Victor Hugo, Lamartine, Alfred de Vigny and Alfred de Musset. Well the hour must have done me some good because that useful structure has stayed firm in my head ever since, despite seriously disliking *Les Miserables* and never having had any further engagement with the others, apart from learning a comic verse about the last named. Which brought the total to five up and furthermore I was now free to bolt for the bus stop. There at least one of the five points had to be deducted, if not two. For a snooty young man, who must have been a prefect since he seemed to be controlling the queue, sauntered in my direction and drew attention to my bare head. I stuttered my explanation but as soon as he had gone began to seethe more than somewhat. Indeed I was outraged. Caps had gone out at Glossop when clothes rationing came in and in the sixth form you could surely do what you liked with your own head and did not have to put up with being publicly bawled out by somebody your own age. Anyway nobody had said anything about uniform when I was smuggled into MGS and I had not even been allocated a cloakroom peg, so where would I put the bloody thing even if I knew where to get one. Definitely two down.

In the debate about MGS, girls were the big deal not caps. But a cap was something parents could understand so at teatime I played it big. That was a mistake because things then started to escalate, like they do, and not long after Alvar Liddell signed off a very big storm indeed was gathering, comparable in intensity with the hurricanes of my infancy, like the one revolving around the attempted assassination of my new-born sister. They thought all that was all over. It wasn't though. As it happened we were not alone in the kitchen that evening, for my St Anne's grandparents were in residence. Grandpa Dick was in a state of sad decline. The cheerful playmate who had once let me 'help' him in the dark room, while he discoursed freely about life and art, had become a confused old man. He had never properly recovered from a bout of shingles suffered, just after D Day, three years earlier, and now he was all but blind, unsteady on his feet and less than compos mentis. Which was a pity because to him

I just might have been able to unburden myself. That nonconforming Nonconformist loved to fly a kite, to pursue a promising idea without bothering much about what 'they' might think. 'I'll fear not what men say', the motto of Bunyan's Pilgrim, might have been his as well. So he would have understood about the difference between the free and independent learning I had come to value and the intellectual pack drill I feared might be in store for me at Manchester Grammar School. And of course he would have understood about girls. He had delighted in the company of women to an extent that disconcerted Dad and, I think, continued to anger his wife. For Granny had not lost her wits. Nor had she lost sight of destiny – the vision of family progress inherited from her father, the Rawtenstall grocer. Its path lay from the rough and tumble of trade into the gentility of professional occupation, first at a lower then at a higher level. Thus her brother had risen to become an optician and her sister became a domestic science teacher. Then a change of gear as her favourite son became a grammar school head and another as her only grandson now grasped the torch that would surely light us all to Christ Church and the Woolsack! Was it coincidence that doting Dad had his mother to stay with us in the very week I was to take my first step on the ladder to fame? Hadn't we done well? Wouldn't we do even better? So the debacle at the tea table must have appalled Granny. She hated 'words'. Scream quietly or the neighbours will hear. Soon therefore she took her stricken spouse upstairs to the refuge of the spare room. Helen too must have disappeared, perhaps pleading homework. Which left the two principals and Mum, who no doubt busied herself with the washing up. During a brief lull we adjourned to the study where, having drawn the curtains against the neighbours, he installed himself with stylised humphing on his leather fireside throne, at the foot of which I slumped in lesser but defiant state. Soon Mum appeared to bear witness from the other side of the hearth and probably took up some knitting. There, between eight and late, Dad and I fought the first and bloodiest battle in a thirty years war that lasted for the rest of his life. Sure, there were truces but none of them lasted, not anyway until his last bleak year in a 'care' home.

We soon left the cap behind and some real issues emerged, although not of course the one that really mattered – that is girls. In all the storm and stress of that black night at Holly Wood we never got to the heart of the matter. Which makes you despair of the family as a medium of communication. We covered a lot of other ground however. They thought I was wickedly turning down a great opportunity because at my wonderful new school I would have to wear a cap and put up with plain fare in the canteen. That was not what I meant at all. What I was trying to say was that I was being asked to make a radical adjustment to my way of life that was not of my choosing, was in my view unnecessary and which had been sprung upon me without any semblance of consultation. Even though they knew nothing about the girls bit, let alone the Sylvia bit, you might have thought they could empathise with the rest of the agony I was experiencing. The last few days had been all but unbearable. If this was what growing up was like, then let me go back to the box room and scream and scream. There was no sympathy from either parent for the sheer *pain* I was suffering. Yet Dad seemed to think I should be grateful for landing me in this mess. And, to the exclusion of his son's feelings, he seemed obsessed with audience reactions to my wilfulness. If I did not stick it out, what would 'they' think? 'They' included her upstairs, the staff and governors of Glossop Grammar School and, unbelievably, Eric James. I could not let down the great High Master whose favour Dad had so deftly canvassed. Why not? What was he to me or me to him? If by opting out I made Dad look a fool, then it served him right. You … you …! I do not suppose I actually uttered the obscenities that buzzed my heated brain. I was still only fifteen and thumbing a nose at the Gauleiter would have taken more guts that even the present occasion lent me. And so it went on. He persisted in self-righteous ranting while I gave way to naked hysteria. I shouted, screamed and wept. I must have smashed things as well for broken ornaments soon littered the carpet and Mum fetched the Hoover. When I wiped a tear-stained face I found blood on my hands. I had rubbed slivers of glass into my cheeks. The whole household must by now have been very frightened. Even curious neighbours might have noted something happening at the big house behind the rhododendrons. And so to bed.

In the morning Dad gave in. The capitulation was as sudden as the original announcement of the MGS plan. Actually I woke up strangely refreshed and expecting to go to Manchester. I felt quite calm at the prospect. The tension having been released and my position – or part of it – having been stated, I was now better disposed to the scheme than at any time so far. If Dad had not blinked I should probably have caught the 8-09 without fuss, the second day would probably have turned out better than the first, and over the weekend a different perspective might have emerged. Before very long I might have settled down sufficiently and responded positively to what was obviously a good school. Eventually no doubt I would have gravitated to Oxford or Cambridge and quite liked it there because I would have been better prepared for Oxbridge ways and anyway would have found solidarity in the company of fellow Mancunians, who lay among the ivory towers as thick as the deep deposit of Etonians. In due course I might have fetched up, not on the Woolsack, but probably in some comfortable academic niche, perhaps even finding a modest chair at a new 1960s university, like the one at York that Lord James of Rusholme came to preside over. In the process I would been liberated from the Gauleiter and also weaned from Dad, for whom eventually, from a position of mature autonomy, I might have come to feel suitable affection. That happy outcome would not have been very different from what he had planned. That the MGS plan was basically sensible has never been disputed. My achievements would have been less dramatic than those in Dad's fantasies but they would have been enough to cheer him. Thus over some golden years we might have sunk some happy pints. On the other hand it might not have worked out like that. In particular how would I have met girls? There were none at MGS. They did not do National Service. They were thin on the ground along the banks of the Cherwell and the Cam. I would have found that deprivation very hard.

Anyway, the morning after Armageddon, Dad did capitulate. He said to stay at home. Later he telephoned my mother, who said I was to go back to school after dinner – to *Glossop* Grammar School. So, fortified no doubt with pie, beans and chips, and also with Granny's blessing – no more raised voices, please – I set out along the familiar trail across the Royle and this time did not pull up at the top of Fitzalan Street. That afternoon in Room 7 I joined Mr Hodgett's Geography class. They let me do that favourite subject as part of my Higher School Certificate despite not having done it for School Cert, because then it had clashed with History. Dad today was free with his concessions. Since, for reasons of economy, first and second year sixth formers were sometimes taught together, I even got to sit with Jas, with whom I had never before been in the same class. It was one of the local curricular imperfections Dad had wanted to save me from but the expedient seemed to work OK. 'Dodder' Hodgett's eccentric approach suited me although it showed scant respect for the full range of the syllabus. For the next two terms we made an intensive study of the topography of Alsace and Lorraine. Metz, Toul and Nancy became as familiar as Glossop, Hadfield and Charlesworth. People said Dodder was boring but I liked his way. It was like looking and thinking, with a Baedeker to hand, in the drawing room at Southport. It lacked the zip of the lesson I had experienced the previous day at MGS – French Romantic Literature buttoned up in one hour flat – but it suited me.

But if things went back to normal, they were never the same again. It became apparent that relations between Dad and me had become permanently dislocated. I had not convinced him in debate and he still did not know what I meant – not surprisingly perhaps since I had failed to present my principal argument. Yet, I realised to my astonishment, that I had shown greater resolution, or at least a greater capacity for bloody-mindedness. He had given way. Which was of course a bitter humiliation to him, on account of which he nursed an anger that seethed beneath the surface of our lives and was apt to break through without warning. As for me, I was torn by conflicting feelings. I felt guilt because I had defied my father and also because feeling guilty had become habitual. I felt doubt because I knew his scheme for my future had had a lot going for it. Yet I also felt liberated. It was not independence, not even autonomy, but I certainly had more space to manoeuvre. I despaired of a meeting of minds with Dad but I knew that in a clash of wills I had a better than even chance of prevailing. The upshot was a state of permanent rebellion in which I wasted much of the rest of my life. In particular it hampered my dealings with authority figures. Bosses, for me were liable always to take on Dad-like qualities. That is not a recipe for happiness or even success.

The first crisis came a few weeks after my re-entry. It was triggered by an incident in the school Hall, the baroque masterpiece more than once celebrated above. Miss Hughes, who shared our English teaching with Dad, and whose dealings with the sixth form were relatively informal, was proceeding down, or perhaps up, the girls' staircase – I doubt if even teachers were permitted use of a staircase allocated to the opposite sex. At that very moment it happened that I was making my way up, or down, the boys' staircase. She must have remembered something she wanted to say to me, for she called across. Now, if it is rude, undignified or anaesthetic to call out to someone across a public space then the misdemeanour was surely hers not mine. But it was my response – I know not what it was but I remember believing it inoffensive – that the Gauleiter, emerging from his office, overheard and objected to. My rejection of his rebuke signalled a total silence between us that lasted a full week. Once again it was he who sued for peace – outside the garage while I was putting my bike away. That episode set a pattern. Something would happen, like things inevitably do. It might be something at school. The MGS affair had intensified his unease at having his son as a pupil at his school. Avoiding it had been a major part of his purpose in shipping me out. He said I mocked him to my friends. He fretted, as we know, about his dignity and fair enough, headmasters need plenty of that, but he was wrong to suppose I set out deliberately to prick the bubble he moved in. Well ... he was fairly wrong. The party skit about his speech day report was surely legitimate satire in the Christmas season of 'misrule'. But it was not only incidents at school that bugged us. Once, shortly after he had delivered a tea table polemic against birthday rituals I failed to acknowledge his fiftieth. He had said it meant nothing to him. He could have fooled me. Indeed he did fool me.

Our confrontations followed a predictable pattern. Something would happen. It would prompt an initial shouting match in which both contestants held their ground. When it subsided the not-speaking competition would begin. Once we kept it up for three weeks before he duly blinked. Mealtimes were the worst. Even Mum and Helen, the neutral parties, were abashed so we all munched stolidly and, in obscene parody of monastic custom, pretended to listen to Alvar Liddell. At school it was not so bad for a tacit convention permitted formal exchanges during lessons. Until he found ways of undermining it. We were studying *King Lear*, the theme of which, he heavily insisted, was 'filial ingratitude'. As he declaimed, he fixed me in a glance pregnant with hurt and fury.

How sharper than a serpent's tooth it is, to have a thankless child!

Yet it was always him who gave in. Meanwhile the situation had advantages for me since while the silence lasted I was immune to criticism. It was a poor kind of freedom.

The cold war between Dad and me began at much the same time as the actual Cold War between the super-powers, and it lasted almost as long. When I finally left school – in 1950 to begin National Service before going up to Oxford [he let Eric James know and got a gracious reply] – the prevailing air of volatile animosity was not cleared. Subsequent changes of life made no difference either. The habit of confrontation survived births, marriages and deaths and proved resistant to graduations and promotions, migrations and retirements. It ruined his seventieth birthday party and almost erupted at my mother's funeral. Our last quarrel came in 1978, the year he reached eighty, and it provoked a silence that lasted for almost a year. The casus belli quite escapes me. Then Dad made his last surrender. He embraced senility. And in the last year of his life something a little better happened. I got to stop hating him and even began to like him again, just a bit anyway.

I think I am appalled.

EPILOGUE

One dank November afternoon in 1991 I was jogging around the Manchester suburbs of Didsbury and Burnage. In a way that others thought peculiar, if not perverse, the time of year and the grey weather, as well as the location, delighted me. Indeed it was on a sudden whim that I was that day pounding the wet pavements, instead of thumping as usual on a treadmill. The light had suddenly put me in sharp touch with my earliest memories. It reminded me of when I was very young and we lived, not far away, in Chorlton-cum-Hardy, and my mother used to take me for walks to the 'village' and the park. The prevailing weather remembered from those distant days was just like now – not exactly raining and not exactly foggy but a miasma highlighted in fifty shades of grey. So I left the gym behind and went on the streets. At that time I was coming to the end of the first draft of this book. I had reached 1947 so the events just narrated were much in my mind. And jogging gets you thinking – which is a good reason for doing it. So it is not surprising that, as I avoided the dual carriageway and took refuge in an arcadia of inter-war semis, like 11 Polruan Road, Chorlton, the bijou home in which my infancy was spent, I became aware that a shadowy companion had fallen in beside me. To call him my father's ghost – Dad had been dead for over a decade – would be melodramatic. We were navigating the purlieus of the A34 to Cheadle, not patrolling the ramparts at Elsinore. And there was nothing frightening or even surreal about the presence that kept step with me. It was just my Dad, the nice, 'holiday' Dad, not the stern Gauleiter. I felt entirely at ease and began to talk to him more comfortably than at any time since the cold war between us had broken out. It might have been fifty years earlier and Hitler might just have invaded Russia and we might have been stepping out along Southport beach discussing the implications of that momentous new twist to the war. I had plenty to say today about public events and current trends, like the fate of the grammar schools, but the new lowering of inhibition between us allowed me to talk also about him and me. In less than an hour I got more off my chest than I knew was lying there. When I got home I turned it into a posthumous letter. It did not seem an odd thing to do.

Here then is my delayed farewell to Dad. I have made some amendments to the original text where the sense of the original seemed obscure but I have not substantially altered it. This is what he and I talked about that day. I cringe at some of the phrasing and have changed my mind since 1991 on several of the issues encompassed. I would for example be less harsh about the historic ruling class and the schools they sent their children to. I was already a Thatcherite, and lamenting the lady's recent departure, but since then I have become something of a proper Tory as well. But if the wording is sometimes awkward, some judgements now seem simplistic, and there is a long disconcerting digression, that is how conversations go. This then is what I said to my dead Dad that enticingly grey Manchester day.

Hello Dad!

I seem to be getting to know you better. I am getting to like you better too. Particularly when I think of you as a boy. I can see how, being small, you felt you had to keep up with your manly dad and your lofty brother. Your growth spurt in the trenches was remarkable, wasn't it? I can also see why books so mattered to you in those days. Boys' stories were not only exciting but they were manuals of manliness, showing you how to play up and play the game. What a lot you read! You consumed a whole library of classics, as well as comics by the ton, well before the age I first mastered a single page of that boys' book of aeroplanes you got Uncle Leslie to buy me – the one I memorised and spilled out as all my own work for the Scholarship exam. You never believed that story but it is true. As a boy I was more into looking than reading and I know that bothered you. You thought I might be backward. I wasn't though, just different. I am making amends. The older I get the more I turn to books. Mind you, I am not sure all that boyhood reading was invariably good for you. It made you such a macho little terrier. And I wonder about that stuffy code of honour you picked up from

Tom Brown and Harry Wharton. It was very stern. Pity you did not have comic comics in those days – you know, like the Beano, with strip cartoons laughing at pompous grown-ups. I could never understand why you banned the Beano and the Dandy so I had to look at them surreptitiously. Too many pictures, not enough text, I suppose. But I would never have managed a densely packed comic like the Hotspur which Chris Gillings quaffed greedily every week. He was an even bigger reader than you. Did you know he fetched up on the Bullock Commission, the 1970s government enquiry into national literacy? He became an HMI on the strength of it. Not bad for a 'B' former! I didn't like him though and I don't think you did either. Too pushy by half.

I am glad Miss Tebay persuaded Granny you were bright and deserved to go to grammar school. What they gave you at Blackpool Grammar and then at Bacup and Rawtenstall seems to have been OK. Well, much more than that actually. It seems to have been very like what you gave us at Glossop and, remembering how it was at GGS, I have come to like that a lot better than I ever thought I was going to when I started writing about it. You gave us orderly routines, filled our heads with facts, got us to think about what we had learned and lifted up our hearts with poetry. It was a great formula and I am sorry I was not more appreciative at the time. Thank you very much. Abolishing the grammar schools was crazy. Yes, I know I was in favour of it but I was wrong. It was a pity though that grammar schools, not just yours of course, came in fancy dress. I think you and your fellow grammarians were soppy about the public schools you copied. I am not insensitive to the beauty of that scene – blades on a feather, breathless hushes in the close and so on but there were a lot of things wrong with the public schools of your day. They were brutal and aggressively nostalgic. They pretended the Industrial Revolution had not happened and turned out empire builders instead of businessmen. Perhaps it was their excess of manliness that dragged you and five million lads like you into an unnecessary war and did for a lot of you in the process. You went along with all that. You never doubted your country needed you and at the same time you disapproved of businessmen as a species. Making money was not an honourable calling. Remember how you bristled whenever Uncle Albert arrived with his retinue – he of "t' biggest bloody gas bill i' Morecambe". Despite him being Mum's favourite brother you loathed him and all you thought he stood for. Yet he ran a successful company making useful things, creating jobs and paying dividends – to Mum among others, an 'unearned income' she spent on the rest of us, you included. A book I read a few years ago identified a conflict in English culture between 'northern' and 'southern' values. Well your family went southern. First they took refuge from the smoke in rural Poulton then went off to live in London. Not Mum though, or her parents. They stayed northern and I am glad some of their bluntness rubbed off on me. Inside my head I feel a north-south split. I am not complaining. I like living on a cusp. Borderlands are stimulating.

I think you were wrong about the Great War as well. I am not even sure you were right about the Second. By that I do not mean I don't admire your courage. I have found out exactly how brave you were. I know now that, towards the end, in 1918, you seldom enjoyed the relative safety of a trench but were caught up in a war of movement and that was much more dangerous. I have followed the steps of the 5th Borders and have come to have a better idea what it was like for you. For a while, in those days, you and your mates must have known each dawn might be your last, for they constantly sent you over the top, sometimes more than once in a single week. But you pressed on over the canal, through the Hindenburg Line and on to victory. Wow! By the way, I think it was the St Quentin Canal you leapt over, not the Canal du Nord, as you used to say. But what's in a name? It surely took guts. So in querying the need for the war I am not casting aspersions on the heroism it generated, in you as in so many others. But does the making of heroes justify mass carnage? Did you know the combined death toll for the two wars is now reckoned to be about sixty million? Did you ever think about what it was you were training your ATC boys to do at Hamburg and Dresden? To burn babies. Sure, like so many others, you put your faith in Winnie to know what had to be done. But was he right and did his patriotism not smack of jingoism? You used to be pretty hard on Germans who excused themselves by pleading unthinking patriotism. That's another bone I might pick with you. Your rants about Germans were just plain ignorant. Your mocking talk about Jews was worse. Yes, I know you were not alone in either outrageous attitude but you were bang out of order.

Not that I am disparaging patriotism as such. We could do with some of it in Britain today. No, I never thought I would think that either. But I don't think what they now call a 'multi-cultural' society can work. Instead of each group doing its own thing we need a core of shared values to rally round. So you were right to love your England, the one you found particularly in Shakespeare. I just don't think the England you loved was in danger from the Kaiser's Germany.

England and Germany in 1914 were not all that different from one another and there was plenty of room for both to flourish. Do you remember that film we saw during the war? I am surprised it passed the censor and apparently it really annoyed Churchill. In it the future Colonel Blimp is in Berlin before the first war and he falls in with a thoroughly decent Prussian brother officer. There was no need for them to come to blows. And did you know the Hohenzollerns had absurdly English tastes? I wish you could have been with Su and me when we went to Potsdam a few years ago, while the Cold War was still on. They took us to the Cecilienhof, the palace where Churchill, Stalin and Truman got together in 1945 to complete their carve-up of Europe. But it wasn't a grand palace. It was a modest English country house. Honestly, but for a view of the Berlin Wall from the terrace, you could have believed you were in the Cotswolds or Devon. If they had said the architect was Lutyens it would have been no surprise and nor would it if Siegfried Sassoon had trotted up from the stables or if Rupert Brooke had emerged from the library licking honey from his fingers. On the front lawn we found the only geraniums in the German Democratic Republic, although it is true they were planted to form a hammer and sickle. And guess who this little piece of old England had been built for. The Crown Prince! – the same 'Little Willy' you all used to fall out of your bivouacs giggling over in the trenches. But I digress. My point is that when you condemned 'Prussian militarism' as something unique you were deluded. There was not much to choose between boar-sticking Junkers and fox-hunting squires. Of course I am not saying you could have worked all that out when you were a teenager, what with your country so insisting it needed you. Anyway if you had not volunteered you would have been called up anyway. So off you went to do your bit like brother Bertie in the song. 'We think you ought to go' they warbled in another song. But were they right? Need you have gone? Need millions like you?

But back to courage. Being lamentably lacking in that quality myself, I have come to salute your bravery. I guess you realised long ago that I am not well endowed in the moral fibre department. Your disappointment at my deficiencies in manliness must have gone back long before that terrible day when I chickened out of Manchester Grammar School and afterwards you and I were never the same again. You probably spotted I was yellow when I was scarcely five and couldn't hack it at Moss Park Infants. Then there were my tantrums before that at Polruan Road. Like that night I screamed in the box room and ruined your trip to the pictures. I am sorry I spoilt your evening and hope it did not lead to a big row. Mum wouldn't have liked it, you going off on your own like you did.

Thinking of it has made me cry, fifty nine years old though I am. I really am a wimp. But at least thinking about guts, and you having them and me never finding any, has made me face up to an episode I have suppressed for nearly twenty years. Can I tell you about it?

It was the year Mum died. That summer you came to stay with us in Holland at that house we borrowed. Do you remember how hot it was? It was the week of the golf Open and in the middle of a baking polder you were glued to the car radio. You may remember too that I was having problems at work and the story had even got into the national press, as we discovered when we bought The Times in Amsterdam. There was a witch hunt going on, the target being my friend Philip, who was also my boss. They wanted him out. I could have defended him but I was scared and let discretion be the better part of valour. Oh dear! I had better start at the beginning. It was during the time of the dissolution of the grammar schools. Yes, I am using that word in allusion to Henry VIII and his destruction of the monasteries. Getting rid of the grammar schools, in the service of which you and many like you had spent the best years of your lives, was a comparable act of state-sponsored vandalism and it too had massive consequences, most of them unforeseen. Well, all the local education authorities had to submit plans for closing their socially divisive grammar schools and 'going comprehensive'. Our lot came up with a novel idea that made them briefly famous. They would lop off the sixth forms of their superannuated grammar schools and send the displaced students, with some of their teachers, to the local technical college. Putting all post 16 education and training into a single 'tertiary college' was supposed to promote social harmony, combat elitism and bring about economies of scale. Which was ... well, bullshit. The scheme bristled with flaws. Academically minded sixth form teachers resented being drafted into the philistine tech. Horny-handed trade instructors resented the intrusion of poncey 'A' level studies into their proudly vocational establishment. And furthermore we were kept short of funds and space – we did not have enough room to accommodate the extra students and staff. About the only thing the authority provided by way of extra resources was me. I was appointed to a new post with the fancy title 'Vice Principal [Academic] and Director of Studies'. You may remember that one of the unsuccessful candidates was your successor at Glossop. Small world. However getting a job is one thing but doing it is another and I was not suited to this one. It is true I had a trendy CV, with spells in 'education' as well as teaching, but I had no experience of technical colleges and that of course attracted the scorn of old sweats training plumbers, cooks and secretaries. Furthermore, as I managed to disguise from the panel, I possessed neither guts nor social skills. Perhaps they would have done better to trust the guy now running the comprehensive cobbled together at Glossop when they merged GGS and West End. That must have hurt! But I did my best in the circumstances and launched a new tutorial system to support students who might otherwise have felt lost in a big organisation operating in a mini skyscraper. It worked well enough in the end – but, as is the way with innovation, not in the short term. In the short term crisis, panic, anger and whinging enveloped us.

Inevitably complaints flooded into the education offices, speeches about us were made at council meetings and the local paper began to take a lurid interest in what was going on at the tech. Also an ambitious local politician had a parliamentary seat in his sights and wanted publicity. Someone must have blundered. Somebody must be to blame. The can must be carried. So the council sent in a 'Committee of Enquiry' to find a scapegoat. The Principal, that is my friend Philip, was a shoo-in for that role. He too was quite new to the place and, like me, came from what they called 'up country', so was not to be trusted. They didn't like his style. So at session after session they had him on his toes, fending off charges of inefficiency and also countering innuendoes about his private life. He deftly stood his ground. Like you, he had guts. He had a lot of other good qualities as well. He was good looking, well dressed, elegant even. He had dash and daring as well as a sharp mind. He could think on his feet and fly by the seat of his pants. You would have liked him. He was like one of your favourite head boys – 'Lycidas' for example, whose death at the very end of the war upset you so much. Philip also was ex-aircrew, although he finished his training too late to see action. We used to call him 'Biggles'. Guys like that are rare. Our employers were lucky to have him and they would have done better to find his gallantry engaging rather than threatening. He did not mean any harm, although I am not saying he hadn't done a few silly things. Nothing dishonest. They would never have got him on that. But he was cavalier. And he had discovered he was living in swinging Britain and, although it was a bit late for him, he had some catching up to do. I was to know the feeling myself. Not just yet. In those days I was, 'sea-green incorruptible', as you never tired of quoting in respect of Robespierre. But a few years later, as you tried not to notice, I flipped alright. However back to 1972. If there were peccadilloes to be taken up with poor Philip then hauling him in front of a kangaroo court was not the way to do it. What was happening was unfair and I could and should have done something about it.

When the Committee began its work I assumed that, along with Philip, I must be a prime suspect. They must be out to get me as well as him. It was me that had brought in the changes that were the cause of discord. So surely my job too was on the line. I was one of two vice principals and I know they discussed whether or not two was too many. Thus throughout that chilly spring I expected to be summoned before the tribunal. Had that happened, as I can see in retrospect, I could have given a very decent account of myself. I would have piped up along the lines just indicated. The authority had given us a tough job and we deserved their support not their animosity. Not only would I have expatiated on the difficulty of the task before us and the lack of support we were getting but I could have demonstrated that my 'progressive' innovations were in fact highly practical. They were economical and took account of limited resources. They respected traditional objectives, like getting the best possible exam results. And they were not just dreamed up on the back of an envelope. The arguments, which were extensively worked out on paper, were coherent and the supporting evidence was carefully marshalled. My schemes would actually have been difficult to refute. I had another asset as well. I was 'sea green incorruptible'. If Philip was into what, in the 1970s, was known as 'personal growth', in those days there was nothing swinging about me. So I had moral clout! I had nothing to fear from the inquisition. However the summons never came. If they really were stalking me they failed to pounce. Which is odd because they grilled every other office-holder in the college hierarchy. I could have taken their neglect as an insult. Did I not count? Was I not the VP/DOS? But instead I was cravenly grateful and that is what mortifies me. I kept my profile low, my fingers crossed and my breath bated until, in July, the inquisitors went the way of the cuckoo. Before they left they had even thrown down a gauntlet. Anybody else who had anything to say was invited to come and speak up. But of course I did not respond. I chickened out. I was a coward. I abdicated my moral duty.

You were always quoting Brutus – or was it Cassius? – about there being a tide in the affairs of men. It delivers the jackpot if taken it at the flood. Well, here was mine and I missed it. Here was a golden opportunity to explain what I meant. It would have gone down well because what I meant was not what the inquisitors thought I meant but rather something quite close to what they meant themselves. So they might have been convinced and I would have acquired authority – authority to protest at the whole proceedings, to defend my friend against unjust charges and to demand a better deal for a pioneering venture doing its best under difficulty. Not only would I have come through with enhanced credibility but would have fetched up on better terms with myself – like you when you came home after winning the war and thumped that bastard of a caretaker who was persecuting your boss. I would have gone forward full of confidence not only in my principles but also in my persuasive powers. That did not happen. Instead, in lacking the courage to take a stand, I wrecked my career. I degenerated into a mere 'ideas man' easily marginalised. Not only did colleagues not believe in me but increasingly I did not believe in myself. My once practical schemes got wilder and wilder. In 1972 I was not a crazy progressive but ten years later I had become one. All, I think, because I lacked the guts to confront those mischievous inquisitors. Thus I lost touch, turned away from work altogether and lapsed into mental breakdown spiced with promiscuity – 'personal growth'! Not only a chicken but a headless one.

I didn't tell you much about all that at the time. We didn't do much real talking in those days, did we? In any case you were mourning Mum and spectacularly not coping with life on your own. You couldn't boil an egg or make a cup of tea. Or you said you couldn't. But today, feeling I can once again confide in you, my long-ago agony has resurfaced and gushed out. For twenty years I have been sitting on the shame of not facing that Committee, without, until now, acknowledging it. Thank you for serving as a catalyst. Ducking a challenge is no way to deal with it. You did not duck in front of the Hindenburg Line? Not that you had any option, I suppose, other than a firing squad! Anyway you found guts when you needed some and I did not. I salute you.

There is so much else we could talk about but perhaps that is enough for one day. There is sex for example. A suitable reward for aircrew but an unfortunate weakness in everybody else? Well, I certainly got screwed up in that respect and you passing on attitudes like that did not help. But I expect you had been screwed up in your turn and never overcame your own embarrassment. Nobody is embarrassed about sex any more – except me that is – but I wonder whether we deal with the facts of life any better than your lot did. Today sex has become a religion. You turned away from God and took up Eng Lit instead. We have turned away from God and taken up sex instead. Salvation lies in forever doing whatever turns you on. That does not seem a recipe for happiness either. In particular sexual freedom along with feminism had undermined the family. Discuss!

367

Next time we might put religion on the agenda too. You confused me about that as well as about sex. You would come home to tea, having just favoured your pupils with beautifully delivered cadences from the Book of Common Prayer, and launch straight into a rant about 'bloody parsons' and how Christianity was as a load of superstition consoling to old maids but no use to real men. I found that bewildering and unconvincing too. You may have left the chapel behind but it never left you. Right to the end of your life you oozed Nonconformity. The way you wrote about your chapel days at Poulton in that interesting little book you wrote – I am sorry you never got it published but it has helped me a lot in my own efforts at memoir writing – shows you were deeply dyed in Nonconformity. Did you really think, when you came back from the war, that you could put all that behind you? You were kidding yourself. Look how, thirty years later, you and Mum were utterly discombobulated when Maud, long after Leslie died, went to live with her still-married lover. Yet those two were as well suited as any couple I have ever come across. I suppose you thought you could hang on to the ethic while rejecting the mumbo jumbo of belief. Plenty of folk have tried that. George Eliot for example or even Darwin – I do tutoring for the Open University and in the process have got to know several of the Victorian greats. They could see the value of church-going to the social order but were at a loss to reconcile science with the bible. You too, I expect. Also, having known the Western Front, I suppose it was difficult to believe in a benevolent God with a benign plan for humanity. But can the ethic work without the faith? It doesn't seem to in the world I find around me, where the Ten Commandments seem honoured only in the breach. Particularly the Ninth, the one about false witness. Modern Britain seems to revolve around people deceiving each other while deceiving themselves as well. Actually I would like to go to church. I don't find belief too difficult, in a general way anyway. And recognising that Christianity is only one valid faith among others does not deter me either. It suits us westerners because our culture is founded in it. The English literature you taught me to love is essentially a body of Christian scriptures. Again, discuss! So what stops me? One thing is a sense I trail from childhood that there is something naff about going to church. For old maids but not for real men, that sort of thing. Guess who put that rubbish into my head!

I do not mean to show a lack of respect for your atheism, if that is what it was. You bravely maintained it to the end, as befits an old soldier. Your coolness when you must have known you were dying is an example to me. I wish I had acknowledged the situation and behaved with appropriate honesty and decorum instead of trying to chatter inconsequentially, something I am no good at anyway. At the end I am afraid I let you down yet again and I am sorry. But at least in the previous year we had done better, hadn't we? We had begun to talk again, like we used to before the distressing events of 1947, to an account of which I fear I must now return. I am so glad we managed a late reunion.

It has, as they say, been good to talk. So well ... Cheerio! You taught me that valediction when I was very young. At least we never said 'TTFN'.

Oh ... and love to Mum.

I do like him better now. I have even come to think that maybe he did not deserve his nick-name. He was an inspiring teacher. And when he was not ranting, blustering and domineering, he was excellent company. Furthermore he loved his wife and children. And he had guts.

Which is the end of what I have to say. I have not told you everything. A measure of inhibition must temper even the frankest of memoirs. But I have told you a lot, much more than I knew myself when I started writing. Remembering how it was, thinking about what emerges and then writing it down, is wonderfully satisfying. If you haven't done it yourself, you might try it. You get to know yourself more than you would think possible. Like a course of analysis? Anyway it is very rewarding. So much so that, even if nobody ever reads these pages except people I know, then it will have been immensely worthwhile. It has taught me so much about me.